TIPPECAN★E
AND TYLER TOO

TIPPECAN★E
AND TYLER TOO

Famous Slogans and Catchphrases in American History

JAN R. VAN METER

THE UNIVERSITY OF CHICAGO PRESS

Chicago and London

JAN R. VAN METER is retired from his position as a regional president and senior partner at the international communications firm of Fleishman-Hillard,
Inc., concluding a career that included specialized work in corporate and
institutional crisis communications. Earlier he worked as a CIA intelligence
analyst, an assistant professor of English at the University of Texas at Austin,
and a freelance speechwriter. This is his first book.

The University of Chicago Press, Chicago 60637
The University of Chicago Press, Ltd., London
© 2008 by The University of Chicago
All rights reserved. Published 2008

Printed in the United States of America

17 16 15 14 13 12 11 10 09 08   1 2 3 4 5

ISBN-13: 978-0-226-84968-3 (cloth)
ISBN-10: 0-226-84968-6 (cloth)

Library of Congress Cataloging-in-Publication Data

Van Meter, Jan R.
Tippecanoe and Tyler too : famous slogans and catchphrases in American
history / Jan R. Van Meter.
p. cm.
Includes bibliographical references and index.
ISBN-13: 978-0-226-84968-3 (cloth : alk. paper)
ISBN-10: 0-226-84968-6 (cloth : alk. paper)
1. United States—Politics and government—Miscellanea. 2. Political
slogans—United States. 3. Political culture—United States—History—
Miscellanea. 4. Political campaigns—United States—History—Miscellanea.
5. United States—History, Military—Miscellanea. 6. Popular culture—
United States—History—Miscellanea. 7. Slogans—United States. 8. United
States—History—Miscellanea. 9. English language—Terms and phrases.
I. Title.
E183.V36 2008
973—dc22
2008005186

∞

CONTENTS

ACKNOWLEDGMENTS

Researching and writing are never completely solitary work. It just seems that way. My debts are great to many for their help, their enthusiasm, and their patience over the past few years:

To all the libraries in New York City, especially to the New York Public Library, to the Brooklyn Public Library, to the library at Columbia Teachers College, with its fine collection of history textbooks, and most of all to the New York Society Library, whose stacks I have prowled for years and whose fine collection of rare old books was made available with the invaluable assistance of Aravig Caprialian, the library's rare book librarian.

To Fleishman-Hillard, Inc. I am particularly grateful to John D. Graham, chairman of Fleishman-Hillard, and to Dave Senay, CEO, for allowing me to occupy an office long after my retirement, thereby giving me a place to work.

To Tim Peters in San Francisco, to Paul Kaplan in Atlanta, and to Jayne Davis in Columbus for their assistance in doing research, and to Elizabeth D. Sansalone for her help in getting the manuscript ready for publication.

To David Duffy and Marcelline Thomson for their valued support and aid.

To Robert Devens and Emilie Sandoz of the University of Chicago Press for their enthusiasm and guidance and to Alice M. Bennett for her sage suggestions and changes.

But most of all, I could not have written this book without the encouragement, assistance, and editorial acumen of my wife, Elena Sansalone, and the constant interest of our son Ben. An obsession, after all, needs more than toleration.

INTRODUCTION

Slogans and Catchphrases in American History

> History is not another name for the past, as many people imply. It is
> the name for stories about the past.
> **A. J. P. TAYLOR**

The Founding Fathers knew the power of words. Indeed, well before the
Declaration of Independence was written, their words created the possibility of a new nation and turned untrained men with their hunting weapons
into a force that endured to defeat the most powerful nation in the world.
With their pens and their voices they stirred themselves and the world.
"We hold these truths to be self-evident, that all men are created equal,
that they are endowed by their Creator with certain unalienable Rights,
that among these are Life, Liberty and the pursuit of Happiness."

Then and since, public words often became shortened into battle cries,
into rallying points, and eventually into symbols—symbols of historical
moments that had to be remembered if the new nation with its new form
of government were to survive external and internal threats. These short-
hand summaries often became slogans and eventually turned up in school
textbooks and popular histories. As a shared national culture developed,
the accumulation of phrases remembered went beyond political and military slogans to include popular catchphrases. Those slogans and catchphrases from the recalled past can still be heard and read, sometimes to
illustrate a point in an editorial, sometimes to reshape a current cause or
recall to life an older ideal, and sometimes to sell a product.

This book is about many of these slogans and catchphrases in American
history. But it is not just about what those slogans meant—and to some
extent still mean—but about how each arose, was created, and perhaps
endured. As we begin to forget them entirely or use them for purposes that
cheapen them, we threaten the history we all have inherited—by birth or
by adoption.

Catchphrases and slogans are not the same thing, though they serve similar functions in national life. The word "slogan" derives from the term for Scottish battle cries, cries meant to rally armies against the enemy. Slogans are still battle cries, sometimes referring to military warfare, sometimes to the political variety, and they always involve a call to action, explicit or implicit. Most slogans that survive in national memory summarize a moment in history. The moment may be a valiant victory or a heroic defeat that must be ingrained in future remembrance: "Don't fire until you see the whites of their eyes" or "Remember the Alamo." The moment may illustrate a mode of conduct, a value to be sustained, a struggle to be continued: "These are the times that try men's souls" or "I have a dream." Others, once important, seemingly survive for more trivial reasons like their simple folk poetry.

Catchphrases are different. Like slogans, they embody moments in the nation's past, but they do not invoke a remembered call to action. Instead, they give voice to a pervasive cultural belief or characteristic attitude: "Nice guys finish last" or "Frankly, my dear, I don't give a damn." Catchphrases arise from a widely shared cultural medium—a book, a movie, a sport—that yielded a phrase that held and still holds the mind. The specific stimulus has gone, but its capturing of a general spirit remains ingrained in some significant part of the cultural psyche.

Yet the slogans and catchphrases should not and cannot stand alone. They are history encapsulated; if they are to be understood, they must be memory devices for a larger story. When they get detached from their history, they lose their meaning and become prey to satire, to advertising, to ignorance. So too might the history they are meant to bring alive for present use.

That history is vital to a nation or a culture is perhaps self-evident. Governments themselves worry about it. Some national governments resist the mention of certain past events in the history textbooks, while others have laws forbidding any public mention of specific acts. Groups that have been or still are omitted from a national history agitate to be included. Shared history conveys accomplishment, pride, and agreed-on values. For these reasons, almost every revolutionary government moves quickly to rewrite its history books.

Before the American Revolution, there were no American history books. There was no America, only thirteen colonies. Yet even as the Revolution was in progress, with its outcome in doubt, people had begun to concern themselves with an American history, a history of the United States.

Noah Webster seems to have begun it, with some brief pages on American history in his 1787 schoolbook. He included these pages for a frankly patriotic reason. A nation just eleven years old needed to develop a wide-spread sense of patriotism: "A love of our country," Webster wrote, "and an acquaintance with its true state, are indispensable—they should be acquired in early life."[1]

Dr. David Ramsay followed in 1789 with a full-fledged history, and when his second edition appeared in 1818, he echoed Webster's concerns. "It is a matter of reproach, that the youth of the United States know so little of their own country, and much more so, that the means of obtaining a competent knowledge of its history are inaccessible to most of them."[2]

In these first decades of the United States, the creation of the nation was a subject more for reminiscence than for study. The revolution was only a generation old, well within the living memory of parents and grandparents. All the presidents until then—and for nearly another quarter-century—had been leaders of the struggle for independence. History of any kind, especially American history, was not a subject for scholarly pursuit and certainly not a subject fit for schools. What schools there were—private or semiprivate academies or one-room schools—tended at the early age level to teach the basic three Rs. After that, most pupils went to work.

History became more important in the 1820s and 1830s, not only because the formation of the nation was now dimming in the past but, more important, because a flood of newcomers was arriving yearly. In every decade the population increased by more than a third, a rate that would continue until 1870: by 1820 the nation had doubled in population since 1790; by the end of the 1830s it had tripled. Memory of the original struggle, indeed of the nation's history, not only was being diluted but was in danger of being lost.

American history textbooks began to be written and used at this time. Added to Webster's rationale was the need to convert the wave of newcomers into citizens by making the nation's history the history of all citizens, new and old. In 1855, in the introduction to his history textbook, Benson J. Lossing stated: "But another question forces itself upon the mind and heart of the enlightened patriot—shall this rich inheritance be long perpetuated and how? The answer is at hand. *Educate every child—educate every emigrant,* for 'education is the cheap defense of nations.' Educate *all,* physically, intellectually and morally."[3] From its early days, intentionally and overtly, the teaching of a shared history was a vital part of preserving and building a still fragile nation.

Many of the textbooks of these years, notably those by Charles A. Goodrich and Emma Willard, sold by the tens of thousands and survived in schools after the authors had died. In their books and others, we find the first mention of the earliest slogans to reach a broad audience: "I only regret that I have but one life to lose for my country" and "Don't shoot until you see the whites of their eyes." The slogans, and their stories, were used to enliven the text for the youthful audience:

> General Putnam told the American soldiers how to manage. "Powder and ball are scarce," said he, "and you must not *waste* them. Don't fire till you can see the *whites* of their eyes—fire *low*—fire at their *waistbands*. You are all marksmen," said he; "you could kill a squirrel at a hundred yards. Take good aim—pick off the *handsome coats*. This they did, and the enemy fell by scores.[4]

Such widely used school textbooks are the first real means of national communication—at least of communicating national values. The same textbook used in New York City could be found in schools in Boise, Chicago, Charlotte, and San Francisco.[5]

If schoolbooks were a form of mass communication, they were a somewhat diffuse one. Their readership was unevenly spread and confined to children, and perhaps to their parents. Combined, they all told the same history and tended to convey the same values and expected behaviors for true citizens. Beginning in the late 1820s, though, a second form of national mass communication emerged: a new kind of presidential election campaign, one that involved far more voters in far more structured activities designed to entertain as much as to illuminate.

The turn began in the election of 1824. There were initially four candidates, all prominent politicians and members of government: John Quincy Adams of Massachusetts, secretary of state and son of a former president; William Crawford of Georgia, secretary of the treasury and a fervent believer in the Jeffersonian ideal of small government; John C. Calhoun of South Carolina, secretary of war, who hated Crawford and believed in a strong national government, but like Crawford was a slaveholder and a defender of slavery; and Henry Clay of Kentucky, the powerful Speaker of the House of Representatives and creator of the "American System" in which the government kept tariffs high, sold public lands, and sponsored vast internal improvements.

Although all the candidates were members of the same party—the old Federalist Party of George Washington and John Adams had withered away for lack of leadership and unpopular policies—they represented hostile factions within that party, and competition was fierce.

Then, nearly without warning and almost as an accident, a fifth candidate emerged, one from outside the traditional political world: General Andrew Jackson, the Hero of New Orleans, a willful individualist and a national figure whose policy views were carefully kept vague. His sudden popularity among citizens well removed from his natural constituency in the newly but rapidly populating West was an immediate threat to the old ways of conducting elections.

Lacking a strong insider power base, Jackson and his supporters had to build one from his unorganized and dispersed supporters. To do that, they put in place the rudiments of a new way of conducting national campaigns and creating the core of a real party system. Though by tradition Jackson could not himself campaign, his supporters organized enthusiastic rallies around the country, held frequent straw polls to demonstrate his growing strength, bought or created a string of supporting newspapers across the country to increase popular support, and stressed his demonstrated leadership rather than his opaque political positions.

When the votes were all in—there were a bit more than 362,000— Jackson had won pluralities in both the popular vote and the votes in the electoral college. He had not, however, won majorities in either. The election would be decided, as the Constitution decreed, in the House of Representatives, where each state had one vote and only the top three candidates in the election would be considered. The power lay with the one loser, Henry Clay, whose influence as Speaker of the House was now pivotal. He could not be elected president, but he could control who would be.

Before the House met, a rumor circulated in Washington that Clay had done a deal with Adams, trading the presidency to Adams in exchange for the position of secretary of state, the traditional stepping-stone to the presidency. While Clay vehemently denied the rumor, and while there was nothing illegal or unconstitutional in horse-trading even at that level, when the House met and the vote was held, Clay did throw his support to Adams; Adams was elected president with Clay's powerful and invaluable assistance, and shortly afterward Clay was named secretary of state.

Jackson and his supporters raised the cry of a "corrupt bargain" and kept it up for four years. Planning began among Jackson's supporters, and soon among the supporters of all the other losing candidates, to organize an opposition to the Adams presidency and all its policies and programs. By the time of the next election, there was beginning to emerge something closely resembling a new political party. It was eventually called "the Democracy," and then the "Democratic Party," but by any name or form,

Adams was not in it. This election would be very different, both in tactics and in outcome.

In that election of 1828, there were only two candidates, Adams and Jackson. Jackson sought to avenge Adams's "theft" of the presidency, and his campaign used the mass tactics and tight organization that were developed in 1824. The general won handily with 56 percent of the popular vote and 68 percent of the vote in the electoral college. But what was remarkable was the voter turnout. The total number of voters increased once the election was a clear contest between two people—dirty, loud, and popular. More than 1.1 million came to the polls. Truly astonishing, however, was the increase in participation by possible voters, from 1824's 26.9 percent to 57.6 percent!

The appeal of the presidential campaigns and their impact as a form of national communication continued to escalate. So too did their ability to articulate policies and programs and, more important, philosophies of government. With a larger and more engaged electorate to appeal to, the political campaigns of the mid-nineteenth century arrived in towns and cities as a combination of religious revival, circus, town meeting, parade, and vaudeville, all mixed with lots of food and drink. At times voter participation rose above 80 percent, and it almost always stayed above 70 percent. The political campaign became both a uniquely American idiom and an eagerly anticipated, widely enjoyed form of entertainment, and it gave birth to slogans like "Tippecanoe and Tyler too," and "He kept us out of war."

As political campaigns reached more and more people, they were soon aided by the development of another communication medium—the national press. Newspapers had always been an important part of American life, but they were largely local and often transitory; their size and importance depended on the size and importance of their locality. Horace Greeley's *New York Tribune,* founded in 1841, became the first truly national newspaper, publishing both daily editions and a special weekly edition for nationwide distribution. Aided by the introduction of postage stamps and federally mandated low postage rates, Greeley's *Tribune* passed 100,000 in circulation by 1852 and 220,000 in 1856. It could be found in eastern cities and in the homes of western farmers.[6]

Greeley strove for more accuracy than was usual for newspapers of the time. The press in general (the *Tribune* too) strove most of all for readership, advertising, and the ability to sway the course of national events. Increasing readership meant, even then, providing entertainment: creating heroes, unearthing corruption, publicizing scandal, waving flags, and wringing out tears. From newspapers came more slogans, going beyond the political, like "Yes, Virginia, there is a Santa Claus," and "Go west, young man." From them came, if not the cause of war, at least the excuse for it: "Remember the *Maine!*"

Then movies, starting in the 1900s, radio, starting in the 1930s, and television, starting in the 1950s, brought more forms of what we more naturally see as mass communication, each altering the nature of all those before it, each changing the nature of the culture itself. And with each medium came new slogans; each spread those slogans with increasing speed and, perhaps, increasing impact. From the movies came such slogans as "Smile when you say that, stranger," "Play it again, Sam," and "Make my day." From radio came "Good evening, Mr. and Mrs. America and all the ships at sea," "T'ain't funny, McGee," and "Hi-yo Silver, away." From television came "Good night and good luck," "Sock it to me," and "I am not a crook."

Slogans, though, are not unique to the United States. Quickly to mind are "Liberté, égalité, fraternité," "L'audace, l'audace, toujours l'audace," and "Après moi, le déluge" among many in France and "This was their finest hour," or "England expects every man will do his duty," or "The life of man, solitary, poor, nasty, brutish, and short" among many in England. Even the Romans remembered "Veni, vidi, vici" and "Ave Caesar, morituri te salutant."

Yet slogans seem to be particularly important to Americans. Nearly a century ago, a prominent American historian, Albert J. Beveridge, noted the effect of slogans on the nation and its history: "'Millions for Defense but not a cent for Tribute' is one of the few historic expressions in which Federalism spoke in the voice of America. Thus the Marshall banquet in Philadelphia, June 18, 1798, produced that slogan of defiant patriotism which is one of the slowly accumulating American maxims that have lived."[7] Whether a particular slogan was actually spoken or written at the time it was supposed to have been or uttered by the individual to whom it is attributed or whether it was created later by others unknown is not, in a sense, important. It is beside the point. Slogans act not to enlighten the past but to recall it; they act not to examine cause and effect but to inculcate values that the nation has tacitly agreed it needs. Indeed, the nation expresses its agreement by the act of remembering. Nathan Hale's "My only regret . . ." teaches sacrifice for the nation in peril; Admiral Farragut's "Damn the torpedoes . . ." teaches bravery; a newsboy's "Say it ain't so, Joe" teaches the despair that will follow the violation of trust, and on and on. Such slogans—such shared values—can be vital to a nation's persistence, even its existence.[8]

The meaning as well as the origin of many of the slogans seems now to be receding from national memory, though they were once common in America. But they are important as a beginning of knowing who we were and how we got here. They are important as a source of key values that we now share or fight about. They are both who we are and, more important, who we sought, and seek, to be. They give us something in common—our history—even as we argue about what we will become.

Slogans, though, are not always uniting; they can be and have been divisive for the nation as a whole even as they unify a particular geographical, political, ethnic, or racial part of it. The slogans of the Vietnam War years—"Hell no, we won't go" and "America: love it, or leave it"—were both uniting and divisive, as was "Tune in, turn on, and drop out." And the ugliest of slogans, one that changes with the time and vitriolic need, never really seems to die: "The only good [insert slur word here] is a dead [ditto]." That slogan too is both uniting and divisive, and it does display "the power of the dark side."

There are obviously far more slogans and catchphrases—both divisive and uniting—in American history than are contained within these covers. I chose these slogans for two reasons. First, I am a child of the 1940s and early 1950s. Many of these slogans, those up to the end of World War II, were ones I learned at school and at home in the books I was given or chose myself at the library. It did not take much to remember them half a century later; I never forgot them. Second, each of the slogans here opens a window to an important moment in American history. Some are military and political moments—indeed, all are until the development of large-circulation newspapers. However, each, no matter how trivial ("Who knows what evil lurks in the hearts of men? The Shadow knows"), illuminates the development of an event or an institution. In total, the slogans do provide a short, though obviously incomplete, history of the United States, most often at its best. To my mind, that was and must still be of great benefit to a nation that is, to its overwhelming advantage, a nation of immigrants.

Two final notes about speeches and speechwriters: First, many of the slogans and catchphrases discussed in this book were first uttered in speeches, and I have often quoted the lines that led up to and followed the specific phrase. To get the most from these quotations, you should read them aloud. In that way you can begin to feel the music of the lines and the excitement of the words.

Second, most, if not all, of the speeches were drafted by someone other than the speaker. Hamilton and Madison drafted some of Washington's speeches, Samuel Rosenman may well have contributed "The only thing we have to fear . . ." to FDR's inaugural address, and Theodore Sorenson wrote the final drafts of many of JFK's best-remembered speeches. Although I have been a speechwriter myself, I have not discussed the role of any speechwriter in the creation of any slogans because a speech belongs to the person who gives it. The ideas and expressions are given life only by the speaker. Who actually wrote a specific line or phrase is in a real sense, and certainly for the purposes of this book, irrelevant. The recurring "Ask not what you can do for your country . . ." evokes Kennedy, not Sorenson, and that particular moment in history that Kennedy led and embodied, for better or for worse.

WE SHALL BE AS
A CITY UPON A HILL

★ 1630 ★

They were Christians, even Puritans, though at one time that had been a term of mockery used by their enemies. They practiced what they believed was the only true religion, a strictly Bible-based Christianity available to anyone who searched the scriptures with clear eyes and a pure heart. The freedom of religion they sought was for themselves, not for others professing different forms or worshiping in different ways.

After the death of Queen Elizabeth I, the two pillars of England, the Anglican Church and parliamentary government, were both involved in power struggles in which the royal authority was challenged by dissenting movements. In the political realm, Parliament was in a constant feud with the king over basic rights and an acknowledged voice in government policy. In the religious realm, the Protestantism that Henry VIII had confined within an English version of Roman Catholicism was increasingly opposed by a small but growing number of disparate groups seeking to rid the Anglican Church of all vestiges of organization and rites that could not be found in the Bible, the only source of truth in earthly or heavenly affairs.

Some of these who wished a thus purified religion—hence "Puritan"—had decided that England's state-supported and protected Anglican Church was hopelessly corrupt. They were willing to defy all royal authority and leave the church to set up their own versions of Christianity—and thus willing, too, to risk fines, prison, or death.

Others, also Puritans, were willing to seek reform of the Anglican Church from within. They attended services as the law required and used the new Book of Common Prayer. They supported ministers, though, whose ideas about God's relationship with man and man's ability to receive God's salvation were increasingly different from those of the bishops whose right to rule their churches they ignored.

John Winthrop was one of these conforming dissenters. He was the son of a prosperous merchant and landowner, and himself a well-educated lawyer with a minor government position. Like all the dissenters, Winthrop believed that England was on the verge of reaping God's wrath for its flagrant disregard of true Christianity. God's presence in the world was real, constant, and watchful; he had set out the terms of his covenant with man in the Bible, and England was violating that covenant. Its declining status in the world was proof of the coming wrath; the king's friction with Parliament and his increasing disregard for the people's ancient rights was proof, too. There was much talk of moving to the new lands — to the New England where small settlements of Puritans scraped out an existence, where the true Christians could preserve the faith until they could return to save their country.

In 1628 a group of dissenting merchants was granted a charter to settle a large area on the Massachusetts coast, land that included the village of Salem, where there was already a small group of Puritans. The grant was confirmed by royal charter in the spring of 1629. Their name in the charter became "the Company of the Massachusetts Bay," and the charter itself was unusual because, unlike all the other such company charters of the time, it did not specify where company meetings had to take place. Through this loophole, a quiet revolution would march.

They would move — charter, company, meetings, and all — across the sea and away from the prying eyes of the king and the church.

The members of the company sought people to join with them, people with proven earthly and spiritual gifts. Not the least of these was John Winthrop. When he was asked to be part of a group that would leave for New England, he agonized about the decision, especially about leaving his fellow religionists — indeed, his fellow countrymen — to face God's imminent judgment alone. "It will be a great wrong to our own Church and Country to take away the good people, and we shall lay it the more open to the Judgment feared."[1]

Searching his heart and the Bible, Winthrop decided that his duty to God lay in using his talents to their utmost, and that could best be done in New England. On August 27, 1629, he and eleven other important dissenters formally signed an agreement to recruit and transport appropriate people for a new settlement in New England by March 1630 — tasks to be accomplished as long as they would be permitted legally to transfer their charter and the governing body to the new settlement. That was accomplished, and on October 20, 1629, a meeting of all the members of the Massachusetts Bay Company (called the General Court) elected John Winthrop governor of the new settlement.

In early April 1630 the first of the Massachusetts Bay Company ships—eventually eleven—began the long voyage across the Atlantic. They left from three assembly points where passengers had been recruited. Winthrop led the way on the flagship *Arbella*, together with three other ships; by June more than a thousand people, of varying trades and occupations picked to ensure the settlement's ability to survive and thrive, and picked also for their religious views, had departed.

It was a wilderness they were traveling toward, not a promised land. They had a mission from God to preserve their true faith against the time when God's anger descended on England and on all of Europe. They would be the true remnant, spared, who could return to a ruined but chastened land and lead the survivors on God's true path.

At some point during the *Arbella*'s two-month voyage, probably near its end, Governor Winthrop preached a sermon to the passengers. In it he laid out the religious basis for the society they were going to build and elaborated on its sacred mission.

The new world, like the old, would have social distinctions: those were ordained by God. God, however, also ordained that the colonists were all linked and had responsibilities to each other—a web of duties that was especially important in the perilous world to which they traveled. At the foundation of these mutual responsibilities, said Winthrop, moving carefully from biblical reference to biblical reference, was love: the love God commands that each person have for his fellow, the love that knits society together, and the love that each has for Christ and that Christ has shown for man through his crucifixion. If the new settlers did not act in accordance with God's laws, "the Lord will surely break out in wrath against us; be revenged of such a [sinful] people and make us know the price of the breach of such a covenant."[2]

He moved to his conclusion, making clear that God's eyes—and man's eyes—were watching what they were about to undertake.

> The Lord will be our God, and delight to dwell among us, as his own people, and will command a blessing upon us in all our ways. . . . We shall find that the God of Israel is among us, . . . when he shall make us a praise and glory that men shall say of succeeding plantations, "the Lord make it likely [like] that of New England." For we must consider that **WE SHALL BE AS A CITY UPON A HILL**.[3] The eyes of all people are upon us. So that if we shall deal

falsely with our God in this work we have undertaken, and so cause him to withdraw his present help from us, we shall be made a story and a by-word throughout the world. We shall open the mouths of enemies to speak evil of the ways of God, and all professors for God's sake. We shall shame the faces of many of God's worthy servants, and cause their prayers to be turned into curses upon us till we be consumed out of the good land whither we are a-going.[4]

The *Arbella* and the other three ships landed at Salem on June 12, 1630, and some four hundred people disembarked. By the end of the summer all one thousand had arrived, and in October Winthrop moved the settlement to a peninsula jutting into the bay. There they built a dock and the town of Boston began.

In the next ten years, these first arrivals would be joined by 19,000 more like them from England. During this time Winthrop was usually, though not always, elected governor each year. The charter allowed him near absolute powers, but those were dangerous among a group of dissenters, dissenters both religiously and temperamentally. Though Winthrop feared democracy, he moved—though sometimes he was pushed—consistently away from autocracy and toward political and religious inclusion, toward persuasion and conciliation. He broadened the vote for governor from only those who were members of the Company to all men, reluctantly allowed the creation of a kind of constitution, "the Body of Liberties," and kept the powers of the church and the state carefully separate. However, Winthrop also guarded against the constant threat of religious division, since it was a danger as much to the needed unity of society in a hostile land as to the souls of its members. Those who threatened division because of their enthusiasm for a different reading of the scriptures—most notably Roger Williams and Ann Hutchinson—were tried and sent permanently away, on pain of death should they return.

Since these were a people who constantly sought guidance as well as solace from the Bible, an early law made parents responsible for ensuring that their children be taught to read. To provide ministers to the next generation, the government founded Harvard College in 1636.

Events in England did indeed take a turn for the better when the Glorious Revolution led by dissenter Oliver Cromwell deposed and beheaded King Charles. Seemingly it was time for those in Massachusetts to return, and some did. Most did not, including John Winthrop. Massachusetts was doing well, growing in wealth, institutions, and population while preserving their form of Christianity. When the British monarchy returned to govern England, the new world Puritans were no longer temporary exiles but perforce settlers, founders, Americans.

Winthrop's words about "a city upon a hill" disappeared for more than three hundred years, kept alive only by historians and scholars of American religion.[5] His words first reappeared in public voice just before John F. Kennedy was inaugurated in 1961, in a speech he gave to a group with the historically evocative name "joint convention of the General Court of the Commonwealth of Massachusetts."

> But I have been guided by the standard John Winthrop set before his shipmates on the flagship *Arbella* three hundred and thirty-one years ago, as they, too, faced the task of building a new government on a perilous frontier.
>
> "We must always consider," he said, "that we shall be as a city upon a hill—the eyes of all people are upon us."
>
> Today the eyes of all people are truly upon us—and our governments, in every branch, at every level, national, state and local, must be as a city upon a hill—constructed and inhabited by men aware of their great trust and their great responsibilities.[6]

The words reappeared again in several speeches given by Ronald Reagan, both before he was elected president and afterward. In his farewell address to the nation, Reagan once more spoke of Winthrop.

> The past few days when I've been at that window upstairs, I've thought a bit of the "shining city upon a hill." The phrase comes from John Winthrop, who wrote it to describe the America he imagined. What he imagined was important because he was an early Pilgrim, an early freedom man. He journeyed here on what today we'd call a little wooden boat; and like the other Pilgrims, he was looking for a home that would be free.[7]

Each man used the reference to Governor Winthrop and the quotation in a different way and for different purposes. To each, it meant something different.

Such is often the fate of slogans in the United States.

NO TAXATION WITHOUT
REPRESENTATION

★ 1763 ★

The year was 1764. The Seven Years' War—known locally as the French and Indian War—had ended with a British triumph and the Treaty of Paris the year before. Although fighting in America to defend both British territory and the colonists who lived there, British commanders had not had the authority to raise troops or money from the colonies without the approval of each colonial assembly. What they got was voluntary and varied widely depending only in part on whether the specific colony was threatened by the French forces and their Indian allies.

Nor was this limitation the only one the British faced. During the emergency period of the war, the local colonial governments had taken advantage of London by assuming local control of budgets, taxes, and patronage. By the end of the war, a tacit compromise had arisen. The king and his Parliament had control over foreign affairs, war and peace, and trade. Parliament, by imposing tariffs and duties, could direct colonial trade to benefit whom they wished, whether in the colonies or at home. In all else the American colonies had home rule, greater than that in places close to home like Ireland, and certainly greater than in the colonies of other European powers. The Americans, accordingly, viewed themselves as Englishmen abroad, with all the rights and liberties of Englishmen in England.

Yet the long war had taken a financial toll on Britain, not least in what it cost the central government to keep its military and civil presence across the Atlantic. In 1748, six years before the war began, that cost had been some £70,000; by 1764 it had risen to £350,000.[1]

Not surprisingly, and not without justification, Parliament thought the colonies should help foot that particular bill. The Americans, also not surprisingly, felt otherwise. The colonies had taken on £2.5 million in debt to pay for their contributions locally. Parliament had assumed some of that debt, but most of it remained to be paid.

In London, the result was the Revenue Act of 1764, often known as the Sugar Act. Benjamin Franklin, there as the representative of two of the colonies, understood the British thinking and did not foresee any problems with it back home.

He was both out of touch and wrong.

Back home, problems arose almost immediately. Boston, a center of commercial activity, rebellious smuggling, and radical politics, was the loudest in its reaction. And the focal point of Boston's reaction was a lawyer and close ally of the leading radical politician, Samuel Adams. His name was James Otis.

Otis was a magnetic and curious personality on the Boston political scene. He had gone to Harvard at an early age and, graduating with a master's degree, read classics at home for another eighteen months. He then studied law and began to practice, first in Plymouth and then in Boston. However, even as a young man, his brilliance and energy were matched by his emotional unpredictability.

Though very successful as a lawyer in Boston, Otis was not motivated either by money or by position. Indeed, in his first major case, undertaken in 1760, he resigned his position as king's advocate general in the Vice-Admiralty Court in Boston to defend a local merchant in that same court, without fee. The issue was the legality of Parliament-authorized "writs of assistance" that allowed the holder to search anyone's property at any time looking for smuggled goods. Otis argued that the writs violated the Englishman's natural right to life, liberty, and property. His fiery four-hour argument forced the court to hold off any ruling until the following year for fear of the public reaction to a ruling opposed to Otis's position.

Less than two years later, when the governor of Massachusetts sought to pay for an armed ship to protect British fishing vessels off the coast of Newfoundland, Otis successfully led the opposition to the move on the grounds that the governor had not sought approval for the expenditure from the colonial assembly. A Tory judge said at the time that Otis was clearly brilliant, but if "Bedlamism [insanity] is a talent, he had that in perfection."[2] The citizens of Boston, though, were not bothered by Otis's mercurial temperament, and in 1763 they elected him to lead their town meetings.

The Sugar Act landed in the midst of this prickly political atmosphere. It was seen as an unwanted major change in British policy. Tariffs and duties had always been imposed by Parliament only to regulate trade. Now the intention was "that a revenue be raised in your . . . Majesty's dominions in America for defraying the expenses of defending, protecting, and securing the same."[3]

In response, Otis wrote and published a pamphlet titled "The Rights of the British Colonies Asserted and Proved." Otis argued that since the colonies had no delegates in Parliament, they could not be taxed. Briefly, the argument ran thus:

That the colonists, black and white, born here are freeborn British subjects, and entitled to all the essential civil rights of such is a truth not only manifest from the provincial charters, from the principles of the common law, and acts of Parliament, but from the British constitution, which was re-established at the Revolution with a professed design to secure the liberties of all the subjects to all generations. . . .

Now can there be any liberty where property is taken away without consent? Can it with any color of truth, justice, or equity be affirmed that the northern colonies are represented in Parliament? Has this whole continent of near three thousand miles in length . . . the election of one member of the House of Commons? . . .

I can see no reason to doubt but the imposition of taxes, whether on trade, or on land, or houses, or ships, on real or personal, fixed or floating property, in the colonies is absolutely irreconcilable with the rights of the colonists as British subjects and as men. I say men, for in a state of nature no man can take my property from me without my consent; if he does, he deprives me of my liberty and makes me a slave.[4]

Otis was not asserting a new right for the colonies but reaffirming an old one, one that the colonists held because they were English and had to be treated as such. Parliament was acting illegally because the colonists were not represented there. The counterargument quickly came from London that the colonists had "virtual representation" because every member of Parliament voted in the interests of all those governed by the king. No one took this argument very seriously.

Nor was Otis making a new argument. Nearly a century earlier, the Massachusetts Bay Colony had refused to obey Parliament's Navigation Acts because "the subjects of his Majesty here not being represented in Parliament, so we have not looked at ourselves to be impeded in our trade by them."

But Otis's position caught the public mood. "The Rights of the British Colonies" pamphlet was enormously popular and highly acclaimed.

However, the force of the argument was short-lived. The farmers in western Massachusetts did not care what happened to the merchants in the eastern part of the colony. The new taxes were important only to a specific class of people who were not numerically dominant, even though they were economically and politically influential. Most important, the more radical of the politicians in the colonies did not want either taxation *or* representation. It was quickly obvious that any elected representatives sent to Parliament would be overwhelmed by the votes of the British MPs and, worse, be too far away in distance, and thus in time, to be in touch with local events or directed by local governments. Otis's arguments might be effective philosophically, but they were hardly effective practically or politically.

What lived on far beyond the immediate cause was Otis's core idea summarized by **"NO TAXATION WITHOUT REPRESENTATION,"** an idea that stimulated increased resistance by colonists to all British attempts to tighten control over them, whether fiscal, civil, or military.

Parliament, though, was not moved. The Sugar Act was quickly followed by the Stamp Act in 1765, which occasioned a boycott of British goods that drastically reduced trade with England, violence in the streets that destroyed the homes of colonial officials, and the colonial Stamp Act Congress. The Congress adopted a set of resolutions, among them an assertion that "no taxes ever have been, or can be constitutionally imposed on [the colonies] but by their respective legislatures."

Finally, faced with this kind of colonial resistance, Parliament repealed the Stamp Act but left the Sugar Act in place and reasserted its right to tax the colonies by passing the Declaratory Act, which affirmed "Parliament's right, as the sovereign legislature of the British empire to bind the colonies . . . in all cases whatsoever."

The Sugar Act was ignored by the colonies and evaded by smugglers, but the real issue remained. The two sides were deadlocked.

As for James Otis, his erratic behavior worsened yearly to the point that he was increasingly distrusted, even by his friends. He had attacked slavery in his pamphlet, but kept his own slave. He had argued and struggled against the British right to tax the colonies but had also written a justification for that right. He publicly rued the day he had become a Whig and then publicly challenged the prime minister of England to hand-to-hand combat on the floor of the Massachusetts House. At night Otis walked the streets of Boston breaking windows. During the day he fired gunshots out his own windows. Finally his family tied him up and took him to a farm outside Boston, where he later died when he was struck by lightning.

Otis's role in asserting much of the philosophical basis for the coming armed struggle with England has been largely forgotten. He is generally credited, though, with first saying "no taxation without representation" in his arguments during the 1761 writs of assistance trial. However, there is no contemporary evidence of it or any mention of it in one place where it might have occurred, Mercy Otis Warren's history of the Revolution. The closest to such a phrase that is recorded is in the reconstruction of his 1761 argument by John Adams nearly sixty years after the fact, and what Adams remembered, or thought he did, was the phrase "the *tyranny* of taxation without representation."[5]

No matter. The slogan is based on Otis's reasoning and uncommon ability as a speaker and on the subject it addresses. It survives because it characterizes, then and now, a basic American belief.

DON'T FIRE UNTIL YOU SEE
THE WHITES OF THEIR EYES

★ 1775 ★

What happened on the hills overlooking both Charlestown and Boston was probably inevitable. The British reaction to Sam Adams's Boston Tea Party—closing the Port of Boston and threatening to strangle Massachusetts economically—galvanized most of the colonies, increased tension, and heightened the need for action to relieve it. Indeed, the combination of British arrogance and geography proved fatal in that hot summer of 1775.

It is important to remember that more than two hundred years ago Boston was virtually an island, connected to the mainland of Massachusetts only by a thin neck of land. When the British forces occupied the city, they trapped themselves. They had the port, but they were surrounded by a hostile countryside that was busily arming itself. Major General Thomas Gage, for the moment both governor of the colony and commander of the British forces, was aware of the danger and wrote to his superiors in London: "The Country People are exercising in Arms in this Province, Connecticut and Rhode Island, and getting Magazines of Arms and Ammunition in the Country and such Artillery as they can procure good and bad. They threaten to attack troops in Boston."[1]

But London was thousands of miles away. Gage's dispatches took seven to eight weeks to be received and answered; he was essentially on his own. When Gage learned of a store of military supplies in nearby Concord, he sent out troops to seize and destroy them. A show of force, he was sure, would cow the colonists and lessen the threat to his men. Indeed, it seemed a risk-free mission. His troops were disciplined, battle-hardened regulars. In the eyes of the British, the rebel militias were a rabble, easily frightened.

But the rebels had the advantage of constant leaks of information. When Gage had decided to land 1,800 men, more than half the Boston garrison, in a show of force on April 19, 1775, word got out almost immediately. On the night before the attack, Paul Revere and Will Dawes were sent out to alert the militias in towns along the route from Boston to Concord. When the British got to Lexington, they found only a token force strung out on the town green. The British fired almost by accident, killing ten and wounding nine. After a long delay they moved on to Concord, but by that time militiamen from a number of towns had gathered and kept coming. Indeed, by the time the British had searched for the reported arms cache and found little, more than a thousand rebels could be seen on the hills above the town. Firing began, killing four British officers and three soldiers — a pattern that would continue in the fighting to come.

The British began to retreat in the face of the unexpected opposition. The rebels, though, did not fight in the traditional European manner, standing up in straight rows to fire and receive fire. These, after all, were men more used to fighting Indians and doing it from behind the cover of trees, walls, and buildings. By the time the British reached the safety of Boston, seventy-three of them had been killed and nearly two hundred wounded. Their mission had gained them nothing; it had gained the rebels everything, not least the confidence that the British could be beaten and the news value of Britain's intention to put the colonies forcibly in their subordinate place.

The news spread fast because Samuel Adams made sure it did. The Massachusetts Committee for Safety sent Israel Bissel to spread the word. Leaving even before the British had retreated from Concord, Bissel reached Worcester in the center of the colony at noon on April 19. On the twentieth, Bissel was in New London at the Connecticut shore. By April 23 he was in New York, and by the next day he was in Philadelphia.

The colonial reaction was equally swift. In the next month, the hills around Boston filled with colonial militiamen from Massachusetts and the surrounding colonies of Connecticut, Rhode Island, and New Hampshire — some 15,000 of them. Nor were these all inexperienced rabble, no matter what the British officers might imagine. The British seemed to have forgotten that some 11,000 colonials had fought with the British army in the French and Indian War. Indeed, approximately 3,800 of the colonials now overlooking Boston had served with Commander Jeffrey Amherst in his campaign against Fort Niagara. They might not have been versed in British military traditions, but they were well versed in warfare.

The colonials, though, were not used to being centrally organized. The army was an army in name only, with no one clearly in charge of anything. Discipline was loose; sanitation was terrible; food and supplies were constantly lacking. The situation was made more complicated for both sides as those loyal to the British fled from the countryside to the safety of Boston and those hostile to the British fled in the opposite direction.

By the end of May the situation had become intolerable. William Howe, the new general sent from England to relieve Gage of one of his responsibilities, knew that time was not on his side. Against the advice of at least one of his commanders, he decided to make a direct assault across the bay to destroy Charlestown and the rebel headquarters at Cambridge.

Again, news of the planned attack leaked out, and the colonials moved to fortify Bunker Hill above Charlestown. Units led by Colonel William Prescott and Israel Putnam were sent to build the defenses. They moved out on the evening of June 16 with wagonloads of picks, shovels, barrels to be filled with dirt, and bundles of stiff sticks used to absorb the expected cannonballs. Whether it was because they did not know which of the two hills on the Charlestown peninsula was Bunker Hill or because the lower one was nearer to the shore and the better place to put a defense line, Breed's Hill was the site of their night's work.

By dawn the rebels' fortifications were nearly complete. Unnoticed by the British, the colonials had constructed a dug-in redoubt protected by breastworks from which they could fire without exposing themselves. To protect against being flanked, they had piled hay against a rail fence leading down to the beach. Although the hay gave them something to hide behind, it provided little protection—though it did convince the British that the fence line was protected by something more substantial that they could not see.

Alerted to the work, the British began firing from their ships and from the shore cannon across the harbor, but with little effect. The British staff met, determined to put down this colonial outrage once and for all. They debated their plans again, but Howe was resolved that a direct assault was the only honorable course. He ordered the troops assembled and boats readied to ferry them across the harbor.

Tired and hungry, the Americans continued to improve their fortifications. When no food appeared, some of the men began to drift away. Finally, about noon, some food and, just as important, six cannons arrived and were put in place facing the beach. Though the British preparations to attack were easily seen, massive colonial militia reinforcements never did arrive from Cambridge.

It took far longer than Howe and his staff had assumed for the 2,200 British troops to assemble, be provisioned, and move down to the docks. When they got there, they found that the navy had sent too few boats, so it took two trips to get all the soldiers across to the beach in front of the colonial fortifications. The navy did, however, increase its shelling, this time including the town of Charlestown, which they set on fire.

Finally some additional colonial troops arrived. Those from New Hampshire moved into position with the soldiers from Connecticut at the rail fence. Some New Hampshiremen were sent down to the one place left undefended—the rocky beach itself—where British troops could move unseen by the defenders in the breastworks. With no one clearly in charge, individual groups and officers made their own decisions. By afternoon, more soldiers and even civilians were coming to help. Samuel Adams's closest ally, Joseph Warren, president of the Massachusetts Provincial Congress, came, as did Joseph Otis, James Otis's brother, and James Winthrop, the librarian of Harvard. None of the colonials, though, had enough ammunition for an extended battle; indeed, they had only fifteen musket balls per man, half the usual battle supply.

By the time the British were ready to begin their attack, it was hot— over ninety degrees—and the British soldiers were wearing thick wool uniforms and carrying fifty-pound packs in addition to their guns. The main force moved across the field in front of the main colonial defenses, forming orderly, straight lines led by their officers as they began to move uphill. A second, smaller group, eleven companies, marched in a column along the beach to flank the Americans and get behind them. The New Hampshire defenders, hidden behind the rocks, could not be seen. Marksmen throughout the colonial lines had been designated to shoot at the officers, and each was accompanied by a soldier who would load another musket as the marksman fired the first. Behind the breastworks on the hill, along the fence line, and from behind the rocks, words of encouragement and advice were passed along: aim low, at the point where the belts of the British soldiers crossed, and **DON'T FIRE UNTIL YOU SEE THE WHITES OF THEIR EYES**. The latter advice has been variously attributed, most often to Israel Putnam, but in fact the words had long been a truism in armies throughout Europe.

The first action foretold the rest, but it was too late for any warning to have an effect on the British plans. As a company of Welsh Fusiliers leading the column advancing along the beach neared the New Hampshiremen hiding behind the rocks, the colonials opened fire with devastating effect. The British officers and noncommissioned officers were hit first, and the line recoiled onto the column behind, soldiers falling dead and wounded. The British soldiers broke and ran.

Meanwhile, the lines of British troops advanced up the hill toward the fence line and the breastworks. When the order to fire was given, they wavered, fell, and ran. The first two lines of British troops got entangled in the panic. The first assault had failed.

Howe and his officers reformed the lines with difficulty and charged again. And failed again. As one officer wrote later:

> As we approached, an incessant stream of fire poured from the rebel lines. It seemed a continued sheet of fire for near thirty minutes. Our Light-Infantry were served up in Companies against the grass fence without being able to penetrate—indeed how could we penetrate? Most of our Grenadiers and Light-Infantry, the moment of presenting themselves [within range] lost three-quarters, and many nine-tenths, of their men. Some had only eight and nine a company left; some only three, four and five.[2]

But now the Americans were short of ammunition and men. Some of those ordered into battle refused, while others in the line slowly moved away. Crushed with the losses as he was, Howe ordered yet another assault, and his remaining troops once again moved in line up the hill.

This third assault, though taking heavy losses, broke through the American defenses. Out of ammunition and without bayonets or rein-forcements, the Americans retreated in an orderly manner. The British took only thirty-one prisoners, most of them gravely wounded. By the end of the day the Americans had been driven off the Charlestown peninsula, but they had managed to fortify the hill overlooking the neck of land, pre-venting the British from moving off into the mainland.

For the British, it was an extremely expensive victory, a term they could use only because they had driven their foe off the battlefield. Howe had lost all of his aides and most of his officers. British casualties totaled 1,054, including 226 killed, casualties that amounted to some 47 percent of the troops that began the battle.

The American casualties were high as well. Out of the 1,500 to 1,700 men on Breed's Hill, approximately 450 were either killed or wounded, most during the final assault and retreat. Nonetheless, the real victory had gone to the American "rabble." As one British officer wrote, "From an absurd and destructive confidence, carelessness, or ignorance, we have lost a thousand of our best men and officers and have given the rebels great matter of triumph by showing them what mischief they can do us."[3]

GIVE ME LIBERTY OR GIVE ME DEATH

★ 1775 ★

In the colonists' slow awakening to the inevitability of the struggle for independence from Great Britain, two colonies, widely separated by geography and personality, led the way and forced the pace: Massachusetts and Virginia.

That Massachusetts should have been one of the leaders is obvious. The colony, after all, had been founded by religious dissenters more than a century earlier and had long been a hotbed of resistance to any religious, economic, or political control by a British government in London. Not only was the colony resolutely Protestant, many of its most prosperous citizens were active smugglers to avoid British tariffs, and its town and colonial governing bodies feuded incessantly with the royally appointed governors. Here also lived Samuel Adams, a master organizer and conspirator who pushed toward independence.

Virginia is perhaps a less obvious leader. Aristocratic by nature, it had an economy based on agriculture—and slavery—and its leaders were patrician in habit and speech. Yet this very aristocratic bent also meant that the colony's leaders resented any British interference in their affairs. Moreover, their collective philosophical intelligence, embodied by Thomas Jefferson and James Monroe, their civic weightiness, embodied by Peyton Randolph, and their military experience, embodied by George Washington, meant that they, as a group, were not cowed by British power.

Nor did Virginia lack for radicals to force the issues. Richard Henry Lee was one of these; Patrick Henry was another.

In his early years, Patrick Henry showed little promise, and certainly no desire to follow his father as a farmer. In his teens he showed no inclination to be a scholar despite evident intelligence, preferring his own pleasure to any achievement. Married against his family's wishes, he twice failed as a merchant and finally agreed to try the law. Typically, Henry studied law for six weeks, hating every minute. His adroit mind and ready tongue enabled him to be, almost accidentally, passed for the bar by three examiners, at least one of whom thought the other two had already certified him.

People took notice of the young lawyer, though, in 1763. Henry took on the defense of his county against the king's veto of a Virginia law that uncoupled ministers' salaries from the market price of tobacco. Central to his argument was that "a king, by disallowing acts of a salutary nature, from being the father of his people, degenerates into a tyrant, and forfeits all right to his subjects' obedience."[1] While the idea was not original, the place where it was enunciated—a colony—was.

A few months later, Henry argued in favor of broad voting rights for the colony's inhabitants, another radical statement in the days of strict property qualifications. In 1765 he was elected to fill an open seat in the Virginia House of Burgesses, the colony's legislature.

Henry's appearance in the House of Burgesses came at the perfect moment for him. The colonies had just learned that Parliament had passed the Stamp Act. Violence broke out in a number of colonies, and especially in Boston. More important, by forcing the use of tax stamps on all documents from legal briefs to bills of sale, from newspapers to published sermons, the act enraged the most powerful and vocal of the colonists—the journalists, the merchants, and the lawyers.

Virginia took the lead in opposition. The House of Burgesses met to decide what to do. On May 29, nine days after taking his seat, the newest member of the House, Patrick Henry, rose to move a series of resolutions. The resolutions spelled out the rights of the colonists, stated that only Virginia could tax its citizens, and asserted that anyone who supported the right of any other body to tax inhabitants of the colony should be considered an enemy. His eloquence lit up the meeting and carried the House. His "Virginia Resolves" all passed, though the last one by only a single vote.

A few days later, Massachusetts called a congress in New York to consider what steps the colonies as a whole could take. The congress met in October and passed a set of resolutions that were much more moderate than those passed in Virginia but still maintained that only the colonies could tax themselves. Yet even before the congress convened, a new ministry in London repealed the act, since it clearly could not be enforced, though it reaffirmed its right to govern in all matters everywhere.

In 1767 there was yet another attempt to exert more control over the colonies and to impose new taxes. And again opposition in America was led by Massachusetts and Virginia. Massachusetts, for its trouble, had its legislative assembly dismissed by the governor under orders from London. Virginia passed another set of resolutions in support of its northern compatriots, this time introduced by a former army colonel, George Washington.

Meanwhile in Boston, Sam Adams's group kept up a steady drumbeat of street theater and violence, causing the importation of British troops from Canada. The show of force ended with several deaths and a riot called, by Adams, the "Boston Massacre" that resulted in the trial for murder of the British officer and troops involved. The British were successfully defended by John Adams and Josiah Quincy, both of whom were determined to show the British that the law, not the mob, reigned in the colonies. The governor of the colony removed the troops from the city, and on the same day Parliament repealed the offending laws, except for one significant tax-the import duty on tea.

Calm and prosperity ensued for several years and might have continued were it not for that nearly forgotten commodity. When trouble came again, it came in Boston, and it came because the East India Company was having financial troubles. To assist the Company, Parliament granted it a monopoly on the shipping and distribution of tea throughout the colonies. The Company could now eliminate all the independent (colonial) merchants by selling the tea only through its own agents. Not only was Parliament threatening the livelihoods of a number of prominent colonists, it was once again throwing its weight around economically.

The reaction was swift and violent. One tea shipment was allowed to land in Charleston, South Carolina, but was not put up for sale. In Philadelphia and New York, the tea shipments were rejected and returned to England. In Boston, Sam Adams had a better idea. On December 16, 1773, colonists dressed as sailors and Indians boarded a ship loaded with tea, broke up the tea chests, and threw the tea into the harbor—the Boston Tea Party.

For the British, who valued property above all, the Boston Tea Party was the last straw. In May 1774 Parliament passed a series of Coercive Acts that closed the Port of Boston to all shipping, drastically altered the form of government in Massachusetts, and provided for shipping certain offenders against the government to England for trial. In a further show of force, a senior general in the British army, Major General Thomas Gage, was appointed both commander in chief in America and royal governor of Massachusetts.

If these actions were meant to cow the citizens of Massachusetts—and the other colonies—into instant submission, they had the opposite effect. Here was not a threat to the colonies' asserted sole right to tax themselves; here was not a theoretical threat to their whole independent way of life. Here was an actual threat to the very livelihood of one of the most prosperous and vigorous of the colonies.

The other colonies rallied to the support of Massachusetts. On May 27, having learned of the moves against the northern colony, members of Virginia's House of Burgesses met in the Raleigh Tavern in Williamsburg and called for a congress of all the continental colonies. By August, the colonies agreed to a congress in Philadelphia.

The First Continental Congress opened as scheduled on Monday, September 5, 1774. Virginia's Peyton Randolph was immediately elected chairman, or "president," and Pennsylvania's Charles Thomas was elected secretary.

The first major question to be dealt with was how the colonies would vote. Patrick Henry, part of the Virginia delegation, proposed a complicated formula to weight each colony's vote according to a number of factors. The subsequent debate convinced him, though, that the method was too clumsy, and he withdrew his motion in a speech that ended with the statement, "The distinctions between Virginians, Pennsylvanians, New Yorkers and New Englanders are no more. I am not a Virginian, but an American."[2] The idea was, for the British, a perilous one.

The Congress began considering a plan devised by the Pennsylvania conservative Joseph Galloway for a power-sharing arrangement with Parliament. (Three years later, Galloway would defect to the British.) In the midst of that debate, Paul Revere arrived with a series of far more radical resolutions drafted by Sam Adams's close friend and ally, Joseph Warren, and passed by a convention of towns around Boston. These "Suffolk Resolves" declared the Coercive Acts unconstitutional and void, urged the citizens of Massachusetts to arm themselves and act as a free state as long as the Coercive Acts were in effect, called for a campaign to refuse to obey all orders given by anyone with a Crown appointment, and urged the Congress in Philadelphia to adopt economic sanctions against Great Britain.

Galloway's plan disappeared under the weight of Warren's "Suffolk Resolves," and the deliberations of the Congress were thereafter shifted in the direction pointed by the Massachusetts radicals. Before it adjourned, the First Continental Congress unanimously adopted a declaration of rights and grievances addressed to the people of Great Britain and the colonists in America. It also declared a boycott, effective December 1, 1774, of all products from Great Britain, and agreed to set up something called "the Association," a system of local committees to enforce the boycott. As a sop to the less radical among them, the Congress also drafted its "Olive Branch Petition" and sent it to the king, asking for redress.

Having then agreed to meet again in May 1775, the Congress adjourned on October 22. The work had gone slowly, even tediously, but the pace was necessary to bring everyone along. What was notable, as many present wrote in letters home, was the civic-mindedness and intellectual quality of the delegates and the civility with which they worked together. They might have been revolutionaries, but they were revolutionary gentlemen.

For the next several months, British control eroded throughout the colonies. Boston seethed with unrest. People in New Hampshire seized four cannons from Fort William and Mary and burned tea in Portsmouth.

On March 20, 1775, the leaders of Virginia met at St. John's Church in Richmond to discuss the resolutions adopted by the Continental Congress. As he had done in Philadelphia, the moderate Peyton Randolph chaired the meeting. A few days into the meeting, Patrick Henry rose to move that the colony immediately form its own militia, preparatory to the inevitable war. The moderates protested that such an act was provocative, even treasonable. To defend his motion, Henry rose to give the best speech of his life, one of the finest in the nation's history.

He began respectfully. "No man thinks more highly than I do of the patriotism, as well as abilities, of the very worthy gentlemen who have just addressed the house. But different men often see the same subject in different lights; and, therefore, I hope it will not be thought disrespectful to those gentlemen if, entertaining as I do opinions of a character very opposite to theirs, I shall speak forth my sentiments freely and without reserve."

He touched briefly on the subject of treason. "Should I keep back my opinions at such a time, through fear of giving offense, I should consider myself as guilty of treason towards my country, and of an act of disloyalty toward the Majesty of Heaven, which I revere above all earthly kings."[3]

He moved to a series of rhetorical questions to make clear the impossibility of the current situation and ended with a torrent of language calling for action, calling for war.

> There is no longer any room for hope. . . .
> They tell us, sir, that we are weak; unable to cope with so formidable an adversary. But when shall we be stronger? Will it be the next week, or

the next year? Will it be when we are totally disarmed, and when a British guard shall be stationed in every house? Shall we gather strength by ir-resolution and inaction? Shall we acquire the means of effectual resistance by lying supinely on our backs and hugging the delusive phantom of hope, until our enemies shall have bound us hand and foot? . . .

. . . If we were base enough to desire it, it is now too late to retire from the contest. There is no retreat but in submission and slavery! Our chains are forged! Their clanking may be heard on the plains of Boston! The war is inevitable — and let it come! I repeat it, sir, let it come.

It is in vain, sir, to extenuate the matter. Gentlemen may cry, Peace, Peace — but there is no peace. The war is actually begun! The next gale that sweeps from the north will bring to our ears the clash of resounding arms! Our brethren are already in the field! Why stand we here idle? What is it that gentlemen wish? What would they have? Is life so dear, or peace so sweet, as to be purchased at the price of chains and slavery? Forbid it, Almighty God!

I know not what course others may take; but as for me, **GIVE ME LIBERTY OR GIVE ME DEATH!**[4]

The meeting recommended that each county raise a company of infan-try and a troop of cavalry. They also elected their representatives to the next Continental Congress two months hence.

Less than a month later, on April 19, the British army fought the Massa-chusetts militiamen at Lexington, Concord, and all the way back to Boston. It was, as Henry prophesied, "the next gale that sweeps from the north."

WE MUST ALL HANG TOGETHER, OR MOST ASSUREDLY WE SHALL ALL HANG SEPARATELY

★ 1776 ★

During the year after the "Battle of Bunker Hill," neither the British nor the colonials did anything to heal the breach. For those intent on independ-ence, the crucial task at hand was forging a consensus among the colonies.

That task was vital psychologically, since breaking free of king and country meant breaking long-standing ties to a nation that many called their motherland and to which, as the colonists often asserted in documents to Parliament, they owed children's duties to their parent. That task was also vital militarily, since the colonies that opposed independence were in the middle Atlantic region and, if not brought along, would give the British the means to split the independence-minded North and South.

For years, the most independence-minded of the colonists had always been careful to draw a distinction between King George and the nefarious doings of Parliament. If only the king knew what Parliament was doing, they believed, he would change its policies and right the wrongs. Indeed, the first act of the Continental Congress seated in Philadelphia, on hearing of the pitched battle outside Boston, was to pass the "Olive Branch Petition" to the king and send it to London. Drawn up at the insistence of John Dickinson, a leader of the opponents of immediate independence, and signed by nearly all those who would eventually sign the Declaration of Independence, it was the last attempt by the Congress to heal the dispute by appealing directly to their king.

When King George refused even to receive the plea, all the events that followed, whether initiated by Parliament, by the king's ministers, or by the colonists, moved in the direction of forcing the colonies toward unanimity around the idea of independence.

On August 23, 1775, the king issued a proclamation that the colonies were in a state of rebellion. At the end of December, Parliament outlawed all trade and commerce with the colonies.

Despite these actions from London, the legislatures of North Carolina, Maryland, Pennsylvania, New Jersey, and New York were still on record as opposing independence. Indeed, the king's health was toasted at General George Washington's officers' mess in Massachusetts.

In January 1776 the tide in America began to change rapidly. Tom Paine's *Common Sense* was published early that month. Paine, a native-born Englishman, had emigrated to America in September 1774 after meeting Benjamin Franklin in London. Always politically active, Paine soon published a pamphlet opposing slavery and became coeditor of the *Pennsylvania Magazine.* Dr. Benjamin Rush, one of the most politically important Philadelphians, suggested that Paine write a pamphlet on the necessity of independence.

Paine's pamphlet was an instant success. Within a month it had sold more than 100,000 copies, had been widely pirated, and had been read by or to nearly every white colonist. Brilliantly written, *Common Sense* transformed the issues in the colonies from a quarrel with Parliament to a direct attack on King George, from a local dispute of colonies with the home country to a desire for freedom around the world.

> O ye that love mankind! Ye that dare oppose, not only the tyranny, but the tyrant, stand forth! Every spot of the old world is overrun with oppression. Freedom hath been hunted round the globe. Asia, and Africa, have long expelled her—Europe regards her like a stranger, and England hath given her warning to depart. O! receive the fugitive, and prepare in time an asylum for mankind.[1]

Events moved in rapid (for the times) succession.

In January 1776, colonists burned Norfolk to prevent its falling into the hands of the loyalists and the loyalist governor.

In February, North Carolina farmer-militiamen defeated British troops and loyalists at Moore's Creek Bridge. The following month, the North Carolina legislature instructed its delegates to vote for independence.

In March, the Second Continental Congress voted to begin disarming all Tories in the colonies and authorized the outfitting of privateers to harry "the enemies of the United Colonies." On the twenty-fifth of the month, a letter arrived from General Washington informing the Congress that the British had evacuated Boston.

On April 6, the Congress opened American ports to commerce from all nations except Great Britain.

The Congress worked as a whole and in committees to finance the government and to decide what to do with British prisoners and do about the British treatment of American ones. It authorized the raising of more troops and waited for England's next move. One of the delegates, Carter Braxton of Virginia, had opposed any call for independence, but now he was in the midst of changing his mind. In concluding a long letter to his uncle dated April 14, 1776, he wrote:

> Previous to Independence all disputes must be healed & Harmony prevail. A grand Continental League must be formed & a superintending Power also. When these necessary steps are taken & I see a Coalition formed sufficient to withstand the Power of Britain or any other, then am I for an independent State & all its Consequences, and then I think they will produce Happiness to America. It is a true saying of a Wit—We must hang together or separately.[2]

The words were much later attributed to Benjamin Franklin, the most revered of the delegates and certainly a noted "Wit." If it was Franklin, though, it is odd that Braxton did not say so, since Franklin's name, if not the man himself, was known throughout the colonies. Still, as historian David McCullough observes, the remark has since been attributed to him because it was in character and fit the mood of the moment. The dire nature of what the delegates were about was clear to them all; the punishment for treason was death.[3]

In May the news reached America that King George was sending 12,000 mercenaries to its shores to assist British troops.

In these months the more radical patriots suppressed Tories, got rid of their appointed governors, and established independent governing bodies.

Yet there was still no unanimity. John Adams saw three equal divisions in the Congress: those who were openly or secretly Tory, those who were cautious about taking any position, and those who wanted independence as soon as possible. The country was even more divided than that, and many just wanted to be left alone. There were Tory strongholds in New York, New Jersey, and Georgia, and every colony was home to a significant number who would openly or quietly resist any break with England. Indeed, New York and New Jersey eventually supplied more men for the British armies than they did for George Washington's.

By May, the two most activist colonies, Virginia and Massachusetts, decided to force the issue. On the tenth of the month, Richard Henry Lee of Virginia rose in the Congress to move that "it be recommended to the respective assemblies and conventions of the United Colonies, where no government sufficient to the exigencies of their affairs hath been hitherto established, to adopt such government as shall, in the opinion of the representatives of the people, best conduce to the happiness and safety of their constituents in particular, and America in general."[4]

The motion was seconded by John Adams and passed with little debate.

The Congress then appointed a committee to prepare a preamble to Lee's motion that would make it more than a recommendation. The appointed membership of the committee foretold the result: Lee, John Adams, and John Rutledge.

On May 15 the committee came back to the Congress with a preamble that was basically a declaration of independence. It eventually passed, over objections from the New York and Pennsylvania delegations.

The next steps could be taken only by the colonies themselves, and Virginia was not long in leading. On June 7, 1776, Richard Henry Lee rose in the Congress to read the recently passed "Virginia Resolves" that urged the Congress to "declare that these United Colonies are, and of a right ought to be, free and independent states . . . and that all political connection between them and the state of Britain is, and ought to be, totally dissolved."[5]

Debate in the Congress intensified, but without much progress, since the holdout colonies remained adamant. To give the Congress more time for informal discussion and, more important, to allow the middle colonies an opportunity to seek new instructions from their legislatures, Edward Rutledge proposed that the question be postponed until July 1. His proposal was adopted, but in the meantime the Congress appointed a five-man committee to draft a declaration of independence. The five were John Adams, Benjamin Franklin, Roger Sherman, Robert Livingston, and Thomas Jefferson, who, at thirty-three, was one of the youngest delegates.

How or why Jefferson got the job of drafting the document himself is the subject of various stories. But over the next week or so, he did it, drawing heavily on his voluminous reading, the recently completed Virginia Bill of Rights, and much that was in the philosophical and political air of the times. As he himself later wrote, the declaration was never intended to be an original creation.

> Not to find out new principles, or new arguments, never before thought of, not merely to say things which had never been said before; but to place before mankind the common sense of the subject in terms so plain and firm as to command their assent, and to justify ourselves in the independent stand we are compelled to take. Neither aiming at originality of principle or sentiment, nor yet copied from any particular previous writing, it was intended to be an expression of the American mind and to give to that expression the proper tone and spirit called for by the occasion.[6]

Most of his time was taken up with compiling a list of the offenses of King George, a significant change in the revolutionary tactics. Before this point, the colonists had carefully ascribed their troubles to a hostile government, of whose offenses the king was surely ignorant. Now the die was being readied for casting, and indicting the king was crucial to the psychological as well as the political revolution.

The ensuing draft was only lightly edited by Adams and Franklin. The heavy work was left for the Congress.

As Jefferson was working, events were moving in the reluctant colonies. On June 15, the New Jersey legislature ordered the removal of its royal governor, William Franklin, Benjamin Franklin's illegitimate and estranged son. Moreover, the legislature authorized its delegates to vote for independence. To ensure that they did so, it sent new delegates to Philadelphia.

A week later, a conference of delegates from all the Pennsylvania counties declared that the colony's delegates should vote for independence. However, the conference had no way to enforce its will.

When July 1 arrived, the outcome was still in doubt, except to John Adams. Before leaving for the Congress that morning, Adams wrote, "This morning is assigned for the greatest debate of all. A declaration, that these colonies are free and independent states, has been reported by a committee appointed some weeks ago for that purpose, and this day or tomorrow is to determine its fate. May Heaven prosper the newborn republic and make it more glorious than any former republics have been!"[7]

When the meeting opened at 10:00 a.m., the president of the Congress, John Hancock, called the session to order. Lee's prior motion was read again, and debate resumed. John Dickinson rose to state the case for the opposition. In the lengthy manner of the time, Dickinson argued strongly that any move to declare independence was premature.

After Dickinson had finished, John Adams rose to argue for independence. He spoke as he usually did, without a written text or notes — and he spoke for more than an hour. As he was nearing the end of his remarks, the new delegates from New Jersey arrived and asked that the arguments in favor be summarized. Reluctantly, Adams rose again and did so.

The whole debate lasted nine hours, with a break for lunch. Then a preliminary vote was taken. Nine colonies voted in favor of independence; three were opposed; and one, New York, abstained. South Carolina was prevented from supporting the motion by Edward Rutledge. Delaware was split evenly 1-1, with the third delegate absent. Pennsylvania remained in opposition, 4-3, with Dickinson and his allies remaining unmoved by their colony's shift in public opinion or by the debate.

A rider was sent to find Delaware's missing delegate, and the meeting was adjourned until the next day on a motion by Rutledge, amid hints that ways would be found to achieve the desired unity. That night, the delegates learned that some one hundred British ships had been sighted off New York.

Just as the meeting was about to reconvene on the morning of July 2, Delaware's missing delegate, Caesar Rodney, rushed in, having ridden all night. A strong proponent of independence, Rodney's vote carried his colony into the independence column.

South Carolina followed Delaware in the interest of unanimity.

The Pennsylvania delegation, too, had found a way. Dickinson, and his close friend, Robert Morris, had decided not to take their seats officially, allowing the colony to vote 3-2 in favor.

When the final vote was taken, only New York failed to vote in favor, continuing to abstain in the absence of instructions to do otherwise.

The Congress moved immediately to consider the draft of the declaration submitted by Jefferson and his committee. On July 4, all the delegates except John Dickinson approved the declaration, which was signed only by John Hancock and the secretary of the Congress, Charles Thomson. The declaration was rushed into print overnight, but because of New York's abstention, it was entitled "A Declaration by the Representatives of the United States in General Congress Assembled." Copies were sent to every state and to the army. It was published in full in the *Pennsylvania Evening Post* on July 6, publicly read aloud in Philadelphia on July 8, and read to the troops in New York on July 9.

On July 19 the Congress learned that the New York assembly had voted for independence. The engraver in Philadelphia was instructed to change the document's title to "A *Unanimous* Declaration by the Representatives of the United States in General Congress Assembled."

It was not until Friday, August 2, after a copy had been carefully inscribed on parchment, that the final Declaration of Independence was first signed. No official notice was taken of the event. Since many of the congressional delegates had gone home by then, the signing of the document was strung out. Indeed, the last person to sign, Thomas McKean of Delaware, did not do so until January 1777.[8]

The words quoted in Carter Braxton's letter disappeared for more than sixty years, though they must have been passed down in some form. In 1840, Jared Sparks published his edition of *The Works of Benjamin Franklin*, the first volume of which included Sparks's biography of Franklin. It was there that Braxton's anonymous words reappeared, but altered in form, time, and place.

> There is another anecdote related of Franklin, respecting an incident which took place when the members were about to sign the Declaration. "We must be unanimous," said Hancock; "there must be no pulling different ways; we must all hang together." "Yes," replied Franklin, **"WE MUST, INDEED, ALL HANG TOGETHER, OR MOST ASSUREDLY WE SHALL ALL HANG SEPARATELY."**[9]

The story had never appeared before, but as historian Carl Van Doren wrote a century later, "Thus a traditional anecdote, real or invented, found its way into history, and has since then lived on in legend with authority from Sparks."[10]

I ONLY REGRET THAT
I HAVE BUT ONE LIFE TO LOSE
FOR MY COUNTRY

★ 1776 ★

When the British sailed off in March 1776, abandoning Boston, the apparent rebel triumph was in fact just the start of a long, hard, and discouraging Year. The fight for independence had begun, but the outlook was bright only for the most optimistic.

General George Washington assumed that the British would move immediately to occupy New York City. With his militia-filled army, he moved there in April. But the British, under General William Howe, had sailed north to Halifax in Canada to await reinforcements. Indeed, Howe had warned London that the war would not be a short one and that to succeed he needed an army of at least 50,000.

Once Howe had received some reinforcements in June—he never would have his 50,000 soldiers—he sailed for New York as Washington had anticipated. New York City was important to both sides. It was centrally located to split the rebellious country; it was a Tory stronghold with the promise of local volunteer troops; and it commanded the mouth of the Hudson, a wide and deep river road that could isolate New England. It was also symbolically significant to the new country, since it was an important city in itself. Washington, in part from his own conviction and in part under pressure from the Continental Congress, was determined to defend it, but to do so meant recreating the British situation at Boston but with the positions of the two sides reversed.

New York City was surrounded by water and vulnerable to the large British navy carrying British troops and their Hessian mercenaries. When the British arrived, Washington, who had fortified Brooklyn Heights across the river in preparation, faced more than 30,000 British and Hessian troops backed by more than a hundred British naval vessels.

General Howe and his brother Richard, who commanded the British navy, asked for a meeting with representatives from the Congress to seek a peaceful settlement. The meeting failed; the representatives, who included Benjamin Franklin, found the British so confident of victory that they were unwilling (and lacked the authority) to concede anything that might achieve peace.

Then began the year's almost unceasing calamities for the Americans. On August 22 the British landed on Long Island, looking to surround and defeat Washington's army. In the invasion, they were greatly aided by loyalist farmers. Several days of skirmishing were followed on August 27 by a full-scale British attack. Washington's defensive plan was weak, and his troops were poorly coordinated, untried in battle, and unfamiliar with the terrain. In a decisive defeat, more than 1,100 Americans were captured, and the rest withdrew to the defensive positions in Brooklyn.

Washington's army was in a fatally weak position and was saved by a combination of British inaction and near-miraculous American action.

First, for some reason, Howe did not immediately press on to follow up his victory — a pattern that continued throughout the year.

Second, on August 29, under cover of night and fog and in complete silence, Washington withdrew his army across the river in boats rowed by a contingent of fishermen from Marblehead, Massachusetts. Washington himself took the last boat, which left just at dawn. Admiral Howe had failed to patrol the East River, and the British were taken completely by surprise.

Washington, though, wavered. He believed the British moves might be a ruse to cover their real intention: to invade at the tip of the island and cut him off. Certainly the British demonstrated his vulnerability by sailing a few warships up the Hudson to a point above him and then sailing back. The ships went unharmed despite almost ceaseless bombardment by American artillery from the shore.

It was only a matter of time until the British crossed into Manhattan. Two of Washington's senior generals advised him to abandon New York City and burn it. Washington did neither, though he did withdraw from the lower part of the island, leaving a small force there and some 3,000 men at Kip's Bay, farther up the island on the East River. On September 15, Howe's troops landed at Kip's Bay. Washington's troops immediately fled, and his men in lower Manhattan just managed to escape being cut off, moving northward to the prepared defensive positions at Harlem Heights at the top of the island. There, on September 16, the Americans counterattacked and routed the British, inflicting heavy casualties, though the two American commanders were killed.

Shortly before this action, a young captain from Connecticut, Nathan Hale, volunteered to spy on the British and bring back the kind of information Washington so badly needed. He and his sergeant, Stephen Hempstead, departed for Stamford, Connecticut, to get a boat to take Hale to Long Island, where, disguised as an unemployed schoolmaster, he could gather information in the British camps. He never had a chance.

Nothing is known of what he did on Long Island or what he learned. What is known is that he was quickly discovered with incriminating documents. He was captured on Long Island on Saturday, September 19, and taken to New York Island. The next morning, General Howe ordered his execution.

That night, late on September 20 and continuing into the next day, part of New York City was burned to the ground. The British said American arsonists did it; New York loyalists said New England rebels did it. Washington later called the fire an accident, though he could not have been unhappy at the fate of a largely loyalist city. Though no arson was ever proved, the fire left the Congress silent and the British in a very bad frame of mind. Hale was hanged on September 22, 1776.

Late in the evening of September 22, as smoke still hung over New York City, word came of Nathan Hale. A British captain, John Montressor, who was an aide-de-camp to General Howe, crossed the American lines at Harlem, bearing a flag of truce and a letter from Howe to Washington regarding a possible exchange of prisoners. Montressor told General Israel Putnam and Captains William Hull and Alexander Hamilton that an American captain named Nathan Hale had been hanged that morning as a spy. A later inquiry by an American officer under a flag of truce returned the information that Nathan's brother recorded.

> Nathan, being suspected by his movements that he wanted to get out of New York, was taken up and examined by the general, and, some minutes being found with him, orders were immediately given that he should be hanged. When at the gallows, he spoke and told that he was a captain in the Continental army, by the name Nathan Hale.[1]

Washington, still without adequate intelligence, was forced by superior numbers to continue to fall back and back. The army and the cause continued in dire straits. No official notice of Hale's fate was taken by Washington or his army. The only notice at the time occurred some months later in brief articles in a few local Connecticut newspapers "merely giving the news from camp that one Hale had been executed."[2] But Captain Frederick MacKensie, a British officer in New York, did keep a diary. On September 22, 1776, the day of Hale's execution, MacKensie recorded: "He behaved with great composure and resolution, saying he thought it the duty of every good Officer, to obey any orders given him by his Commander-in-Chief; and desired the Spectators to be at all times prepared to meet death in whatever shape it might appear."[3]

MacKensie's diary was not discovered for a century, though. And at the time, it was several years before fuller accounts began to come out. An article in the *Boston Independent Chronicle* for May 17, 1781, dealt with Hale's demise in the context of the hanging of the British spy Major John André, who had been executed eight months earlier. The *Chronicle* story was reprinted in 1782 in the *London Remembrancer*. In contrasting the treatment and last moments of the two men, the story reported:

> André as he was going to die, with great presence of mind and the most engaging air, bowed to all around him, and returned the respect that had been and was still paid to him; and said: "Gentlemen, you will bear witness that I die with the firmness becoming a soldier." Hale had received no such respects, and had none to return; but just before he expired, said, aloud: "I am so satisfied with the cause in which I have engaged, that my only regret is, that I have not more lives than one to offer in its service." [4]

It was Hannah Adams, author of *The History of New England* published in 1799, who first made Hale an important patriotic figure. She described Hale's last moments:

> Unknown to all around him, without a single friend to offer him the least consolation, thus fell as amiable and as worthy a young man as America could boast, with this as his dying observation, "that he only lamented, that he had but one life to lose for his country." . . . To see such a character, in the flower of youth, cheerfully treading in the most hazardous paths, influenced by the purest intentions, and only emulous to do good to his country, without the imputation of a crime, fall a victim to policy, must have been wounding to the feelings, even of his enemies. So far Hale has remained unnoticed, and, it is scarcely known such a character ever existed." [5]

The words attributed to Hale are close to what we now think of when Nathan Hale comes to mind. Adams credits Captain (later General) Hull for her account, and when his daughter published his biography in 1848, Hale says **"I ONLY REGRET THAT I HAVE BUT ONE LIFE TO LOSE FOR MY COUNTRY."** The statement is very like one in a well-known play of the time, Joseph Addison's *Cato*.[6] While Captain MacKensie's account in his diary does not contradict the later versions of Hale's last words, it seems likely that he would have noted the striking line from a well-known play. More important, the words became a slogan that survives as a core patriotic belief of the country and is true in that sense.[7]

THESE ARE THE TIMES THAT
TRY MEN'S SOULS

★ 1776 ★

Having been pushed off Long Island and to the top of New York Island (now called Manhattan), General George Washington was entrenched on the Harlem Heights. He was vulnerable, and he realized it. At any moment General William Howe could land troops behind him and trap his men on the island. The combination of superior forces and superior strategic position seemed to ordain a complete British victory. Yet as he had done before and would do again, Howe failed to seize his advantage. He did nothing for a month. Nor did the Americans.

Washington was in despair, writing to John Hancock in Philadelphia that the outlook was "gloomy." Washington went on to say that he had no chance of success "unless some speedy and effectual measures were adopted by Congress." These measures included enlistments for at least three years and inducements to enlist, including clothes, a cash bounty, regular pay, a promise of one hundred acres after honorable discharge from the army, and provision for volunteers and their widows. Washington also demanded that there be some system to enlist "gentlemen and men of character" as officers. Officers were elected by their men, and that system just would not work in warfare. Hoping that the citizen militias could defeat a British regular army was romantic at best. As Washington wrote, "to place any dependence upon Militia is, assuredly, resting on a broken staff."[1]

For once, Congress overcame its horror of a regular army and gave Washington what he wanted. That would help eventually, but it could do nothing for the general at the moment. His army continued to deteriorate. Men whose short enlistments ended left for home; others just left. The replacements who arrived were untrained and unsupplied.

Washington could wait no longer. He withdrew his forces northward, and Howe's troops followed him. On October 22 a three-day battle took place at White Plains, twelve miles north of New York City. The two sides fought to no real conclusion, and Washington withdrew across the Croton River. The Americans had suffered one hundred killed and wounded; the British casualties were three times that, but they could afford the losses.

Deciding that the British would eventually cross the Hudson, move through New Jersey, and take Philadelphia before going into winter camp, Washington moved some of his troops across first. However, he left a sizable force at Croton, sent some troops to Peekskill, and decided to defend both Fort Washington, on the New York side of the Hudson River, and Fort Lee, directly opposite on the New Jersey side. It was not a time to split what little force he had.

After a pitched battle, Fort Washington fell on November 16. Nearly 3,000 Americans surrendered, and all their equipment and cannons were lost. Two days later, General Charles Cornwallis surprised the Americans at Fort Lee, and the Americans only narrowly escaped.

For the next weeks, Cornwallis pursued Washington across New Jersey. Howe sent him nine fresh battalions but ordered him to wait at Brunswick until Howe could join him there. The wait, like most of the British waits, was self-defeating.

After Howe joined them, the British pushed on to Princeton, arriving in the town just as the American rear guard was leaving. Stopping in Princeton for eighteen hours to rest and feed his troops, Howe missed yet another opportunity. Washington had boats waiting to convey his army and its weapons across the Delaware River. The crossing was accomplished with difficulty on December 7 and completed on December 8. When the British arrived at noon on the eighth, they could find no boats to continue their pursuit.

For the moment, the Americans were again safe–to rest and to be reequipped and fed.

There were no reinforcements available, though. The British had occupied Providence on December 7, tying up Rhode Islanders who were meant to move to Washington's assistance. Washington repeatedly sent pleas for aid to General Charles Lee with the troops left in Croton, but Lee did not respond.

Nothing seemed to go well for the Americans. On Washington's recommendation, Congress abandoned Philadelphia for Baltimore. Morale both in Congress and in the army was at a low ebb. Many officers talked about resigning their commissions; the enlistments of most of the soldiers in the Continental Army would expire on December 31, and few were expected to extend their service.

But while most were losing heart, Tom Paine began writing again. Paine, whose pamphlet *Common Sense* had turned the tide in favor of independence at the beginning of the year, joined the army as a volunteer aide first to General Daniel Roberdeau's "Flying Corps" and then to General

Nathanael Greene. At night and in his few spare moments, Paine wrote the first of a series of "Crisis Papers," meant to lend new enthusiasm to the flagging cause. Read to Washington's troops in New Jersey and published on December 23, 1776, Paine's brilliant rhetoric rang out.

He began with what became four of his most famous sentences:

> **THESE ARE THE TIMES THAT TRY MEN'S SOULS.** The summer soldier and the sunshine patriot will, in this crisis, shrink from the service of their country, but he that stands it now, deserves the love and thanks of man and woman. Tyranny, like hell, is not easily conquered; yet we have this consolation with us, that the harder the conflict, the more glorious the triumph. What we obtain too cheap, we esteem too lightly; it is dearness only that gives every thing its value.[2]

In a short space, Paine reviewed the past months' action, restated the reasons for independence and the war, castigated the enemy and its allies, lauded General Washington, and reassured the wavering. He ended with a stirring call for bravery and a dire warning if bravery was not forthcoming.

> I thank God, that I fear not. I see no real cause for fear. I know our situation well, and can see the way out of it. . . . By perseverance and fortitude we have the prospect of a glorious issue; by cowardice and submission, the sad choice of a variety of evils-a ravaged country-a depopulated city-habitations without safety, and slavery without hope-our homes turned into barracks and bawdy-houses for Hessians, and a future race to provide for, whose fathers we shall doubt of. Look on this picture and weep over it! and if there yet remains one thoughtless wretch who believes it not, let him suffer it unlamented.[3]

As Paine was writing, Washington was preparing to act, to gain a badly needed military success. On December 14, Howe ordered his army to stop pursuing the Americans and go into winter quarters. That same day, Washington convened a meeting of his generals to plan a strike back across the Delaware.

The plan was risky, depending on secrecy and surprise, but the Americans needed to take risks. On the night of December 25, three columns left the American camp to cross the river. It was raining, then sleeting, and finally snowing. The river crossing was choked by swiftly moving ice that had broken up and was now refreezing. Only the column led by

Washington himself made it across, and the heavy snow slowed it down, preventing a dawn attack on the Hessians in Trenton.

Nonetheless, Washington's column achieved the needed surprise. At 8:00 a.m. the attack began. The sentries were killed or overpowered; the troops, sleeping off their Christmas celebration, were completely unprepared. Henry Knox's artillery swept the streets with grapeshot as the Hessian officers and men emerged from their shelters. Panic ensued, and the Hessian commanding officer, mortally wounded, surrendered.

The Americans had suffered only four casualties in battle. Two more men had frozen to death en route. They captured thirty Hessian officers and more than eight hundred enlisted men, together with six cannons, one thousand muskets, ammunition, and battle flags. Learning of the battle at Trenton, the Hessians pulled out of Bordentown, Burlington, and Mount Holly; Howe could spend the winter with his mistress in New York, and his troops rested in the city's friendly confines.

Washington's 6,500 men moved to a safe haven in the hills near Morristown, New Jersey. Congress was safe for the moment, and the American army could now rest and rearm, with sufficient food and supplies. Many extended their enlistments, and there was time to recruit and train reinforcements.

Once again action had responded to words, but there were long years left to fight.

MILLIONS FOR DEFENSE,
BUT NOT A CENT FOR TRIBUTE

★ 1798 ★

In the 1790s there was a war between France and the United States that is remembered only by historians, who call it "the Quasi-War." Though never declared by either side, it was enough of a war to call George Washington out of his longed-for retirement to be, once again, commander in chief of the army. But the anticipated French invasion never happened; the only fighting that took place was on the high seas between individual ships, only one of which was a regular French naval vessel.

The Quasi-War began with a peace treaty, Jay's Treaty with England in 1795, that aimed to reduce the hostilities between the United States and Britain–a Britain at war, as usual, with France. Washington had declared the United States neutral, but the British had not vacated their military fortifications on the United States' western borders and had taken to seizing France-bound merchant ships for their cargo and impressing some of their crew members. The Jay Treaty only reduced the English actions, but it enraged the pro-France Republicans led by Thomas Jefferson.

The Jay Treaty also enraged the French, who considered the American declaration of neutrality a violation of the United States–France treaties of 1778, not to mention poor thanks for their assistance to America in its revolutionary struggle. Moreover, by overthrowing the French monarchy and becoming a republic themselves, were they not now comrades in ideology?

To make their displeasure known, the French broke off diplomatic relations, refused to pay any debts they had incurred to buy American grain, confiscated American merchant ships and their cargoes in French ports, and made liberal use of French privateers to attack American shipping in the West Indies.

President John Adams responded by calling a special session of Congress in the spring of 1797. He told the assembled congressmen that while he wanted to avoid a war with France, the United States had to build up its defensive forces on both land and sea. At the same time, he announced that he would send a mission to France to find ways to decrease tensions and eliminate hostilities.

Three people were named to the mission: Charles Pinckney of South Carolina, who was already in Europe but had been refused recognition by the French as the United States minister to the country; John Marshall of Virginia, a highly respected and well liked lawyer, and Elbridge Gerry of Massachusetts, a close friend of Adams and known to be sympathetic to the French. All were veterans of the Revolutionary War, but Gerry was known as a contrary character. Indeed, it was said that in a roomful of like-minded men, Gerry would always be in stubborn opposition.

Marshall and Gerry left for Europe on separate ships, and the three would not be heard from again for months. Marshall arrived first at the meeting point in the Netherlands on August 29, 1797, where he found Pinckney and began a friendship that lasted a lifetime. When Gerry did not arrive, the other two moved on to Paris, where Gerry finally met them on October 4.

Four days later, all three met with the French foreign minister, Charles-Maurice de Talleyrand-Périgord. Talleyrand was embarking on a four-decade career in the post, a career in which he survived two governments of the Republic, the Napoleonic empire, and several kings. He had spent several years in the United States and was considered friendly toward the country. Even better, he had nearly complete control over French–United States relations. What the three Americans did not know then, but would soon find out, was that Talleyrand considered public service the ideal place to get rich, and he intended to become very rich.

This first meeting with Talleyrand lasted just a few minutes. He was working on a memorandum on Franco-American relations, he told them, and would be done in a few days. They would meet to begin negotiations once he was done.

They would not meet again for nearly five months.

They would, however, hear from Talleyrand. A week later, Talleyrand's private secretary arrived to inform the Americans that the Directory (the French executive body) was insulted by President Adams's speech and demanded an explanation of the offensive passages. Unless the Directory was satisfied, the negotiations with the Americans would not start.

Four days later Jean-Conrad Hottinguer, the first of three emissaries from Talleyrand, called on the American envoys. Only Pinckney was available, so Hottinguer told him that, although Talleyrand was working on their behalf, there would be a number of preconditions to any negotiations. Specifically:

- The Americans would have to "give satisfaction to the honor of France," that is, apologize for Adams's speech
- The United States would have to pay all the claims that Americans had brought against the French government for lost ships and cargoes
- The American government would have to assume the responsibility for paying for all damage done by French privateers
- The American government would have to lend the French government a large sum of money
- The envoys would have to give £50,000 to Talleyrand as a *douceur* (sweetener)

A day later, Hottinguer returned with the demands in writing.

For the next four months, the nonnegotiations continued. Other emissaries would arrive, the demands would change slightly, but always two things remained: the loan to the government and the bribe to Talleyrand. And over and over the American group, led by Marshall, would refuse. Not only was a loan to the French going beyond their instructions, it would violate American neutrality. And the bribe, while hardly unknown in doing business with the French, was offensive.

Gerry worried constantly that if they did not give in, the French would begin a real war against the United States and drive the Americans into the arms of the England he hated. Every meeting with an emissary was followed by an increasingly heated discussion in which Gerry argued continually against Marshall and Pinckney's refusal. But each time, they prevailed and Gerry went along.

To Hottinguer, their position was incomprehensible and frustrating. As Marshall wrote in his private journal:

> Mr. Hottinguer again returned to the subject of money. Said he, "gentlemen, you do not speak to the point. It is money. It is expected that you will offer money." General Pinckney said we had spoken to that point very explicitly and had given an answer. "No," he said, "you have not. What is your answer?" General Pinckney replied, "No, no, not a sixpence." [1]

In mid-October and again in early November, Marshall wrote long coded dispatches to Timothy Pickering, the American secretary of state. All three envoys signed the dispatches, which were sent off by ship.

The emissaries from Talleyrand now began to imply—and then to state openly—that if the Americans did not give in, they would be expelled, and even that a real war would ensue. Marshall believed both the threat of war and the threat of expulsion were bluffs, and he called the bluffs again and again. Above all, if anything did happen, he wanted the responsibility to be Talleyrand's, not the Americans'.

Then, deciding that Gerry was the weak link in the American group, Talleyrand met with him personally, and Gerry became his emissary to Marshall and Pinckney. When even that did not work, Talleyrand finally met with all three on March 2, 1798. He told them that the Directory was angry not only about Adams's speech, but also about Washington's Farewell Address. Only an agreement to provide the French with a substantial loan would allow things to go forward. He evaded Marshall's question about whether that demand was an ultimatum and ended the meeting.

While all this was going on in Paris, Marshall's coded dispatches finally reached the United States, were decoded, and were read by Pickering and Adams on March 6, 1798. (Pickering took the precaution of substituting the letters X, Y, and Z for the names of Talleyrand's three main emissaries, and the situation in Paris became known as the XYZ Affair.) Adams was loath to show the dispatches to Congress for fear he would endanger the lives of his envoys. Instead, he told Congress that dispatches had arrived saying the mission had failed.

Enraged by what they saw as a Federalist plot against the French, the Jeffersonian Republicans demanded, and the House of Representatives voted, to see the documents. When the documents were sent and, at the demand of the Senate, printed up, they were leaked to the newspapers within days. The furor set off a wave of patriotic solidarity in the country. The best the pro-French Republicans could say was that it was all likely a Federalist fraud. Talleyrand had misjudged the American political scene entirely.

Pickering immediately sent off new instructions to the envoys. If, by the time they received his instructions, they had been officially recognized and were in the midst of negotiations, they should continue. If they had not been recognized, they should demand their passports and come home. Under no circumstances were they to agree to any loan to the government or to any *douceur* for Talleyrand.

But by the time the new instructions reached Paris, Marshall and Pinckney had already made Talleyrand blink. He had ordered them to leave. Gerry was left behind, but with the explicit understanding that he was not empowered to act alone.

Pinckney went to southern France with his sick daughter. Marshall arrived in the United States on June 17, 1798. He hurried to Philadelphia to brief Adams and found himself a hero. While he disappointed many Federalists by agreeing with Adams that war could and should be averted, he had upheld the country's honor, to the applause of all.

At a dinner in his honor shortly after his arrival in Philadelphia, there were 120 guests, including the Speaker of the House, members of Adams's cabinet, and justices of the Supreme Court. Thirteen toasts were made during the meal, the thirteenth by Congressman Robert Goodloe Harper of South Carolina. Harper rose, raised his glass, and spoke so that all could hear: **"MILLIONS FOR DEFENSE, BUT NOT A CENT FOR TRIBUTE."** The crowd roared its approval.[2]

It was not so much a policy as a political war cry. In fact, the United States had been paying tribute money for several years, but they had been paying it to countries that were little known and little regarded: the Barbary States of North Africa, which, without protection money, had seized American ships in the Mediterranean Sea and imprisoned or enslaved their crews. The first such payments had been made by the Washington administration not two years earlier. By the time Jefferson became president on March 4, 1801, the United States had paid nearly $2 million in various forms of tribute to Morocco, Algiers, Tunis, and Tripoli to allow American merchants to sail safely in the Mediterranean.

Even so, Harper had caught the country's and the Congress's imagination. Congress renounced the Treaty of 1778, suspended all trade with France, authorized the capture of French privateers, and began rebuilding the navy.

Realizing he had overreached, Talleyrand soon began negotiations with the Americans, first with the American minister to The Hague and then with a new minister to Paris sent by Adams. The French dropped their demands for a loan, ceased all talk of bribes, stopped asking for apologies for speeches, and ended the depredations of their privateers, already greatly reduced by the revivified United States Navy.

The Quasi-War ended in late 1800, but given the slowness of communication generally, and particularly with ships scattered at sea, fighting continued into 1801. Harper's war cry did not survive long, either. Jefferson's administration once again reduced the army and navy to skeletons. It would take another war, with Britain, to make a real navy a constant in American defense.

FIRST IN WAR, FIRST IN PEACE, AND FIRST IN THE HEARTS OF HIS COUNTRYMEN

★ 1799 ★

When it became clear that a war with England not merely was inevitable but had already begun, John Adams, a Massachusetts delegate to the Continental Congress, sought a military leader who could demonstrate by his very presence that this war would be a national effort. He worked hard to gather support for a Virginian, George Washington, and on June 14, 1775, Washington was unanimously elected commander in chief of what was, at that moment, a New England army. The next day Washington accepted, though in his characteristically self-deprecating fashion: "I beg it may be remembered by every gentleman in this room that I this day declare with the utmost sincerity I do not think myself equal to the command I am honored with."[1]

He immediately left for Boston, and when he arrived days later, he found the American forces in a good tactical position but in vast disarray. Washington needed everything an army needs, but above all he needed time. As luck would have it, the British gave him time.

Having been badly burned at their attempt to break the American circle surrounding Boston, the British sailed north to recover, regroup, and get reinforcements. Washington and his army headed south to defend what the British had already proved could not be defended: a city surrounded by water, with a largely unfriendly population.

And it was at New York, after the series of American defeats there, that Washington developed his strategy for the future. Since he could not fight the British on their own terms, he would trade land for time, temporarily at least, needing only enough success to keep the army willing and the French interested. And he got time, first when a providential fog allowed him to get his badly defeated army off Long Island and out of Brooklyn, and then when General William Howe consistently failed to follow through on his battle victories. He got time with his surprise victories at Princeton and Trenton at the close of 1776, which brought four shiploads of guns and ammunition from the French, with his near victories in 1777 at Brandywine Creek and Germantown in Pennsylvania, and with the British surrender at Saratoga in New York on October 17, 1777, which brought French troops and naval support.

Throughout, Washington triumphed over continual difficulties. Two of his officers turned traitor; the more notable, Benedict Arnold, was a real loss of military talent. He endured squabbles with Congress, which questioned his leadership even as it fled from city to city, and weathered a plot led by Major General Thomas Conway to get him fired. He endured hard winters, most famously at Valley Forge, when men died of illness and others deserted while the loyalist farmers around him hid their cattle, which he needed for food. He endured mutinies over lack of pay and food, and he endured one militia in New Jersey that turned out when called, only to declare itself loyal to the king.

In August 1781 Washington got his chance at a final victory. Learning that the French fleet of twenty-eight ships and 3,000 troops would be available to him on its way to the Caribbean, Washington pulled all but a small force confronting New York out of the line to march with him to attack the British troops dug in on Virginia's York peninsula. He was joined by French troops marching from Rhode Island, and by the time the two groups reached Virginia, the French fleet had beaten off a British fleet coming to the rescue. The ensuing Battle of Yorktown, in early October, ended with a complete British surrender of more than 7,000 men. When the news reached London, the king said to the prime minister, Lord North, "It is all over."

It was. The peace treaty was signed on November 30, 1782, though news of the treaty did not reach America until March of the following year. And in the popular mind, it was Washington's victory. Although it had been a continental war with more than 1,200 battles, large and small, from Florida to Maine, it was the figure of Washington that loomed over all—steady, resilient, determined, and undaunted by internal and external strife. The common wisdom, especially in Europe, was that Washington would now rule the new country.

King George III had said that if Washington "could give up power, he would indeed be the greatest man of the eighteenth century." And to the surprise of all, that is just what Washington did on Tuesday, December 23, 1783, to a packed house of Congress and spectators in Annapolis, Maryland.

For the next five years, Washington lived happily at Mount Vernon, repairing his farms and his fortune. But those five years were difficult ones for the country. Congress governed under the Articles of Confederation and Perpetual Union, which had been adopted in November 1777. There was no chief executive, no president; centralized power was abhorrent to those rebelling against the rule of a monarchy. Even the state governors, with the exception of New York, had little power. Congress did appoint executive departments and people to run them—foreign affairs, finance, war, admiralty, and post office—but there was no federal justice system and hardly any money. Indeed, between 1781 and 1786, the states paid into the national treasury only $500,000, hardly enough to run a government and make interest payments on the foreign loans that had paid for the war.

The states quarreled incessantly over territory, over needed common projects, over trade. While many prospered with the growth of the country, many more suffered with the lack of a hard currency and the burden of domestic debt. The British did not leave their forts in New York and in the Northwest Territory, ostensibly because the Americans were not making good on their reparations to the departed loyalists, and they continued to sell goods and weapons to the Indians. A debtor rebellion in western Massachusetts—Shays's rebellion—had to be forcibly put down by a military force led by the secretary of war.

Washington, in touch with national affairs and involved with his pet project of building a canal from the Potomac to the Ohio River, was deeply disturbed. He wrote to Congressman Thomas Jefferson:

> The want of energy in the Federal government, the pulling of one state and party against another and the commotion amongst the Eastern people have sunk our national character much below par and has brought our politics and credit to the brink of a precipice. A step or two farther must plunge us into a sea of troubles, perhaps anarchy and confusion.[2]

It was not a surprising assessment from a man used to running an army, but it was an opinion widely shared. The immediate result was a convention in Annapolis in September 1786, attended by delegates from only a few states; they recommended that Congress call a constitutional convention.

Congress agreed, and the convention began on May 25, 1787, meeting in Philadelphia in the same Independence Hall that had been the scene of the Declaration of Independence. Washington, who had been reluctant to attend, was immediately and unanimously elected president of the convention. For the next four months, most of the brightest minds in America worked in formal session six days a week, six hours a day. (Only Thomas Jefferson was absent, as ambassador in Paris.) Washington worked behind the scenes but rarely spoke publicly. In the end, Congress gave in to reality; the country needed a strong, centralized executive. The constitution that emerged from Philadelphia had (and has) relatively little to say about the powers of the executive branch, spending most of its words on the way the president would be elected. That it did so is due largely to the general belief that the first president would be Washington, the one man everyone trusted.

Getting a constitution ratified was not easy; indeed, only thirty-nine of the fifty-five delegates even signed the final document. Compromises had to be swallowed, and the distaste for centralized government had to be overcome. But finally, in November 1788, more than a year after the close of the Constitutional Convention, North Carolina, the twelfth state, voted for the new constitution and the Congress declared it ratified. (Rhode Island, which had refused even to send delegates to the convention, did not hold a vote until 1790.) The first capital of the new government would be New York.

And in the election that followed, Washington was indeed unanimously elected in the electoral college with no real opposition and no effort on his part to campaign.

There were problems enough to deal with. The nation's economy was improving, but money for investment was scarce, largely due to the lack of a hard currency. England and now Spain threatened the borders, just as the threat of secession was heard along the crest of the Appalachians from citizens to whom Spain denied the use of the Mississippi River for shipping their goods. The army consisted of just over 670 officers and men; there was no navy. But the biggest problem was that, for the first time, Washington and the country had no model for their new government. Washington had had models for his role as military officer and even as commander of an army. There were books he could read and people from whom he could seek advice on how to be a prosperous farmer and businessman. But no one had ever been a president of a country—anywhere. If there was a model, it existed only in Washington's beliefs and instincts—as well as in his experience as commander in chief.

The English system provided some guidance, and Washington established an English-style cabinet with secretaries in charge of the departments that were already authorized by Congress. The State Department was reluctantly headed by Jefferson, the Treasury Department by an eager Alexander Hamilton. They were important men in critical jobs; they were also destined to be mortal enemies.

The problem of what to call Washington was just as perplexing. John Adams wanted "His Highness, the President of the United States and Protector of the Rights of Same." Others suggested "His Exalted High Mightiness" or "His Elective Highness." Washington insisted on being addressed as just "Mr. President."

With that out of the way, attention shifted to setting up a federal judicial system, which Washington believed was vital to a functioning nation. Congress passed the Judiciary Act of September 24, 1789, as its first major legislation. Washington appointed John Jay as chief justice, and the Supreme Court met for the first time on February 2, 1790.

The first political crisis came in January 1790, when, at the request of Congress, Hamilton proposed a plan to pay the old Congress's debts, which included the unpaid war debts of both the nation and the states, by funding a national debt. The southern states, which had already paid off their debts, balked at paying for those of the other states, and a divisive stalemate threatened. Only a compromise reached over dinner at Jefferson's home saved the day: Congress would pass Hamilton's plan in exchange for building a new capital on the Potomac River.

Washington almost created a panic when he nearly died of pneumonia in May 1790. Jefferson wrote, "You cannot conceive the public alarm on this occasion. It proves how much depends on his life."[3] Abigail Adams wrote to a friend, "It appears to me that the union of the states depends under providence upon his life; at this early day when neither our finances are arranged nor our government sufficiently cemented to promise duration, his death would I fear have the most disastrous consequences."[4]

The second great crisis of the time began in December 1790, when Hamilton proposed that Congress charter a national bank. Again, Hamilton and Jefferson squared off. Jefferson argued not only that chartering corporations was a state function but that establishing such a powerful, centralized body gave far too much power to the federal government. Hamilton, in turn, argued that national economic progress and financial stability necessitated the bank and that the Constitution allowed any measure by Congress as long as it was not specifically forbidden. Washington sided with Hamilton, as he would again and again in the future.

By late 1791 the conflict between Hamilton's vision of the state and the vision championed by Jefferson and Madison not only intensified within the cabinet but spilled out into public polemics on both sides. Hamilton sought a state that helped business develop the nation's economy through a strong, centralized government and the active government policies that would emerge from it; the Jefferson-Madison vision greatly restricted centralized power and emphasized support of the small farmer and the poorer part of the population. Newspapers, both independent and subsidized by each side, took up the fight, and political parties began to coalesce. Because Jefferson and Madison's followers favored the preservation of the republican form of government, they became known as Democratic-Republicans. Hamilton's followers took on the name Federalists.

Washington was in the middle, both as mediator and last court of appeal in his own cabinet and as president. Since his instincts were naturally for an energetic centralized executive, he was increasingly seen as opposed to the Republicans and became the focus of public attacks.

Tired of the constant fighting and often vitriolic newspaper attacks, Washington, with his term of office quickly coming to a close, no longer wished to be president. As both parties realized his mood, they did find one thing they could separately agree on: Washington had to continue as president. "The confidence of the whole Union is centered in you," Jefferson said. "North and South will hang together if they have to hang with you."[5]

With great reluctance and only on condition that he would not have to campaign, Washington agreed. Again, he was unanimously reelected by the electoral college.

Washington's second term was far more stressful than his first. The execution of the French king Louis XVI and his queen Marie Antoinette, coupled with the British declaration of war on France, led to yet another battle in the cabinet and in the country, for France sought United States aid according to treaties made under the king's rule. Washington, after an angry cabinet meeting, sided with the Anglophile Hamilton and formally declared American neutrality.

But neutrality was not to be a shield for the new nation. The British resumed seizing American ships in the Caribbean and impressing the crews. The French seized American ships bound for England, and in one instance they tortured the captain to make him admit his cargo was going to the British. Pro-French Democratic-Republican societies were formed around the country and actively sought to undermine Washington's foreign policies. The treaty negotiated with the British gained the Americans nothing, and riots broke out in several cities.

The troubles of Washington's second term were not limited to foreign affairs. The antitax Whiskey Rebellion broke out in western Pennsylvania in the fall of 1794. Washington himself led a force of 12,000 men that put it down. Settlers in western Kentucky and Pennsylvania threatened to leave the Union unless something was done to gain shipping rights on the Mississippi from the Spanish. Washington's envoy to Spain negotiated a treaty, but what was negotiated was not the right of access but the privilege of it.

Now thoroughly disheartened and exhausted by the strains of office, Washington began, a full year ahead of time, to draft his farewell to the nation. By doing so, he established yet another precedent of his precedent-setting presidency: the two-term limit. The precedent would last for nearly 150 years. He also astounded the world, and his political enemies, by voluntarily relinquishing power.

The Farewell Address, though, was never delivered in person from the speaker's platform in Congress. Instead, it was published in newspapers and in pamphlets throughout the country in September 1796. It was far longer than any speech Washington had given, and he spent much of his time decrying the destructive growth of political parties, advocating national unity, and emphasizing the need to avoid foreign alliances. Although the country immediately ignored his counsel against political parties, it so took to heart his warning against foreign alliances that it was not until 1949 that the United States made such a treaty with a foreign nation.

In March 1797 Washington attended the inauguration of his vice president and elected successor, John Adams. Within weeks he left for Mount

Vernon. And there he stayed, with a brief return to military power in late 1798 when Adams, expecting a French invasion, appointed him commander in chief of the army with the approval of the Senate. Fortunately for all involved, the invasion never materialized.

A year later, on December 3, 1799, the sixty-seven-year-old Washington caught a cold that quickly turned into a throat infection. Treated with a succession of bleedings, Washington's illness worsened. He died on the night of December 14, 1799, and was buried shortly afterward in a joint Christian and Masonic ceremony.

The nation was plunged into mourning, and expressions of grief came from Europe as well, in military salutes from the British fleet, in a ten-day mourning period in France that ended with a eulogy by Napoleon Bonaparte, and in editorials throughout the Continent. Congress, on learning of Washington's death, adjourned immediately and declared December 26 a day of formal mourning. On that day Congressman Henry Lee, selected by Congress to give the formal eulogy, took the pulpit of the Lutheran church where the memorial parade ended. In part, Lee said:

> FIRST IN WAR, FIRST IN PEACE AND FIRST IN THE HEARTS OF HIS COUNTRY-MEN, he was second to none in the humble and endearing scenes of private life. Pious, just, humane, temperate and sincere—uniform, dignified and commanding—his example was as edifying to all around him as were the effects of that example lasting. . . . Correct throughout, vice shuddered in his presence and virtue always felt his fostering hand. The purity of his private character gave effulgence to his public virtues. . . . Such was the man for whom our nation mourns.

Similar ceremonies were repeated throughout the nation for the next seven weeks. More than three hundred eulogies were given in 185 towns, and usually the oration was printed and given to each family that attended.[6]

Lee's words lived on, in some part because Lee was widely quoted, but also because his words became part of school textbooks. In the widely used *History of the United States of America on a Plan Adapted to the Capacity of Youth and Designed to Aid the Memory*, published in 1826, those youths read the following:

> Under Washington, as our leader, we won our independence; formed our constitution; established our government. And what reward does he ask for services like these? Does he ask a diadem? Does he lay his hand upon our

national treasury? Does he claim to be emperor of the nation that has risen up under his auspice? No—although "first in war—first in peace—first in the hearts of his countrymen,"—he sublimely retires to the peaceful occupations of rural life, content with the honour of having been instrumental in achieving the independence, and securing the happiness of his country.

There is no parallel in history to this! By the side of Washington, Alexander is degraded to a selfish destroyer of his race; Caesar becomes the dazzled votary of power; and Bonaparte, a baffled aspirant to universal dominion.[7]

REMEMBER THE ALAMO

★ 1836 ★

In mid-July 1821 Stephen F. Austin arrived in Texas, then a part of Spanish-governed Mexico, with a government contract that his father had willed to him—a contract to bring settlers from the United States. But the contract had been with the Spanish government in Mexico, and the Mexican Revolution had driven out Spain, creating an independent nation. Austin did not speak Spanish, had no government contacts, and did not know the land.

He had one important advantage. Almost no one except Indians and Americans wanted to live in Texas. Even at this point, the Americans who had ventured south and west across the border to settle outnumbered the Mexicans who had moved north.

Before going to Mexico to get his father's contract with the government transferred to him, Austin had advertised for settlers. Finding he needed government approval in Mexico City, he made the long journey and presented his proposal. He would bring three hundred families into Texas, and each would get nearly nine hundred acres plus additional land for each family member and each slave. Initially the land would be free to the immigrants, but Austin could charge a fee of 12.5 cents an acre and get a large grant of land for himself. Although slavery was illegal in Mexico, Austin persuaded the Mexican government to allow it in Texas through a subterfuge whereby entering slaves would be freed and then immediately indentured for life.

There was no shortage of willing immigrants. The land was far cheaper than land in the United States and was free of endemic diseases. In less than a decade, the population of Texas increased by some ten thousand Anglo-Americans, almost all from the South.

The government in Mexico City, though, was unstable, changing from a strongly centralized form to a more federal system that allowed each state considerable freedom to develop. The growing presence of land-hungry Americans outside the Mexican border had been a constant concern. Now many influential Mexicans began to worry about a growing American presence inside their border — a presence different in culture, language, religion, and acceptance of government authority. Their concern was not allayed when a small group of settlers threw the local Mexican officials out of their town in December 1826 and proclaimed the Republic of Fredonia.

Although the two-month Fredonia rebellion was easily put down, the loyalty of all Anglo-Americans now became deeply suspect in Mexico City. One observer sent to Texas by the government wrote to a friend in 1829, "If the colonization contracts in Texas by North Americans are not suspended, and if the conditions of the establishments are not watched, it is necessary to say that the province is already definitely delivered to the foreigners."[1]

In 1830 the Mexican Congress prohibited all immigration from the United States, ended all colonization contracts, outlawed slavery in any guise, and called for customs duties, from which Texas had been exempted. Although Austin worked hard to calm tempers on both sides, several brief and violent conflicts broke out during the next two years whenever Mexican troops or government officials tried to enforce this new "Law of April 6, 1830."

In January 1833, General Antonio López de Santa Anna took control of the national government, and three months later he was elected president by the Mexican states. The development boded well for the Texians, as they called themselves, for Santa Anna was a federalist. Many Texians, particularly the more recent ones, decided they could no longer rely on whatever government happened to be in power hundreds of miles away. They met in the town of San Felipe in 1833 and voted to demand the repeal of all immigration restrictions and push for separate statehood within Mexico.

The response from Mexico City was ambivalent. On the one hand, Santa Anna and the Congress did agree to repeal the immigration prohibition effective six months later, but they did not act on the statehood proposal.

More than a year later, with Santa Anna's approval, the state legislature of Coahuila y Texas liberalized the immigration laws, allowed settlers to buy land from the government on generous terms, made English an official language, and gave its citizens the right to trial by jury, a right not available anywhere else in Mexico.

Then events turned against the Texians. In April 1835, Santa Anna switched political sides and decided to seize absolute power. He replaced the Congress with a more pliant body, abolished the constitution, and replaced the states with departments run by his appointees. When one of the states rebelled, he suppressed the rebellion, killing thousands.

In Texas another rebellion began with a small skirmish in the town of Anahuac in June 1835, when citizens protested the arrest of a local merchant on suspicion of smuggling. A group of volunteers led by William Travis forced the local Mexican troops to surrender, let them leave in return for their weapons, and freed the merchant.

In a natural response, the Mexicans announced they would increase the number of troops in Texas and arrest the troublemakers. In September a force of 500 soldiers led by General Martin Perfecto de Cos left Matamoros for San Antonio to make the arrests. Fighting began in early October with skirmishes at Gonzales, Goliad, and Concepción. Each time, the Texian volunteers were easily victorious. By early November, they exhibited a reckless confidence that victory would be easy and practically bloodless.

On December 5, 1835, the Texians who had besieged San Antonio since October attacked the town, and five days later the Mexican defenders surrendered and were allowed to leave. It seemed just a continuation of the string of victories. Many of the soldiers assumed the war was over and left, leaving only a few hundred as a defensive force at the old mission called the Alamo.

Santa Anna, who called himself "the Napoleon of the West," had had enough. He gathered an army of more than 6,000 and began to move toward Texas. In mid-January 1836, Sam Houston in Goliad got the information that members of an army led by Santa Anna were crossing the Rio Grande and heading northeast. Jim Bowie, also at Goliad, immediately left for San Antonio with thirty volunteers, and Houston sent orders giving the officer in charge at the Alamo the option of destroying the mission and retreating or staying to fight.

There were few men available to fight. The whole Texian army consisted of some 100 men in the Alamo, approximately 400 at Goliad, and 60–70 more at San Patricio. Santa Anna's advancing force numbered in the thousands, including a very good cavalry and twenty-one cannons.

The Alamo commander opted to stay, and small groups of volunteers began arriving to help. When the commander got sick, he turned the command over to William Travis, who shared it with Jim Bowie. By the time Santa Anna arrived, there were only 150 men and nineteen captured cannons in the mission turned fort.

On February 24, 1836, three days after Santa Anna's siege of the Alamo had begun, Lieutenant Colonel and Commandant Travis got a message out:

> To the People of Texas & all Americans in the world:
>
> I am besieged by a thousand or more of the Mexicans under Santa Anna—I have sustained a continual Bombardment & cannonade for 24 hours & have not lost a man—The enemy has demanded a surrender at discretion, otherwise, the garrison are to be put to the sword, if the fort is taken—*I shall never surrender or retreat.* . . . I call on you. . . . to come to our aid with all dispatch. . . . If this call is neglected, I am determined to sustain myself as long as possible & die like a soldier who never forgets what is due his honor & that of his country. VICTORY or DEATH."[2]

Santa Anna's attack began ten days later, before dawn on March 6. At first the defenders, firing cannons and shooting from protected positions behind the heavy walls, inflicted heavy losses on the Mexican troops, who had to advance across open ground. But the sheer number of attackers was overwhelming. A small group reached the north wall, forced open a door, and seized the cannons, which they turned on the Texian positions. The fighting quickly became hand to hand; Travis was one of the first killed, and Bowie was killed as he lay in bed, too sick to get up.

At the end only seven men survived, possibly including the famed scout, Indian fighter, and former congressman Davy Crockett. They were brought before Santa Anna, and the general ordered them killed as traitors, not prisoners of war. When some of the Mexican officers protested, the general's own staff put the survivors to the sword.

The next day the bodies of the Texian dead were piled up and burned. A few women and children, together with Travis's slave, were allowed to leave for Gonzales so they could report what had happened, presumably to terrify any potential Texian opponents. Santa Anna badly underestimated them.

While the Alamo siege was still in progress, a convention of Texians met at Washington-on-the-Brazos. On March 2, without debate, the convention declared their independence, in a document patterned on the

American Declaration of Independence. The delegates named Sam Houston as commander in chief of their entire army, and he left immediately to take command.

When Houston arrived at Gonzales, he found he had an army only of 374 volunteers in that town plus some 400 men at Goliad, to confront the advance of a weakened, but still overwhelming, Mexican army.

Like George Washington decades before him, Houston quickly realized that defending fixed positions against these odds was futile. He ordered the men at Goliad to withdraw toward him so that the two groups could operate jointly. The commander at Goliad, though, delayed his withdrawal for five days and was forced to fight Santa Anna's oncoming troops. Though the Texians inflicted further heavy losses on the Mexicans, they were forced in the end to surrender. Once again, Santa Anna ordered the execution of all but twenty-eight of the prisoners.

Houston, now alone, began a series of retreats, playing for time to train his men, to get reinforcements, and to wait for Santa Anna to make a mistake. His tactics were misunderstood by those put in charge of the newly declared Republic of Texas, and many thought he was a coward. The president ordered him to fight. Yet within a month of his taking charge, new volunteers had increased his troops to 900 men. And Santa Anna made his mistake.

On April 16, 1836, Houston learned that Santa Anna had split his forces and, with only 1,000 men, had crossed the Brazos River to head for Harrisburg, where the Republic's leaders were. Houston raced to confront the Mexicans, a forced march of fifty miles in nearly continuous rain. He arrived too late to save Harrisburg, though the Texian leaders had narrowly escaped. When Houston learned that Santa Anna was turning northward, he again moved to get in front of him.

To reach the Mexican army, Houston had to move his troops across rain-swollen Buffalo Bayou opposite the ruins of Harrisburg. On April 18, 1836, Houston first conferred with his officers and then called the army together. He used few words to tell them that the battle they had been yearning for was near. "The army will cross [the bayou], and we will meet the enemy. Some of us may be killed, and must be killed. But, soldiers, REMEMBER THE ALAMO, the Alamo, the Alamo."[3] As Houston recalled in his memoirs published nineteen years later, "This watchword . . . was caught up by every man in the army, and one simultaneous shout broke up into the sky . . . and the green islands of trees in the prairie sent back the echo."[4]

After a hard overnight march on April 19–20, the Texian army reached Lynch's Ferry on the San Jacinto River, a ferry Santa Anna would have to use in his advance. As they had done in earlier fights, the Texians camped among the trees and put their only two cannons where the enemy could see them easily. The Mexicans would need to cross open ground to fight.

Though the Mexican army arrived just three hours later, Santa Anna was convinced that the Texians would not attack until dawn, and he spent the rest of the day and much of the night preparing fortifications.

On the morning of April 21, 1836, Santa Anna received some 550 reinforcements, bringing his numbers to 1,350 men to oppose Houston's 900. But the Texians did not attack at dawn, so Santa Anna ordered his exhausted men to eat and rest, leaving only a few troops to keep watch.

It was at 3:30 in the afternoon that Houston's men began their attack, moving quietly across the plain, under orders to hold their fire. The Mexican sentries spotted them, but the groggy Mexican soldiers fired ineffectually. Houston and his horse were both hit, but he and his men kept moving forward.

When they had gotten within two hundred yards of the Mexican positions, Houston ordered one organized volley and a wild charge. Screaming "Remember the Alamo" and "Remember Goliad," using muskets as clubs and fighting with pistols and knives, the Texians overwhelmed the invaders. Within eighteen minutes the battle was over, though the killing went on despite Houston's attempts to stop it. By nightfall the Mexicans had more than 600 dead, with 730 more captured. The Texians had two dead and six fatally wounded.

The next day, troops bringing in more Mexican prisoners noticed one being saluted by the others. Santa Anna was now accounted for. He was taken to Houston and addressed him arrogantly. "That man may consider himself born to no common destiny who has conquered the Napoleon of the West; and it now remains for him to be generous to the vanquished."

"You should have remembered that at the Alamo," Houston answered.[5]

Many demanded that Santa Anna be executed. Instead, Houston forced the general to sign an armistice to end all the fighting in Texas and ordered him to withdraw all the Mexican forces. Eventually they withdrew across the Rio Grande, thus instilling the idea–the conviction–that the Rio Grande formed the real border of Texas. It would take another war to settle that question.

The temporary government of the Republic of Texas arrived at San Jacinto and took over. Santa Anna was forced to agree to two treaties, one public and the other secret, in exchange for his freedom. The public treaty, the Treaty of Velasco signed on May 14, 1836, officially ended the war. The secret treaty obliged Santa Anna to use his influence to have the Mexican government accept the first treaty and to recognize the Republic of Texas as an independent state with its southwestern boundary at the Rio Grande.

Elections were held to choose a president and a congress for a permanent government of Texas, to approve the constitution, and to recommend annexation by the United States. Houston was easily elected the first president of the Republic. A congress was elected, and the constitution was accepted unanimously. Annexation was supported 3,277 to 91.

Annexation to the United States, though, was a decade in coming, mixed up in international affairs, United States presidential elections, the Panic of 1837, and the slavery question. Texas struggled along, enduring Indian hostilities, badly conceived financial measures, the threat of continually shifting capitals, and administrations that changed every two years. Throughout, though, Texas grew and grew. When the Republic began, it had an estimated population of 30,000 Anglo-Americans, 5,000 black slaves, 3,500 Mexicans, and 14,500 Indians. By the time it became a state nine years later, on December 29, 1845, the white population had reached 102,000; there were 39,000 slaves.

I'D RATHER BE RIGHT
THAN BE PRESIDENT

★ 1839 ★

From 1811 until 1851, Kentuckian Henry Clay caught and kept the eye and mind of the whole nation with his legislative and party leadership, his intellect, his foresight, his genius for finding compromise solutions to seemingly intractable problems, and not least his oratory. His most prominent achievements in those forty years were monumental, vital to the survival of the nation, but doomed to eventual failure.

Though he had twice filled out others' unfinished terms in the Senate, Clay was first elected to Congress in his own right in 1810 at age thirty-three. And when he arrived to take his seat in the House of Representatives in November 1811, he was promptly elected Speaker. For Clay, the speakership was not the nominal role it had always been. He made it into a position of national power, which it has been, to varying degrees, ever since. Clay concentrated power in himself, assigning his allies to all the important committees, coming to the House each day with a clear agenda, a decided strategy for dealing with any challenges, and a ready ability to mesmerize audiences with his words. It was as if he arrived on the national scene already master of his congressional world.

The first real test of his mastery did not take place for nearly a decade. It was in 1820 that slavery—a long-simmering domestic issue that had been deliberately ignored for thirty-three years—threatened the nation, which was still less than a generation old.

The North and South had had, since the Federal Convention of 1787, a tacit agreement that the Ohio River and the Mason-Dixon line, 36°30′ north latitude, constituted the division between the states and territories that allowed slavery and those in which slavery either had been abolished or was quickly dying. It was a necessary political compromise to ensure the stability of an always-fragile union, for it gave the South the security of relatively equal population and thus relative equality of representation in the two houses of Congress. By 1820, though, the North was outpacing the South in population and had a significant edge in the House of Representatives: 105–81. Yet as Congress carefully admitted new free states and slave states alternately, the South kept its equality and its balance of power in the Senate. In 1819, Alabama was admitted as a slave state, bringing the balance to eleven states in each camp.

In 1819 Missouri applied for admission as a state. Part of the territory lay above the dividing line, and the state had been partly settled by southern slave owners. Missouri's move was seen as a southern power grab. In response, Representative James Tallmadge proposed an amendment to the Missouri statehood bill that prohibited the introduction of new slaves into Missouri and required that all slaves newly born there be freed when they reached age twenty-five. The bill and its amendment ignited hot tempers and furious debate. Representative Thomas W. Cobb of Georgia shook his fist at New York's Tallmadge and yelled, "If you persist, the Union will be dissolved. You have kindled a fire which all the waters of the ocean cannot put out, which seas of blood can only extinguish." "So be it!" screamed Tallmadge. "Let it come!"[1]

The importance of the moment was not lost on acute political observers. Former president Thomas Jefferson wrote, "This momentous question, like a fire bell in the night, awakened and filled me with terror. I considered it at once as the knell of the Union." In his diary, John Quincy Adams wrote, "I take it for granted that the present question is a mere preamble—a title page to a great, tragic volume."[2]

It was now that Clay inserted himself into the middle of the fight, as he would do again and again for the rest of his life. His attitude toward slavery was complicated. He hated it and thought it a great evil, but he also believed that immediate emancipation endangered both whites and blacks and threatened the very existence of the nation. His only solution— ultimately and inevitably unacceptable to either side—was gradual emancipation and resettlement of the freed slaves back in Africa. Yet embodied in his position here, as it was in many of his future legislative actions, was his most cherished value: that the Union had to be preserved at all costs.

For that reason, Clay first fought the Tallmadge amendment on the grounds that it was unconstitutional. Despite his leadership, the amendment passed in the House 79–67, only to fail soundly in the Senate, 31–7. Congress adjourned with the status of Missouri still unresolved and seemingly irresolvable.

An opening appeared at the start of the next session when Maine, then a part of Massachusetts, applied for statehood as a free state. The Senate tied the two statehood bills together and added an amendment prohibiting slavery in the Louisiana Purchase territories north of the old 36°30′ line—with the exception of Missouri. In the House, Clay worked doggedly to support the compromise, but tempers ran too high and positions were still too rigid for a resolution. The House rejected the Senate compromise; the Senate replied that it would agree only to its original bill.

For the first of many times, Congress turned to Clay, appointing him to head a joint committee. Clay in turn appointed the members of the committee, a majority of whom supported the compromise. With Clay's driving leadership, the committee reported in favor of the Senate compromise, which passed in the House by three votes.

At this point Clay's sometimes outrageous leadership revealed its naked power. When his mortal enemy, Representative John Randolph of Virginia, moved to reconsider the vote on the compromise, Clay postponed the motion on the grounds that the hour was late. The next morning Randolph again rose with his motion, but Clay ruled him out of order until the House had completed its routine business. As that routine business was being done, Clay signed the Missouri bill and had the clerk deliver it to the Senate. Thus, when Randolph was able to rise for a third time with his motion, Clay announced that it was too late: that the bill had been signed and sent to the Senate, there was no way to get it back, and the Missouri vote was final. The House, presented with a fait accompli, voted 71–61 against reconsideration.

But the matter would not stay resolved. In between congressional sessions, the Missouri legislature wrote a constitution that included a clause forbidding free blacks from entering the state, a clear violation of the United States Constitution. When Clay arrived back in Washington in January 1821, everything had come undone. Both sides appealed to him, and he went to work with his usual tirelessness. He formed a new committee to find a solution, got named to it only those who were amenable to compromise, was named head of the committee, and in early February presented a report of his "Committee of Compromise." The report called for admitting Missouri on condition that the state legislature would never pass a law preventing any person from settling in the state who was or could be a citizen of any other state.

After much maneuvering and voting, the compromise was rejected in a series of close votes. In the impasse, the antislavery side considered that Missouri's actions voided their statehood; the pro-slavery side considered Missouri a state.

Clay swung into action. Again, he got a joint committee created, and again, under his own direction, the committee voted nearly unanimously in favor of the just-rejected compromise. This time it worked. The compromise passed the House 87–81, and two days later, the Senate approved it 28–14. In August, Missouri became the twenty-fourth state of the Union, keeping the balance intact.

Clay's determination to let nothing endanger the future of the nation called into play his singular ability to find compromises, however reluctantly accepted, which became a lifelong theme in his political career. It was also the ground on which he built his ideas for an ever-stronger Union, ideas he called the "American System." The system included a strong and unified currency, protective tariffs for the growth of specific areas of agriculture and manufacturing, and federal spending on internal improvements that would, even if initially confined to one state, connect the country, enable a flow of commerce in all directions, and create greater prosperity for all. That some areas of the country might suffer in the short run and thus oppose his ideas would only mean he would have either to persuade them of his logic or to find compromises that all would understand and agree to. Clay, then, was willing to gamble the power of his vision against the shifting political winds.

Barely a year after his victory in the Missouri Compromise, the Missouri legislature named Clay as its candidate for president for the election of 1824. The legislatures of Kentucky and Ohio followed. In the event, though, it was a crowded field of candidates because a new two-party system had yet to emerge after the demise of the old Federalist Party a decade earlier. Eventually four candidates ran, all with the Democratic-Republican label: Clay with what he thought was broad, national support; John Quincy Adams of Massachusetts with overwhelming support from the Northeast; Andrew Jackson of Tennessee with exceedingly strong support from the western states that threatened Clay's support there; William H. Crawford of Georgia with the support of the southern states where Clay, too, hoped to do well.

Clay's real hope, he felt, was that no candidate would win a majority of the electoral votes and that the election would go to the House of Representatives, where he was the undisputed master. The one contingency he did not foresee was that, should the election end up in the House, the House could choose only among the top three candidates.

And so it came about. No candidate won the election of 1824. Jackson drew the most votes in the electoral college, with 99. Adams came in second with 84; but Crawford, who had suffered a stroke and was partly blind and an invalid, came in third, four electoral votes ahead of Clay. Clay's strategic vision was correct except in one important detail: he was the one loser in the field of four.

Yet Clay still had a key role to play. The position of secretary of state had always been the stepping-stone to the presidency. Clay detested Jackson, whom he saw as a danger to the Bank of the United States, a key part of the American System, and as completely unfit for the highest political office. There was no way he would assist Jackson, but Adams was another matter. The two met on January 9, 1825, to discuss their ideas on future policy and Clay's willingness to participate in the right role. They reached a tacit understanding, and Clay's presidential hopes must have seemed certain, if somewhat delayed.

The Kentucky legislature instructed its delegation in the House to vote for Jackson. Clay responded that the Kentucky delegation was legally free to vote for whom it wished, and shortly afterward, it announced that it would vote for John Quincy Adams. So too did the Ohio delegation, over which Clay had considerable influence. The political temper of Washington rose to new heights, whipped up by rumors and intrigues. When the election was held in the House on February 9, Adams was elected president on the first ballot.

The screams of the Jackson supporters grew even shriller when, less than two weeks later, Clay accepted the position of secretary of state in the future Adams cabinet. The event became notorious for the rest of Clay's life as the "corrupt bargain." It probably cost him any future chance of being president and was, as he admitted years later, the stupidest thing he had ever done.[3]

Thereafter Clay would render exceptional service in Washington and experience consistent rejection whenever he tried for the ultimate reward for that service—the presidency.

He ran again against Jackson in 1832, getting the unanimous nomination of the National Republican Convention. With high hopes to defeat "King Andrew," as Jackson was called by his opponents for his high-handed administration, Clay battled in the Senate to embarrass Jackson and throughout the country to crush him at the polls. But it was Jackson who did the crushing, doing even better against Clay than he had done against Adams. It was Clay's second national political defeat.

No sooner was the election over, however, than Clay's commitment to the Union and his support of tariff reform were called into action. A new tariff law had been bitterly opposed by the southern states, and now South Carolina took legislative steps to enable it to secede if the federal government attempted to enforce the law and previous hated tariffs. President Jackson, enraged by the challenge, sent a bill to Congress authorizing him to use force to make the state comply. When the Senate approved Jackson's bill, civil war loomed—for the second time in just over a decade.

Again Clay worked furiously behind the scenes to create a compromise and get it through both houses of Congress. And again he was successful. Jackson signed the Tariff Compromise of 1833, and South Carolina withdrew its challenge to federal authority.

Clay withdrew from the nomination to oppose Martin Van Buren, Jackson's hand-picked successor in the 1836 presidential election, believing he lacked sufficient support. As the election of 1840 neared, he again felt the call. But he had been on the stage so long, and been the creator and expediter of so many compromises, that he was distrusted everywhere. He was attacked in the South as being a secret abolitionist and in the North as being pro-slavery. Moreover, while it looked as if a Whig triumph in the upcoming election was all but inevitable, many in the party increasingly felt that he just could never win on a national level. Clay disagreed, believing that, if everyone just understood his position on slavery, he could and would win.

Accordingly, he prepared to give a major address on the issue in the Senate early in February 1839. To test his ideas, he called several people to a meeting to ask their opinion of the speech. Senator William C. Preston of South Carolina told him that the speech might not settle anything, that it might merely antagonize both sides of the question and end by hurting him politically everywhere. As Preston described the moment in a speech a month later,

> After stating what he proposed, I suggested whether there would not be danger in it, whether such a course would not injure his own prospects, as well as those of the whig party in general. His reply was, "I did not send for you to ask what might be the effect of the proposed movement on my *prospects*, but whether it was *right; I HAD RATHER BE RIGHT THAN BE PRESIDENT.*"[4]

So it was to be. At the party convention in December, though Clay had the greatest delegate strength overall, the party leaders in Pennsylvania and New York made sure he never got close to the nomination. Instead, the Whigs nominated William Henry Harrison, who won easily.

Frustrated and in poor health, Clay resigned from the Senate. His political career and his service to the nation were not over, though. Two years later, in 1842, Clay again began to think of running for president, buoyed by the declared support of fourteen state Whig conventions. Then, just before the Whig convention in May 1844, Clay declared himself opposed to the unilateral annexation of Texas. Nonetheless, he was almost immediately and unanimously nominated the Whig candidate.

Texas became the key issue in Clay's campaign against James K. Polk, and Clay wavered on the issue, or at least seemed to. In a published letter, he wrote, "Personally I could have no objection to the annexation of Texas, but I certainly would be unwilling to see the existing Union dissolved or seriously jeoparded [jeopardized] for the sake of acquiring Texas."[5] As with his position on slavery, his position on Texas convinced no one of anything except that he was trying to have it both ways. Yet he was again right. The annexation of Texas together with the war and territorial acquisitions that ensued did indeed imperil the Union. And Clay would, for one last time, be called into action to save it.

The election of 1844 was very close, so close that it was the votes for the abolitionist candidate in New York that cost Clay the state and the election for the third time. Polk was elected with just 49.6 percent of the popular vote and an electoral vote of 170–105. New York's thirty-six votes made the difference.

Clay sought the Whig nomination for the last time for the 1848 election, in the midst of the Mexican-American War. He almost succeeded despite his unwillingness to commit formally to his candidacy, coming in a close second on the first ballot. In the end, though, Zachary Taylor won the nomination and eventually the presidency, though like Harrison, the last Whig who had beaten Clay for the nomination and been elected president, Taylor died in office.

In February 1849 Clay was once more elected to the Senate by the Kentucky legislature. He returned to Washington at the end of the year to find everything at an impasse brought on once more by the slavery issue. The Mexican War had led to the sudden acquisition of California and New Mexico (including what would become Arizona). The South was feeling threatened by antislavery agitation and an uncertainty over the slave state/free state balance, which stood at fifteen apiece. Three years earlier David Wilmot, a Pennsylvania member of the House, had proposed an amendment to a presidential bill stating that in any territory newly acquired by the United States, "neither slavery nor involuntary servitude shall ever exist." While neither Wilmot's Proviso, as it was called, nor President Polk's proposal that the Missouri Compromise slave state/free state boundary of 36°30′ should be extended across the continent was accepted, California, New Mexico, and Utah were clearly ready for admission to the Union. But how?

The fat was thrown into the fire by California, which held a convention in September 1849, drafted a state constitution prohibiting slavery, and was knocking on the statehood door. The North rejoiced, the South was up in arms, and secession was once again in the air.

Newly inaugurated President Taylor recommended the immediate admission of California as a state and the organization of New Mexico and Utah as territories without any mention of slavery. When Georgia's senators complained, Taylor made it clear that any moves toward secession would be met by the force of the army. The ailing Senator John Calhoun of South Carolina wrote, "I trust we shall persist in our resistance [to the admission of California] until the restoration of all our rights, or disunion, one or the other, is the consequence."[6]

Then, at the end of January 1850, Henry Clay proposed a series of compromise resolutions that attempted to give each region something, and then defended his compromise in a speech that lasted over two days. The resolutions included admission of California and organization of the territories of New Mexico and Utah as Taylor recommended, settled the border of Texas to exclude any claims on New Mexico, declared that ending the slave trade in Washington, DC, was "expedient" but ending slavery there was "inexpedient," and acknowledged the need for a more effective fugitive slave law. His compromise gave to and took away from everyone.

The debate over Clay's compromise took six weeks, and when Clay agreed to put the resolutions into a single bill, the debate continued. Finally, at the end of July, the effort seemed to have failed when individual senators introduced amendments that gutted the compromise piecemeal. Clay, again in poor health, left to recuperate in Newport, but Senator Stephen A. Douglas reintroduced each part of Clay's compromise singly. By the time Clay returned to Washington, all the resolutions had been passed except one, and that was passed two weeks later. Douglas refused to take the credit he deserved, instead giving it to Clay, who had indeed done the lion's share.

Still in poor health, Clay resigned from the Senate at the end of the next year and died six months later.

What had Clay really achieved? To some, his career may seem a failure. He was most often right, but he was never president. Yet his legislative actions put off the inevitable war for nearly three decades, time that enabled the North unknowingly to prepare for its narrow, bloody victory and gained, in the end, the salvation of Clay's beloved Union.

TIPPECANOE AND TYLER TOO

★   1840   ★

That the slogan "Tippecanoe and Tyler too" survives is hardly a testament to the men to whom it refers. The first died after one month as president; the second was repudiated, while in office, by his own party. Perhaps it is because the election campaign that featured the slogan was, according to some historians, the first modern presidential campaign. More likely, it survives for the simpler reason that the slogan both scans and rhymes.

The first two political parties that emerged after George Washington's presidency, the Federalists and the Republicans, slowly died as the Federalists became increasingly noncompetitive. Over the two decades 1820 to 1840, new parties began to come together around powerful national figures. The first to emerge strongly was the Democratic Party, whose eventual hero and leader was Andrew Jackson and whose ideology, if it had one, stressed electoral and governmental involvement of all free white men and opposed elitist control of the country, symbolized by the Bank of the United States.

The second party, in both popularity and power, was the Whig Party, and it too coalesced around strong figures, like Senators Henry Clay and Daniel Webster. But the Whigs remained in opposition because they could not find a national leader or a national cause to call their own beyond opposition to "King Andrew." That failure was not surprising, because the party was composed of many groups with diametrically opposed views. As Millard Fillmore, a young Whig stalwart from Buffalo, New York, wrote in 1839:

> Into what crucible can we throw this heterogeneous mass of old national republicans, and revolting Jackson men, Masons and anti-Masons; Abolitionists and proslavery men; Bank men and anti-Bank men with all the lesser fragments that have been, from time to time, thrown off from the great political wheel in its violent revolutions, so as to melt them down into one mass of pure Whigs of undoubted good metal?[1]

So great was the problem in the election of 1836 that the Whigs ran four candidates for president, hoping to split the vote and throw the election into the House of Representatives. All they accomplished was to give the presidency to the Democrat Martin Van Buren.

In part because of Democratic policies before Van Buren's presidency, Van Buren faced the Panic (what we now call a depression) of 1837, and he was held responsible. "Van Ruin," as his enemies called him, did not help matters when he was widely quoted restating the then conventional idea that it was not the job of the federal government to relieve business distress.

The election of 1840 looked very promising for the Whigs. The problem was whom to nominate. The most obvious candidate was the well-known and powerful senator Henry Clay, who had run, and lost, twice before. Many party leaders, though, opposed Clay as part of the failed past. Daniel Webster wanted the nomination, but he had little support outside his home state of Massachusetts.

Two other figures emerged, both military heroes: William Henry Harrison and Winfield Scott. Of the two, Indiana's Harrison had more real appeal. As one of the four failed Whig candidates in 1836, he had run surprisingly well, carrying seven states that represented every section of the country except the Old South. Moreover, Harrison was known for several military victories. The first was his costly victory over the Indians led by Chief Tecumseh near the confluence of the Tippecanoe and Wabash Rivers. Harrison later achieved a significant victory over the British in Canada, but it was the earlier battle that gave him his nickname.

A late entry was Virginia's General Winfield Scott. Scott was deservedly famous for his military victories in the War of 1812 and for his diplomatic efforts in soothing the border tensions between Canada and the United States during the winter of 1838–39.

Early in December 1839, the Whigs assembled in Harrisburg, Pennsylvania, for their first-ever national convention. The Whig leaders wanted a candidate who could win without provoking all the old controversies that had tripped them up in the past. They worried too that the party would once again splinter over candidates, and for that reason they adopted a number of convention rules to avoid that peril. The most important of these was a "unit rule," requiring that each state delegation poll itself and report the candidate who received a majority vote of the delegation as the candidate of the whole.

In the first several ballots, Clay led all candidates but could not gain a majority. After several days of intense backroom politicking, Harrison surged ahead and won. The Clay forces were furious, as was Clay himself, but they were somewhat mollified when John Tyler, who had been born in the same Virginia county as Clay, was named the Whig vice-presidential candidate.

Significantly, the Whigs did not adopt any platform, in part to avoid taking positions on issues, but also because it was not customary then.

Nearly five months elapsed between the Whig convention and the Democratic convention, an interval that proved fatal to the Democrats. Those five months gave the Whigs both time to mobilize mass grassroots support and time to exploit an opening that the Democrats inadvertently provided. A Baltimore newspaper editorial snootily observed that, given his past record of mediocrity, Harrison would be happy on his backwoods farm if he had a pension, a log cabin, and a barrel of hard cider. Thus were launched the major symbols and themes of the coming campaign.

When the Democrats finally met in Baltimore in May 1840, they calmly renominated Van Buren. But there was no calm outside their meeting place, because the Whigs had organized a massive rally of their supporters. With some 75,000 people watching, between 8,000 and 25,000 (estimates vary) Whigs from all over the country marched in a procession that was said to be three miles long. The torch-bearing marchers pulled floats bearing log cabins with cider barrels on their porches, rolled massive balls down the street ("Keep the ball rolling"), passed out hard cider, roared in approval for speeches they could not possibly hear, and chanted endless doggerel and slogans. The only memorable one was **TIPPECANOE AND TYLER TOO**.[2]

The campaign was on, and in a way that anticipated many, if not most, of the twentieth-century presidential campaigns. It was a grassroots campaign because the eligible voters had grown in number and changed in character over the years. In the original colonies, voters had to own property to vote. Over the decades since, more and more states had changed the qualifications and thereby expanded the voting rolls. Indeed, by 1840 twenty-three of the twenty-six states had what amounted to white male suffrage. Blacks had the vote only in Maine, New Hampshire, Vermont, and Massachusetts; women had the vote nowhere. Changed, too, was the method for choosing the delegates to the electoral college, so that in all the states, the electors were selected by popular, not legislative, vote. Both changes increased the number of potential voters, and as a consequence there was a tremendous increase in voter participation. In fact the turnout in 1840 was phenomenal.

The campaign was not a campaign of issues, of careful consideration of the candidates. It was a campaign of empty, though resonant, rhetoric and name-calling. Mud was slung by the wagonload. Van Buren was lampooned as an aristocrat who sat in a palatial White House eating dinner off gold plates while sipping rare French wines. In sharp contrast was the log-cabin-living, cider-drinking, homespun-wearing Indian fighter Harrison. The campaign images of both candidates were almost completely fictional. The White House, then and now, was hardly palatial, and there were no gold plates. Harrison, like Van Buren, was an American aristocrat, born on the Virginia estate of his father, who had signed the Declaration of Independence. He had a college degree and was both a former governor of the Indiana Territory and a former minister to Colombia.

But image was all, and Harrison adhered to the advice given to his campaign managers in his first presidential run in 1836. "[Let Harrison] say nothing—promise nothing. Let no Committee, no Convention, no town meeting ever extract from him a single word about what he thinks now and will do hereafter. Let the use of pen and ink be wholly forbidden as if he were a mad poet in Bedlam."[3] And for a long time Harrison did say nothing. A committee was formed to answer his correspondence with innocuous platitudes. Indeed, Harrison was nicknamed "General Mum" by the frustrated Democrats who tried to counter the emotions of the mass rallies and the slanders of the stump speakers with reason—which did not work—and with similar tactics, which had some success but not enough.

Even clothing changed, as Whig speakers appeared only in homespun clothing and emphasized their common-man origins. In place of Harrison on the stump, the Whigs featured such luminaries as John W. Baer, the Buckeye Blacksmith; Tom Corwin, the Wagon Boy; Henry Wilson, the Natick Cobbler; and not least, Honest Abe Lincoln, the Rail Splitter.

Finally Harrison, perhaps stung by his General Mum nickname, embarked on the first-ever speaking tour by a presidential candidate. He made twenty-three speeches, lasting one to three hours, in various cities and towns. Reprinted in pamphlets, the speeches were widely available. Even here, though, Harrison remained faithful to Biddle's advice. He said nothing controversial or offensive.

Harrison's campaign managers also made great use of the exploding modern medium of the time: newspapers. In the decade from 1830 to 1840, the number of newspapers grew from 900 to 1,600, including a growth of daily newspapers from 100 to 200.[4] The campaign made great copy for readers who looked to the newspapers for entertainment as much as news.

Politics had become an important form of entertainment for a nation that was still largely rural or small-town. The torchlight parades, songs, chants, speeches, and free food and cider made a wonderful break for hardworking men. Such rallies were held everywhere the Whigs sensed they had a chance.

When November came, 2.4 million voters went to the polls. Turnout had risen from 57.8 percent of the eligible voters in 1836 to an astounding 80.2 percent. Records were set for voter participation in every state; in New York, nearly 92 percent voted.[5]

Harrison won easily with nearly 53 percent of the popular vote. His margin was far larger in the electoral college, where he gained 234 electoral votes from nineteen states to Van Buren's 60 votes from seven states. The Whigs also gained control of both the Senate and the House. For the first time in history, they had a complete victory.

But the victory was short-lived. One month after his inauguration, on April 4, 1841, Harrison died from pneumonia. "Too" became president— "His Accidency," as the Democrats called him.

Tyler first established the important precedent that the vice president inherited the full office of the presidency: powers, title, and the White House as residence. He also accepted Harrison's full cabinet and approved an increase in the tariff that was important to many in the party. But then he began to veto a number of bills passed by the Whig Congress, one after another. His cabinet resigned en masse, with the exception of Daniel

Webster, who also resigned shortly thereafter, and the party in Congress read him out of its ranks. Tyler eventually went over to the Democrats.

Only the slogan survived.

FIFTY-FOUR FORTY OR FIGHT!

★ 1844 ★

The War of 1812 and its concluding Treaty of Ghent, signed by both parties in 1814, left a number of potentially irritating issues unresolved. Not the least was where the border between Canada and the United States actually lay.

The resolution of this critical issue began where the United States began, in the East. The Rush-Bagot agreement in 1817 settled the boundaries of Maine on the east and established the boundary between the two countries west to Lake of the Woods in what would become Minnesota along the line of the forty-ninth parallel. In the Convention of 1818 the boundary was extended farther along the forty-ninth parallel, to the "Stony Mountains" at the western border of what is now the state of Montana, covering all the land in President Jefferson's Louisiana Purchase of 1803.

But there the border stopped, at least geographically. West of it lay the vast Oregon Territory, claimed entirely or in part by four countries: Spain, Russia, Great Britain, and the United States.

Both the British and the Americans claimed the whole of the Oregon Territory, since both had discovered it based on brief visits by naval or whaling ships. The Lewis and Clark expedition explored it. Only the British Hudson's Bay Company and John Jacob Astor's American Fur Trading Company had made any real use of it, taking as many furs as they could while the animals lasted. The United States was too busy expanding into what it clearly owned to pay a great deal of attention to this faraway region. After all, a U.S. Army expedition in 1819 had said the Great Plains were unfit for habitation.

Since neither nation had an overwhelming interest in or need for the Oregon Territory, the Convention of 1818 agreed to defer the problem. (The Spanish and Russian claims were just ignored.) Instead, the region would be jointly occupied in a "condominium" arrangement, with the area open to citizens and ships of both countries. If there was any governing body in the Territory, it was the Hudson's Bay Company.

By the mid-1820s, both Spain (by sale in 1819) and Russia (by treaty in 1824) had relinquished any claims on Oregon. The British and Americans agreed in 1827 to continue their condominium for another ten years.

Two things made this joint arrangement unstable, at least for the United States. The first was a dominant national mistrust of the British and their motives. Two wars in fifty years plus an immigrant population, many of whom held historical enmity for the English, provided plenty of fuel for this suspicion, if not paranoia.

The second cause of instability was the relentless growth of the United States and the ever-westward push of its people. Between the end of the War of 1812 and the start of real friction over Oregon in 1840, America had added eight states to the eighteen that existed at the start of the war. With the single exception of Maine, all those states pushed west, either in the northern part of the country (Illinois, Indiana, Michigan) or in the south (Alabama, Arkansas, Mississippi), with Missouri in the middle. Texas was applying for membership, and Iowa loomed.

Nor were distance and time as great a problem as they had been. Steamships were increasingly seen on the nation's rivers. Canals and railroads were knitting the East together; the telegraph was beginning to bring instant communication.

Then, in 1834, a group of American missionaries and their families settled in the Willamette Valley in the Territory. An American Society for Encouraging the Settlement of the Oregon Territory was formed and published flyers and prospectuses extolling the climate, resources, and available land. By 1840, pioneers were beginning to push west in large numbers.

The issue of the Oregon Territory was ready to heat up. In 1842 Oregon fever struck Iowa, Missouri, Illinois, and Kentucky. Wagon trains of prairie schooners began leaving from Independence, Missouri, and from 1843 to 1845, four to five thousand new settlers arrived in the Territory. Many others did not survive the crossing.

This new westward movement spurred debate in Congress. Calls were made to put forts along the Oregon Trail, to give every white male settling in the Territory 640 acres, and to extend United States law all the way from 42° north latitude to 54°40′ (from what is now the northern border of California to well north of Vancouver Island, nearly three hundred miles north of the current U.S. border). Arguments were made that the

British in the Territory threatened United States borders, business expansion, and national destiny. A bill to annex Oregon up to 54°40′ was passed in the Senate but died there.

By now the Americans greatly outnumbered the British in the Territory, and in July they set up a provisional territorial government, adopting the laws of Iowa. Also, in July more than one hundred Democrats, seeing a potent political issue they could own, gathered in Cincinnati. The meeting demanded that the United States provide security for the Oregon Territory by force and defined the northern limits of Oregon to be 54°40′. Even President John Tyler, in his annual message to Congress in December, said that the United States would never compromise on its claim to the whole Oregon Territory and asked for money to build Oregon Trail forts. Tyler failed to mention that his government had already informally told the British it was willing to compromise.

The issue of free American expansion was beginning to dominate American politics. President Tyler, trying to gain some political momentum for himself in the upcoming 1844 election campaign, in which he hoped to run as the Whig standard-bearer, moved to satisfy the rising sentiment for territorial expansion. He opened negotiations with Texas over annexation and statehood and instructed his new secretary of state, John C. Calhoun, to open negotiations with the British in Washington over Oregon. Calhoun was to offer to divide the territory at the forty-ninth parallel. Tyler was not the first president to make that offer. John Quincy Adams had proposed the same thing several times. The British minister, though, declined the offer now, as the British had before.

At that point, seemingly out of the blue, Tyler submitted to the Senate a treaty signed with the Republic of Texas in mid-April 1844. Unfortunately for Tyler, Secretary of State Calhoun, trying to secure ratification, had passed the treaty on to the Senate, together with a number of supporting documents. Included was a letter intended for the British minister to Washington, a letter saying that the motivation for the treaty was to protect Texas against "the desire of Great Britain to see slavery abolished in Texas." The slavery fat was in the fire, and a combination of antislavery northern Democrats and Whigs eventually defeated ratification. Expansion, though, would continue to be a potent political issue.

In the midst of this furor, both parties were about to hold their nominating conventions for the 1844 presidential elections. The Whigs were clearly going to name Henry Clay, senator from Kentucky, but Clay opposed the Texas treaty, and the Whigs would also avoid taking any position on future expansion in either Oregon or Texas because of the increasing antislavery sentiment in a large part of the party. Annexing Oregon meant going ahead with annexing Texas, and annexing Texas meant increasing the number of slave states.

The Democrats seemed set to nominate the former, and unpopular, president Martin Van Buren. Van Buren, though, made a crucial mistake when, in a letter published in the *Washington Globe,* he stated that he opposed all of Tyler's moves toward reaching a treaty with the Republic of Texas. He left open a future Texas state, but only if the Mexican government agreed. The southern Democrats were angry. More important, former president Andrew Jackson, still a force in the Democratic Party, was furious.

Jackson summoned James K. Polk to his home, the Hermitage. Polk, a Kentuckian and now out of political office, was a longtime Jackson stalwart, having served as a member of the House of Representatives for fifteen years and as Speaker of the House for five. Jackson told Polk that Van Buren had proved himself hostile to further expansion of the country. Indeed, the Democrats needed a pro-annexation candidate from the Southwest if the party was to be successful in the upcoming election and if the nation was to continue to grow as it must. Van Buren, he said, was "the most available man." This statement may sound like the least ringing endorsement of any candidate in history, but "available" was, at the time, slang for "electable." Accordingly, plans were laid to present Polk as a compromise candidate if Van Buren and others were unable to secure the nomination.

The Whigs met on May 1 and nominated Clay by acclamation. The Democrats met on May 27 and, within a day, fell into a deliberately deadlocked convention. Van Buren led all other nominees on the first ballot but could not get more votes. Senator Lewis Cass of Michigan overtook him on the sixth ballot, but he too stalled out. The convention adjourned until the next morning.

That night the Polk forces decided to strike, and Polk was put on the ballot the next morning, garnering enough votes to lead all other nominees. On the next ballot, the ninth, Polk's victory was assured, and he was nominated unanimously. As the official record of the convention stated, "The enthusiasm which now filled the convention was indescribable, and continued to increase up to the hour of adjournment."[1]

Whereas the Whig Party platform did not mention any annexation issue, the Democratic platform mentioned it with a vengeance:

> Resolved. That our title to the whole of the Territory of Oregon is clear and unquestionable; that no portion of the same ought to be ceded to England or any other power, and that the reoccupation of Oregon and the

re-annexation of Texas at the earliest practicable period are great American measures, which this Convention recommends to the cordial support of the Democracy of the Union.[2]

Strangely, that was practically the last that was heard of Oregon for the whole of the election. Texas captured the limelight, along with other issues.

It was in congressional debates during 1844 over expansion issues that Oregon continued to surface. During a speech in the Senate that summer, Senator William Allen of Ohio, a stalwart supporter of westward expansion, declared, **"FIFTY-FOUR FORTY OR FIGHT!"** and that slogan captured the mood of the expansionist Democrats. "Fifty-four forty" was seen painted on the canvas covers of the wagon trains leaving for Oregon.

But the slogan was not used during the election; the issue remained largely out of sight. The best the Whigs could do was to cry, "Who is James K. Polk?" and allege that his grandfather had been a loyalist during the Revolution. Polk, noted for his integrity and dogged hard work, was invulnerable; indeed, he hardly campaigned at all and promised that he would serve only one term. His victory in November was a narrow one, 90,000 votes out of 2.7 million cast, but his victory in the electoral college was decisive—170-105.[3]

In Polk's inaugural address on March 4, 1845, he warned Mexico not to disrupt the coming annexation of Texas and informed Great Britain that the United States' claim to the entire Pacific Northwest was "clear and unquestionable." His statements were backed by his enduring belief that foreigners, particularly Great Britain, must be dealt with firmly and from a position of strength. In the months that followed, he proved willing to go to war—actually in the case of Mexico and potentially in the case of Great Britain.

After his inauguration, Polk attempted to resolve the Oregon dispute at the same time as he tried to deal with Texas and Mexico. An offer in July to open negotiations was rejected by the British minister in Washington, who never told London of Polk's opening offer to cede a small part of Vancouver Island to Britain.

Internal events in Great Britain, though, did not let the issue lie there. If the United States annexed Texas, the Americans would have a near monopoly on cotton production, threatening the British textile industry. A famine in Ireland had increased British reliance on American wheat. Polk's campaign promise to reduce the tariff had the support of the British manufacturers. In this context, Polk's December 1845 call on Congress to end the agreement on joint rule of Oregon and enact a land policy that could stimulate even more settlers was both a direct threat and an immediate stimulus to negotiations.

In January 1846 the British offered to submit the dispute to international arbitration. Polk refused. But when Polk learned from the American minister in London that thirty British warships were about to sail for Canada, he quickly instructed him to inform the British government that the United States government would agree to a compromise on the forty-ninth parallel as the border with Canada, along with limited access to the Columbia River for British ships.

The British delayed a response until the Senate voted to end the condominium agreement in mid-April. As war broke out with Mexico in May, unknown to the British, London made a new offer, accepting the forty-ninth parallel if Vancouver Island remained under British control. Polk got the offer in early June. While it was not all of what he wanted, he did not want to fight two wars at the same time. He presented the British offer to his cabinet to get their support and only then sent it to the Senate. Despite furious opposition from Senator Allen and his allies, the Senate passed a resolution of acceptance and, a week later, ratified a formal treaty 41–14. Allen remained a bitter opponent and, in protest, resigned his chairmanship of the Senate Foreign Relations Committee.

The attention of the administration, and the nation, now turned to the war in Mexico—and to Mexican-ruled California.

The survival of the phrase "Fifty-four forty or fight" is curious. It was not a campaign slogan, and the sentiment did not rule the actions of the government except as a reminder of the threat to go to war. Its continuing presence in the American memory can best be attributed to alliteration.

GO WEST, YOUNG MAN

★ 1851 ★

Almost from the beginning, the new country was about land. To be sure, it was also about freedom of religion (yours, but not always theirs); about prosperity; about freedom from the restrictions of the Old World; and

almost always about beginning anew. But land brought about these desired things, made them possible, perhaps inevitable. After all, those
who arrived both early and late came from places where the only real
security and the only path to respect and independence came with owning land.

The new country had more land than any single person could imagine,
and it was there for the taking. The quest for land had a frantic quality,
often violent, always aggressive, and always with the belief that owning
land was a right as important and as integral as any right one could ration-
ally think about.

In 1713 the population of the original twelve colonies was only some
360,000. In 1760, with the addition of the thirteenth colony, Georgia,
America's population was closing in on 1.6 million. Some of the increase
came from the large families of the time. Most of it came from immigration, and not just from England. The mother country was unusual among
colonizing nations in that it allowed non-English (white) peoples to enter
as full-fledged participants, either immediately or after the end of their
indenture.

The pressure for land and the consequent hostile counterpressure from
the French and the indigenous "Indians" brought conflict both minor
and major. In vain did the king in London try to establish a permanent
boundary at the crest of the Appalachians. By 1769 the boundary had been
breached, and land was being sold in the western parts of Pennsylvania,
Virginia, and Kentucky.

In this first major advance of the frontier, the pattern of future movement
was clear, a pattern that would continue for more than a hundred years.
Land would first be explored by hunters and Indian traders, who would
bring back word of new fertile territory. Pioneer settlers would then culti-
vate scattered farms. By treaty, by violence, or by legal or illegal purchase,
land would be opened to speculators and settlers alike, who would quickly
establish themselves. Farming methods or an increase in demand, or both,
would create pressure for new land, and the cycle would begin again.

These cycles would take less and less time as the population pressure
mounted, immigration increased, and the dream of land and independence, even riches, grew brighter. The process has become known as westward expansion; from the viewpoint of the original inhabitants, it could
just as easily be known as westward contraction.

When the American Revolution began, the pressure to settle more
land—and to get out from under British control of land policy—was strong
and getting stronger. The Revolutionary War, however, by removing all

British protection from the settlers, put a halt to the movement west. Once the war ended, though, the movement resumed and increased.

By 1790 the United States had a population of nearly four million, equal to the combined populations of Britain, France, Germany, Spain, and Italy. In 1795 a treaty with the Indians gave the country the last of the northeast territory up to the Mississippi. The area was quickly settled, and the remaining Indians were pushed out.

Congress had to institute its own land policy. Movement of settlers was quickening in all regions of the country. The national population had begun the greater than 30 percent annual increase that would continue for the next six decades. Vermont, Kentucky, and Tennessee had already become states. New York had doubled its population with its expansion westward; Pennsylvania increased by 70 percent. In the South, movement into the new lands in the 1790s was so great that thirteen counties in Maryland and twenty-six in Virginia actually lost population.[1]

The congressional debate in 1796 largely dealt with two issues: What would be the manner of settlement—in centralized townships like New England, or in scattered settlements, as had been the general practice elsewhere?—and who could buy land from the government and for how much? The Federalists wanted no part of chaotic settlement and ungovernable citizens, but President George Washington, though a western landholder through his own earlier speculative purchases, wanted a price low enough to enable individuals to buy land but high enough to deter new speculators.

The result was mixed. The price settled on, $2 an acre, was too high for most would-be settlers, and the minimum acreage for purchase was too large. Over time, the minimum amount of land was lowered and the credit terms extended. For those left out, the old way sufficed: they squatted on empty land until they were forced out by owners or until the land became exhausted or the wildlife disappeared. Then they moved on. It would be left for a future generation to change the system.

Although the land policy was settled, at least temporarily, two major obstacles to continuing growth remained. The first was the Indians, who represented a constant danger to individual settlers and occasionally a serious threat to the country as a whole.

The second was a political one, which Washington, from the beginning, had worried about: the existence on every border, to the north, west, and south, of potentially hostile foreign powers. The English had not withdrawn from their forts in the northwest, under the pretext that the United States had not lived up to the peace treaty that ended the

Revolutionary War. The French, who had taken back Louisiana from the Spanish, owned all the lands west of the Mississippi and often abetted the Indians in staving off American settlements. The Spanish sat to the south in the Floridas.

The French problem was solved first, and with unexpected ease. In 1803 the French foreign minister Charles-Maurice de Talleyrand-Périgord, at Napoleon's instructions, casually asked the American minister to Paris, Robert Livingston, "What would you give for the whole of Louisiana?" It took only nineteen days to sign a treaty giving the United States the Louisiana Territory in exchange for approximately $15 million. The formal transfer was made in New Orleans on November 30, 1803.

The English problem was solved with a war. The War of 1812, though tactically a loss to the British (at best, a stalemate), ended in 1814 with both sides agreeing to a status quo ante bellum. The British agreed to leave their forts, and, this time they did. They also tacitly gave control of the Iroquois to the United States.

The Spanish problem was solved when Spain, recognizing the impossibility of defending the Floridas—General Andrew Jackson had led two invasions there to put down Seminole attacks across the border—sold all its possessions east of the Mississippi, together with its claim on the Oregon lands, for $5 million. Though the treaty and sale were agreed to on February 22, 1819, political maneuverings on both sides delayed ratification of the treaty for two years.

The problem of the Indians was both easier and harder to solve. It was harder because there were no concentrated entities to deal with, and neither the Indians nor the Americans seemed capable of making a treaty last in the face of constant pressure from determined settlers. It was easier because the ravenous, politically irresistible need for land by migrants and immigrants alike meant that an Indian policy simply evolved. The Indians were to be removed, by violence, subterfuge, or treaty, to any land that the Americans did not want. The policy was first suggested by Jefferson and was most notoriously carried out by President Andrew Jackson, who successfully defied a Supreme Court decision in order to do so.

No matter what, the people kept coming—from the older states to the newer, from the newer to the frontier, and from northern Europe to everywhere.

From 1800 to 1840, the country's population more than tripled, from 5.3 million to 17 million. Ten more states were admitted to the Union. So great was the money to be made in land and in investments in manufacturing, canals, and banking that money flooded in from overseas, particularly from England. Domestic banks freely gave credit to rich and not so rich alike, far beyond anyone's ability to pay.

And then, in 1837, the bubble burst. European banks, worried about the vast overextension of debt, pressured British banks and investment houses for repayment of loans. The British, in turn, demanded repayment of their short-term loans from American banks and businessmen. The wheat crop in the United States failed in 1836, and wheat had to be expensively imported from Canada and even England. American farmers could not pay their loans, nor could businessmen. American banks throughout the country failed. In New York City, one-third of the workingmen were jobless.

In New York, Horace Greeley was the editor of the *New Yorker*, an influential weekly journal. Though Greeley had worked his way up from poverty himself, his frantic work habits and his always precarious personal finances had insulated him from what was going on around him. The Panic of 1837 put an end to that insulation, and Greeley was shocked and scared by what he saw in the streets and slums of his city. On June 3, 1837, he began a campaign to solve the problem:

> Mechanics, artisans, laborers, you cannot with safety give heed to those who prophesy smooth things. . . . We say to the unemployed, you who are able to leave the cities should do so without delay. You have a winter in prospect of fearful, unexampled severity. Do not wait to share and increase its horrors. Fly—scatter through the land—go to the Great West. . . . The times are out of joint. . . . Let all who can, betake themselves to the country. . . . Away, then, hardy adventurers, to Ohio, Michigan, Illinois, Indiana, or Wisconsin, if you have money to go so far.[2]

In every issue for the next eighteen months, Greeley wrote on this theme, so much so that he became known as "Go West Greeley." The irony of the epithet was not noticed. Greeley's family had taken the well-trodden path from New England to western New York to Illinois and had failed everywhere they settled. Greeley, as a teenager, picked up and sought his future by reversing the direction, moving back East.

The depression that followed the Panic of 1837 ended in 1840. The westward movement that had slowed picked up again, aided by the growth of the canal system that brought would-be settlers west and farm and mining products east; the newly established riverboats carried the same products south, for domestic consumption and for export. Cities like Cleveland, Cincinnati, and Chicago grew from villages into metropolises. Immigrants from abroad went north and west, but almost never south.

The year 1840 also saw the establishment of a Permanent Indian Frontier, which began in what is now northern Nebraska at the bend of the Missouri River and went due south roughly along the forty-fifth parallel to the Red River. Here the eastern tribes were moved, with the Plains tribes moved west of them. The project was doomed, since the eastern and Plains tribes could not peacefully coexist, the eastern tribes could not farm in the semiarid environment, and, most important, the Indian Frontier intentionally blocked the inevitable movement of the pioneers in their search for new, cheap land.

For the moment, though, the movement of settlement went around the Indians, first by the migrants in the north, to flow toward the new fertile lands in Oregon, and then by the settlers from the south toward the welcoming arms of the government in Texas. California became a place to settle, with people moving south from Oregon. So fast was this movement that all three places became states before 1860: Oregon's statehood was enabled by settling the border dispute with Britain in 1846, Texas was admitted in 1845 after it had broken free of Mexico and had become its own republic in 1836, and California became a state in the aftermath of the Mexican-American War in 1846.

Meanwhile, Greeley had started the *New York Tribune*, which published both a daily edition and a special national weekly edition. In 1852 the circulation of the *Tribune* passed 100,000, and the newspaper was being read throughout the country. Greeley himself had become influential in politics in support of Henry Clay and the Whig Party. And he was still promoting the West as the place for young men to seek their fortunes. "If any young man is about to commence in the world, with little in his circumstances to prepossess him in favor of one section above another, we say to him publicly and privately, Go to the West; there your capabilities are sure to be appreciated and your industry and energy rewarded."[3]

In 1853 Josiah B. Grinnell sought Greeley's advice personally. Grinnell reported that Greeley said to him, "Go West, young man, go West." It did not take long for Greeley's message to be shortened to "GO WEST, YOUNG MAN," and he was quoted that way in small towns and large cities.[4] Six towns and two counties in the West are named for him, presumably by citizens who had heeded his advice.

Even the outbreak of the Civil War in 1861 did not halt the movement west, any more than economic depressions did. In the two decades before the war, the nation's population increased nearly 14.5 million, or 85 percent. By the end of the Civil War the population still increased, if only by another 7 million, 22.6 percent. For those moving west, the war was usually something happening far away that did not concern them, and if it did, moving allowed them to avoid it. Movement slowed, but it continued.

By the end of the Civil War in 1865, the United States presented an odd political geography. The Union consisted of states on both coasts and on both northern and southern borders, but there was lots of empty land in between—empty of people who were not Indians. Yet the advent of a national railroad system, the invention and rapid acceptance of new ways to fence, farm, and harvest the semiarid lands in the middle of the nation, and the discovery of mineral riches, not the least of which was gold, ensured that it would not take long to fill in the void. Once again the Indians were moved; once again the settlers moved west. Indian wars continued sporadically. In his annual message to Congress in 1877, President Rutherford B. Hayes expressed some guilt for the state of affairs:

> The Indians were the original occupants of the land we now possess. They have been driven from place to place. The purchase money paid to them in some cases for what they called their own has still left them poor. In many instances, when they had settled down upon lands assigned to them by compact and begun to support themselves by their own labor, they were rudely jostled off and thrust into the wilderness again. Many, if not most, of our Indian wars have had their origin in broken promises and acts of injustice on our part.[5]

It was true, but it did not matter in any practical terms. The settlers kept coming.

The national census of 1890 reported that the country's population was 63 million, an increase of 12.8 million in the past decade, indeed an increase of 24.4 million people since 1870, 64 percent for the period. Accompanying this news, however, was a more astonishing announcement. "Up to and including 1880 the country had a frontier of settlement, but at present the unsettled area has been so broken into by isolated bodies of settlement that there can hardly be said to be a frontier line. In the discussion of its extent, its westward movement, etc., it can not, therefore, any longer have a place in the census reports."[6] In 1827 James Barbour, President John Quincy Adams's secretary of war, had publicly said that there was so much land in the West that it would take five hundred years to fill it up. It had taken sixty-three.

Westward movement did not stop in 1890. Much of the western land was thinly settled. There were only 60,000 people in Wyoming, 143,000 in Montana, 88,500 in Idaho, and 47,000 in Nevada.[7] Government land was still in demand. Four times as many acres were homesteaded after 1890 as before.[8]

To this day, the country is still moving west—as well as south. An argument can be made that the growth of the suburbs after World War II was made possible by cheap loans to veterans and cars for all, and the continuing movement west and south by the invention of the air conditioner; but the motivation to move out of the city to what passes for country in 1950 or 1990 is the same as the motivation to move 150 years earlier—land.

A HOUSE DIVIDED AGAINST
ITSELF CANNOT STAND

★ 1858 ★

Henry Clay may have thought the Compromise of 1850 that he and Stephen Douglas engineered in Congress had put an end to the nation's chronic problem of slavery, but it merely deferred the problem—or deferred a solution. A compromise, after all, works in the long run only if both sides are comfortable about what each has given up.

If Clay thought he had achieved something more lasting, it was because he fervently believed that slavery would die naturally as long as it was confined geographically. Yet because both the abolitionist side and the pro-slavery side believed at some conscious or unconscious level that Clay was right—that slavery had to expand into new territories or it would wither—the compromise inevitably could not hold. Continued conflict over the issue was inevitable, and Clay's hallowed Union would continue to fray.

In Washington, sectional tensions were made worse because of the generational change in the Senate since 1850. The House of Representatives had always been volatile, but the Senate, filled with men who either remembered the struggle for independence or had parents who had been fervently involved, acted as a moderating force. But those men were either dead or dying—most notably Clay and Daniel Webster. John Calhoun, too, was dead, but his was never a moderating influence, and unfortunately his were the ideas that lived on in the South. When crises came now, there were no "national" voices of reason.

The national party system, too, became sectional. The Whig Party virtually disappeared, largely because it had no strong leader once Clay had died, and that made it vulnerable to the split over slavery. Indeed, so many Whigs who opposed slavery left the party before the election of 1852 to form the Free-Soil Party that the Whigs, who had gotten just over 200,000 votes fewer than the Democrats in the presidential race, lost in the electoral college 254 to 42. The Free-Soil Party had drawn enough votes to lose key states for the Whigs.

And as the center failed to hold, the South became increasingly defensive about its right to continue the slave system, and the abolitionists in the North became increasingly aggressive in opposing it. There were more and more calls by the South that the North had to silence the abolitionists by any means. Threats of secession came from both North and South.

Both sides agreed on only one thing: slavery was an issue that only a state could decide; the federal government could not forbid it. Yet that agreement meant that the territories, governed by the federal government, became the flashpoint for all conflict.

Meanwhile, an Illinois lawyer and politician named Abraham Lincoln was making himself more and more visible. Although he had been elected to the House of Representatives only for a single term, Lincoln's reputation for honesty and intellectual integrity, his background as a self-made man, and his battles against Senator Stephen Douglas brought him notice around the country. What was often obscured by his somewhat uncouth physical presence and irrepressible country humor was Lincoln's incredible ability as a politician.

It was Stephen Douglas who precipitated the crisis. In January 1854 he introduced a bill to organize the Great Plains as the Territory of Nebraska. Douglas's Democratic Party was as split over the slavery issue as the Whig Party had been. Seeking to resolve that party split, to enhance Douglas's support among the southern pro-slavery Democrats for his own political ambitions, and to reach yet another national compromise over slavery, Douglas's bill included his own idea that the people of the new territory, not Congress, should decide whether their territory would be slave or free ground. He called the idea "popular sovereignty."

Douglas's Kansas-Nebraska Act might have sounded like a compromise, but it effectively repealed the Missouri Compromise, which forbade slavery north of 36°30´. Three months of bitter debate followed. And when the bill passed, only dire things happened. As Senator Charles Sumner, a staunch abolitionist, stated, "It is at once the worst and best Bill on which Congress ever acted." It was the worst because it gave a victory to slavery, but it was the "best, for it annuls all past compromises with slavery, and makes all future compromises impossible. Thus it puts freedom and slavery face to face, and bids them grapple. Who can doubt the result?"[1]

The crisis worsened. Enforcement of the runaway slave laws became impossible in the North. The Republican Party was created at a convention in Jackson, Michigan, and resolved to oppose the extension of slavery. A federal land office opened in Kansas, setting off a land rush by both those opposed to slavery and those in favor. After all, the status of the territory would be decided by vote. Fighting broke out between armed bands, and within a short time the area became known as "Bloody Kansas."

Back in Illinois, Lincoln was increasingly troubled by what was happening. His feelings about slavery were changing, though they were still basically those of his late hero, Henry Clay—that slavery was evil but that, if confined, it would eventually die out. Still, he was sympathetic to the people of the South: he had been born there, he had grown up in a border state, and his wife came from the South and had family there. Yet he wrote to a friend, "There is no peaceful extinction of slavery in prospect for us. . . . The condition of the negro slave in America . . . is now as fixed, and hopeless of change for the better, as that of the lost souls of the finally impenitent." He continued, "The Autocrat of all the Russias will resign his crown, and proclaim his subject free republicans sooner than will our American masters voluntarily give up their slaves." And more, "Can we, as a nation, continue together permanently—forever half-slave and half free?" But further he could not go—yet. "The problem is too mighty for me. May God, in his mercy, superintend the solution."[2]

The violence in Kansas continued and worsened. So too did the rhetoric in the nation's newspapers and legislatures. On May 19, 1856, Senator Sumner delivered a typically violent speech on the floor of the Senate, a speech that personally attacked Senator Andrew Pickens Butler of South Carolina. Three days later a relative of Butler's, Preston Brooks, assaulted Sumner as he sat in the Senate, beating him unconscious with his cane while Douglas and Senator Robert Toombs watched. Violence had come to Congress itself.

The presidential election of 1856 brought no respite. There were now three parties and three candidates: the Democrats with James Buchanan; the Republicans with John Frémont, and the American Party with

Millard Fillmore. The South announced that if the abolitionist Frémont won, it would secede rather than accept the result. Buchanan won, but with substantially less than a majority of the popular vote. The Union was saved, but not for long.

To make matters even worse, on the heels of Buchanan's inauguration, the Supreme Court announced its decision in the Dred Scott case. Scott, a slave, had sued for his freedom on the grounds that he had twice been a resident of Illinois and Missouri, both free states. Chief Justice Roger Brooke Taney and the four southern associate judges denied his suit on the grounds that as a Negro, he could not be a citizen of the United States, and as a resident of a territory he could not be emancipated by Congress because Congress had no right to deprive any citizen of his property without due process of law. The Missouri Compromise, then, was itself unconstitutional and void.

The uproar in the North was deafening, and the noise further convinced the pro-slavery South that more protections were needed. Demands for legalizing the slave trade again were heard from politicians and editors alike. In the fall of 1857, a rigged election in Kansas elected a pro-slavery territorial legislature, which in turn drew up a pro-slavery constitution and submitted it to Congress. Facing an election campaign himself the following year, Senator Douglas, in an about-face, opposed this expression of "popular sovereignty" and led the successful fight in the Senate against the Kansas constitution, thereby managing to alienate his supporters in the South while leaving his opponents in the North unappeased.

It was in this heated atmosphere that the Republican Party in Illinois met on June 16, 1858, to pick its candidate to oppose Douglas in the coming senatorial election. Lincoln's friends had worked hard to gather support for him, and the result of the convention was assured. Lincoln was nominated unanimously on the first ballot.

That evening, Lincoln rose to give his acceptance speech. It was, in fact, a speech his friends opposed as too radical, even if courageous. He began with a series of logical statements of his beliefs, beliefs that centered on the key, the only real issue facing his state and, indeed, the nation. He spoke first of Douglas's Kansas-Nebraska Act, and then moved more broadly.

> We are now far into the *fifth* year, since a policy was initiated, with the avowed object, and *confident* promise, of putting an end to slavery agitation. Under the operation of that policy, that agitation has not only, *not ceased,* but has *constantly augmented.*

In *my opinion*, it will not cease, until a *crisis* shall have been reached, and passed. **"A HOUSE DIVIDED AGAINST ITSELF CANNOT STAND."**

I believe this government cannot endure, permanently half *slave* and half *free*. I do not expect the Union to be *dissolved*—I do not expect the house to *fall*—but I *do* expect it will cease to be divided. It will become *all* one thing or *all* the other.[3]

In the election that followed—for the state legislature, which in turn elected the United States senator from the state—Lincoln lost. However, the popular vote was close, with the Republican candidates for the legislature winning nearly 50 percent of the vote as opposed to 47 percent for the Democrats. Still, the Democrats won narrow control of the legislature and voted 54-46 for Douglas.

Though Lincoln had lost, his stature and his fame increased. His words resounded, to the hostility of the South and the approval of the antislavery North. True, the statement "A house divided against itself cannot stand" was not original. It came from the Bible, where it occurs in three of the Gospels, particularly in the Gospel according to Matthew. As such, it was familiar to practically everyone who heard or read it; as such, it had enormous weight. Nor was it the first time the statement had been made: Lincoln himself had used it before, both orally and in writing, and others had used it as well. But it was Lincoln's statement, made at a tense time and by a man known for his integrity and courage, that left the words resounding in the popular mind as the nation careered toward war.

DAMN THE TORPEDOES, FULL SPEED AHEAD

★ 1864 ★

When Rear Admiral David Farragut arrived off Mobile Bay, Alabama, in January 1864, he was sixty-two years old and had been in the naval service for fifty-two of those years. At age twelve, he had been in combat in the War of 1812 and had served as the captain of a captured prize ship. Farragut, despite his age and his longevity in the service, was known as a relentless combat commander.

More than a year and a half before arriving at Mobile Bay, Farragut had achieved a signal victory, defying the received wisdom that New Orleans could be captured only once the forts defending the entrance to the Mississippi River had been destroyed. Instead, he had run his ships by the forts, eluded Confederate combat and fire ships, and lost only one of his vessels, together with casualties of 37 men killed and 146 wounded out of the 4,000 men in the attack.

His reward was promotion to rear admiral, the first person in America's history to hold that rank.

Once New Orleans had been seized in April 1862, Farragut had wanted to move immediately against Mobile, taking advantage of his momentum and the relative weakness of the defenses at the head of the Alabama River. The Union wartime leaders, however, were focused on closing the Mississippi for good and worried about ship losses that would weaken the blockade along both the Atlantic and Gulf coasts. Mobile would have to wait.

Now, at the beginning of 1864, Mobile had become the only significant port left to the Confederacy on the Gulf of Mexico. Its importance for trade and blockade runners had increased. It had developed a growing manufacturing capability and was connected to the interior of the South by rail as well as by river. Even more important, combat ships were being built upriver and could be sent to Mobile for completion. There was a rumor, soon confirmed, that the largest, most powerful ironclad ram ship yet was under construction 150 miles north of Mobile and would soon be sent to wreak havoc on the Union ships blockading the Confederacy's southern coast.

The key to the city of Mobile was Mobile Bay, miles downriver. Once the bay was controlled, the city would be useless. On arriving off the bay, Farragut began the routine careful planning that underlay all his bravura attacks. With his flag lieutenant, he boarded a gunboat and personally reconnoitered the defenses. Inside the bay, there was little to fear: a small squadron of gunboats that were converted river steamers. Outside the bay, though, were three forts. The most powerful, Fort Morgan, had more firepower than any two of the Mississippi River forts he had faced, and its guns were all trained on the entrance to the bay.

For the next few months, Farragut's ships tightened the blockade around Mobile Bay as he waited for a response from Washington. He had requested 5,000 army troops to attack the rear of the forts while he forced his way in, as well as at least two ironclad monitors. If he could not seize the forts after moving past them, his fleet might get as bottled up as the Confederates were now.

The Navy Department in Washington, though, was slow in making up its mind, occupied with the blockade and with action elsewhere. When the existence of the Confederate ironclad ram, now launched and christened *Tennessee*, was confirmed, the Department suddenly found more monitors to assist than Farragut had requested and supplied some, though not all, of the troops.

The *Tennessee* promised to be a real threat. More than two hundred feet long and forty-eight feet wide, it drew only fourteen feet of water and could operate in shallower coastlines than Farragut's larger sloops of war. More important, it was reputed to be impervious to cannon fire from opposing ships.

The *Tennessee* had two weaknesses, though. First, its engine, cannibalized from an abandoned riverboat, was not powerful enough to drive it more than six miles an hour. Second, its steering mechanism ran in open stern channels and was perilously vulnerable. Farragut, however, was not aware of the weaknesses, only the strengths.

On May 18, 1864, the *Tennessee* entered Mobile Bay, ready for action. When it made a few trial runs, both the ship's captain and the observing Farragut learned that the *Tennessee* could not operate in open seas, especially rough water. It was solely a defensive weapon.

On May 24, Farragut and his flag captain again boarded a gunboat to inspect the avenue of attack more closely. They watched as small boats began laying torpedoes (an early version of what we call contact mines) to narrow the entrance channel to the bay. The mines were being laid at the end of a long sandbank that reached into the channel, ensuring that only one ship at a time could enter and, on entering, would face the firepower of Fort Morgan. That small channel had been left for Confederate blockade runners.

For the next month, while waiting for his ironclads and troops, Farragut meticulously planned his attack using small wooden replicas of his ships on a map, arranging and rearranging his forces and refining his tactics. On July 12, 1864, he issued General Order no. 10, laying out his battle plan. He would use fourteen steam-powered wooden ships and four monitors to make the attack. The remaining ships would bombard the forts from the gulf and prevent any Confederate ship that might appear from joining the battle.

The attacking ships were to be arrayed in two columns. Each wooden ship was to be lashed to a gunboat, partly to protect the smaller gunboats from the cannons of the defenders and partly to give the larger ships the power of two engines. The monitors were to go slightly in advance but in a parallel line, closer to Fort Morgan, since they were better able to withstand the firing of the large guns. Once past the forts, the ships would attack the small Confederate gunboats and particularly the *Tennessee*. Farragut emphasized the danger posed by the torpedoes, though they were clearly marked by buoys, and strongly stressed the necessity for the column to keep moving. Any halt or confusion under the guns of Fort Morgan would be devastating.

As always, Farragut planned to lead the column in his flagship *Hartford*. For once, Farragut's commanders convinced him that his ship should go in second, behind the *Brooklyn*, which had more bow guns and had a torpedo-sweeping mechanism on its bow.

It took two weeks to prepare the ships, rehearse lashing them together, and practice moving in columns. On August 5, 1864, the fleet was awakened at 3:00 a.m. After eating a quick breakfast, the crews maneuvered the ships into position. At 5:30 a.m. the columns began to move.

At 7:00 a.m. the *Brooklyn* got within range of the Fort Morgan guns and firing began. At the same time, Union troops moved behind the only other fort that posed a real threat on the opposite side of the channel and used cannons to destroy or disable all its guns.

As more ships moved within range, the smoke of the cannons began to obscure the action. Farragut, as was his custom, climbed into the rigging of the *Hartford* to get above the smoke. He shouted directions to his pilot, also in the rigging with a voice tube to communicate to the deck. Farragut's flag captain worried about his now sixty-three-year-old admiral and sent a seaman after him with a line. As Farragut later said, with characteristic understatement: "You understand, I was only standing in the rigging with a rope that dear boy Watson had brought me up, saying that if I would stand there I had better secure myself against falling; and I thanked him for his consideration, and took a turn around and over the shrouds and around my body for fear of being wounded, as the shots were flying rather thickly."[1] Suddenly the *Brooklyn* signaled that the monitors were getting ahead of it and that it could move forward only if it passed them. Farragut ordered the *Brooklyn* to keep moving and ignore prior orders. The columns had to keep moving.

Then one of the Union monitors, the *Tecumseh*, spotted the *Tennessee* moving as if to escape and immediately turned in pursuit. But in doing so, the *Tecumseh* turned into the minefield and, almost at that moment, blew up. The captain of the monitor behind it later reported, "[Its] stern lifted high in the air with the propeller still revolving, and the ship pitched out of sight like an arrow twanged from a bow."[2]

Before the suddenly silenced Union guns, ninety-three men were trapped in the iron ship and died. Amazingly, twenty-one escaped. Farragut immediately ordered a boat to pick up any survivors, and the commander of Fort Morgan and the captain of the *Tennessee* both ordered their gunners not to fire on the rescue boat.

But firing elsewhere continued furiously. The *Brooklyn*, whose bow the *Tecumseh* had crossed into the minefield, reversed engines and stopped. The current caught it and swung its stern into the channel, blocking all movement behind it. With the tide flowing inshore, the column began to bunch up. Farragut watched, astonished. The Union ships behind him were frantically firing grapeshot and shrapnel into Fort Morgan to drive the Confederate gunners away from their guns, but return fire was hitting nearly all the ships in the Union column.

As Farragut said later, he was at a loss for what to do. There was the minefield close at hand to his left, cannon fire from above, and ships behind him. He offered a quick request for divine guidance: "Oh God, who created man and gave him reason, direct me what to do. Shall I go on? And it seemed as if in answer a voice commanded, 'Go on!'"[3] The *Hartford* moved forward, close to the *Brooklyn*. Farragut yelled to his pilot in the rigging just above him, "What's the trouble?" The pilot responded, "Torpedoes."

The answer was immediate. "Damn the torpedoes." To his flag captain, "Four bells, Captain Drayton." To the captain of the gunboat lashed to the *Hartford*, "Go ahead, Jouett, full speed."

And at full speed, they plunged into the minefield. The crew below could hear the torpedoes hit the bottom and side of the ship, even the primers snapping. But there was no explosion. Farragut had gambled that the torpedoes had been disabled by their long exposure to seawater, and he had won.

His entire fleet quickly entered the bay, safe from the firing from Fort Morgan. Only the *Tecumseh* had been lost, though one of the ships had been disabled with a shot into its engine.

Once inside the bay, the Union ships quickly disposed of the Confederate gunboats. The ironclad ram *Tennessee* did damage to the entering ships, then withdrew under the Fort Morgan guns for a time. Finally, knowing the battle was lost, the *Tennessee's* commander ordered his ship to attack. Farragut ordered the whole fleet to sink the oncoming ram, and every ship converged on it, firing cannons and ramming it when they got close enough. So close did the ships get that fighting occasionally became hand-to-hand, with sailors throwing loose hardware at each other, firing pistols, and even in one case stabbing with bayonets. So great was the noise, smoke, and confusion that the *Hartford* was accidentally rammed by another Union ship.

By 10:00 a.m., though, the fight was over. Two Confederate gunships escaped by fleeing upriver where the Union ships could not go. The *Tennessee* had its smokestack shot off, its command center penetrated, and its exposed steering gear demolished. The *Tennessee* surrendered. Farragut was seen crying as he viewed the dead laid out on the deck of his ship.

The Battle of Mobile Bay was the last naval combat Farragut ever saw. His health was failing, and he was recalled to New York with his flagship for a hero's welcome. On learning of the victory, President Lincoln ordered every navy yard to fire a hundred-gun salute and issued a proclamation to be read at every religious service throughout the Union.

On December 22, 1864, Congress created the rank of vice admiral, and Farragut was promoted to it. Two years later he was again promoted and became the first full admiral of the navy in American history. But he never fully regained his health and died in 1870, five weeks after his sixty-ninth birthday.

Did Farragut actually yell **"DAMN THE TORPEDOES, FULL SPEED AHEAD"**? The whole incident was never mentioned in his dispatches to the Navy Department, which naturally focused on the actual fighting in the bay and the result—the purpose, after all, of the mission. Farragut was also not a self-promoter and would not have stressed any such action of his own. Newspaper accounts, at first taken from Confederate sources, since no reporters were present at the battle, did not cite the incident. Nor did Horace Greeley's history of the war written two years later.

Indeed, the incident was not mentioned until the publication of *The Battle of Mobile Bay* fourteen years later. The author, although a naval officer, was not present at the battle.[4] The story was repeated the following year by an eyewitness, Lieutenant John Coddington Kinney, who was detailed from the army to the *Hartford* as one of its signal officers. Kinney was reluctant to accept or reject the story.

> As [Farragut] passed the *Brooklyn*, a voice warned him of the torpedoes. This is the current story, and may have some basis of truth. But as a matter of fact, there was never a moment when the din of the battle would not have drowned any attempt at conversation between the two ships, and while it is quite probable that the admiral made the remark, it is doubtful if he shouted it to the *Brooklyn*.[5]

The next year Loyall Farragut, Admiral Farragut's son, published his biography of his father. Since he had access to many of those on board and to his father's journal and letters, the biographer's retelling of the events at Mobile Bay carries some weight. He writes:

> The *Brooklyn* began to back; the vessels in the rear, pressing on those in the van, soon created confusion, and disaster seemed imminent. "The batteries of our ships were almost silent," says an eye-witness, "while the whole of Mobile Point was a living flame."
>
> "What's the trouble?" was shouted through a trumpet from the flag-ship to the *Brooklyn*.
>
> "Torpedoes!" was shouted back in reply.
>
> "Damn the torpedoes!" said Farragut. "Four bells! Captain Drayton, go ahead! Jouett, full speed!" And the *Hartford* passed the *Brooklyn*, assumed the head of the line, and led the fleet to victory. It was the only way out of the difficulty, and any hesitation would have closed even this escape from a frightful disaster.[6]

One reason for the slogan to have lived—beyond its obvious exhortation to bravery in the face of danger—is that Farragut's use of swear words was famously unlike him. His words, then, would be the product only of extreme stress and might well have been remembered by those on the ship who revered him. And being remembered, the moment was passed from ship to ship, becoming a naval legend before it reached print years later.

WITH MALICE TOWARD NONE, WITH CHARITY FOR ALL

★ 1865 ★

The Civil War had already begun when Abraham Lincoln was inaugurated on March 4, 1861, though the fighting had not started. South Carolina had formally seceded the previous December, setting off a rash of followers in the Deep South. A Confederate government had been formed in February.

Two attempts at reconciliation had failed. Yet there seemed hope, if only because the Confederate capital had been moved to Richmond, Virginia, some one hundred miles from Washington. It appeared to be an easy target, one that many believed could be easily captured, leading to a quick and decisive victory.

Lincoln's hero, Henry Clay, had known better and had warned the South and the nation over a decade earlier. In the debates over his proposed Compromise of 1850, Clay prophesied that secession would bring on a "furious . . . bloody . . . implacable" war.[1] Practically alone in the midst of the excitement, General Winfield Scott, the best military mind left to the Union, foresaw a long war too, and he gave the new president a plan that required hundreds of thousands of troops (though even he underestimated how many), great generalship, and a strategy of encirclement.

But Clay was long dead, and Winfield Scott was old. Popular and political opinion thought otherwise. Lincoln, unschooled in military affairs, partook of the popular wisdom, but after the early disaster at Bull Run, he never again thought a direct strike at the Confederate capital would bring victory.

Remember that Lincoln was a minority president, elected with only 40 percent of the popular vote. Indeed, until the newly rebellious states withdrew from Congress, the Republicans did not have control of the legislative bodies. While Lincoln had a war to fight, he faced domestic battles that loomed just as large, constantly threatening his ability to lead the Union in that war. But that threat brought to the fore his hitherto unrecognized talents as a master politician.

Lincoln formed a cabinet not of friends and supporters, but of representatives of all the factions in what remained of his precious Union. They were not only men who were better known and more widely experienced than he was, but even men who were his rivals and who often disliked and belittled him. Yet in the years before the next election, he kept them in line and in office.

It was vital to keep the wavering border states in the Union if he was to avoid broadening the military conflict or seeing his lines of communication cut. If keeping the border states meant enraging the abolitionists by not freeing the slaves or even announcing abolition as a war aim, Lincoln would do that.

Simultaneously, he needed to keep the European nations out of the conflict and keep the doors open to a resolution, and he did so by refusing even to recognize that a state of war between two powers existed. That there was a conflict was undeniable, but it was a conflict between a sovereign state and a few wayward parts that could return at will.

He needed constantly to balance the demands of hostile internal constituencies—the so-called War Democrats in the North, who supported maintaining the Union but who were at best ambivalent regarding slavery; the Radical Republicans, who demanded both abolition and severity toward the rebellious states; and the Republican moderates, who wanted peace on almost any terms.

He needed to secure popular support for an abstract ideal, the Union, while the Southerners fought for something far more real and tangible: their land, their independence, and their way of life.

And Lincoln had to do all this in the face of far too frequent military defeats, long casualty lists in the newspapers, and generals who never understood what needed to be done or were willing to do it.

Yet Lincoln succeeded by sheer force of will and an ability to convey to the public the importance of the inhuman effort necessary.

And inhuman it was, because the war, which began as a traditional European-style military conflict, became something new. At least it did so in the hands of the generals Lincoln found at long last, generals who understood what had to be done. General Benjamin Franklin Butler at Hatteras Inlet, and a few months later, General Ulysses S. Grant at Fort Donelson, called for their defeated enemy to surrender in a new and different way.[2] Grant replied to the opposing commander who had asked to negotiate surrender terms, "No terms except an unconditional and immediate surrender can be accepted."[3]

Just as implacably, Grant wrote of his plan for his Virginia campaign, "I determined to hammer continuously against the armed force of the enemy and his resources, until by mere attrition, if in no other way, there should be nothing left to him but submission."[4]

For two years the war ground on. With only occasional successes amid many bloody defeats and with continual calls for more recruits, more draftees, and more sacrifices, Lincoln and the Republicans faced midterm elections with little hope. Indeed, the congressional elections of 1862 went against the Republicans, though they did manage to hold on to a majority in both houses. Lincoln, however, was unmoved, and he began planning for an eventual victory in the war despite the almost relentless negative news from the battlefield. The major good news, of course, was the Union victory at Gettysburg, though General George Meade, despite Lincoln's almost frantic urging, let Robert E. Lee and his troops escape intact, or as intact as 25,000 men killed and wounded would allow. Lee was still loose, and the outcome of the war was far from certain.

It was in this year that Lincoln began to unveil how the nation could be reunited after the war. He clearly wanted to make reunion as easy as possible for the rebellious states—for he had always thought of them as states, no matter what they thought themselves. Accordingly, in his "Proclamation of Amnesty and Reconstruction," issued in December 1863, he offered a general amnesty to anyone who would take an oath of loyalty to the United States and, by doing so, acknowledge the actions taken during the war concerning slavery. The only people excluded from this quick reentry into citizenship would be those who held high office in the Confederate government and senior officers in the military, though the way was left open to their eventual pardon as well. In addition, whenever 10 percent of those who had voted in a state in the 1860 election swore the oath of allegiance, they could set up a new state government and send representatives to Congress, thereby fully reentering the Union.

Opposition was quick. Led by Thaddeus Stevens of Pennsylvania in the House and Benjamin Wade of Ohio in the Senate, the Radical Republicans passed a bill that was far more punitive. Lincoln, as was his wont, outmaneuvered them, employing the "pocket veto" by failing to sign the bill after the close of the congressional session.

But still the war continued badly, and the casualties on both sides continued to mount. As the presidential election of 1864 approached, it was far from clear that Lincoln could even be renominated or, if he was, that he could win an election. There was rebellion in his own party, even from within his own cabinet, but again Lincoln the politician triumphed. In June 1864 he was renominated by acclamation at a convention of the newly created National Union Party, a party that combined the Republicans with the War Democrats who supported Lincoln's efforts.

This time the war began to turn in the Union's favor. A Confederate thrust at Washington, DC, had been turned back, and General Philip Sheridan was rolling up the Confederates in the Shenandoah Valley of Virginia. Most important, Lincoln's opponents had forgotten Lincoln's tremendous popular support and his ability to mobilize it. In the November election Lincoln and his policies were triumphant, winning 55 percent of the popular vote and 91 percent of the electoral vote.

It was in his inaugural address on March 4, 1865, that Lincoln most vividly enunciated his vision for the future. It was a rainy, windy day, but the crowd assembled was huge. When Lincoln stepped forward to give his speech, the sun broke through the clouds and lit up his unmistakable figure. Like his speech at Gettysburg, this speech was short, no more than five minutes.

Lincoln began by telling his listeners that he would not spend their time reviewing what had happened in the four years since his last inaugural speech. They knew that well. Nor would he make predictions about the future—that was still unclear. He did, though, stress that the war and its horrors were a divine judgment on both sides for the evil of slavery.

Nor might the judgment be ended:

> Yet, if God wills that [the war] continue until all the wealth piled by the bondsman's two hundred and fifty years of unrequited toil shall be sunk, and until every drop of blood drawn with the lash shall be paid by another drawn with the sword, as was said three thousand years ago, so still it must be said, "The judgments of the Lord are true and righteous altogether."[5]

The war, then, was God's will and God's judgment on all Americans. No one had the right to punish the other, for God was punishing the nation itself. Once that idea was clear, Lincoln moved to his famous conclusion:

> WITH MALICE TOWARD NONE, WITH CHARITY FOR ALL, with firmness in the right as God gives us to see the right, let us strive on to finish the work we are in, to bind up the nation's wounds, to care for him who shall have borne the battle and for his widow and his orphan, to do all which may achieve and cherish a just and lasting peace among ourselves and with all nations.[6]

Later that month, Lincoln convened a meeting on board the president's flagship, the *River Queen*, of Generals Ulysses S. Grant and William Tecumseh Sherman and Admiral David Porter to outline what he wanted surrender terms to be when the time came. "Let them once surrender and reach their homes," he said, "[and] they won't take up arms again. Let them all go, officer and all, I want submission, and no more bloodshed. . . . I want no one punished; treat them liberally all round. We want those people to return to their allegiance to the Union and submit to the laws."[7]

And that is what happened. When General Grant met with General Lee at the Appomattox Court House some six weeks later, Lee asked Grant to write down his terms for surrender. Grant followed Lincoln's ideas. The officers and men would sign statements that they would not fight anymore, and then they could go home. Although the men would have to surrender their weapons, the officers could keep their sidearms and horses. When Lee asked if those who owned their own horses could take them, enlisted men as well as officers, Grant agreed to "let all men who claim to own a horse or mule take the animals home with them to work their little farms."[8]

And at the surrender parade, both sides silently saluted each other. As General Joshua Chamberlain, eventually to be the president of Maine's Bowdoin College, wrote, "On our part not a sound of trumpet more, nor roll of drum; not a cheer, nor word nor whisper of vain-glorying, nor motion of man standing again at the order, but an awed stillness rather, and breath-holding, as if it were the passing of the dead! . . . How could we help falling on our knees, all of us together, and praying God to pity and forgive us all."[9]

But it was not to last. Lincoln's assassination, just five days later, unleashed the forces of retribution that he had kept at bay. Lincoln had likely planned to accomplish his reconstruction plan while Congress was out of session. The succeeding President Andrew Johnson had neither the power nor the will to follow through—with repercussions that would last for more than a century afterward.

WAR IS HELL

★ 1880 ★

As he watched his troops decimate the attackers during the sixth Union frontal assault on his lines, General Robert E. Lee was heard to say, "It is well that war is so terrible, or we should grow too fond of it." It was a remark that only a general could make.

That anyone thought the Civil War—or the War Between the States, as it was and is often called in the South—would be either glorious or short is evidence of the blind optimism inherent in the war spirit of the time. There existed neither the officers, nor the men, nor the weapons, nor the terrain, nor the tactics that would make it so.

West Point, from which the senior officers of both sides at the outset had graduated, was really an engineering school that dabbled in military studies. It taught no course in military strategy or the management of large armies in the field. Nor was there any opportunity to learn these skills elsewhere. Field training maneuvers on a large scale were impossible, since the whole regular army consisted of just 16,000 men and officers. The Mexican-American War, in which many West Pointers had served, had been won by a force of some 10,000 men.

The soldiers who would fight on both sides were volunteers, civilians who were sent into battle with at best only a few months of training. Their weapons were largely rifles, front-loading muskets, and bayonets. The gunpowder they used gave off so much smoke that battlefields were often obscured within minutes. Moreover, they fought over ground that was hilly, dotted with woods, and bordered with forests. There were fearsome kinds of artillery to support or oppose them.

The war in the first years was one of occasional pitched battles involving thousands of men punctuated by long periods of rest and replenishment. The tactics almost always involved frontal assaults by men in long—often very long—lines two deep charging at defenders drawn up two deep in equally long lines. Although such tactics not only were destructive to the combatants and rarely decisive, they were inevitable because there were no dependable means of rapid communication to coordinate anything more complicated. Organizing flanking attacks or sending large forces around the enemy to attack from the rear was nearly impossible for commanders miles apart or merely out of sight of each other.

The result was huge casualties on both sides. At the Battle of Shiloh, where the Union army under Ulysses S. Grant was caught by surprise, the Union won but suffered 13,000 killed and wounded out of 63,000 men, a casualty rate of 20 percent. The Confederate army under the command of General Joseph Johnston, which nearly won the battle, lost 11,000 killed and wounded out of 40,000, a rate of 28 percent. Other battles were bigger, but the casualty rates for both sides remained necessarily high.

Moreover, such battles often had a devastating effect on soldiers. Two memories will give a sense of what it was like.

> We saw caissons hit and blown up, splinters flying, men flung to the ground, horses torn and shrieking. Solid shot hit the hill in our front, sprayed battalions with fountains of dirt, and went plunging into the ranks, crushing flesh and bone. . . . The shock from a bursting shell will scatter a man's thoughts as the iron fragments will scatter the leaves overhead.[1]

> The 26th Mich. was the first to reach the breastworks, and as the line scaled the bank it was met by a volley from close quarters & recoiled with fearful loss, but only for an instant, for we pushed on, and the works were ours. The men, infuriated and wild with excitement, went to work with bayonets

and clubbed muskets, and a scene of horror ensured for a few moments. It was the first time I had been in the midst of a hand to hand fight, and seen men bayoneted, or their brains dashed out with the butt of a musket, & I never wish to see another scene.[2]

Nor was life between battles comfortable and safe. Sickness was rampant, and the state of medical knowledge and the level of care available were such that disease and wounds were as destructive as any attacking force. The men suffered from illnesses ranging from cholera and typhoid to tuberculosis and chronic diarrhea. Twice as many men died of disease during the war as died in battle: an estimated 224,000 in the Union army and 160,000 to 180,000 in the Confederate forces.

Yet to win the war, the South needed only to achieve a stalemate. A stalemate would render the civilian population in the North willing to negotiate a peace in which the Confederacy would be allowed to go away. The North had to conquer or lose.

To conquer, the North had to change the way it was fighting, and the harbinger of those changes was in the western armies under the command of General Ulysses S. Grant. Grant had decided that if his major advantage militarily was his seemingly endless source of replacement soldiers, then a strategy of continuous war would grind the Southern forces to exhaustion, if not extinction. Moreover, Grant knew that winning meant destroying opposing armies, not occupying cities. Occupying the Confederate capital of Richmond would no more bring victory to the Union than occupying Philadelphia or burning Washington had brought victory to the British.

In March 1864 Lincoln promoted Grant to the rank of lieutenant general, the first since George Washington, giving him command of all the Union armies. Grant sent for William Tecumseh Sherman, promoted him to head of the Military Division of the Mississippi, and laid out his strategy for the rest of the year. Grant would take charge of the fighting in the East, with the goal of destroying the forces under Lee. Sherman would focus on destroying the armies under General Joseph Johnston. The Union forces already controlled the Mississippi and had cut the Confederacy off from its states across the river, denying it both men and supplies, especially food. Sherman would further cut up the enemy by denying it its Deep South territory. Both armies would initiate action on the same day, May 5, 1864.

Grant's written orders to Sherman, issued from Washington in April, gave Sherman the plan for all the armies in general and a short order for Sherman himself: "You, I propose to move against Johnston's army, to break it up and to get into the interior of the enemy's country as far as you can, inflicting all the damage you can against their war resources."[3] The details were left up to Sherman. His 100,000 men would move on Johnston's 65,000.

Obviously, Johnston could not afford heavy casualties. Instead, he retreated slowly, trying to stretch out Sherman's forces until he could be attacked. Sherman, though, was no longer playing that game. Each time Johnston blocked him, he sent forces to flank the Confederate forces or let off a furious artillery assault. And each time he was flanked, Johnston retreated. Only once did the two face off, at Kennesaw Mountain, some twenty miles southeast of Atlanta, when Johnston's forces had a slight advantage in numbers and a great advantage in position. There Sherman's army suffered 2,000 casualties to Johnston's 270. It was the only time Sherman let that happen.

Finally the Confederate president Jefferson Davis tired of Johnston's tactics—although Grant later stated that Johnston was using his only real option——and relieved him. His successor, General John Bell Hood, notorious for his reckless fighting spirit, promptly lost three battles against Sherman. After the third, on July 28, 1864, Sherman was close enough to Atlanta to mount a siege, moving to surround the city and shelling it constantly to force its surrender. Direct assault was hopeless.

After six weeks, Hood was nearly encircled and abandoned the city. Sherman's forces entered it on September 7. The question was, What would come next? The Confederate army had not been destroyed, and Sherman had no intention of occupying a city. Grant's original thinking had left two options. Sherman could head south to Mobile or east to Savannah. The question was argued in Washington for more than a month, though Admiral David Farragut's victory at Mobile Bay made the answer obvious. Finally, the decision was made. Sherman would march his forces to the sea at Savannah.

Hood's army began to move north, so Sherman sent some of his forces to deal with him, selecting 60,000 men to undertake a march that was both risky and innovative. He forced the evacuation of all civilians from Atlanta, tore up the rail lines that connected it to the rest of the Confederacy, burned anything of military value, and marched away with only a few days' food. His army would have no means of communicating with Grant and no food except what it could find along the way.

Sherman moved in four columns, marching roughly in parallel ten miles apart so that, if there were trouble, one could come to the other's assistance. The lure of fresh food and firewood was irresistible to soldiers who felt that anything was fair game if it would help them and hurt "the Sesesh." The general had tried for years to forbid his troops to loot, but with little success. Now he gave up. Looting and burning became a tactic of war. More and more, his troops had been attacked by Confederate irregulars and squads of guerilla fighters. As far as Sherman was concerned, all of them, civilian and military, were the enemy. Besides, he had struck on a new way, he thought, of punishing the Confederacy. His troops would "eat out" a territory, thereby denying his enemy vital military supplies—food and horses. As he said in a speech shortly after the war's end:

I know there are parties who denounce me as inhuman. . . . I care not what they say. I say that it ceased to be our duty to guard their cities any longer, and had I gone on stringing out my column, little by little, some of your Illinois regiments would not have come home, but would have been crushed. Therefore I determined to go through their country, and . . . we destroyed Atlanta, and if we had destroyed all the cities of the South in order to bring about the result in view, it would have been right."[4]

So Sherman disappeared from Union view. To get to Savannah, just 100 miles away on a straight line, his troops marched more than 350 miles, meeting little resistance. In doing so, his army cut a swath sixty miles wide through the Georgia countryside as the men foraged for whatever they could eat or carry. But little resistance, from troops led again by General Johnston or from irregulars and even bandits, did not mean none, and what there was, was dealt with quickly and brutally.

Some of our foragers were out yesterday and had killed some hogs when they wire [were] fired upon by some bushwackers. As most of their guns were empty our boys ran for camp which was not far away. One of our boys, Charles Ellis of CoB, was shot down while begging for his life. While moving out this morning we saw the lifless bodies of several citizens swinging from trees with a placard upon each which read:

"This is done in retaliation for the unwarranted attact made upon my foragers yesterday. Any repletion of this offense will be similarly punished, and in addition, all building upon ten square miles of ajecant territory will be destroyed.
(signed) W T Sherman,
General Commanding"

We have no more trouble and our scouts say that every one of those hung were in the gang that fired on our men.[5]

Sherman arrived at Savannah on December 10, 1864, twenty-nine days after leaving Atlanta, to find that he was a hero in the North. He paused there for a while and then moved his army north and then east through South Carolina and North Carolina, ending at Raleigh two days after Lee's surrender to Grant on April 9, 1865. There he met with General Johnston to negotiate a peace. The agreement went so far beyond what he was allowed to do that it had to be renegotiated with Grant present.

Years later, though, as the nation was wearying of Reconstruction and of government corruption, Sherman's opinion of the war changed. The inventor of "total war" did not regret his actions; they were justified by the supreme good of the cause: saving the Union of the United States. On August 11, 1880, he appeared at a gathering of five thousand Union veterans accompanying President Rutherford B. Hayes. After Hayes had spoken, the veterans shouted for Sherman to speak, and he did.

The war now is away back in the past and you can tell what books can not. When you talk you come down to the practical realities just as they happened. You all know this is not soldiering here. There is many a boy here to-day who looks on war as all glory, but, boys, **IT IS ALL HELL.** You can bear this warning voice to generations yet to come. I look upon war with horror, but if it has to come I am here.[6]

Subsequently, the phrase was changed in the repetition to "war is hell."

But the best judgment of the war, at least from the Union point of view, was written in his diary by a private, Ted Upson.

We returned to our homes. But all did not return. Of the thousand officers and men who started out with us four hundred and seventy four were not with us now. Many had met death on Southern battle fields; some in hospitals far from home and friends had given all they had to give—thier lives. They sleep thier long last sleep neath whispering pines. Others, unable to stand the strains, trials, and exposures of Army life had left us before the end of the war and came home—some to die, others to linger along broken in health. But from those who have lived to return comes no words of regret. They are content thier duty is done, and well done. What matters the loss of all these years! What matters the trials, the sickness, the wounds! What we went out to do is done. The war is ended, and the Union is saved.[7]

GIVE ME YOUR TIRED, YOUR POOR

★ 1883 ★

The Statue of Liberty was initially conceived in 1865, at a celebration of the end of the American Civil War. And as seems fitting for a French initiative, it began at a dinner in a small village outside Versailles. The host was Edouard-René Lefebvre de Laboulaye, a prominent liberal in Napoleon III's empire, the former head of the French Anti-Slavery Society, a fervent admirer of the United States, and a critical figure in keeping the French government from recognizing the Confederacy. One of his guests that night was a thirty-one-year-old sculptor, Frédéric-Auguste Bartholdi, who was working on a bust of Laboulaye and was entranced by the concept of monumental sculptures. In the course of dinner, Laboulaye told his guests,

> The Frenchmen who fought in the United States spilled their blood for the principles they hoped to see prevail in France and the world. . . . In that struggle for independence [there was] a fraternity of feelings, a community of efforts and of emotions, and when hearts have beaten together, something always remains among nations as among individuals.[1]

He proposed that to honor that eternal bond the French create a statue, a "Monument to American Independence: Liberty Enlightening the World," and donate it to the United States. If no one else at that dinner listened to him, Bartholdi did. He began to think, and then to create sketches of what such a monument would look like. In 1871 Bartholdi came to the United States armed with letters of introduction from Laboulaye, traveling first down the east coast to Washington and then west to all the principal cities. As he wrote to his sponsor, "In each town I look for some people who might wish to participate in our enterprise. Up to now, I've found them everywhere. Things will be prepared; it will need only a spark from France."[2]

To provide the spark, Laboulaye organized the Franco-American Union to raise funds to build a statue. By August 1875 Bartholdi had completed a four-foot model of his creation, the statue as we now know it. The design was approved by the Union and exhibited at a fund-raising kickoff dinner in Paris. By year's end, 200,000 francs had been raised. Construction had already begun; the arm and torch were exhibited at the Philadelphia Centennial Exhibition to the acclaim of great crowds, and by 1880 the French had raised their goal of 2 million francs ($400,000) to complete the statue and ship it to the United States—where nothing had been done.

The American Committee now faced the need to raise the money to build the pedestal for the statue and to reassemble the pieces that had been dismantled at its Paris construction site for shipping. The initial estimate for these tasks was $100,000, preposterously low, as it turned out. The committee made its initial public appeal for funds in January 1882; two years later only $85,000 had been raised, and Congress had voted down a bill that would have appropriated another $100,000.

One of the New York fund-raising events was a Pedestal Fund Art Loan Exhibition in December 1883. Admission was fifty cents, or five dollars for twelve tickets; a catalog was also on sale. The opening reception, on December 3, 1883, was a major social event.

> Fifteen hundred invitations were issued to the reception which opened the Art Loan Exhibition in aid of the Bartholdi statue pedestal fund at the Academy of Design last evening. From 8 o'clock to 10 a steady stream of people poured through the doors of the Academy. Probably two-thirds of those invited were present at some time during the evening. The galleries were well-nigh impassable at 9:30, and every room occupied by the exhibits was thronged. Most of the gentlemen wore evening dress and many of the ladies were arrayed in elegant costumes.[3]

On exhibit were more than two hundred paintings by European and American artists, sculpture, stained glass, ivory carvings, lace, glass, jewelry, and "aboriginal art" by American Indians—all from private collections. There was even the original telegram sent by Samuel Morse—"What hath God wrought"—and the key to the City of London given to General Ulysses S. Grant.

There was also a poem by an emerging young New York poet, Emma Lazarus. The head of the Pedestal Fund Committee had asked her to donate a poem for a Loan Collection Portfolio that would contain contributions from writers like Bret Harte, Walt Whitman, and Mark Twain. The portfolio would be raffled off to raise money.[4] A member of New York's Jewish aristocracy, Lazarus had been until recently, like most of her family, an unobservant Jew, as assimilated into the New York world as it was then possible to be. That had changed dramatically when a group of refugees from the murderous Russian pogroms landed in New York. With others on a relief committee, Lazarus had visited the group in its temporary quarters on Ward's Island in the East River and had been transformed into a social activist in both her civic and her creative life.

At first Lazarus had declined the invitation to contribute something. She did not, she said, "write to order." Shortly thereafter, though, she sent her poem, which was read aloud at the reception.

> Shortly before 9 o'clock the Esperance and Helvetian Singing Societies were grouped upon the main staircase, and, accompanied by Theodore Thomas's orchestra, sang Gounod's "Hymn to Liberty" with good effect. Then, Mr. F. Hopkinson Smith, director of the exhibition, stepped upon a small platform and in a graceful speech gave the ladies of the various committees the credit of having built up the exhibitions. He then read a poem written by Emma Lazarus for the *Portfolio* of the Art Loan Collection which was entitled "The New Colossus."[5]

It was the first time anyone had ever heard her poem.

> Not like the brazen giant of Greek fame,
> With conquering limbs astride from land to land;
> Here at our sea-washed, sunset gates shall stand
> A mighty woman with a torch, whose flame
> Is the imprisoned lightning, and her name
> Mother of Exiles. From her beacon-hand
> Glows world-wide welcome; her mild eyes command
> The air-bridged harbor that twin cities frame.
> "Keep, ancient lands, your storied pomp!" cries she
> With silent lips. **"GIVE ME YOUR TIRED, YOUR POOR**
> Your huddled masses yearning to breathe free,
> The wretched refuse of your teeming shore.
> Send these, the homeless, tempest-tost to me:
> I lift my lamp beside the golden door."

Unlike his comment about the choral performance, the *New York Times* reporter made no comment about the reception given to "The New Colossus." It is hard to imagine the social and financial elite in the audience—a group that included names like Drexel, Morgan, Harrison, and Sayre—thrilling to Lazarus's lines or her transformation of Lady Liberty into Mother of Exiles. And indeed, the poem disappeared from sight for twenty years.

The cornerstone for the pedestal was laid in August 1884, but work ceased two months later because the committee had run out of money. It was saved only by the intervention of Joseph Pulitzer, himself an immigrant and the owner of several newspapers, not least the *New York World*. He had tried two years earlier to raise money for the pedestal but had given up after two months. On March 16, 1885, the *World* ran a front-page editorial that concluded:

> We must raise the money!
>
> *The World* is the people's paper, and it now appeals to the people to come forward and raise the money. The $25,000 that the making of the statue cost was paid in by the masses of the French people—by the workingmen, the tradesmen, the shop girls, the artisans—by all, irrespective of class or condition. Let us respond in like manner. Let us not wait for the millionaires to give this money. It is not a gift from the millionaires of France to the millionaires of America but a gift of the whole people of France to the whole people of America.
>
> Take this appeal to yourself personally. *It is meant for every reader of The World.* Give something, however little. Send it to us. We will receive it and see that it is properly applied. We will also publish the name of every giver, however small the sum given.[6]

The committee itself joined in the public effort. In six months the goal of $100,000 was reached. Some 120,000 people had sent in money.

The statue arrived in June 1885; the pedestal was completed in April of the following year. With additional money from Congress, the statue was erected and unveiled on October 10, 1886.

That the poem disappeared after its initial reading in 1883 is not surprising, because it showed only one aspect of the American attitude toward immigration. Immigration was viewed as a mixed blessing, and steps were taken early to keep out or send back those seen as undesirable. And undesirables were usually those who had dangerous religions, like Catholicism or Judaism, who spoke different languages, who looked different, who might have strange ideas about politics and power, and, worst of all, who tended to live in cities. Those immigrants who sought land to farm were more often the objects of fun than fear.

With the Naturalization Act in 1795, America began a slow process of limiting who could legally become a citizen by restricting citizenship to "free white persons" who renounced their prior national allegiance. The Alien and Sedition Acts of 1798, enacted in the fear of pro-French revolutionary agitation, allowed the president to expel any aliens he thought dangerous, but the acts were unpopular and soon expired.

As the Statue of Liberty was being built and the American Pedestal Committee dawdled in its fund-raising, Congress passed the Chinese Exclusion Act of 1882, preventing any further immigration from China. A series of contract labor laws that followed then prohibited immigrants' entering the country under a labor contract made before they arrived, thus preventing an influx of the always-feared cheap foreign labor.

As the late decades of the nineteenth century and the early ones of the twentieth saw waves of immigration from southern and eastern Europe—almost all destined to live in the cities—immigration laws were increasingly tightened. The Reed-Johnson Act of 1924 set the pattern for the following forty years, establishing quotas for countries of origin and setting annual limits of 150,000 immigrants. More than half of those allowed to come were from Great Britain and Ireland; only 5,800 were from Italy and 6,500 from Poland. Indeed, it was not until 1965 that national quotas were abolished.

The Statue of Liberty, then, was unveiled just at the beginning of the new influx of Jews, Poles, Russians, Italians, and other "different" peoples. Whatever the statue meant to its French donors or its American recipients, the steerage passengers on those thousands of ships that passed it in the following years gave it their own meaning, a meaning far closer to the words of Emma Lazarus, words that neither they nor the citizens of their new land were aware of.

Lazarus died of cancer in 1887, having never seen the statue. Her poem, though, received new life on May 5, 1903. The next day the *New York Times* carried a short article with the headline "IN MEMORY OF EMMA LAZARUS; Tablet on Liberty Island to the Poetess Who Sang of the New Colossus." The article quoted the poem, but first it explained:

The memory of Emma Lazarus, a writer of note in her day, has been revived by her friend, Miss Georgina Schuyler, by a graceful act. Yesterday a memorial bronze tablet was unveiled on Bedloe's, or Liberty Island as it is now called, just inside the entrance to the pedestal of Bartholdi's gigantic statue of Liberty Enlightening the World.

The choice of this place rests on the interest which Emma Lazarus took in the Liberty Statue as a symbol for a land where the down-trodden and despised have found a chance to develop their own careers, an interest which found one expression in her verses on "The New Colossus." They were written in 1883 and are inscribed on the tablet which Miss Schuyler has dedicated to her shade.[7]

Thereafter, visitors to the popular attraction saw the poem, and slowly its words seeped into the popular consciousness. They became the expression of what the nation wanted to believe about itself, rather than what it was.

IF NOMINATED I WILL NOT RUN; IF ELECTED I WILL NOT SERVE

★ 1884 ★

By the time the presidential election of 1884 began heating up, reform was definitely in the air. The nation was tired of the stench of corruption emanating from Washington. Grant's two terms had been rife with scandal. The following presidents had been reformers, as far as they could be with easily corrupted forces in charge of both houses of Congress. Moreover, boss-led machines dominated politics in nearly every populous state, so that even when the Democrats seized control first of the House in 1875 and then of the Senate in 1879, scandals kept recurring.

The Democrats in this election year had a strong favorite, Grover Cleveland, who had an imposing track record of reform as sheriff, then mayor, of Buffalo, New York, and now as governor of the state. The GOP had a small but growing body of reformers too, which included the young Theodore Roosevelt. President Chester A. Arthur was in ill health and refused to run again. The candidate the party leaders clearly favored was James G. Blaine of Maine, who had been in Congress from 1863 to 1881, first as a representative and Speaker of the House, and then as a senator. Blaine, though, had been tainted with corruption in his private financial dealings and was seen as part of the problem, not as a solution.

It looked to be a tight election, and many Republicans sought a candidate who was both nationally known and regarded as invincibly honest. The recently retired William Tecumseh Sherman was now, as he had been in 1875, an obvious choice.

Yet Sherman was also an odd choice. True, he was honest, forthright, and well-spoken, but he was just not suited to the role of politician. He hated—truly hated—the press, detested politicians, distrusted the masses, and disliked Congress, especially when it disagreed with him. Though not a Catholic himself, he was married to a fervent one at a time when anti-Catholic prejudice was strong. One of their children had become a Jesuit priest.

Ulysses S. Grant, elected president in 1868, picked Sherman to succeed him as commanding general of the now-shrunken army, thus forcing him to live in Washington, DC. Sherman's first act was to order a reorganization of the staff reporting to him, an effort quickly thwarted by the staff's relationship with the press and with Congress. He fought with Grant's secretary of war and with each succeeding secretary over reporting and control. Worst of all, he refused to lobby Congress over the military budget or military policy. "I cannot and will not condescend to importune members to obtain any special end, no matter how desireable." He explained, "By my office I am above party."[1]

Finally, in self-defense, he moved his headquarters from Washington to St. Louis, removing himself from the fetid air—both climatic and political—of the capital. But he also removed himself from any possibility of getting anything accomplished.

When Republican control of the White House had been in jeopardy eight years earlier, in the election of 1876, Sherman was actively discussed as a candidate. He was also on an extended world tour that kept him in the news and out of the action. When he returned, he wrote to former congressman and current supporter James S. Rollins that if the presidency was offered he would refuse it: "You may argue that none before has done such an act, then, if the case arises, I must be the first of a series."[2]

Though out of the political action between 1875 and 1884, Sherman still had managed to make even more news and even more political enemies. His two-volume *Memoirs* had become the sensation of 1875. Up to then, Southerners had remembered Sherman for his decency to them as defeated foes, a decency embodied in the treaty he had negotiated and signed with General Joseph Johnston, which was far more generous to the Confederacy than Grant's treaty with Lee. Indeed, it was so generous that it had been repudiated by the government and had to be renegotiated in Grant's presence. His book now managed vividly to remind Southerners of his exploits in Georgia and the Carolinas. He became the never-to-be-forgotten destroying devil of the war.

In 1884 Sherman was again a potential political force, and his allure for the Republican Party did not diminish. Friends and politicians kept bringing up the subject. Not the least of these was James G. Blaine himself, who was friendly with Sherman and who needed to know what Sherman really wanted in order to assess his own chances for the nomination. It was inconceivable to Blaine that Sherman would not want to lead the nation.

A bit more than a week before the Republican convention in Chicago was due to convene on June 3, 1884, Blaine wrote to Sherman:

> It is more than possible, it is indeed not improbable, that you may be nominated. If so you must stand your hand. . . . If it comes to you it will come as the ground-swell of popular demand, and you can no more refuse than you could have refused to obey an order when you were a lieutenant. . . . It would in such an event injure your great fame as much to decline it as it would for you to seek it.[3]

The argument clearly troubled Sherman, for he wrote several letters in reply, but in one he stated that he would refuse even if it would be seen as an "offense to the convention which construes itself the people . . . whose mandate was the voice of God."[4]

On his way to the GOP convention in Chicago where he would be the presiding officer, General John B. Henderson stopped in St. Louis to see Sherman. As later reported in an updated version of Sherman's *Memoirs*,

> He urged, by every argument at his command, his acceptance of the nomination. The answer to this appeal may be gathered from the conclusion of a telegram to General Henderson written on June 3d after the work of the convention had begun. "Please decline any nomination for me in language strong but courteous," followed by a letter on June 5th which concludes with equal firmness: "there is no shadow of excuse to call on me to make a sacrifice of interest, inclination, or conviction of what is right in the premises."[5]

Word of the telegram got out. A reporter saw him at his home on June 5 and asked about the "rumored telegram" to Henderson. The "interview" is typical of Sherman.

> "I sent no telegram to Chicago," he said, "but three days ago I mailed a letter to Gen. Henderson. He telegraphed me last night, and I presume my letter reached him to-day, and I am glad it got there."
> "You would not accept, then, a unanimous nomination?"
> "No, I would not."
> "What are your reasons?"
> "I have plenty of them, but keep them to myself."[6]

That evening, while Sherman was entertaining some friends in his library, yet another cable from Henderson arrived. Sherman's son, Thomas, later told the story.

> I was at his side in his library on Garrison Avenue when he received the telegram. . . ."Your name is the only one we can agree upon, you will have to put aside your prejudices and accept the Presidency."
>
> Without taking his cigar from his mouth, without changing his expression, while I stood there trembling by his side, my father wrote the answer, "I will not accept if nominated and will not serve if elected."
>
> He tossed it over to me to be handed to the messenger and then went on with the conversation he had been engaged in. In that moment I thought my father a great man."[7]

As time went on, his words were changed to **"IF NOMINATED I WILL NOT RUN; IF ELECTED I WILL NOT SERVE."** The statement is more euphonious and balanced and thus more memorable. It was a rare moment in American political history, at least in the public's eyes.

Henderson's warning of an impending draft by the convention on June 5 was only a dream in his own mind. Sherman's name was placed in nomination that evening, but whether owing to his cabled reply or not, on the first ballot, the general received just two votes. Blaine won on the fourth ballot and went on to face Cleveland in a furiously dirty campaign.

Blaine was discovered to have finagled a stock deal, which kept the press and partisan speakers busy, especially with the evidence of a letter from Blaine that concluded, "Burn this letter," an instruction that had not been followed. Then Cleveland was revealed to have fathered an illegitimate son ten years earlier. Blaine never really managed to explain his financial actions, but Cleveland was found to have voluntarily supported his son and the mother. The hecklers on both sides romped.

> Blaine, Blaine, James G. Blaine,
> The continental liar from the State of Maine
> *Burn this letter!*

And hecklers at Democratic rallies chanted,

> Ma! Ma! Where's my pa?
> Gone to the White House,
> *Ha! Ha! Ha!*[8]

As one of the Republican reformers who supported Cleveland said, "We are told that Mr. Blaine had been delinquent in office but blameless in private life, while Mr. Cleveland has been a model of official integrity, but culpable in personal relations. We should therefore elect Mr. Cleveland to the public office which he is so well qualified to fill, and remand Mr. Blaine to the private state he is admirably fitted to adorn."[9]

That is what happened—but barely. Cleveland won the election by just 25,000 votes out of more than 10 million cast—0.3 percent more than Blaine. His margin in the electoral college—219 to 182—was supplied by his own state of New York, which he carried by a mere 1,149 votes.

YOU SHALL NOT CRUCIFY
MANKIND UPON A CROSS OF GOLD

★ 1896 ★

Political campaign issues, in retrospect, often seem trivial. The charge in 1840 that President Martin Van Buren kept a lavish, even royal, lifestyle in the White House or the controversy in 1952 over the gift of a vicuña coat to the wife of vice-presidential candidate Richard Nixon hardly affected the future of the nation. Yet the trivial issues usually stand for much larger ones, indeed so large and complex that they are avoided. But in being avoided, they lend heat to their trivial stand-ins.

So was the issue of "free coinage" of silver that dominated politics in the last decades of the nineteenth century. Coupled with the emergence of the most powerful public speaker since the death of Daniel Webster in 1852, the silver issue galvanized the electorate in 1896 with the most heated controversy since the Civil War, dividing regions and parties.

The orator was William Jennings Bryan, a native of Illinois who moved to the booming city of Lincoln, Nebraska, at age twenty-eight to take advantage of the opportunities there for a young lawyer. A devout Christian, Bryan's biblically founded beliefs, coupled with his hero worship of Thomas Jefferson, easily led him to Democratic politics. His political beliefs were fused into what he devoutly saw as Christian duties to aid the workingman and the poor. He was defeated in his first try for Congress but discovered that not only could he speak well from the platform, he could also move an audience with his evident sincerity. Although Nebraska was a largely Republican state, Bryan was elected twice to the House of Representatives. There his oratorical abilities gained him recognition and a following in his party within Congress. In his first major speech, on the dry subject of tariff reform, his performance led one of his Republican opponents to move to allow him more than his allotted hour. He continued for another two hours, and his audience grew as he spoke. So did his reputation.

The issue of free silver, as it was called, arose after the end of the Civil War. Before the war, both gold and silver had monetary value, with silver worth approximately one-sixteenth the value of gold by weight, and coins were minted of both. During the conflict, however, the Union paid for the war by issuing paper money backed only by the good faith of the government. Coins, the currency of most members of the working class, were in very short supply. But there were a few transactions for which only gold was accepted.

When the war ended, the paper money was again redeemable in either gold or silver, but gold, with its partial recognition during the war, was seen as preferable. Then in 1867 much of Europe established gold as the sole basis for its money and the official medium for payments between countries. In 1873 the United States followed suit, without any controversy or even notice. The government purchased no silver and minted no silver coins. Soon afterward the economy went into recession and prices fell, especially prices for farm products. Farmers and silver miners alike charged that the government had gone on the gold standard because of a conspiracy—the "Crime of '73"—and demanded that it return to "bimetalism." Several halfhearted attempts to do so were made, but prices and wages continued low. Agitation grew for "free coinage" of silver, requiring the government to buy all the silver presented to it and thereby increase the money supply and improve the economic life of the working classes.

The heated debate roiled the nation. A third political party, the Populist Party, built itself into a power, largely on its advocacy of free silver. The Democratic and Republican parties both began to fissure, with strong minorities in each favoring silver. The parts of the country whose economies were increasingly industrial—largely the Northeast and the Midwest—stood fast for gold and for high tariffs. The parts of the country that depended on farming and mining for a living—the South and the

West—called out for silver. Early in his congressional career, Bryan took the side of silver.

In 1894 Bryan announced that he would not run for reelection to the House of Representatives but would instead run for the Senate. In addition to advocating free coinage of silver, Bryan came out in favor of a graduated income tax, federal insurance for bank deposits, and the right of workers to unionize and strike. Since Grover Cleveland, the only Democratic president since the Civil War, had just sent troops and federal marshals to break the Pullman rail strike, Bryan was formally opposing his own party leader.

The worsening state of the national economy led to a national sweep for the Republicans. In the House alone, the GOP gained 121 seats. Bryan lost his Senate bid, though he did easily win a popular nonbinding preference vote for the Nebraska Senate seat. Nebraska's senators were chosen by the state legislature, which the Republicans controlled.

The election, and Bryan's campaign, increased his following within the Democratic Party and his region. Moreover, they increased Bryan's own belief that he could and should play a role in the presidential election of 1896. In his last days in Congress, he spoke often, trying out campaign themes. In December 1894 he spoke in opposition to further pro-gold action.

> The money centers present this insolent demand for further legislation in favor of a universal gold standard. I, for one, will not yield to that demand. I will not help to crucify mankind upon a cross of gold. I will not aid them to press down upon the bleeding brow of labor this crown of thorns.[1]

Returning to Nebraska, Bryan found he was in such demand as a public speaker that he could earn more money on the rapidly developing speaking circuits than he could as a lawyer. He quit the law and spoke on a variety of topics throughout the country, often at venues that would prove politically advantageous in the future.

During the year and a half before the 1896 election, liberals felt increasingly embattled. The Supreme Court invalidated the small income tax enacted in 1894. It prohibited applying the new Sherman Anti-Trust Act to manufacturers but later upheld using the same act against striking unions and their leaders. The economic depression continued. Any reform that might help the working classes seemed impossible.

When Bryan went to the Democratic convention in Chicago in July 1896, he was still just one of many candidates for president. The party was controlled by an old guard that largely opposed anything but the gold standard and by big city machines, which saw no advantage to their industrial base in the silver issue.

The convention delegates, though, were looking for change and anxious about the future. From the very first, the insurgents won the battles—over the convention officials, the makeup of state delegations, and the party platform. Indeed, each plank in the platform represented a repudiation of their own President Cleveland and his policies.

In the key fight over the first plank—that dealing with money—the insurgents succeeded in passing wording that opposed a gold standard because it put the nation under the control of foreign nations and had resulted in lower prices and higher taxes. The old guard wrote a minority report and insisted on debating the issue before the whole convention. To demonstrate their democratic principles, the majority agreed to the debate.

On July 9, the day scheduled for the debate, the convention hall was packed. Spectators, journalists, and delegates all jammed together in a room the size of a football field. The first three speakers were disasters. The first pro-silver speaker antagonized the crowd with his vituperative racist attitude and equally clear hatred of almost everyone else. The two minority pro-gold speakers bored everyone with their calm, logical, fact-filled addresses.

Then Bryan walked slowly to the podium from his seat with the Nebraska delegation, and the audience quieted to attention. He spoke, as he always did, from a clear memory of a well-rehearsed speech, and he began quietly. The issue under debate might be free silver, but it was larger than that.

He spoke of the rising tide of dissent among the people of the West, of the conspiracy of the large economic interests, and of the Supreme Court's thwarting of Congress. He rebutted the points made by each of the minority speakers and addressed the primacy of the free silver issue rather than the tariff question. He spoke ever more loudly about the coming election as a contest between two ideas of government and said that the silver issue was a reflection of that contest. It was implicitly another battle in the struggle between Jefferson and Hamilton that was as old as the Republic. It was a struggle of section against section within the now rapidly industrializing nation.

> You come to us and tell us that the great cities are in favor of the gold standard; we reply that the great cities rest upon our broad and fertile prairies. Burn down your cities and leave our farms, and your cities will spring up again as if by magic; but destroy our farms and the grass will grow in the streets of every city in the country.

As he moved toward his closing with escalating fervor, Bryan reasserted the idea that the struggle was one of American independence, individual and national, and was fundamental to the soul of the party.

> Having behind us the producing masses of this nation and the world, supported by the commercial interests, the laboring interests and the toilers everywhere, you will answer [the] demand for a gold standard by saying to them: You shall not press down upon the brow of labor this crown of thorns, **YOU SHALL NOT CRUCIFY MANKIND UPON A CROSS OF GOLD**.[2]

With these last lines of his twenty-minute speech, Bryan brought his hands to his head and then, at the end, stretched them out and held the crucifixion pose. The gesture was, for Bryan—and for most of his audience—not a pose, not a piece of oratorical theater, but a statement of his belief in the congruence of Christianity and social reform.

The audience sat stunned as Bryan left the podium for his seat. And then, the *New York World* reported, "The floor of the convention seemed to heave up. Everybody seemed to go mad at once. . . . the whole face of the convention was broken by the tumult—hills and valley of shrieking men and women.[3]

The *New York Times,* like most urban newspapers, was hostile to Bryan, calling him "a wild theorist filled with a desire of personal advancement," but it also reported at length on the demonstration following his speech.

> The demonstration at the close of Bryan's speech struck terror into the hearts of the Bland and Boies and MacLean and Stevenson boomers. The declaration by him that the people must not be crucified on the cross of gold was the signal for an avalanche of measureless outburst. As he started for his seat one policeman stood ready to clear the way and another to prevent the crowd from closing in upon him. Their efforts were unavailing.[4]

The marching and the cheering lasted forty minutes—twice as long as the speech. The balloting for presidential candidates could not be held until the following day. When it was, Bryan, who began the voting more than one hundred votes behind the leader, triumphed on the fourth ballot, when he secured the needed two-thirds vote.

It was Bryan's last triumph. Though also endorsed by the Populist Party a week later, Bryan was outspent ten to one by the Republicans, and his campaign was swamped by its nearly sole reliance on his own efforts. The GOP fielded hundreds of speakers while William McKinley stuck to his front porch and made only one speech—to a local Ohio garden club. Bryan campaigned tirelessly. Beginning in August, he traveled from Maine to Nebraska, concentrating on what he thought would be swing states around the Great Lakes. In three months he gave more than 250 speeches, not counting impromptu stops at stations where a crowd gathered to see his train go through. His campaign made news because it was the only campaign to report on, the only candidate who was doing anything to cover. Few papers in big cities, though, treated him sympathetically.

When the votes were counted, McKinley won with 7 million votes—51 percent of the total—and 271 electoral votes to Bryan's 6.5 million popular votes and 176 electoral votes. Bryan carried the South and much of the West but none of the Great Lakes states he had counted on. The GOP won control of both houses of Congress.

Bryan would retain his hold on his followers and run again, twice, as the Democratic Party's candidate, but he would never again come as close or get more votes. By the end of the 1890s, higher prices for farm products returned along with national prosperity, and the discovery of huge gold deposits in Alaska and the Yukon Territory eased the metal shortage.

Early in 1900 the Republican Congress passed a bill to put the United States on the gold standard for good. President McKinley signed it. For the rest of his life, Bryan made his living giving speeches throughout the country, often being called on to give once more his "Cross of Gold" speech.

YES, VIRGINIA,
THERE IS A SANTA CLAUS

★ 1897 ★

The figure of Santa Claus as an integral part of Christmas seems as if it must go back to antiquity. Yet not only was Santa Claus created, he was created in the United States–and fairly recently at that.

At some point in the fourth century AD, the Christian church began to celebrate Christ's birth on December 25. The date was not arbitrary, even though there was never any historical indication of the date of Christ's birth. December 25 was the date of the pagan festival honoring the sun god on the day of the winter solstice. Thus the church could use the existing celebration with transformed content to attract new converts with a mix of old and new symbols and festivities. The word "Christmas" first appeared in England about the eleventh century as the term "Christes maesse" entered the language. Shortly thereafter, "Xmas" came into general use, from the Greek letter chi (x) for Christ.

Yet the links to the old festivities meant that the holiday was too often marked by ribaldry and drink, so much so that Cromwell's Puritan Commonwealth declared that Christmas could only be a day of penance and, in 1652, prohibited its observance entirely. In the American colonies, the split continued. In Puritan New England, Christmas was not recognized; the Quakers in Pennsylvania concurred. In the southern colonies and in rural areas, Christmas was an occasion for celebration, entertaining, and sometimes riotous parties. By the eighteenth century, though, even the Massachusetts dogmatists began to hold December 25 as a recognized date for staid and solemn church observances.

In fact the American colonies and then the United States had few generally observed holidays until well into the 1800s. Thanksgiving and the Fourth of July were for family and civic celebration, but nothing more than that. When the change began to a more general recognition of Christmas as a family celebration, it began in New York.

Although Saint Nicholas had been a Protestant favorite in Europe, particularly in Holland, he had no presence in the United States except as the patron saint of the old Dutch families in New York. Indeed, in 1773 New York's *Rivington's Gazeteer* wrote that Saint Nicholas's birth anniversary had been celebrated on December 20 by "a great number of Sons of that ancient Saint . . . otherwise called St. a Claus."[1] The next year the same publication noted the saint's celebration on December 8.

By 1810, Saint Nicholas had been adopted by the New-York Historical Society and particularly by John Pintard, one of its founders. At its annual meeting in December 1810, the Society gave out a woodcut that pictured the saint with a purse in one hand and a switch in the other.

It was Pintard's friends who took Saint Nicholas further. In 1809 Washington Irving described him as the patron saint of New York. In 1822 Clement Clarke Moore wrote a poem, "An Account of a Visit from St. Nicholas" for his family's enjoyment, setting the visit on Christmas Eve. A year later the poem was reprinted in the *Troy (New York) Sentinel,* and it then began to appear annually in newspapers around the country. And when New York artist and caricaturist Thomas Nast illustrated Moore's poem in an

1862 edition, he established forever the likeness of Santa, complete with reindeer and sleigh.

America took up Christmas with a vengeance. When the Pennsylvania Dutch brought their Christmas trees to the United States sometime in the second decade of the nineteenth century, the custom was written up in magazine articles and the always popular "Annual" books so that the idea spread quickly.

Traditional English Christmas carols were followed by American ones. Edward Hamilton Sears, a Unitarian minister from Massachusetts, wrote the lyrics for "It Came upon a Midnight Clear" in 1849, and Richard Storrs Wills, a New York organist, wrote the music the next year. John Henry Hopkins Jr., the rector of Christ's Church in Williamsport, Pennsylvania, wrote "We Three Kings of Orient Are" in the late 1850s; Henry Wadsworth Longfellow wrote "I Heard the Bells on Christmas Day" in 1863; Episcopal rector Phillips Brooks wrote "O Little Town of Bethlehem" in 1865, and in 1868 his organist, Lewis H. Redner, added the music; and in 1885 came "Away in a Manger," whose authorship is unknown.

Christmas cards were introduced into the United States from Germany by Louis Prang in 1875, and the next year he could not keep up with the demand. By the beginning of the next decade, post office officials were complaining about the volume of mail during December.

That Christmas quickly became important to the public is evidenced by its being made a legal holiday. Louisiana was the first to make the move in 1837, soon followed by Arkansas. By 1860, fourteen states had officially recognized Christmas, and by the end of the Civil War, thirty-one states and territories joined the crowd. On June 26, 1870, the United States Congress declared Christmas a federal holiday.

Early on, the commercial side of Christmas made itself felt. By 1860 more and more stores began carrying special Christmas gift items. By the 1880s special store displays were attracting crowds of onlookers and shoppers. As the *New York Tribune* noted in 1882, "One of the signs of the approach of Christmas is the crowds of 'sidewalk spectators' that gather around the windows to watch mechanical toys."[2]

Before the century closed, there were more and more complaints about commercialism. "The modern expansion of the custom of giving Christmas presents has done more than anything else to rob Christmas of its traditional joyousness. . . . [M]ost people nowadays are so fogged out, physically and mentally, by the time Christmas Day arrives that they are in no condition to enjoy it. . . . As soon as the Thanksgiving turkey is eaten, the great question of buying Christmas presents begins to take the terrifying shape it has come to assume in recent years."[3]

And through it all, the figure of Santa reigned. His dual aspect of bringing presents for the good children and punishments for the bad withered away. Though his name was generally "Santa Claus," remnants of the older figures remained in his other less used, but still recognizable names: Kris Kringle and Saint Nick. The latter, of course, is a clear reference to the ancient Saint Nicholas and also remained in the "Claus," a shortening of Nicholas. Kris Kringle has an even stronger religious link. The German immigrants and their descendants were visited by a Santa Claus figure named Christkindel or Christkintle—in English, Christ Child. The figure slowly disappeared, except in name, as Kris Kringle.

Into this now nationally recognized holiday of Christmas with its now nationally recognized patron saint stepped a young New Yorker named Virginia O'Hanlon. Surely, for as long as a never-seen Santa Claus had been delivering presents to homes, older children had been spilling the secret to their younger brothers, sisters, and schoolmates–and breaking their hearts. In 1897 the eight-year-old, on the advice of her father, wrote a letter to the *New York Sun*.

> Dear Editor,
>   I am 8 years old. Some of my little friends say there is no Santa Claus. Papa says, "If you see it in The Sun, it's so." Please tell me the truth, is there a Santa Claus?

Francis P. Church, one of the editors of the paper, responded with an editorial titled **"YES, VIRGINIA, THERE IS A SANTA CLAUS."** It appeared, unsigned, in the third column of editorials, just below one on "The Chainless Bicycles." It is as much a defense of religion as of Santa Claus.

> Virginia, your little friends are wrong. They have been affected by the skepticism of a skeptical age. They do not believe except they see. They think that nothing can be which is not comprehensible by their little minds. All minds, Virginia, whether they be men's or children's, are little. In this great universe of ours, man is a mere insect, an ant, in his intellect as compared with the boundless world about him, as measured by the intelligence capable of grasping the whole of truth and knowledge.
>   Yes, Virginia, there is a Santa Claus. He exists as certainly as love and generosity and devotion exist, and you know they abound and give to our life its highest beauty and joy. Alas! How dreary would be the world if there were no

Santa Claus! It would be as dreary as if there were no Virginias. There would be no childlike faith then, no poetry, no romance to make tolerable this existence. We should have no enjoyment, except in sense and sight. The external light with which childhood fills the world would be extinguished. . . . .

You tear apart the baby's rattle and see what makes the noise inside, but there is a veil covering the unseen world which not the strongest man, nor even the united strength of all the strongest men that ever lived could tear apart. Only faith, poetry, love, romance, can push aside that curtain and view and picture the supernal beauty and glory beyond. Is it all real? Ah, Virginia, in all this world there is nothing else real and abiding.

No Santa Claus! Thank God! he lives and lives forever. A thousand years from now, Virginia, nay 10 times 10,000 years from now, he will continue to make glad the heart of childhood.[4]

This was Virginia's only brush with fame. She became a teacher and principal in the New York City school system, retiring after forty-seven years on the job. She died in 1971, seeing her letter reprinted somewhere every year—as it is to this day.

REMEMBER THE *MAINE!*

★ 1898 ★

In the last years of the nineteenth century, two academic events signaled a coming change in America's view of itself and its role in the world. In 1890 Captain Alfred Thayer Mahan, head of the new Naval War College in Newport, Rhode Island, published *The Influence of Sea Power upon History, 1660–1783*. In it he examined six characteristics that were needed for the growth of maritime might, essential for any nation wishing to be an international power. All six characteristics could be found in the United States, though it had not yet emerged as a power in the world. Still, Mahan argued, the time had come. "Whether they will or no," he wrote, "Americans must now begin to look outward."[1]

Three years later, in July 1893, Frederick Jackson Turner delivered his paper "The Significance of the Frontier in American History" to an audience largely composed of scholars at the World's Columbian Exposition in Chicago. Turner took as his stepping-off point a passage in the U.S. Census Bulletin no. 12, issued in 1891, which stated that there was no longer a frontier line in the United States. In Turner's view, the existence of a frontier and the need to extend and settle it had created a distinctive American character and special political and social institutions. Now the end of the frontier meant that if the nation was not to atrophy, the United States needed a new frontier—an external frontier.

Both Mahan's and Turner's ideas fell on fertile ground. Since the end of the Civil War, the United States had exploded demographically and economically. By 1890 its national wealth exceeded $65 billion, making the nation economically larger than Great Britain, the reigning world power. The population, at 75 million, had doubled in the decade since 1880, with the increase coming largely through immigration. Militarily, however, the nation lagged behind—deliberately so. It was felt that a powerful military encouraged foreign adventures and that wars were bad for the domestic economy. Consequently the army was small, some 20,000 men whose duties were largely Indian fighting. The navy had shrunk from the largest in the world at the end of the Civil War to twelfth, behind China and Chile.

Yet there were signs that things were about to change. As Theodore Roosevelt, then a police commissioner of New York City, wrote to the equally pugnacious senator from Massachusetts, Henry Cabot Lodge, "The country needs a war." [2]

Events near to home provided one.

Cubans had been sporadically and violently pushing for independence since 1868, when the Ten Years' War for Cuban Independence was launched by a planter, Carlos Manuel de Céspedes, with his Pronunciamento de Yara, and 147 men including his own 30 freed slaves. While never managing to gather more than 20,000 rebels to fight the Spanish, Céspedes did succeed in forcing a settlement in 1878 that appeared to gain the rebels amnesty, freedom for the slaves in the rebel forces, and some land. The pact, however, did not end slavery on the island, and the Spanish government defeated the reforms.

The ensuing disillusionment among the Cuban middle class soon led to the rise of a new independence movement, this time led by José Martí. After a prison term at hard labor for his radical activities, exile in Spain, and more Spanish repression of dissent in Cuba, Martí moved to New York City to organize a new rebellion. Funded in large part by Cuban tobacco workers in the United States, Martí founded a newspaper, recruited two important military figures from the previous effort, Maximo Gómez and

Antonio Maceo, and established a strong group of lobbyists and propagandists in New York City and Washington, DC.

On February 25, 1895, Martí's followers in Cuba began a new war for independence, and by April Martí, Maceo, and Gómez were all in Cuba and formed a military government to prosecute the war. Martí was killed in battle in May, but what he had started continued.

The war went badly at first, but the Cubans were assisted by confusion in Spain, which sent only some inadequately prepared additional troops. By midyear the Cuban rebels had declared a Republic of Cuba and were achieving significant success with a combination of tactics that included direct attacks on Spanish troops and the destruction of the agricultural economy. The Spanish responded by forcing the rural population into fortified towns and conducting a scorched-earth campaign to deny the rebels manpower and food. The only result was widespread starvation and intensified poverty among the Cuban people.

By the latter part of 1897, the war was at a complete stalemate. Spanish troops controlled only the urban areas and the railroad lines; the rebels controlled the rest of the country.

American popular opinion strongly favored the Cubans in their independence struggle, a struggle people could easily identify with no matter how new they were to the United States. While the official government policy under the Democratic presidency of Grover Cleveland was one of nonintervention, both the efforts of the Cuban lobby in the United States and the frenzy of the Hearst and Pulitzer newspapers kept the issue in the forefront of the news. The news, some of it invented by reporters and illustrators, got so inflammatory that the Spanish government repeatedly protested to the State Department. The coverage continued; Cuba was good for circulation.

The Republican Party strongly favored the Cuban cause, yet when the Republican William McKinley defeated the Democrat William Jennings Bryan in November 1896, the official neutrality policy did not change. The strong business influence in the GOP opposed any involvement as bad for business. Quietly, however, the U.S. Navy had put together contingency plans in case war with Spain ever became a reality. The final plan, reviewed by the Cleveland administration and again by the McKinley administration, focused on an attack on Cuba and Puerto Rico, with a subsidiary effort on Manila in the Spanish-held Philippines. A slow buildup of naval forces was also under way, with the building of modern battleships beginning in 1890. The first two were the *Texas* and the *Maine*.

McKinley continued Cleveland's efforts to resolve the war in Cuba through diplomatic efforts and offers of mediation. The Spanish government wavered between reluctant small compromises and outright hostility. The United States newspapers, though, did not waver. William Randolph Hearst, angry because Joseph Pulitzer's *New York World* was able to make news and increase sales, sent reporter Richard Harding Davis and illustrator Frederick Remington to Cuba in January 1897 with orders to send back stories. After a short while, Remington got restless and wired Hearst, "Everything is quiet. There is no trouble here. There will be no war. I wish to return."

Hearst wired back, in a famous reply, "Please remain. You furnish the pictures and I'll furnish the war." [3]

Late in 1897, the McKinley cabinet discussed sending a warship to Havana for a courtesy visit. President Cleveland had stopped all such visits for fear of provoking an incident, but McKinley thought the tense situation warranted a show of power.

In January 1898 rioting in Havana seemed, at least to the newspapers, to indicate intensified strife, but by the end of the month the crisis abated. McKinley decided to move forward with a naval visit. The Spanish government was notified, reluctantly agreed, and in turn announced a similar series of courtesy visits by the Spanish cruiser *Vizcaya* to United States ports. On January 24 the second-class battleship *Maine* was ordered to Havana.

The *Maine* was the first of its kind in the rebuilding navy. Because it was designed to ram enemy vessels, its heavy guns were concentrated forward and aft, with little ability to fire broadside. Its major weapons were four ten-inch guns and six six-inch guns. The design did not really work and was not continued, but the *Maine* was modern and it was a battleship.

Arriving the next day, the *Maine* anchored in Havana harbor. The commanding officer, Captain Charles Sigsbee, made his official calls on the Spanish officials and, although he saw no sign of public hostility, ordered a high level of security on the ship. Sigsbee also refused to grant the enlisted men shore leave, fearing incidents with the civilian population.

All remained quiet in Havana for the next three weeks. Sigsbee even attended a bullfight as the guest of the Spanish naval commander. On February 1, though, the Spanish government rejected another McKinley proposal to end the Cuban stalemate, telling the United States that affairs in Cuba were none of America's business. The *Maine* remained in Havana harbor.

The evening of February 15 was very hot and humid. Captain Sigsbee was writing a letter in his compartment when he heard two noises: the first sounded to him like a rifle shot, and the second was a tremendous explosion. A huge column of fire and smoke rose 150 feet above the ship, and debris landed half a mile away.

Within minutes, the *Maine* sank. Of its 355 crew members, 252 were killed outright and 8 others died later of injuries. Of the surviving 96, only 16, including Captain Sigsbee, were unhurt, taken to safety by other ships in the harbor, including Spanish ships.

Sigsbee immediately cabled the Navy Department, carefully avoiding any speculation about what or who had caused the explosion. Indeed, the Spanish naval officials rushed to assure him that they knew nothing about it, and Sigsbee believed them.

The newspapers had no doubt, though. The New York papers carried pages of coverage for an entire week, stating that the *Maine* had been purposely blown up and that the Spanish had done it. Hearst's *New York Journal*, on February 18, carried the headline:

REMEMBER THE MAINE!

TO HELL WITH SPAIN!

Within days, the U.S. Navy dispatched a court of inquiry to Havana to investigate. The Spanish government held its own investigation. While the investigations were going on, tensions ran high. The U.S. Navy sent reinforcements and ammunition to the Pacific fleet; ships in Key West and on the East Coast were put on alert. McKinley got congressional approval for $50 million in emergency funding for national defense, most of which went to the navy.

War fever spread throughout the United States. The slogan "Remember the *Maine!*" was shouted by schoolboys and imprinted on young women's hair ribbons. Displaying the flag became nearly mandatory. The Pledge of Allegiance, written only six years earlier, became part of the ritual in all classrooms. The most popular toy was a replica of the *Maine* that, at the touch of a spring, fell apart as though blown up.[4]

The Spanish concluded their investigation by mid-March. Their divers found the Maine's hull plates bent outward, indicating an internal explosion. The divers failed to note that the ship's keel had been bent inward and up through the armored deck plates. Spain's official conclusion was that the explosion had been an accident.

The Navy Court of Inquiry delivered its report to the Navy Department on April 25. The court concluded that there had been two explosions, one external, causing the keel to buckle inward, and the second internal, causing the hull to rupture outward. Only a mine, said the court, could have caused the first explosion, which had detonated the ship's magazines. However, the court found no evidence of any Spanish involvement, nor any direct proof of a mine.

In the ensuing weeks, McKinley sought to avoid the war that the public and the newspapers were increasingly demanding. He insisted on an immediate armistice in Cuba, a repeal of the civilian concentration in armed towns, and an acceptance of the United States as the final arbiter of peace terms. The Spanish continued to rebuff the efforts, delaying responses whenever possible.

Finally, a frustrated and harried McKinley delivered an ultimatum to Spain in a congressional address on April 11. Within days, both the House and the Senate passed resolutions recognizing the Cuban Republic but including in a joint resolution a formal disavowal of any desire to annex the island. McKinley signed the joint resolution and sent it to the Spanish on Wednesday, April 20, demanding a satisfactory answer by Saturday.

War was in the wind. The Spanish ambassador closed the embassy and left for Canada. The American ambassador to Spain departed for France. On Friday, McKinley declared a Cuban blockade; on Saturday he called for 125,000 men to volunteer to fight.

On Monday, April 25, McKinley requested a formal declaration of war from Congress, since the Spanish government had refused to receive the joint resolution of Congress and had severed diplomatic ties. Congress declared war within the hour.

FIRE WHEN READY, GRIDLEY

★ 1898 ★

On April 25, 1898, the day Congress formally declared war on Spain, a telegram from Secretary of the Navy John D. Long to Commodore George Dewey, commanding officer of the Asiatic Squadron, was rushed from Hong Kong to nearby Mirs Bay, where Dewey and most of the squadron were preparing for possible action. The telegram contained orders to initiate the first combat of what was to be known as the Spanish-American War.

That Dewey was in charge and soon to be the first hero of the war was in large part due to a chance relationship with the fast-rising star Theodore

Roosevelt, then an assistant secretary of the navy. They belonged to the same Washington club.

Dewey, born in Vermont in 1837, entered the navy as a midshipman directly after graduating from the Naval Academy in 1857. Promoted to lieutenant in 1862, he served under Admiral David Farragut in the Civil War and gained an excellent combat record. After the war Dewey held a number of peacetime navy jobs, as a commander of sloops in the Pacific, as lighthouse inspector, and as president of the Lighthouse Board in the Treasury Department. In 1895 he obtained the presidency of the navy's Board of Inspection and Survey, responsible for quality control of all the navy's ships, and was promoted to commodore. Dewey was resigned to a life in Washington and eventual retirement without ever seeing action again.

A widower, Dewey regularly ate dinner at the Metropolitan Club. When Roosevelt was offered the position of assistant secretary of the navy in spring 1897, he too joined the club, and the two often rode to dinner together. Roosevelt, always on the lookout for talent and energy, took a great liking to the commodore.

Soon afterward, the news spread that the post of commander in chief of the Asiatic Squadron would become vacant later that year. Only two people were obviously in line for the job: Dewey and Commodore John Adams Howell. Howell was barely senior to Dewey and had both Navy Department and some congressional support. All Dewey had was a strong war record and Theodore Roosevelt.

It was enough. Roosevelt did not like Howell.

With Roosevelt's backing and the support of a Dewey family friend, Senator Redfield Proctor of Vermont, Dewey got the position. But he did not get the promotion that normally went with the job. As a punishment for using political influence, Secretary Long left him as commodore.

Dewey assumed command on January 3, 1898, in the harbor of Yokohama, Japan, where his flagship, the *Olympia*, was anchored. His flagship captain was Charles V. Gridley.

In the last days of January, Dewey received the Navy Department's order to retain all men whose enlistments were ending. Recognizing the order as a sign that events between Spain and the United States were worsening, he worried about needing more ammunition. Fortunately, new supplies arrived in mid-February, and Dewey ordered the *Olympia* to steam to Hong Kong, a better center for any operations against the Spanish. He learned of the sinking of the *Maine* only after arriving in Hong Kong.

On February 26, Secretary Long decided to take an afternoon off and warily left Roosevelt in charge, with specific instructions: "Do not take any such step affecting the policy of the Administration without consulting the President or me. I am not away from town and my intention [is] to have you look after the routine of the office while I get a quiet day off. . . . I am anxious to have no unnecessary occasion for a sensation in the papers."[1]

Construing his instructions in his own fashion, Roosevelt took the opportunity to wire an order to Dewey in Hong Kong: "Order the squadron except *Monocacy* to Hong Kong. Keep full of coal. In event of declaration of war, Spain, your duty will be to see that the Spanish Squadron does not leave the Asiatic Coast and then offensive operations in Philippine Islands. Keep *Olympia* until further orders."[2]

Dewey quickly obeyed, getting the cruiser *Boston* from its station off Korea and the cruiser *Raleigh* from the European Squadron, which transited the Suez Canal on previous orders.

That the Philippines should be a focus of American attention was natural. Like Cuba, the Philippines had been in a sporadic state of rebellion for years. A truce between the rebels, led by Emilio Aguinaldo, and the Spanish had been concluded in December 1897 with promises of reforms and an end to the often-brutal repression. Aguinaldo and his fellow rebel leaders were in voluntary exile in Hong Kong, but as usual the reforms never came and the repression remained. Aguinaldo offered the rebels' assistance to the United States in any conflict with Spain and sought assurance that the Americans did not intend to succeed the Spanish as rulers. He got oral promises, but never the written declaration he asked for. Dewey, in particular, never took the rebel leaders seriously.

Instead, Dewey worried about the lack of good information on the Spanish positions in their Philippine capital, Manila, or in Subic Bay to the north. What information he had was either old or anecdotal; there were rumors of minefields in Manila Bay. He bought whatever naval charts were available in Hong Kong, since the navy had no recent ones.

Events continued to worsen through April. The United States ships were repainted in their battle color of gray green. The cruiser *Baltimore* arrived as an additional reinforcement as Dewey received word of the Cuban blockade. On April 23 the United States consul to the Philippines closed the consulate and left for Hong Kong. That same day, Great Britain declared its formal neutrality in any conflict between the United States and Spain, and the governor-general of Hong Kong ordered Dewey to leave with all ships by Monday, April 25.

On Sunday Dewey sent most of the Asiatic Squadron north to Mirs Bay, where they could continue to prepare for action. On Monday, two hours after Dewey and the *Olympia* had left Hong Kong, a telegram from Secretary Long arrived and was rushed to Mirs Bay. "War has commenced," the wire read, "between the United States and Spain. Proceed at once to Philippine Islands. Commence operations at once, particularly against the Spanish fleet. You must capture or destroy. Use utmost endeavors."[3]

Dewey and his commanders reasoned that the Spanish fleet would be in either Manila Bay or Subic Bay, thirty-five miles northwest. They discounted any reports of mines and felt strongly that their forces would prove superior to anything the Spanish could offer. Just as the Asiatic Squadron was about to leave on April 27, Dewey got a report from the former consul to the Philippines that the greater part of the Spanish fleet was in Manila Bay and that new guns had been placed overlooking the harbor.

In fact, the Spanish presented little to fear. The Philippines had been too distant and unimportant an outpost for the Spanish government or the Spanish military to take seriously. Most of their artillery was obsolete, some guns were improperly sited, there were no modern mines to defend the harbors, and the preparations to fortify Subic Bay were never completed. Of the ships available to Rear Admiral Patricio Montojo y Pasarón, only two were cruisers and two were gunboats. Of the others, only one had guns, and it had to be towed.

Montojo had always believed that Subic Bay was the place to confront the Americans. He took his fleet there only to discover that nothing was ready to support him in a battle, and nothing could be ready for months. When he learned that the Americans had left Hong Kong, heading first for Subic and then for Manila, Montojo returned to Manila, where defenses were ready.

Once back, though, Montojo and the governor-general decided to confront the Americans at the worst possible place for the Spaniards—an inlet of Manila Bay where they had little room to maneuver and where the shore batteries could not fire at short range. On the other hand, confronting the enemy in front of the city, where far better shore based artillery could support the Spanish ships, risked destruction of the city itself.

As the Asiatic Squadron steamed toward the Philippines, the ships completed their battle preparations, stripping off as much woodwork as possible and dumping all flammable liquids overboard. Arriving at Subic Bay on April 30, Dewey found that the Spanish had left. He told his captains they would immediately go to Manila and engage the enemy that night.

The Squadron entered the Boca Grande Channel of Manila Bay just before midnight, but the defenders did not see them until 12:10, when the guns guarding the entrance opened fire. Dewey's ships replied, and minutes later all ships of the squadron were safely inside the bay. Just before dawn, the Americans ate a meal of coffee, beans, and hardtack.

By sunrise, May 1, the American ships were within six miles of Manila. Though they expected to see the Spanish fleet in front of the city, they were spotted well south, in their confined inlet. At 5:00 a.m. the Spanish guns on shore began firing, but their shells fell short. Two mines exploded, but they too were short of the lead flagship. The Americans held their fire. At 5:15 the Spanish ships joined the firing. Dewey had taken up his post on the open bridge of the lead ship, *Olympia*. Gridley, trying to prevent both commanders' being killed by a lucky shot, was at his post in a steel conning tower just below the bridge.

At 5:22 a.m., with the range less than five thousand yards, Dewey spoke to the *Olympia*'s captain. **"YOU MAY FIRE WHEN YOU ARE READY, GRIDLEY."**[4]

The flags gave the signal, "Engage the enemy," and the battle began in earnest. As bands on the *Olympia* and the *Baltimore* played "The Star-Spangled Banner," the American ships opened fire.

Almost immediately the Spanish flagship was sunk, with nearly half its crew killed or wounded. Within two hours, almost all of the Spanish fleet was sunk or disabled.

Dewey, erroneously informed that the *Olympia* was running out of ammunition, pulled the squadron back to take stock. Discovering the error, he ordered that everyone be fed before going back into action. Then the squadron attacked again, destroying the shore batteries and the one cruiser left fighting. By 1:20 p.m. all firing had ceased, and the American fleet anchored off the city.

News of the battle reached United States newspapers on May 2, but the information came from the official Spanish cable to Madrid and did not convey the completeness of the disaster. Dewey's message, which had to be sent to Hong Kong by ship before being cabled to the United States, did not arrive at the Navy Department until May 7.

Dewey was hailed as one of history's greatest naval heroes and the Battle of Manila Bay as the greatest naval victory ever. Congress gave Dewey his promotion to rear admiral.

In a book published a year later by John Barrett, a diplomat and journalist, Dewey's command was used enshrine the hero:

> The supreme incident in the train of events, beginning with his first coming to Hong Kong up to the hour of the battle which showed the remarkable deliberation and readiness, was the giving of the famous command: "You may fire when you are ready, Gridley." There you have the man: what

composure and yet what strength, what confidence and yet what decision of character are shown in the words, which must be immortal as well as the memory of the man who uttered them.[5]

SPEAK SOFTLY AND
CARRY A BIG STICK

★ 1901 ★

With the end of the Civil War in 1865, the nation turned inward, eager to move from relentless destruction to relentless construction—of buildings, of cities, of railroads, of the country. Instead of fiery politicians, mediocrities were elected no matter what the cost in corruption. For thirty-five years the major figures of the times were outwardly bland—solid, taciturn men focused on financial or political power, often for their own enrichment.

Onto this scene burst Theodore Roosevelt—called Teddy only by those who did not know him or who sought to belittle him. Roosevelt was unlike anyone ever seen before in public life. Born to an old and wealthy family, Roosevelt came to move easily among all classes and ranks of American life. A prolific author, a highly respected historian and naturalist, a war hero, a friend to anyone who interested him, he was also an idealist who could move among political bosses and be liked by them, however reluctantly. And perhaps most important, he was a flamboyant self-promoter with endless, relentless energy.

Though he had been elected to a single term in the New York State Assembly some years earlier, Roosevelt began his real political career with his political appointment as one of two Republicans among the four commissioners of the New York City Police Department. From the first day, he took control of the commission and began his real education as a politician and as a citizen. His friendships with Jacob Riis and Lincoln Steffens, both reporters covering parts of the city that the aristocratic Roosevelt barely knew existed, gave him an insight into the lives of the poor and the effects of government corruption on those lives. Roosevelt used the press to generate public support for himself and his actions—the beginnings of a lifelong mutual, and mutually enjoyed, relationship. In that first year in office he was everywhere: making arrests, rousting sleeping policemen, forcing out corrupt senior members of the force, and above all generating news. News, Roosevelt instinctively knew, generated both public knowledge and public support. For a city grown used to official corruption as the cost of urban living, Roosevelt was a revelation.

He was also a revelation to the political machines, both Republican and Democratic, since he threatened the financial relationships, illegal and legal, they had built with business and thus jeopardized the way they used power to stay in power. One of them, New York State Republican boss Thomas Platt, found a way to stymie Roosevelt and impede the work of the police commission. When another commissioner, the son of former president Ulysses S. Grant, went to Platt for support to break the deadlock on the commission, Platt turned him down. "I'd like to please you, Colonel Grant, but I don't care nearly [as much] to please you as I do to worry [harass] Roosevelt." [1] It was Roosevelt's first run-in with Platt, but it would not be his last.

By 1896 Roosevelt was thoroughly frustrated by his struggle to get anything more accomplished. He was now nationally known as a fighter for reform and against corruption. He directed his energies into campaigning successfully for William McKinley that year and asked for a senior position in the Department of the Navy as a reward. McKinley was wary of Roosevelt's fervent belief in naval power and of his reputation for being uncontrollable, but he was willing. First Roosevelt had to mollify Platt, who would be elected senator from New York early in 1897. Ever a realist in politics, Roosevelt turned his back on one of his earliest supporters and backed Platt. With that demonstration of party loyalty, Roosevelt was named assistant secretary of the navy, a position in which the party felt he would be reined in by his superior. Once again the political establishment failed to know the man.

Even as second in charge of the navy, Roosevelt was able to espouse the cause of a powerful navy, a need he understood well. At age twenty-four he had written the first of his many books, *The Naval History of the War of 1812*, and he avidly read the writings of Captain Alfred Thayer Mahan, whose work on the subject was becoming increasingly influential in the United States and indeed throughout the world. The need for such a peacetime navy was increasingly important in Roosevelt's eyes, and in the eyes of his political mentor Senator Henry Cabot Lodge, because of two crises, one in Hawaii involving Japan and another in Venezuela involving Germany and Great Britain. As Lodge wrote to a friend at this time, Americans "must make up our minds whether we are to be dominant in the Western Hemisphere and keep it free from foreign invasion or whether we are to stand aside and let it be seized as Africa has been."[2] Roosevelt was so convinced of the inevitability of a war with Spain over its rebellious possessions in the Caribbean and the Pacific that he wrote a war plan for the navy and presented it to McKinley.

When the United States battleship *Maine* blew up in Havana harbor in 1898, war was sure. Roosevelt, despite the requests of McKinley and of his own wife, resigned to join the First United States Volunteer Cavalry—the Rough Riders—as second in command. The success of the navy—which the Department of the Navy had championed and built up—nearly cost Roosevelt his chance for glory; the war was virtually over once Admiral George Dewey destroyed Spain's navy in the Battle of Manila Bay on May 1, 1898. In Cuba, though, Spain offered enough resistance that Roosevelt was able to demonstrate his leadership and bravery under fire and become a national military hero. Here too Roosevelt's relationship with the press was crucial, for his exploits made headlines and his picture was on the cover of *Harper's Weekly*.

He arrived home in time for the nominating conventions for the New York State governor's election, and the only person who stood in his way for the Republican nomination was again Thomas Platt. Platt had a problem. The current governor, a Republican, wanted to run again but was badly tainted with scandal. The reformers in the party were aroused and might help elect a Democrat. Platt, though, had learned his lesson about Roosevelt and wanted none of him. As far as he was concerned, Roosevelt was "a disturber of political harmony," and if there is anything a political boss wants it is "harmony." As Platt wrote to one of the Republican county committee chairmen:

> If he becomes Governor of New York, sooner or later, with his personality, he will have to be President of the United States, and nobody can foretell how the problems growing out of the Spanish War will work out, and, aside from the question of whether he will be fair to me and our organization, I am afraid to start that thing going.[3]

He had, though, no choice. Platt wanted the party to retain the governor's chair more than he did not want Roosevelt to occupy it. Though he tried to keep him to a McKinley-like front-porch campaign, Roosevelt rebelled in the last three weeks and, in a whirlwind campaign, was able to win the tight election by 17,000 votes.

Platt came to tolerate Roosevelt, even to like him, but Roosevelt indeed proved just as uncontrollable as ever. In his first annual message to the legislature, he called for legislation to clean up the sweatshops and for better factory inspections. He began a series of reforms ranging from better pure-food laws and an eight-hour day for all government workers and workers on government contracts to forest and park protection and appointing blacks to state positions. As he felt more sure of his ability to get his way in the legislature, he was increasingly willing to oppose Platt and able to win.

When Roosevelt fired a key Platt ally, the aptly named Louis Payn, as superintendent of insurance, Platt made a last-ditch effort to fight back. The insurance industry provided large sums to Platt, as well as to individual legislators, and wanted a controllable superintendent. Accordingly, Platt mobilized his forces in the business community and declined to approve any replacement. Platt also began an effort to get Roosevelt out of Albany by having him nominated as the Republican candidate for vice president in the upcoming presidential election. If nothing else, Platt could shift his problem to McKinley, who would be a shoo-in for reelection, and to Marcus Hanna, the national Republican leader. By spreading rumors that Roosevelt would not be around much longer, Platt also hoped to weaken the governor's hold on his legislative strength.

Platt's first line of attack failed when Roosevelt refused to be threatened with political ruin if he pushed his choice of a successor to Payn. Fresh evidence of Payn's corruption surfaced, and the next day Platt approved Roosevelt's nominee. A few days later, on January 26, 1900, Roosevelt wrote to a friend in the legislature:

> Your letter of the 25th really pleased me. Of course, I shall not feel real easy until the vote has actually been taken, but apparently everything is now all right. I have always been fond of the West African proverb: "Speak softly and carry a big stick; you will go far." If I had not carried the big stick the organization would not be gotten behind me and if I had yelled and blustered . . . , I would not have had ten votes.[4]

But this first known use of the phrase by Roosevelt was in a private letter, and nobody besides the addressee noticed it.

Platt's second line of attack proved much more successful: he started supporting Roosevelt for vice president. In this effort Platt was aided by Roosevelt's friend, the increasingly influential Senator Lodge, for an entirely different reason. Platt wanted Roosevelt out of New York; Lodge wanted Roosevelt on the GOP ticket and in Washington. Roosevelt was ambivalent. The job, after all, did not give him the scope for action he craved.

Still, the time was ripe. Roosevelt was overwhelmed by popular support in the party, and the lure of national office was strong. Even Hanna, who really did not want the irrepressible Roosevelt on the ticket, got no support from the affable McKinley. In sheer frustration, Hanna was heard to exclaim, "Don't any of you realize that there's only one life between this madman and the Presidency?"[5]

Evidently not, though Platt must have grinned in relief when McKinley and Roosevelt were nominated and swept the election of 1900. Roosevelt, as usual, had done most of the campaigning, with the help of a contingent of his Rough Riders veterans.

But the vice presidency was not much of a job, and his formal duties in the Senate lasted only days before the session closed. And so Roosevelt began speaking around the country on his two favorite topics: a strong navy and the Monroe Doctrine. The Monroe Doctrine, first announced on December 2, 1823, in President James Monroe's message to Congress, forbade any European colonization in the Americas and warned that any attempt to do so would be considered "dangerous to our peace and safety." Enforcement of the doctrine in the past had largely been passive, since the European powers were busy colonizing other parts of the world. Now Roosevelt, among many, had long believed that it was vital to United States interests and could be enforced only with a naval force that was the equal of any.

On September 2, 1901, Vice President Roosevelt spoke at the opening of the state fair in Minneapolis. To what the *New York Times* termed "a large and enthusiastic audience," Roosevelt spoke on naval preparedness, among other things.

> "Our duty," he said, "may take many forms in the future as it has taken many forms in the past. Nor is it possible to lay down a hard-and-fast rule for all cases. We must ever face the fact of our shifting national needs, of the always-changing opportunities that present themselves. But we may be certain of one thing: whether we wish it or not, we cannot avoid hereafter having duties to do in the face of other nations. All that we can do is to settle whether we shall perform these duties well or ill."[6]

The newspaper, though, did not print the following paragraph; after all, the story ran on page 10 with a headline, "Col. Roosevelt[7] talks to the Minnesotans." The unreported paragraph that followed contained the following:

> Right here let me make as vigorous a plea as I know how in favor of saying nothing that we do not mean, and of acting without hesitation up to whatever we say. A good many of you are probably acquainted with the old proverb: "Speak softly and carry a big stick—you will go far." If a man continually blusters, if he lacks civility, a big stick will not save him from trouble; and neither will speaking softly avail, if back of the softness there does not lie strength, power.[8]

Still, it was only a speech by a vice president, and again, outside the immediate audience, no one really noticed. Four days later, McKinley was shot after giving a speech in Buffalo, New York. Roosevelt was sworn in hours after the president's death on September 14. In brief remarks at the time, Roosevelt pledged to continue McKinley's policies. The pledge did not console Mark Hanna. "I told William McKinley," he said to newspaper owner H. H. Kohlsaat, "it was a mistake to nominate that wild man in Philadelphia. I asked him if he realized what would happen if he should die. Now look, that damned cowboy is President of the United States."[9]

On October 3, 1901, the *Chicago Tribune* ran the full text of McKinley's last speech on page 9 next to the full text of his vice president's last speech four day's earlier. The text was dense, and Roosevelt's affection for the West African proverb went unremarked.

It was on April 3, 1903, that now president Roosevelt gave another speech in the Midwest. In his eighteen months in the White House, he had been instrumental in peacefully settling a major coal strike in Pennsylvania, had confronted Great Britain, Germany, and Italy over their demands on the Venezuelan government, and had faced down the German kaiser, forcing the Germans to stop shelling the coastal cities in Venezuela and to withdraw their ships.

Roosevelt's Chicago speech was, again, on his favorite themes, both domestic and international. As befitted a major speech given locally by a president of the United States, the news ran on the *Chicago Tribune's* front page with large headlines. This time the headline ran, "SPEAK SOFTLY; CARRY BIG STICK; SAYS ROOSEVELT." In addition to providing the news about the speech, the section of the speech containing the proverb was reprinted in a special box below a photo of the president and with a small title for the boxed section, "SPEAK SOFTLY AND CARRY A BIG STICK."[10]

Not only had the reporters and editors paid attention, the paper internalized the phrase. Ten days later it carried a page 3 article headlined "Speak Softly, Carry a Big Stick, and Wear a Fierce Mustache, Is the Advice of Inspector Shea to the West Side Policemen."[11]

Eight days after that, a *Tribune* editorial on the need for improving the navy was headlined, "Is the Stick Big Enough?"[12]

And the following year, Judge Alton B. Parker was nominated as the Democratic candidate to run against Roosevelt in the 1904 election. In the speech nominating Parker, Martin Littleton said that Parker was "a man who puts against the stealthy hunt 'with the big stick,' a faithful observance of constitutional restraints."[13]

The slogan had now entered the popular lexicon. Not only was it colorful, it epitomized the man the public knew, fit his style, and gave voice to the mood of the times.

HIT 'EM WHERE THEY AIN'T

★   1902   ★

Willie Keeler was born in 1872 in one of the urban hotbeds of baseball— Brooklyn, then the fourth-largest city in the country. It was in Brooklyn that Candy Cummings was credited with inventing the curve ball, Eddie Cuthbert had first stolen a base, and Dicky Pearce created the bunt. And it was a Brooklyn ball club, the Brooklyn Atlantics, that in 1870 defeated the first professional team, the Cincinnati Red Stockings, ending the touring club's eighty-four-game winning streak.

Keeler, the smallest among several brothers, began to play baseball as soon as he could throw a ball and swing a bat. Baseball was far more fun than anything else he could do, or was supposed to do, like go to school or work. At age fourteen he began to play regularly on one of Brooklyn's many amateur teams, most often as a left-handed third baseman, unusual then as now. Because of his size, "Wee Willie" choked up on the bat so far that at least a foot of wood showed beneath his fists, but he could hit hard and often.

A year later Keeler's father sent him to work, but that did not suit him. At age sixteen he was playing for money in Brooklyn, in Queens, and even in New Jersey. He moved up quickly from the Plainfield Crescents in the Central New Jersey League to the Binghamton Bingos in the Eastern League, and then, at age twenty, to the New York Giants in the National League (the only major league there was in 1892).

At first Keeler stumbled in the big league. He was played sparingly, and in 1893 he broke his ankle sliding into second base. He was sold to Brooklyn but was quickly sent down to Binghamton.

And then lightning struck Keeler and baseball. In 1893 the new manager of the Baltimore Orioles, Ned Hanlon, was trying to resurrect the failing team by putting together a new kind of baseball club. Hanlon believed he could revolutionize the game and the Orioles by playing a different kind of baseball than the traditional "large men hitting away at all times" that dominated the game. He wanted what came to be known as "scientific" baseball, baseball that would emphasize strategy, speed, and exploiting opponents' weaknesses. By the end of the year, Hanlon had acquired the kind of players who could play his way.

When the 1894 season began, Hanlon's Orioles included six future Hall of Famers: first baseman Big Dan Brouthers, third baseman John McGraw, shortstop Hughey Jennings, catcher Wilbert Robinson, outfielder Joe Kelley, and Willie Keeler. He had a solid pitching staff and a hard-hitting outfielder, Walter Brodie.

Not needing a left-handed third baseman, Hanlon moved Keeler to the outfield and drilled the club on his way of playing baseball: strong defense with fielders covering each other on all plays; aggressive hitting with an emphasis on the hit-and-run, bunting for hits, hitting foul balls until a good pitch came along, and the "Baltimore chop," in which the batter hit down on the ball to create a very high bounce that allowed the batter to reach first base before the ball could be fielded. Keeler immediately excelled at this kind of hitting.

In his very first full year as a regular, Keeler batted .371, with 219 hits in 129 games. Three-quarters of his hits were singles, but he could drive in runs—ninety-four of them that year. Nor did Keeler lead the team. Kelley did, with a .393 average, but McGraw and Jennings hit too, for averages of .340 and .335.

The new kind of baseball—aggressive, speedy, and often pugnacious—was led by the fiery McGraw, who sharpened his spikes, fought with the umpires, and tripped opposing runners when he could get away with it. It paid off. Yet for all his roughness, McGraw was also the brains of the team and constantly sought to create new ways of winning. The previous year the Orioles had finished eighth in the league, with a record of sixty wins and seventy losses. In this breakout year, they finished first by three games, with a record of eighty-nine wins and thirty-nine losses.

The fans (known then as "cranks") loved Keeler. In a group of players who were on the small side, he was the smallest. (Keeler said he was five feet four, but he never allowed himself to be measured.) In a group of fast, quick-hitting batters, he was the swiftest and most reliable hitter. In a group of fine fielders, Keeler could track down the hardest hit and throw with anyone.

Hanlon's Orioles won again in 1895 and yet again in 1896, each time finishing further in front of the league. Keeler's average improved as well: .377 in 1895 and .386 in 1896. *Sporting Life* wrote, "To think that so small a man as Keeler should lead all the League sluggers! Truly it is the eye and not the size."[1]

In 1897 the Orioles finished second to the delightfully named Boston Beaneaters,[2] but Keeler hit his career high that year, batting .424, with 239 hits. In 1898 Keeler's average declined to a still-astonishing .385, but the club again finished second to the Beaneaters. By the next year, the heart of the club was gone.

It was an era of trusts—the steel trust, the oil trust, the beef trust—and eventually of the trustbusters, but baseball caught the trust bug too. Early in 1899 the baseball owners allowed themselves the luxury of joint club ownership, thus pooling their player assets. The Brooklyn and Baltimore club owners formed such an arrangement, and since Brooklyn was a bigger market but had a club that lost games and money, the owners decided to shift some players around. Eight Orioles and their manager Ned Hanlon moved north, while ten Dodgers moved to Baltimore. Among the Orioles who moved were Kelley, Jennings, and Keeler, who was delighted to go home. McGraw and Robinson refused to move, so they stayed as the core of the Orioles, with McGraw as manager, a role he would fill spectacularly for the next thirty-three years.

For the Dodgers and for Keeler, the move paid off financially and in the standings. The Brooklyn team, now named the Superbas after a Broadway company called Hanlon's Superbas, won the league title for the next two years. Keeler's average continued on a slow slide from his amazing high: .379 in 1899 and .362 in 1900.

In 1901 the Superbas faded to third place as the war began between the newly created American League and the established National League. Yet Keeler kept loyal to Brooklyn and stayed a favorite of the fans. On

August 6, as the team struggled to finish in the top four, a *Brooklyn Eagle* reporter, much later reported to have been Abe Yager, the future sports editor of the paper, approached Keeler after the day's game had been rained out. Keeler was discussing the bet he had made that Brooklyn would finish ahead of the Giants (betting on baseball was common and unremarkable at the time):

> "Lucky Willie," remarked a bystander.
>
> "Lucky nothing," said Wee Willie. "It's one of the great people I am. Why, they're all looking to me for information. Here's one of the few communications that I've received this year. I'll have to hire a secretary if this thing keeps up."

And Keeler produced a letter from faraway Littleton, North Carolina:

> Mr. William Keeler:
> Dear sir:
> Have you any treatise on the art of batting written by yourself? If so, please inform me where I can obtain such and the price thereof. I inclose stamp for reply.
>
> I have always considered you the best batter in the country and from your work this year I am thoroughly satisfied that you are. Hence, wishing to become a batter myself, you can readily see why I wish to obtain information from the country's best batter."

"Wouldn't that make you chesty," remarked Keeler. "I've already written that treatise, and it reads like this: 'Keep your eye clear and HIT 'EM WHERE THEY AIN'T.' That's all.[3]

And Keeler won his bet, too, since the Giants finished only one game out of the cellar. Willie hit .339 that year, completing a string of eight straight seasons with two hundred or more hits.

The next year Brooklyn finished a far distant second in the league, twenty-seven and a half games behind Pittsburgh. After the season, Keeler was badly injured when a wagon overturned during a hunting trip in California. On his return, he announced he was jumping to the American League. Although the National and American leagues made peace before the start of the 1903 season, Keeler joined the new New York Highlander club.

Though hurting, Keeler still managed to hit well. By the 1907 season his career was coming to an end. He had fewer than a hundred hits, and his average was now just .234. But baseball was all he knew or cared about. He struggled on until the end of the 1909 season, when he was released by the Yankees, as the Highlanders were now known. His old teammate and friend John McGraw hired him as a player-coach for the New York Giants. For the last time, Keeler hit .300, though he appeared in just nineteen games and got only five hits. He did make one new record, though, as the only major leaguer to play for all three New York teams.

Keeler lived out the rest of his life in Brooklyn and died on New Year's Day 1923. He left an incredible playing record. With a career batting average of .341, compiled with 2,932 hits in 2,123 games, Keeler was the first Oriole player elected to the Hall of Fame, in 1939. Only McGraw, elected in 1937 for his managerial brilliance, preceded him.

THERE'S HONEST GRAFT AND THERE'S DISHONEST GRAFT

★ 1903 ★

The intercabinet struggles between the followers of Alexander Hamilton and Thomas Jefferson soon became the dreaded party "factions" nominally called the Federalists and the Democratic-Republicans (or Anti-Federalists) and then, by 1828, full-blown though still evolving political parties—the National Republicans and the Democratic-Republicans. These political organizations, even in their earliest forms, created the part-time, and eventually full-time, profession of politics at the state and local levels.

The working politician was not interested in political philosophy or even the broad issues facing the city, state, or country. The working politician was interested in winning elections, often—perhaps usually—by whatever means necessary. Power became his central aim in life, and the money it brought became his personal and organizational lifeblood.

Until the late 1820s, though, the political struggles at the state and national levels were largely between factions among the old landholding families and their retainers. But the erosion of the property qualification for voting, coupled with a large increase in immigrants who settled in cities, changed that pattern. This new polity increasingly needed services that government could not or would not provide in the urban areas that became increasingly powerful for the votes cast by people the older elites disdained. And the growth of the cities was phenomenal. By the beginning of the Civil War, for example, Boston had grown from 26,000 at the turn of the century to nearly 170,000; New York from 61,000 to nearly 800,000; and Philadelphia from 41,000 to 500,000. Cincinnati, which had only 3,000 people in 1810, had grown to 161,000; and Chicago, which had 5,000 in 1840, had 109,000 in 1860.

For the immigrants who swelled the cities, the conditions were beyond deplorable. Housing was rudimentary, growth was chaotic, policing was nominal and corrupt, food and health measures were nonexistent, employment was sporadic, and there was no civic leadership. The sole ray of light for many, if not most, was in the developing political machines and their leaders, the machine bosses. As Martin Lomasney, the boss of Boston's Eighth Ward, said, "I think that there's got to be in every ward somebody that any bloke can come to—no matter what he's done—and get help. Help, you understand; none of your law and justice, but help."[1]

The best known of the urban political machines was New York City's Tammany Hall. Created in 1789, Tammany Hall ruled the city because it stepped in to provide the services a poor, immigrant population needed: jobs, navigation through government laws and regulations, housing, bail money, and relief in times of dire need. But Tammany was not a welfare organization whose members worked out of civic obligation. Tammany's efforts were exchanged for votes from grateful citizens. Its funding came from graft: skimmed bribes for the police to overlook legal infractions, enforced contributions from officials who needed votes, and payments by businessmen who wanted contracts or protection from the government. Such money not only funded the smooth operation of Tammany, it also enriched senior officeholders and Tammany "sachems," as the leaders of the Hall were called.

Similar political machines developed in every city of any size as it grew, in every part of the nation, and they survived well into the twentieth century. In the nineteenth and early twentieth centuries, the machines were characterized by graft and theft. Tammany was their unwanted symbol, but its depredations were characteristic, not exceptional.

Such outright thievery manifested itself early. In 1829 sachem Samuel Swartwout was appointed collector of the Port of New York by President Andrew Jackson, whose early and ardent supporter he had been. It was a post known for its opportunities to steal, and steal he did. In 1838 Swartwout fled to Europe, and he was found to have taken more than a million dollars in less than ten years. His was not the first Tammany financial scandal, merely the biggest up to that time.

Tammany did not control the votes of the city only through its benevolence. It often controlled the polls through violence (using people termed "sluggers") or through fraud (ballot box stuffing, having "repeaters" vote early and often, and importing "mattress" voters from other cities). Still, these voting frauds, while occasionally significant in the outcomes of elections, represented a minority of the votes, albeit a sizable one. For example, in 1868, estimates at the time asserted that "at least 25,000 of the 156,000 votes cast were fraudulent," 16 percent of the total.[2]

The power to survive financial scandals, the occasional voter revolt, and the resulting reform administrations stemmed from the machine's ability to provide services that were crucially needed and rarely supplied by government or volunteer organizations, and never as a matter of government policy. The dominance of Tammany continued despite even the most corrupt of bosses: William Tweed.

"Boss" Tweed is best known through the cartoons of his mortal enemy, *Harper's Weekly* cartoonist Thomas Nast, cartoons that Tweed particularly hated, since even the most illiterate of voters could understand them. Tweed, like many of Tammany bosses, had worked his way up from the depths of New York City's poverty, and he acceded to the leadership of Tammany in 1860. As one early historian put it, "This is his immortality. He was a chair maker by trade, a vulgar good fellow by nature, a politician by circumstances, a boss by evolution, and a grafter by choice."[3]

There was no form of graft and thievery that Tweed did not engage in, not for Tammany's sake, but to enrich a small group of cronies. In his actions he was crude, as the times were crude—brooking no opposition, reaching into every pot of gold, and himself holding only those offices that could bring him money. Tweed, after all, had learned his skills as a junior member of a board of aldermen known in the press as "the forty thieves." He was president of New York City's board of supervisors, from which he controlled all the city's financial policies and practices. For a time he was state senator, and from that position he could direct private and public favors to his city and, most important, to those corporations he owned or controlled.

The height of his plundering came with the authorization, in 1858, to build a new county courthouse in New York City. Its original budget was $250,000; it was to be completed in two years. In fact the building was started four years late and completed twelve years late, and the total cost came to an estimated $12.5 million—a budget overrun of 50,000 percent. What money was not stolen directly went to pay bills padded as much as two or three times. The contractor got 35 percent of his bill; the rest went to Tweed and his friends.

Though rumors and even published articles about the massive theft abounded, it was not until a disaffected member of the conspiracy, outraged at not getting his share, brought proof to the *New York Times* that Tweed was toppled. Two of his top lieutenants left for Paris, and Tweed eventually died in jail.

Tammany, though, did not die. Tweed was succeeded by "Honest John" Kelly, who reformed Tammany to eliminate the grossest abuses and bring discipline to its actions. After Kelly came Richard Croker and then William Murphy, who brought the organization to the height of its respectability. No longer did stealing enrich the sachems, though the lower ranks still battened off organized police graft and business bribes. A reform mayor or an activist police commissioner like Theodore Roosevelt would intervene and make some small headway, but within a few years Tammany would be back in power. Croker, testifying to an investigating commission, presented Tammany's justification.

> We have thousands of men who are alien born. They are alone, ignorant strangers a prey to all manner of anarchical and wild notions. Tammany looks after them for the sake of their vote, grafts them upon the Republic . . . and although you may not like our motives or our methods, what other agency is there by which so long a row could have been hoed so quickly or so well.[4]

In the beginning of the new century, after Croker exiled himself to a castle he had bought in Ireland, a newspaper reporter named William L. Riordon found a Tammany sachem who fascinated him. George Washington Plunkitt had once been, simultaneously, city magistrate, a member of the board of aldermen, a member of the board of supervisors, and a state senator, collecting three salaries. He was also Tammany's leader of the Fifteenth Assembly District.

Plunkitt's office was at a shoeshine stand outside Boss Tweed's county courthouse. There he held audiences with people who needed something, and he talked about politics, particularly politics as practiced by Tammany Hall, "the most perfect political machine on earth."[5]

> Everybody is talkin' these days about Tammany men growin' rich on graft, but nobody thinks of drawin' the distinction between **HONEST GRAFT AND**

DISHONEST GRAFT. There's all the difference in the world between the two. Yes, many of our men have grown rich in politics. I have myself. I've made a big fortune out of the game, and I'm gettin' richer every day, but I've not gone in for dishonest graft—blackmailin' gamblers, saloonkeepers, disorderly people, etc.—and neither has any of the men who have made big fortunes in politics. . . .

Just let me explain by examples. My party's in power in the city, and it's goin' to undertake a lot of public improvements. Well, I'm tipped off, say, that they're going to lay out a new park at a certain place.

I see my opportunity and I take it. I go to that place and I buy up all the land I can in the neighborhood. Then the board of this or that makes its plan public, and there is a rush to get my land, which nobody cared particular for before.

Ain't it perfectly honest to charge a good price and make a profit on my investment and foresight? Of course, it is. Well, that's honest graft.[6]

As far as Plunkitt was concerned, his epitaph should be "George W. Plunkitt. He Seen His Opportunities, and He Took 'em."[7]

Eventually Riordon collected twenty-three of Plunkitt's curbside lectures, and in 1905 he published them as *Plunkitt of Tammany Hall: A Series of Very Plain Talks on Very Practical Politics.* It was a success. New Yorkers were both horrified and captivated by Plunkitt's good-humored self-justification. They knew the realities of what lay behind Plunkitt's descriptions and what he left unsaid, but the Tammany Hall of Boss Tweed was long dead, and the Tammany Hall of William Murphy was different both in kind and in quality. Besides, there is nothing New Yorkers love better to this day than sheer, bald-faced effrontery.

Nor did they forget him. When he lay terminally ill in 1924 at age eighty-two, the *New York Times* ran an article with the headline, "G. W. Plunkitt Ill, Famous Politician." The subhead was even more telling: "Former Tammany leader of Fifteenth District and the Exponent of 'Honest Graft.'"[8]

After his death a short time later, the *Times* ran three more articles, two on his life and one covering his funeral. Though he did not get his self-written epitaph, a paragraph in the *Times* story on the massively attended funeral mass might have served: "Though no confirmation could be obtained, it was said by intimate friends that the Senator's estate will amount to considerably more than $1,000,000."[9]

Opportunities indeed.

WE STAND AT ARMAGEDDON, AND
WE BATTLE FOR THE LORD

★ 1912 ★

The incredible growth of the United States in the decades after the Civil War—in population, industry, and wealth—had been accompanied by equally incredible growth in political corruption, urban squalor, waste of resources, and poverty. The traditional government institutions that worked well in a relatively small, simple agrarian democracy simply had not kept pace with the nation's development into an increasingly urban, industrial, populous society.

Beginning in the last decades of the nineteenth century, journalists, academics, social critics, and novelists began exposing the growing dangers and inequities of America's economic, political, and social life. They were joined by reformist politicians at the local and state levels and eventually by national figures, first William Jennings Bryan and then Theodore Roosevelt, president at age forty-three after the assassination of William McKinley.

The new president was a man of great enthusiasms, wide-ranging friendships, and decided opinions. He believed the president should be an active force in changing the fabric of national life. And he was controlled only by the force of his ideas and the strength of his will.

Almost immediately he began changing the role of the president and instituting as many reforms as possible. Within his first term, Roosevelt revived the dormant Sherman Anti-Trust Act by instructing his attorney general to bring an action against one of the railroad trusts, intervened to settle a major coal miners' strike in Pennsylvania, initiated the Forest, Land, and River Reclamation Policy, began building the Panama Canal, created the Department of Commerce and the Bureau of Corporations, and resolved a dispute with Canada over the boundary of Alaska.

Easily nominated for a full term in 1903, Roosevelt won with equal ease against his Democratic opponent, with 56 percent of the popular vote and 72 percent of the electoral college vote, both totals exceeding McKinley's of four years before. The Republicans had firm control of both houses of Congress, but Roosevelt made a critical mistake. On election night in November 1903 he announced, "On the fourth of March next I shall have served three and a half years, and this three and a half years constitutes my first term." He went on to say, "under no circumstances will I be a candidate for or accept another nomination."[1] From that moment, he was a lame duck.

The second term was eventful and occasionally successful. Roosevelt's active negotiation ended the Russo-Japanese War (an action for which he received the Nobel Peace Price in 1906). But making progress in domestic reform was getting harder. As Roosevelt told Congress in a special message near the end of his term, "Every measure for honesty in business that has been passed during the last six years has been opposed by these men with every recourse that bitter and unscrupulous craft could suggest and the command of almost unlimited money secure."[2]

But Roosevelt had promised to leave office, and as his successor he picked William Howard Taft, his vice president, who really did not want the job. Taft, though somewhat weak, was tremendously loyal and would continue the work that Roosevelt had started. Or so Roosevelt believed as he left for an African safari to give Taft a clear field.

Things began to go wrong almost immediately. Taft, who had promised to keep Roosevelt's cabinet in place, changed his mind and appointed his own. Then, trumpeting an effort to revise the tariffs, Taft found himself under the sway of the very men Roosevelt had warned him about. The resulting Payne-Aldrich tariff bill not only did not lower the tariffs generally as the progressive Republicans and Democrats wanted, it raised them almost across the board as business and industry desired. Worse, Taft praised the bill publicly as "the best bill that the Republican party ever passed."[3] In the congressional elections that followed soon after, the Democrats won control of the House for the first time in fifteen years and picked up twelve seats in the Senate. Administrative moves to weaken conservation measures further increased Roosevelt's feeling that he had been betrayed.

Talk now began of nominating Roosevelt as the Republican candidate for president in 1912 or, failing that, organizing a new party with him at the head. Roosevelt tried to put down such talk, but his speaking tour of the West on his return from Africa only stimulated it. In Osawatomie, Kansas, Roosevelt spoke on the need for a "New Nationalism" that would put the needs of the whole nation ahead of the demands of a section of the country or a group of individuals. The struggle, as Roosevelt outlined it, took on historic proportions: "At every stage, and under all circumstances, the essence of the struggle is to equalize opportunity, destroy privilege, and give to the life and citizenship of every individual the highest possible value both to himself and to the commonwealth."[4]

Clearly, Roosevelt was beginning to change his mind about running. In December 1911 he wrote to a friend, "While I am absolutely sincere in saying that I am not a candidate and do not wish the nomination, yet . . . I do not feel it would be right or proper for me to say that under no circumstances would I accept it if it came, because while wildly improbable, it was yet possible that there might be a public demand which would present the matter to me in the light of a duty which I could not shirk."[5]

In fact, Roosevelt believed that Taft would get the nomination and the Democrats would win the presidency in 1912. Only he could beat both the Democrats and the increasingly popular Eugene V. Debs, the perennial Socialist candidate. By early January 1912 he stated publicly that "if the people make a draft on me, I shall not decline to serve."[6] And two weeks later, "If it is the sincere judgment of men having the right to know and express the wishes of the plain people that the people as a whole desire me, not for my sake, but for their sake, to undertake the job, I would feel in honor bound to do so."[7] Five weeks later, Colonel Roosevelt announced his candidacy for the Republican nomination.

In the fight for convention delegates, Taft led early, largely because the early states were not ones that held primaries. When the primary states began to weigh in, Roosevelt surged. Even in Taft's home state of Ohio, Roosevelt won easily. A total of 540 delegate votes were needed to win the nomination, and while Roosevelt was ahead, 254 delegates were contested, and the Republican National Committee, closely controlled by the old guard, would decide.

Roosevelt was doomed. The Republican National Committee ruled consistently in Taft's favor, giving Taft 235 of the contested seats and awarding Roosevelt only 19. The fight became bitter and personal. Roosevelt told a crowd that "the receiver of stolen goods is no better than a thief. . . . It is a naked fight against theft and thieves, and the thieves shall not win."[8] Taft called his former leader a demagogue, a dangerous egotist, and a liar. Roosevelt called Taft a fathead, stupid, a liar, and a traitor to the party.

Finley Peter Dunne weighed in. Dunne, a political observer and humorist, wrote in the Irish dialect of a fictional Chicago saloon owner named Mr. Dooley:

> Am I goin' to th' convintion? What a question to ask a spoortin' charakter. If a fellow was to come to ye an' say: Here's a free ticket fr a combynation iv th' Chicago fire, Saint Bartholomew's massacree, the battle iv th' Boyne, th' life iv Jesse James, an' th' night iv th' big wind, an' all th' victims will be

ye'er thraditional inimies," wud ye take it or wud ye not? . . . I'll get a seat somewhere that I can see th' sthruggle fr human rights goin' on but fur enough away so I won't be splashed.[9]

The only chance Roosevelt had left was the vote on the floor of the convention ratifying the decisions of the Republican National Committee. But there the old guard was leaving nothing to chance, even if it meant splitting the party and losing the election. As President Taft wrote in a letter to William Barnes, the Republican boss in New York, "Victory is by no means the most important purpose before us. . . . It should be to retain the party."[10]

On the night before the convention opened with its first business of ratifying the decisions on the contested delegates, Roosevelt addressed a packed house of 5,000 supporters in Chicago's Auditorium. The streets outside were jammed with some 10,000 more who could not get in but who cheered whenever they heard cheering from within.

Roosevelt began by immediately attacking the leadership of the Republican Party and enlarging the struggle against their actions into a struggle for democracy and the nation itself.

Tonight we come together to protest against a crime which strikes straight at the heart of every principle of political decency and honesty, a crime which represents treason to the people, and the usurpation of the sovereignty of the people by irresponsible political bosses, inspired by the sinister influences of moneyed privilege. We here in this hall are engaged not only in a fight for the rights of every decent Republican, we are engaged in a fight for the rights of every decent American whatsoever his party may be.[11]

Roosevelt spoke for well over an hour and was constantly interrupted by cheers.

"Bully for you!" Hit 'em hard!' "Go at 'em!" "Knock out the steam roller!" and a dozen other whoops greeted each appeal. Above them all rose the great cry of "Teddy—Teddy—Teddy!" That was the easiest thing to say, and men and women yelled it until they were hoarse. The cheering as he entered kept up until the organ broke into "America," then picked up again, and only the colonel's outstretched arms and beaming smile stopped it.[12]

Roosevelt detailed the actions of each individual who had acted to deny him the nomination. He stressed that wherever a primary had been held, large majorities voted for him, and wherever no primary had taken place, Taft had won. It was a situation that could not be accepted. And coming to the end of his speech, Roosevelt returned to his theme of a national struggle, sending the crowds inside and outside the hall into a frenzy.

> What happens to me [in this struggle] is not of the slightest consequence; I am to be used, as in a doubtful battle any man is used, to his hurt or not, so long as he is useful, and is then cast aside or left to die. I wish you to feel this. I mean it; and I shall need no sympathy when you are through with me, for this fight is far too great to permit us to concern ourselves about any one man's welfare. If we are true to ourselves by putting far above our own interests the triumph of the high cause for which we battle we shall not lose. It would be far better to fail honorably for the cause we champion than it would be to win by foul methods the foul victory for which our opponents hope. But the victory shall be ours, and it shall be won as we have already won so many victories, by clean and honest fighting for the loftiest of causes.
>
> We fight in honorable fashion for the good of mankind; fearless of the future; unheeding of our individual fates; with unflinching hearts and undimmed eyes; **WE STAND AT ARMAGEDDON, AND WE BATTLE FOR THE LORD.**[13]

The next morning's *Chicago Daily Tribune* carried news of the speech on its front page and, in a boxed section on page 2 printed the final paragraphs of the speech with the headline, "We Stand at Armageddon, and We Battle For the Lord."

But it was not to happen. Each contested delegate was allowed to vote on all the contested delegates except himself, and Taft's nomination was assured. California governor Hiram Johnson, at a meeting of Roosevelt supporters, jumped on a table and declared that a new political party would be born. Roosevelt's key financial backers assured him that he would have the money if he ran for president on a third-party ticket.

On Saturday morning, June 22, a statement from Roosevelt was read, once again asserting that the nomination was being stolen and that anyone who accepted the nomination under these conditions "would have forfeited the right to ask the support of any honest man of any party on moral grounds."[14] Fistfights broke out on the floor, and it took twenty minutes to restore order. The balloting for the nomination took place, with Taft getting 561 votes. Roosevelt got 107, and Robert La Follette got 41. Ominously for the Republicans, 344 delegates refused to vote.

Later that day the disaffected delegates met in Orchestra Hall, nominated Roosevelt for president, and received his enthusiastic acceptance. Back at the main convention, "when the tickets had been completed, the one question asked the outsider by the leaders was: "How do you think Roosevelt will run?"[15]

The answer would be "Better than Taft"—but not well enough.

A month earlier, in May, the Socialists, meeting in Indianapolis, had again nominated Eugene V. Debs after a fierce intraparty fight between a radical wing and a more conservative one. Debs spent much of his campaign attacking Roosevelt.

On July 2, in Baltimore, the Democratic Party nominated Woodrow Wilson, the increasingly progressive Democratic governor of New Jersey. It had taken forty-six ballots. Wilson believed that the real election contest would be between him and Roosevelt, not Taft.

Finally, on August 7, Roosevelt formally accepted the Progressive Party's nomination at a huge convention in Chicago. After a tumultuous fifty-minute demonstration, Roosevelt gave his acceptance speech, once again concluding with his increasingly famous declaration, "We stand at Armageddon, and we battle for the Lord."

The campaign was hard fought, at least by everyone except Taft, who gave only one speech, and that to a county Republican Club in New Jersey. Both Wilson and Roosevelt lost their voices temporarily, and Roosevelt was wounded by an assassin's bullet—though he went on anyway, showed his bloody shirt to the crowd, and finished his speech. Only then did he go to the hospital.

When the voters went to the polls in November, Wilson emerged the winner. Though he received only 42 percent of the popular vote with nearly 6.3 million votes, Wilson easily won in the electoral college, with 435 votes. Roosevelt came in second with 4.1 million popular votes and 88 electoral votes. Debs, the Socialist, came in fourth with nearly 1 million votes and 6 percent of the total, the highest percentage a Socialist candidate would ever get.

Taft came in third with 3.5 million votes, some 23 percent of the total, and only 8 votes in the electoral college. The old guard had kept control of the party, but they would not occupy the White House again until 1920.

The real winner was reform. Reform candidates received more than 11 million popular votes—75 percent of the total, and the agenda for Wilson, and progressives of all persuasions, was clearly set.

HE KEPT US
OUT OF WAR

★ 1916 ★

MAKE THE
WORLD SAFE FOR
DEMOCRACY

★ 1917 ★

Woodrow Wilson, first elected in 1912, was the first southern-born president since the Civil War—indeed, the first since Zachary Taylor in 1848—and the first Democratic president to be elected to successive terms since Andrew Jackson, whose second term ended in 1836. Under his leadership, more far-ranging domestic reforms were passed than ever before, and until Franklin D. Roosevelt's first term twenty years later, Wilson stood as the leader in governmental and social change.

Son and grandson of Presbyterian ministers, Wilson grew up in the South in the aftermath of the Civil War. He left to attend the College of New Jersey, later renamed Princeton and long known as the northernmost southern university. He became an academic, earning a PhD from Johns Hopkins University, and went on to be a popular professor of history and government and a respected, well-published scholar. Rejoining Princeton in 1902 as its president, Wilson embarked on a campaign to dramatically change its educational program and upgrade its student body. Attracting new kinds of faculty, administrators, and students, he enjoyed quick success, but he underestimated his opposition among the existing faculty and alumni. After years of internal strife, Wilson resigned to accept the Democratic nomination for governor of New Jersey.

Elected governor, Wilson entered the office as he had done at Princeton, with a plan to transform the state, one of the least progressive and most machine-dominated in the nation. Combining the ideas of the increasingly important Progressive movement with his own, Wilson succeeded in taking control of the party in the state legislature. With frequent appeals to the public, he passed a series of transforming laws: a direct primary system to take more power away from the bosses of both parties, a public utilities commission to regulate the power and water companies in the state; and a corrupt practices act to make government more honest and more responsive to the needs of the public. Again, though, Wilson underestimated the growing internal opposition to change. The Democrats lost seats in the next election, and the party bosses looked for revenge. Yet Wilson's efforts here, as at Princeton, had attracted national attention for the 1912 presidential election.

Though still a newcomer to politics, with only two years in elected office, Wilson gained the Democratic nomination for president, but only after a struggle and forty-six ballots. It was a long shot, a desperate gamble by the party, for the Democrats had not elected a president in twenty years.

The Republicans helped. The GOP split wide open, renominating President William Howard Taft in the face of a Progressive movement headed by former president Theodore Roosevelt. Roosevelt took his followers, started the Progressive Party (called then and now the Bull Moose Party), and was nominated as its candidate. The Socialist Party, then at its high-water mark in American politics, nominated the highly respected Eugene V. Debs, and even the prohibitionists, opposed to all forms of alcoholic drink, nominated a candidate.

In this crowded field, Wilson was elected with a distinct minority of the voters—just under 42 percent of the vote. Roosevelt and Taft combined to get more than 7.5 million votes, 50.5 percent, but so great was the appeal of Wilson's ideas and speeches nationwide that he gained 435 electoral votes, and, more important, his party gained control of both houses of Congress for the first time in two decades.

Again, Wilson began a new job with a rush. Inaugurated in March 1913, he spearheaded and secured passage of the first tariff reform in decades; the Federal Reserve Act that established the Federal Reserve System and allowed the federal government a key role in controlling credit and interest rates; the Clayton Act that revised and tightened up the old Sherman Anti-Trust Act while exempting labor unions from its provisions and freeing them to organize; and the Trade Commission Act that set up the Federal Trade Commission as the watchdog of business competition and the safeguard against monopolies.

Before the end of his first term, Wilson turned his attention to social reform and secured passage of legislation that supported farm credit, workman's compensation for job-related injuries, child labor protections, and the eight-hour day. He also, as he had in New Jersey, nominated and pushed through the Senate ratification process the first Jewish member of the Supreme Court, Louis D. Brandeis.

It was foreign policy that provided the most testing problems for Wilson. There were ill-advised military interventions in Nicaragua, the Dominican Republic, and Haiti and a near war with Mexico. Yet these were overshadowed by two events: the death of his beloved wife, Ellen, in August 1914 and the first shots of World War I.

For Wilson the decision to declare the United States neutral in the conflict was an easy one. The country had a long-standing philosophy enshrined by George Washington in his warning against "entangling alliances" in his 1796 Farewell Address. Moreover, taking sides in the struggle could alienate important segments of the American population, most notably the large German and Irish minorities.

Involvement carried another risk. Engaging in a war would render the nation less liberal in its domestic policies and more brutal in its politics. As Wilson told the editor of the *New York World* several years later, war "would mean that we should lose our heads along with the rest and stop weighing right and wrong. . . . Once lead this people into war and they'll forget there ever was such a thing as tolerance. To fight you must be brutal and ruthless, and the spirit of ruthless brutality will enter into the very fibre of our national life, infecting Congress, the courts, the policeman on the beat, the man in the street."[1]

Less than two weeks after his wife's death, Wilson publicly appealed to the public to show the "true spirit of neutrality," to act in a manner "[which] neither sits in judgment upon others nor is disturbed in her own counsels and which keeps herself fit and free to do what is necessary and disinterested and truly serviceable for the peace of the world."[2]

While Wilson's concept of neutrality held out the pledge that the United States could and would be available to bring about peace among the warring powers, it also contained a contradiction, for it implied not only that the country would not take sides but also that it actively asserted specific rights that neither side could violate with impunity. Among them were the right to conduct commerce with all the warring parties and the right to be safe from any harm to its citizens or its property.

Such rights would have been easier to assert and even maintain a century earlier when the seas were wide and the ships were slow. The existence of submarines and steam-powered warships made that kind of neutrality difficult at best, particularly when one of the warring nations, Germany, had already invaded France through a neutral country, Belgium, and remained there as an occupying power. Moreover, Americans seemed to believe that their lives were inviolate even when sailing on a ship that flew the flag of one of the warring nations.

Over the next few years both sides, to a greater or lesser degree, violated America's neutrality. Within a year of Wilson's declaration of neutrality, a German submarine sank the British passenger liner *Lusitania* off the coast of Ireland. More than 1,100 people were killed, including 128 Americans.

With the backing of substantial public opinion, former president Taft asserted that Congress would approve a declaration of war.

Wilson took two actions. Three days after the sinking, he spoke to an audience of newly naturalized citizens. In praising them for coming to America to find the life, liberty, and freedom to pursue happiness that they were unable to secure in their former homes, he talked about the special role of their new country.

> The example of America must be a special example. The example of America must be the example not merely of peace because it will not fight, but of peace because peace is the healing and elevating influence of the world, and strife is not. There is such a thing as a man being too proud to fight. There is such a thing as a nation being so right that it does not need to convince others by force that it is right.[3]

That same day, May 11, 1915, Wilson talked with his cabinet about the note he was about to send to the German government. He called for the Germans to cease all submarine warfare against civilian ships. The Germans, faced with an ever-tightening blockade by the British navy, declined, and Wilson replied with a much stiffer note.

While the diplomatic exchanges were going back and forth and the two governments argued over what to do, the Germans sank another British passenger liner on August 19, killing, among others, two Americans. Faced with mounting American impatience and hostility, the Germans agreed not to sink unarmed ships without warning. And indeed none were sunk for the rest of that year.

The United States, though, began to rebuild a seriously depleted army and navy, neither of which had seen real combat since the Civil War. Wilson justified the increases by asserting both parts of his concept of neutrality in a speech given in January 1916.

> I know that peace is not always within the choice of the nation, and I want to remind you, and remind you very solemnly, of the double obligation you have laid upon me. . . . : "We are relying on you, Mr. President, to keep us out of this war, but we are relying upon you, Mr. President, to keep the honor of the nation unstained."
>
> Do you not see that a time may come when it is impossible to do both of these things? Do you not see that, if I am to guard the honor of the nation, I am not protecting it against itself, for we are not going to do anything

to stain the honor of our own country. I am protecting it against things I cannot control—the actions of others. . . . You may count upon my heart and resolution to keep you out of the war, but you must be ready, if it is necessary, that I should maintain your honor. . . . And the nation's honor is dearer than the nation's comfort and the nation's peace and the nation's life itself.[4]

Then, in March, a German submarine attacked an unarmed ferry in the English Channel, killing eighty, including four Americans. The Germans denied any responsibility, though few believed them. Wilson sent yet another note in protest, demanding an immediate abandonment of such tactics, and that same day he called a special session of Congress to read them his note. Reluctantly and ambiguously, the kaiser agreed.

Wilson received national and international acclaim, just in time for the political conventions to nominate candidates for the presidential elections of 1916. The Republicans nominated Supreme Court justice and former New York governor Charles Evans Hughes. The Progressives again nominated Theodore Roosevelt, who declined the nomination to support Hughes. Wilson sought, and was assured, the Democratic nomination, and he planned and controlled all aspects of the convention and his platform. The dominant theme would be his accomplishments over the past four years.

What Wilson could not control was the reaction of the convention delegates. The keynote speaker was former Ohio governor Martin H. Glynn, who began with a routine recital of the domestic accomplishments of the Wilson administration and in return received perfunctory applause. However, when Glynn turned to foreign policy, the reaction was far different.

> For vain glory or for selfish purpose, others may cry up a policy of blood and iron, but the President of the United States has acted on the belief that the leader of a nation who plunges his people into an unnecessary war, like Pontius Pilate, vainly washes his hands of innocent blood while the earth quakes and the heavens are darkened and thousands give up the ghost.

He then, at the insistence of the cheering crowd, cited instance after instance, from Washington to Grant, when presidents had refused to go to war.

> This policy may not satisfy those who revel in destruction and find pleasure in despair. It may not satisfy the fire-eater or the swashbuckler. But it does satisfy those who worship at the altar of the God of Peace. It does satisfy the

mothers of the land at whose hearth and fireside no jingoistic war has placed an empty chair. It does satisfy the daughters of this land from whom bluster and brag has sent no loving brother to the dissolution of the grave. It does satisfy the fathers of this land and the sons of this land who will fight for our flag, and die for our flag when reason primes the rifle, when honor draws the sword, when justice breathes a blessing on the standards they uphold.

To prolonged acclaim, he concluded,

One name will shine in golden splendor upon the page that is blackened with the talk of Europe's war, one name will represent the triumph of American principles over the hosts of darkness and of death.

That name will be the name of the great President who has made Democracy proud that he is a Democrat, and made Americans proud that he is an American.

It will be the name of the statesman who has kept his country true to its faith in a time that tried men's souls; the name of the student and the scholar who has championed the cause of American freedom wherever he found it oppressed; the name of the patriot who has implanted his country's flag on the highest peak to which humanity has yet aspired; the same that carried the torch of progress to victory once and will carry it to victory again; the name of Woodrow Wilson, President and President to be.[5]

And so the course and nature of the coming campaign changed on the spot. When the final draft of the party platform was issued, plank 27 stated, "In particular, we commend to the American people the splendid diplomatic victories of our great President, who has preserved the vital interests of our Government and its citizens, and kept us out of war."[6]

No one knew, or could remember, just who inserted that last clause in the platform. But with the constant control Wilson kept over the platform committee, he certainly had to have known about it and approved.

At rallies throughout the campaign, there appeared everywhere signs that read, **HE KEPT US OUT OF WAR**, and the speakers all dwelled on that theme.

Events at home and abroad roiled the election campaign. Wilson narrowly avoided a war with Mexico only because the Mexican government did not retaliate for the American occupation of Vera Cruz. There was a nationwide rail strike. Britain kept up its interference with neutral shipping to Europe and incited increased Irish American hostility when it bloodily put down the Irish Rebellion.

The campaign must have provided Wilson with a sense of respite, but it was an extremely close election. In fact, when Wilson went to bed, not only was Hughes in the lead, but the *New York Times* had conceded him the election. The late-arriving returns from the West, particularly from California, won the day–barely. Wilson had gained a popular vote margin of just under 700,000 votes and an electoral college margin of 277-254. He had won California by only 3,806 votes, and that state made the difference. Wilson was still a minority president with 49.4 percent of the vote, but he had gained nearly 3 million more votes than in 1912. It was largely the peace theme that had done the job, since it appealed most strongly in the middle and far West, where the election was won.

After the election, the war in Europe dominated Wilson's attention. He made several quiet attempts to mediate, but both sides had sacrificed too many men and too much of their resources to listen to anything but victory. Wilson went public to try to go over the heads of the warring countries. On January 22, 1917, he made an address to the Senate in which he called for a "peace without victory" in the world.

> Victory would mean peace forced upon the loser, a victor's terms imposed upon the vanquished. It would be accepted in humiliation, under duress, at an intolerable sacrifice and would leave a sting, a resentment, a bitter memory upon which terms of peace would rest, not permanently, but only as upon quicksand.[7]

Wilson was prophetic, as he had been before and would be again, but nothing happened, nor could it have. Then the Germans made two disastrous moves. The first, helpfully revealed to the United States by British intelligence, was a telegram sent in code to the German ambassador to Mexico from the German foreign secretary in Berlin. Known as the "Zimmerman telegram" from the name of its author, it instructed the ambassador to propose to the Mexican government that if the United States entered the war, Mexico and Germany could join forces. At a German victory, Mexico would be given back its lost territories of Texas, New Mexico, and Arizona. Wilson kept the information secret—for a time.

The second German move was the announcement at the end of January that Germany would resume unrestricted submarine warfare. The move, hotly debated in Berlin, was determined to be the only way to loosen the noose of the British blockade.

Wilson revealed the contents of the Zimmerman telegram and broke off diplomatic relations with Germany to make his displeasure clear. Yet the situation in Europe worsened still more. In March the Russian revolutionaries ousted the czar and signed a harsh peace treaty with the Central Powers, putting even more pressure on the Allies. By the end of March the German submarines had sunk four vessels, causing fifteen American deaths. America's entry into the war was now assured.

Wilson called an extraordinary joint session of Congress on April 2, 1917. That evening the senators and representatives were joined by the Supreme Court justices, members of the cabinet, and a large delegation from the diplomatic corps. Wilson began by reviewing recent events, the steps he had taken to avoid becoming involved, and the decisions of the German government. And in the middle of his address, he spoke a sentence that became a watchword for America's troops and civilians in the days to come and a touchstone for the peoples of Europe.

> We are now about to accept the gage of battle with this natural foe to liberty and shall, if necessary, spend the whole force of the nation to check and nullify its pretension and its power. We are glad, now that we see the facts with no veil of false pretence about them, to fight thus for the ultimate peace of the world and for the liberation of its peoples, the German peoples included: the rights of nations great and small and the privilege of men everywhere to choose their way of life and of obedience. **THE WORLD MUST BE MADE SAFE FOR DEMOCRACY.** Its peace must be planted upon the tested foundations of political liberty. . . . We are but one of the champions of the rights of mankind. We shall be satisfied when those rights have been made as secure as the faith and the freedom of nations can make them.[8]

And for this ideal, America went to war. For this ideal, Wilson was to spend the rest of his political life and, ultimately, give his life itself.

LAFAYETTE, WE ARE HERE

★ 1917 ★

In 1777 a wealthy teenage French aristocrat, the Marquis de Lafayette, resigned his captain's commission in the French army, bought a ship, hired a captain and crew, and sailed for America to take part in its revolution against Great Britain. The Continental Congress commissioned him as a major general, but only after he had offered to serve at his own expense. At first taken on as yet another foreign staff aide to Washington, Lafayette proved himself in battle, was given a division of troops to command, and then proved himself again as a successful military leader. While leading troops to harry General Charles Cornwallis's army that threatened Virginia, Lafayette recognized the opportunity to trap the British on the coast. He persuaded Washington to move troops south and to arrange for a French fleet, then sailing from the West Indies up the American coast, to head for the Yorktown peninsula as well. When the French infantry reinforcements arrived, Lafayette cut off Cornwallis on the peninsula, and with the arrival of Washington and his troops a week later, Cornwallis was in the bottle. On October 19, 1781, the British surrendered.

Lafayette became an important hero to the young republic, and when he was invited back in 1824 by President James Monroe, he toured all the states and major cities with a hero's welcome. Congress awarded the now-impoverished Lafayette $250,000 and a grant of land in Florida. He died ten years later at age seventy-eight and was buried next to his wife in the Picpus Cemetery in Paris. Soil from Bunker Hill that he had brought back from his visit was sprinkled on his grave.

One hundred and forty years after Lafayette arrived to assist America in its battle against England, the first United States troops arrived in France to help in the war against Germany. True, the immediate motivation for the United States' declaration of war against Germany, and later against Germany's chief ally, Austro-Hungary, was not to defend England and France but to assert its rights as a neutral power against Germany's declaration of open submarine warfare on all vessels from any country. But the motivation did not matter to the Allies. Fresh troops were needed badly—by both sides.

Indeed, the situation in Europe was increasingly desperate. Trench warfare had destroyed much of a generation of young men. The bitter winter of 1916–17 had left civilians short of food and fuel. The British blockade had greatly reduced German food supplies. There had been mutinies in the French and German armies and labor strikes in both countries as well. Only the politicians and the generals were eager to continue.

At the moment it declared war, the United States presented a threat more possible than real. Its army ranked seventeenth in the world in size, with just over 100,000 men, and had had no experience in major-power warfare since the Civil War. It had no tanks and virtually no artillery; there were fewer than 1,500 machine guns, of four types whose parts were not interchangeable, and only 285,000 Springfield rifles. True, the army was supplemented by 132,000 national guardsmen, but these were poorly trained and still controlled by state governors. In fact, the only first-rate troops the United States had were the 15,500 men in the Marine Corps.[1] Moreover, the nation had no armaments industry of any size, and the car and truck manufacturers had neither the ability nor the desire to produce trucks for the military.

President Wilson and Congress moved swiftly where they could. The National Guard was put under the control of the federal government, and the Marine Corps was "lent" to the army. Within a month of declaring war, Congress passed the Selective Service Act, instituting the draft for the first time since 1865. Almost immediately, the United States moved to supply Great Britain and France with food and with merchant ships for transport and destroyers to deal with the German U-boat menace. But more than anything, troops were needed. The newly named commander of the American Expeditionary Force, General John J. Pershing, initially estimated that he would need one million men.

Enthusiasm for the war ran high, even though Wilson had won a second term in large part on his policy of keeping the country neutral and out of European wars. But popular sentiment had shifted, aided by British publicity about German atrocities both real and fictional. Equally important in the change was the German announcement that it would resume unrestricted submarine warfare, attacks that had already taken American lives on freighters and passenger liners.

Not only was there little public furor over the resumption of the draft, but, in a tragicomic episode, former President Roosevelt appeared at the White House, with much publicity, volunteering to raise a division of troops to be sent to the war under his command. Later Wilson and Pershing politely but firmly declined to let the Rough Riders ride again. This war was not, like the war against Spain twenty years earlier, an amateur affair.

The first American troops landed in France on June 13, 1917. It was a small, symbolic contingent led by General Pershing, largely officers, and they were met at Boulogne-sur-Mer by a host of dignitaries including Colonel Jacques Adelbert de Chambrun, a direct descendant of the Marquis de Lafayette. Almost two weeks later, the first real contingent arrived, four transports carrying the U.S. First Division, including the Fifth Marine Regiment.

The American troops were hardly ready for combat, but the British and French public were ecstatic at their arrival. To show them off, the

French implored Pershing to take part in a massive celebration of America's Fourth of July. Reluctantly, because he worried about their untrained military appearance, Pershing agreed and named the Second Battalion of the Sixteenth Infantry to represent the whole division.

The result was electric. Under its headline INDEPENDENCE DAY CELEBRATED IN BOTH LONDON AND PARIS, the *New York Tribune* wrote:

> But the greatest celebration of the Fourth held anywhere took place in Paris, where the entire city greeted with wild enthusiasm a battalion of the American expeditionary force which tramped through her streets. To England, still calm in her strength, the day was merely the opportunity to extend courtesy to an ally.
>
> To France, it was the chance to embrace the savior.[2]

Years later, General Pershing wrote:

> This first appearance of American combat troops in Paris brought forth joyful acclaim from the people. On the march to Lafayette's tomb at Picpus Cemetery the battalion was joined by a great crowd, many women forcing their way into the ranks and swinging along arm in arm with the men. With wreaths about their necks and bouquets in their hats and rifles, the column looked like a moving flower garden. With only a semblance of military formation, the animated throng pushed its way through avenues of people to the martial strains of the French band and the still more thrilling music of cheering voices. By taking parallel streets, I was able to gain several successive vantage points from which to watch this unique procession pass. The humbler folk of Paris seemed to look upon this few hundred of our stalwart fighting men as their real deliverance. Many people dropped on their knees in reverence as the column went by. These stirring scenes conveyed vividly the emotions of a people to whom the outcome of the war had seemed all but hopeless.[3]

The American troops marched through the cemetery gates. Gathered about the burial ground were several hundred dignitaries, both French and American. A delegate of the Sons of the American Revolution placed a wreath on Lafayette's grave, and the American ambassador to France, the American minister to Belgium, and the French minister of war all spoke briefly. Pershing, who disliked public speaking, had designated Colonel Charles E. Stanton to speak on his behalf. Stanton's speech, noted briefly in the American newspapers, was brief and in English.

Stanton had written a speech that reviewed how and why the United States had come to join France in the war, but given the crowds and the emotions of the day, he scribbled a shorter version of it that concentrated instead on the historical relationship between the two countries, pledging that in this struggle "what we have of blood and treasure are yours." Then, surrounded by politicians, military men, and ordinary citizens of Paris, he concluded:

> Therefore it is with loving pride we drape the colors in tribute of respect to this citizen of your great Republic, and here and now, in the shadow of the illustrious dead, we pledge our hearts and our honor in carrying this war to successful issue.
> **LAFAYETTE—WE ARE HERE!**[4]

It would be months before the Americans saw combat, months in which troops were drafted and given their basic training in the United States, then shipped to France for more extensive training using their own rifles but having to learn to use French machine guns and artillery. There were battles, but these were between Pershing and his French and British counterparts.

Neither the French nor the British could understand why it should take so long to train American troops. Trench warfare, after all, required little more than the ability to shoot and the willingness to advance when ordered. Attacks and defense were planned in voluminous detail, leaving little room for initiative by small groups or individuals. All the Allies wanted was fresh American bodies to fill the increasing gaps left by shrinking, and often unwilling, British and particularly French troops. These American troops, the Allies envisioned, would be filtered into existing French and British units to act as morale boosters and "stiffeners," always under non-American command.

Pershing, with Wilson's strong backing, wanted something very different. He believed that American troops would fight better under American command. Further, he did not believe that the rudimentary training for trench warfare could produce winning tactics. Pershing was committed to "brief orders and the greatest possible use of individual initiative by all troops engaged in the action." Indeed, much later in the war, when Pershing and his American First Army took over the forty-mile sector around Saint-Mihiel, Pershing was given the French plans for attack and for the defense of the positions the Americans were inheriting. Each plan was hundreds of pages. But Pershing had already issued his own plan to his officers. The plan for attack consisted of eight pages; the one for defense took six.[5]

So determined was Pershing to maintain American methods and unit cohesion that the French, until the final months of the war, regularly and unsuccessfully tried to have Wilson remove him as the commander.

Though the Americans first saw action in October 1917 and suffered their first casualties then, they were used as American units and in relatively quiet areas to give them experience. The flow of American troops increased monthly, as did the intensity of their training. However, in late March 1918 the Germans began a major offensive to bring the war to a close before the Americans could appear on the battlefield in any real numbers. By May they had forced a wedge between the French and British armies. The time had come for American troops.

The first major engagement for the Americans began at the end of May when the First Army Division helped the French retake an important position at Cantigny and part of the First Marine Division stopped the Germany advance at Chateau-Thierry, closing the gap between the British and French lines. Though the Americans suffered heavy losses, their relentless fighting spirit and subsequent victory established their worth with both their allies and their enemies.

It was at the battle for Belleau Wood that a Marine Corps legend was born. An officer of French troops who were moving back under fire advised the Marine officer in charge that the Marines should retreat as well. Captain Lloyd Williams answered, "Retreat? Hell, we just got here."

Their offensive having ground to a halt, the Germans believed they had one last chance. Their troops were exhausted, increasingly ill with influenza, and in a mutinous mood. Using 2.3 million men in three attacking armies, the Germans attacked the French in two places, on a thirty-mile front between Reims and Verdun and across the Marne east of Chateau-Thierry. The attack was to begin in mid-July, and its object was to seize control of the road to Paris, and then of Paris itself by the end of the month.

But Pershing had finally gained his objective, the concentration of American troops into a single force under his command. This force, the First American Army, attacked the Germans south of Verdun and forced them out of their positions, capturing 2,900 guns and more than 13,000 men. The end was coming, though it would take several months of hard, bloody fighting before the Germans surrendered. Indeed, as one marine later recalled, "Many months later, that battalion of the Sixteenth U.S. Infantry, shredded after severe fighting, would sing out to the Doughboys relieving them 'We've paid our debt to Lafayette, who the hell do we owe now?'" [6]

Though the Americans suffered 53,000 dead in combat and more than 200,000 wounded, the cost of the war for the other combatants was far higher—more than 11 million dead from all causes on both sides. Whole villages had lost their entire population of young men; countries had lost much of an entire generation. Never again would a war feature the senseless battering of trench warfare. If the enormous casualties would not ensure that, then the weapons introduced in the war—the tank and ground-support aircraft—would.

Yet for many Americans—and Europeans too—the war was lost because of the peace. The experience had been so bitter, the losses had been so great, and the means of warfare so destructive that the peace conference enforced punishment rather than peace. Wilson's cry that this would be "a war to end all wars" and that the allies should create a "peace with no victors" made him a hero in the streets and an ignored pest at the conference table. The terms of the peace went a long way toward ensuring that the war would be fought again—just twenty years later.

SAY IT AIN'T SO, JOE

★ 1919 ★

In 1919 the United States was looking for relief. World War I had ended in November 1918, and the troops were coming home. Also coming home were the thousands of wounded, but not the more than 53,000 who died as a result of combat nor the equal number who had died of other causes, many from influenza.

Also just ended was the influenza epidemic in the United States, which had swept the nation in just four months of late 1918, leaving a million dead out of the twenty million cases and devastating such major cities as Boston, New York, Philadelphia, and San Francisco.

A wave of labor strikes was sweeping the nation as workers, whose demands had been held in check by the national war effort, sought shorter hours and better working conditions. The police struck in Boston; the actors struck in New York; there were massive steelworker and coal miner strikes in the Midwest and a general strike in Seattle—and more. The strikes were beaten back with frequent use of troops, police, and privately hired strikebreakers.

On July 27, 1919, a race riot broke out in Chicago when a white mob at the beach stoned and drowned a young black man who was swimming in what was considered whites-only water. In the five days of rioting that followed, 38 people were killed, 291 were injured, and a thousand were left homeless.

Baseball was a place people could turn for relief, and professional baseball was on the verge of its first golden era. The powerhouse team to watch was Charles Comiskey's Chicago White Sox.

The White Sox, American League champions in 1919, looked to ease through the nine-game World Series against the National League's Cincinnati Reds. (The owners had lengthened the series to allow them to make up for their poor financial results of the 1918 war year.) The White Sox had a team batting average of .287, led by Joe Jackson's .351, Eddie Collins's .319, and Nemo Leibold's .302. The team also featured three fine pitchers, with Eddie Cicotte (29–7; ERA 1.82), Claude "Lefty" Williams (23–11; ERA 2.64), and rookie Dickie Kerr (13–7; ERA 2.88).

Cincinnati, despite popular opinion, was not going to be a walkover. It had won the National League championship by nine games, and though the team batting average was only .263, the team had such hitters as Eddie Roush (.321) and Heinie Groh (.310). The Reds' real strength was in their pitching staff, with a combined earned run average of 2.23, nearly a run less than the White Sox's 3.04.

Ominously, the White Sox were not a happy team. The players were divided into two cliques that barely spoke. They were vastly underpaid, and there was nothing they could do about it—the rules of baseball allowed them two choices: play for their team at the salary their owners chose to pay them or not play baseball at all. Joe Jackson, for example, earned $6,000 in 1919, less than a third of what his near rival Ty Cobb was making that year. Mostly country boys with little education, professional players found that baseball was both their occupation and their trap.

Out of this situation was born an incredibly clumsy and amateurish plot for some of the players to get more money. Sure that the White Sox would win the American League pennant, first baseman Chick Gandil approached John J. "Sport" Sullivan, a gambler he knew, in a hotel in Boston. Gandil had a plan to fix the World Series if Sullivan would come up with $80,000 to pay the players.

While Sullivan went off to get the money, Gandil recruited seven players to go along with his plan: star pitchers Eddie Cicotte and Lefty Williams, shortstop Swede Risberg, third baseman Buck Weaver, and outfielders Joe Jackson and Happy Felsch. Utility reserve infielder Fred McMullin had to be included, since he had overheard Gandil and Risberg talking. Only Cicotte demanded his money—$10,000—in advance.

Sullivan, meanwhile, was talking to so many gamblers to secure the money that word of the fix began to leak out almost immediately. Moreover, Gandil and Risberg began to gamble on Cincinnati and told players on other teams to do the same. Premier gambler Arnold Rothstein at first turned down the opportunity but later changed his mind. Money and orders were coming from at least two sources, neither knowing clearly about the other.

Not only were rumors flying almost from the beginning, the double-crosses were too. Sullivan got an initial $40,000 for the players but secretly kept $30,000 for his own betting and promised the players that more would be coming. Gandil had no choice but to give the remaining $10,000 to Cicotte, who was to be the starting pitcher for the first game.

On the night before the series started, there were so many rumors and so much betting on Cincinnati that the odds favoring the White Sox were shifting dramatically. The star sports reporter for the *Chicago Herald and Examiner* wired all the newspapers that took his copy, "Advise All Not to Bet on This Series; Ugly Rumors Afloat." [1]

The 1919 World Series opened in Cincinnati on October 1 to a full house at Redland Field. Cicotte's second pitch of the first inning hit a batter, the signal that the fix was on. With the Reds leading 1-0 in the fourth inning, the Reds scored five runs. Cicotte and Risberg botched a double play that would have ended the inning without any scoring, and Weaver came up short on a ball hit past him. The White Sox manager lifted Cicotte with the score 6-1, but the damage had been done. The White Sox lost 9-1. Gandil's group had batted .210 for the game.

Worried about the rumors and telegrams reporting more rumors, Comiskey went to the National League president, and together they approached the American League president, Ban Johnson. Johnson, though, scoffed at the idea. At the same time, the gamblers told the players that all their money was out on bets but promised more after the second game.

The second game began the next day, with Lefty Williams starting for the White Sox. The Chicago team threatened in the first inning, but the threat died when Gandil grounded to short with Jackson on third and one out, followed by Risberg's fly ball to right to end the inning. In the fourth inning, the White Sox threatened again, with Weaver and Jackson on second and third and one out. Again, though, Gandil grounded to first, and Weaver was caught trying to score. Risberg ended the inning again with a pop fly to first.

In Cincinnati's part of the fourth inning, the Reds scored three runs while Williams, who had held the team scoreless until then, issued three walks and two hits. That was all the Reds needed, though they scored again in the sixth. The White Sox scored two runs in the top of the seventh inning on a throwing error but never scored again. The Reds won the game 4–2. Gandil's group game batting average was a far better .363, but they had left seven men on base.

After the game, the players got their $10,000, though it was far short of what they thought they had been promised. The players were also told to win the next game. Even though they were not getting what they thought they were owed, the players had no choice but to continue—and to win for a pitcher they disliked, the rookie Dickie Kerr.

And win they did, in a packed Comiskey Park in Chicago, with Kerr pitching a three-hit shutout, 3–0, in just ninety minutes. Two of the runs came as Chick Gandil batted in Joe Jackson and Happy Felsch in the second inning. Again, after the game, one set of gamblers refused to give the players any more money. The players agreed to continue, but only if they got their money before each game they were to lose. The money appeared.

The fourth game, also in Comiskey Park, opened to another packed crowd. Cicotte again started for the White Sox. Each time the White Sox threatened to score, one of the Gandil group managed to end the inning. Cicotte held the Reds scoreless until the fifth inning, when they scored two runs on errors by Cicotte, one a wild throw to first and the other a fielding error that deflected a Jackson attempt to throw out a runner trying to score. That was all the scoring; the Reds won 2–0. The Gandil group batted .143.

Between the fourth and fifth games, Gandil got another $20,000 for the players. He gave $5,000 each to Risberg, Felsch, Williams, and Jackson. Weaver was out of the group and out of the fix. McMullin, being marginal anyway, would have to wait for his money.

It rained in Chicago on Sunday, October 5, so the game was postponed. On Monday, Lefty Williams started and held the Reds hitless for four innings. Hod Eller, on the mound for the Reds, gave up two hits but no runs, so the Reds came up in the sixth with the score tied 0–0. Eller himself led off the inning with a fly ball that fell between Jackson and Felsch, and Risberg misplayed Felsch's throw to allow Eller to get to third base. Williams then gave up a run-scoring single and a walk to put men on second and third. The top Reds hitter, Eddie Roush, hit a long fly that Happy Felsch could not catch up to, scoring the two men on base. Cincinnati scored one last time on a sacrifice fly, and the Reds led 4–0. The White Sox never scored, and the game ended. The Reds now led in the series four games to one. The Gandil group, now excluding Weaver, had no hits in fifteen at bats.

The action shifted to Cincinnati for the sixth game. The promised money for the players never arrived. Dickie Kerr started for the White Sox, but this time he was not as effective, and the Reds led 4–0 after five innings on the strength of good hitting, three White Sox errors, and Dutch Reuther's pitching. But in their half of the fifth inning, the White Sox tied the game and chased Reuther from the mound.

The score stayed tied until the tenth inning, when singles by Weaver, Jackson, and Gandil put the White Sox ahead 5–4. Kerr retired the side in the bottom of the tenth, and the White Sox had narrowed the Reds' series lead to 4–2. The Gandil group had a game batting average of .294 and batted in three of the White Sox's four runs.

Game seven, also in Cincinnati, saw Cicotte starting for the third time. This time the White Sox won easily, 4–1. The Gandil group got only four hits (for a batting average of .200) but accounted for all the runs batted in. Cicotte's pitching was masterful; he allowed only the one earned run and three walks.

Once again the action shifted back to Chicago, but this time with the White Sox needing only one win to tie the series. And at least one major gambler was getting nervous. Back in New York, Arnold Rothstein called in Sport Sullivan to suggest that enough was enough. The next game should be the last of the World Series. A suggestion was sufficient; Sullivan made a call to Chicago, and that night a man approached Lefty Williams and, according to Williams, threatened his wife if Williams did not make sure the Reds had the game won in the early innings.

On October 9 Comiskey Park was jammed, as it always was. Williams started for the White Sox, got the first man out, and then, pitching only fast balls, gave up four successive hits and three runs before being removed for a relief pitcher. By the end of the inning, the Reds led 4–0. They got another run in the second, another in the fifth, three more in the sixth, and their last, and tenth run, in the eighth inning.

The White Sox scored one run in the third inning and mounted a big threat in the eighth, but the score was 10–1, and after they scored three runs, the inning ended. One inning later, so did the series. The winning players each got a check for approximately $5,200 as their share; the losers' shares were about $3,200 each.

For their efforts, the Gandil group was unevenly rewarded, as much by the ringleader as by the gamblers. Gandil kept a total of $35,000. Cicotte and Risberg each got $10,000. All the others received $5,000, except Weaver, who got nothing.

Comiskey and his manager were sure that the rumors of a fix were true and were equally sure who the fixers were. Comiskey started a private investigation and held back the World Series checks for the players he thought were involved. By November, though, the talk of a fix had died down, and Comiskey sent the checks. Hugh Fullerton of the *Chicago Herald and Examiner* tried to keep the story alive, but his own paper refused to run his copy, and the *New York Evening World* watered down what it took. The assembled owners shrugged it all off, and everything seemed to go back to normal.

But it was not all normal. While Comiskey re-signed most of the White Sox players for the 1920 season, there was one notable exception; Chick Gandil refused and got out of professional baseball. In January the Yankees bought Babe Ruth from the Red Sox and started their first dynasty. True, attendance at major league baseball in the new season was nearly double that for 1919, but the influence of gambling on the games continued and seemed to be more public. In September 1920 a grand jury was convened in Cook County, Illinois, to investigate an alleged fix of a recent Cubs-Phillies game. One of those called to testify, New York Giants pitcher Rube Benton, told the grand jurors that he had seen telegrams relating to the fix of the 1919 World Series and named four of those involved. The barn door was opening.

Within the month, Cicotte, Jackson, and Williams had confessed and testified to the fix. Felsch told a reporter that he had taken money. Weaver claimed complete innocence. The day after Jackson testified, the *Chicago Herald and Examiner*'s story contained the legendary words:

> As Jackson departed from the Grand Jury room, a small boy clutched at his sleeve and tagged along after him.
>   **"SAY IT AIN'T SO, JOE,"** he pleaded. "Say it ain't so."
>   "Yes, kid, I'm afraid it is," Jackson replied.
>   "Well, I never would've thought it," the boy said.[2]

The incident with the unnamed boy has a distinctly made-up flavor, far from unusual at the time. However, the words spread and survived because they embodied a general feeling of betrayal.[3]

Rothstein met with two of the major gamblers involved, Sullivan and Abe Attel, and suggested they all go on foreign vacations that he would pay for. Sullivan went to Mexico, Attel to Canada, and Rothstein to Europe. In the end, only Rothstein testified in Chicago—and he claimed that he was entirely innocent and Attel was the key figure.

Public opinion, led by newspaper stories, was increasingly hostile. Many of the baseball owners felt some changes were needed. On October 7 the president of the National League and eleven owners agreed to form a new governing body for professional baseball. One month later the new structure was formed, and Judge Kennesaw Mountain Landis accepted the job as commissioner of baseball, even as he retained his federal judgeship.

The Illinois grand jury formally indicted the eight White Sox players and four gamblers, as well as New York Giants first baseman Hal Chase, who had recently been barred from baseball for fixing games and gambling. Shortly thereafter the Illinois state's attorney's files that mentioned Arnold Rothstein, and those that contained the original signed confessions of Cicotte, Jackson, and Williams, were stolen, given to Comiskey's attorney, and disappeared.

The trial began during a heat wave in mid-July 1921 and concluded with verdicts of "not guilty" for everyone. Proving "intent to defraud" was just too difficult. Not for Commissioner Landis, however. His statement to the press read, "Regardless of the verdict of juries, no player who throws a ball game, no player that undertakes or promises to throw a ballgame, no player that sits in conference with a bunch of crooked players and gamblers where the ways and means of throwing a game are discussed and does not promptly tell his club about it, will ever play professional baseball."[4]

None of Gandil's group ever did. Shoeless Joe Jackson, a minor actor in the conspiracy, never made it into the Hall of Fame, even with his lifetime batting average of .356.

THE BUSINESS OF AMERICA
IS BUSINESS

★ 1925 ★

Jazz was a noun, a verb, and an adjective. Jazz was a style and a mood, an inward-looking mood. The jazz age was a time of domestic excitement, of professional and college sports stars, of intrepid fliers, of girls called flappers with immodestly short dresses, and the passage of a constitutional prohibition on alcohol that seemingly made everyone feel the need for a drink.

But it was not like that for everyone, even for most everyone. For many people the age seemed to offer constant prosperity, but for just as many it was full of fear and insecurity, both political and economic.

The United States had entered World War I with the belief, the conviction, that it would bring peace, prosperity, and above all democracy to the tired nations of Europe. The high hopes raised by the termination of this "war to end all wars" died with the cold realities of the peace brought about by the cynical old men at the peace table in Versailles. Partly in disgust and partly in relief, the United States turned its back on the rest of the world to face rapid transition and turmoil within.

Over half the nation lived in cities of more than 100,000, and the continuing troubles of Europe were bringing more and more new people. In the five years between 1919 and 1924, more than a million new immigrants flooded in, including some 600,000 from southern Europe, another 200,000 from eastern Europe, 150,000 from other European countries, and nearly 175,000 from Mexico. The newcomers engendered fear—fear of the "Bolshevism" they might bring, fear of competition for work, fear of the continued growth of the cities so opposed to the national ideal of farmer democracy, and just fear of foreignness.

In a reaction of fear, the McCarran Act of 1924 strictly limited immigration of undesirables: Jews, Poles, Russians, and other non-Anglo-Saxons. The quota for immigrants from Germany was more than 51,000; from Italy, just under 4,000; from Great Britain and Northern Ireland, 34,000; from Russia, a bit more than 2,000.

Another sign of fear was the resurgence of the Ku Klux Klan to defend the embattled white race, particularly its women. At its height, the Klan claimed nine million members and was strongest in the South and in rural Midwestern states, where it strongly influenced political candidates and the outcome of elections.

Yet there was no reason for fear. The country was increasingly prosperous, or seemed so. The turn inward led to a conservative turn in politics with an overwhelming business orientation. The Democrat Woodrow Wilson, a stout internationalist who had, even as he was dying, led the doomed fight for a League of Nations (doomed because uncompromising), was succeeded by Republicans Warren G. Harding and Calvin Coolidge, both of whom believed that the function of government was primarily—

if not solely—to encourage America's business development. Business, Coolidge said, was "one of the greatest contributing forces to the moral and spiritual advancement of the race." [1]

That Coolidge was in office to make that statement was, as even his friends said, part of his lifelong luck. He had become president of the Massachusetts state senate when the powerful incumbent unexpectedly lost his bid for reelection. He was able to run for lieutenant governor when the incumbent in that job made a bid for the gubernatorial nomination and lost. After two terms he was elected governor, just in time for the Boston police strike that began on September 9, 1919. Coolidge refused to intervene until the mayor acted successfully, then he took over the police force by executive order, stating, "There is no right to strike against the public safety by anybody, anywhere, anytime." Overnight, Coolidge was nationally known as "the man who defied Bolshevism and won." [2]

It was later that year that the Republican National Convention met to nominate its candidates for the upcoming presidential election. After the delegates were deadlocked, the party's old guard met late at night in a smoke-filled room and chose Warren Harding, whom the delegates dutifully nominated the next day. However, when the same group tried to dictate the vice presidential candidate, the convention rebelled and stampeded for Coolidge. The ticket was easily elected.

Coolidge's final stroke of luck came three years later as the Harding administration began to crumble under the weight of scandal. Harding was weighed down by the betrayal of the very friends he had put in office, and on a trip to the West he collapsed and died on August 2, 1923. Coolidge was president.

Coolidge was publicly laconic, outwardly dour, puritanical, uncompromisingly honest, and firm in his belief that the government's job was to do as little as possible. And that was fine with the voters, or most of them. He was, many said, safe. And given the national mood and the changes occurring in society, safe was, well, safe.

The next year was a presidential election year. Coolidge was nominated easily. The Democrats, on the other hand, took 103 ballots and two weeks to come up with a nominee, John W. Davis, a candidate not markedly different from Coolidge. It was hardly a race; Coolidge won with 54 percent of the vote. The Republicans used two slogans: "Keep Cool with Coolidge," which makes little sense but survives, probably because of its advertising-like resonance, and "Coolidge or Chaos," which has not survived despite its alliteration, probably because of its time-sensitive reference to the Democratic mess in finding a candidate.

Coolidge proposed a few things to Congress, but little got done. Although the Republicans had a majority in both houses, the party, which contained a virulent split between the old progressive wing and the conservatives, could not act easily or at all. The country, though, did not really care. Business was booming.

Big business developed with nation-transforming force. Cars rolled off the assembly lines to change where and how people lived. More and more homes, at least in the cities, had electricity and telephones, household appliances, and the newfangled radio, all of which changed family life more quickly and profoundly than ever before in the nation's history. Output in manufacturing rose nearly 32 percent between 1923 and 1929, and the gross domestic product increased more than 35 percent, from $70 billion in 1919 to $95 billion in 1928.[3] A belief spread, at least among the middle class, that everyone not only could become prosperous but should. And why not? Business was not just an economic institution; it had become a force for social and cultural good. The president himself said so. "Business rests squarely on the law of service, reliance on truth, faith and justice. The growing tendency of American business to correct its own abuses has left the Government free to advance from problems of reform and repression to those of economy and construction."[4]

For 1924, Coolidge proposed to cut taxes, reduce the national debt, and reduce government spending to the lowest level in a decade. In presenting his budget message to Congress on December 6, 1923, Coolidge went even further. America, it seemed, was one large corporation. "I have in mind that the taxpayers are the shareholders of the business corporation of the United States, and that if this business is showing a surplus of receipts the taxpayer should share therein in some material way that will be of immediate benefit."[5]

A little more than a year later, on January 17, 1925, Coolidge gave a rare public speech, addressing the American Society of Newspaper Editors. The speech was typically noncontroversial, discussing the importance of a free press to a democratic society. Coolidge talked about the need for newspapers to balance their business needs with their public educational role, a balance he believed they maintained very well.

There does not seem to be cause for alarm in the dual relationship of the press to the public, it is on one side a purveyor of information and opinion and on the other side a purely business enterprise. Rather, it is probable that a press which maintains an intimate touch with the business currents of the nation is likely to be more reliable than it would if it were a stranger to the influences.

After all, the chief business of the American people is business. They are profoundly concerned with producing, buying, selling, investing and prospering in the world. I am strongly of the opinion that the great majority of people will always find these are moving impulses of our life.[6]

It was, for the time, accurate, obvious, a commonplace—as long as the Americans being described were middle and upper class. As time went on, the phrase got shortened to **"THE BUSINESS OF AMERICA IS BUSINESS"** and, wrongly interpreted, became an object of ridicule.

Below the middle class there were troubling signs. In 1926 the average worker brought home a bit more than $26 for a forty-nine-hour workweek. Farm income was just as bad, if not worse, having never recovered from the bust that followed the end of World War I. Estimates of the minimum wage needed for a family to maintain health and "decency" varied from $1,800 to $2,080 a year, yet the average worker never made more than $1,500 during the whole decade.

While worker output rose 32 percent in the decade, hourly wages rose only 8 percent. The average workweek remained about fifty hours, and in some industries it was far higher. In the steel industry, for example, tens of thousands worked seven days a week. Because of relentless employer pressure, union membership declined from more than 5 million in 1920, or 12 percent of the workforce, to 3.4 million, or 7 percent, in 1929. Purchasing power in this new consumer economy was increasingly concentrated among the relatively few at the top.

For those above the working class, riches seemed almost within reach, if only one knew how to get them. In California, right after the end of World War I, there was a land boom. In 1919 the total value of real estate development permits was $28 million; by the end of 1923 it exceeded $200 million—far more development than there were possible buyers, and by the end of 1924 the boom had died. But the fever had not died. In 1925 Florida became the promised land, with two thousand real estate offices housing twenty-five thousand agents. Again there was more development than possible buyers, and when a massive hurricane swept the state and killed four hundred people, the bubble popped here too.

If not in land speculation, perhaps riches could be found in the stock market. And in 1924 stock trading and stock prices began to rise. For the year, the average daily number of shares traded increased 19.2 percent, and the Dow Jones Industrial Average for the end of the year was 26.2 percent over 1923. In 1925 average daily trades increased even more, 61.6 percent, and the Dow by year-end was up 30 percent. The next year things leveled off, but 1927 saw more frenzy as more and more people got into the market: average daily volume up 28.5 percent and the Dow up 28.8 percent. Activity fed on itself. In 1928 the average number of shares traded daily was up from just over 2 million to 3.4 million shares—61.8 percent—while the Dow ended the year 48.2 percent higher. Truly the stock market was the place for easy wealth. Investors were cheered on by the relentless enthusiasm of distinguished professors and high government officials who saw nothing but blue skies and higher prices ahead.

On August 2, 1927, while on vacation out west, President Coolidge issued what may be the shortest news release in American presidential history. At a press conference carefully timed for after the close of the stock market in New York, Coolidge announced, "I do not choose to run for President in nineteen twenty eight."

Over the next few days the stock market fell 4.5 percent and then rose to new highs. On reflection, if players in the market then ever really reflected, investors were reassured that whoever was elected president in 1928 would be a Republican and things would remain unchanged in the country and in the stock market.

For Coolidge, though he would have been the unanimous choice of the following year's Republican convention, his surprise decision was the culminating piece of his political luck. He would miss "the Crash," or vice versa.[7]

PROSPERITY IS JUST AROUND THE CORNER

★ 1930 ★

THE ONLY THING WE HAVE TO FEAR IS FEAR ITSELF

★ 1933 ★

In accepting the Republican nomination for president in August 1928, Herbert Hoover was excited about the future. "We have not yet reached the goal, but given a chance to go forward with the policies of the last eight years, we shall soon with the help of God be within the sight of the day when poverty will be banished from the nation."[1] He won in a landslide with 58 percent of the vote, and in his inauguration speech he exuded confidence. "I have no fears for the future of our county. It is bright with hope."

Yet underneath the booming economy and stock market there were signs, largely ignored, that all was not well. The world economy was burdened by war debts now a decade old, and probably uncollectible, since foreign trade and foreign economics were suffering. Billions of dollars of private investment were in default. High tariffs in the United States prevented foreigners from selling their products, thus keeping them from earning the money to pay their war debts or to buy American goods in return.

Even at home, things were not good. The agricultural sector was suffering, since there were few exports of massive crop surpluses to offset the low prices farmers could get at home. While speculative profit had boomed, wages had barely risen, and lower-income families were struggling to stay where they were economically. More and more people, sure that the stock market could only go up, were borrowing money to buy more and more shares. On September 3, 1929, Americans had taken out $8 billion in brokerage loans to gain what were surely easy profits just ahead.[2] There was a sharp decline in residential construction, down more than a billion dollars from 1928. More and more goods were going unsold; inventories had more than tripled from the previous year as consumer spending slowed.

Nor had domestic poverty nearly been banished. A Brookings Institution study of the economy of 1929 stated, "At 1929 prices a family income of $2,000 may be regarded as sufficient to supply only basic necessity." As one historian has noted, "One might reasonably interpret this statement to mean that any income below that level represented poverty. *Practically 60 per cent of American families were below it.*"[3]

The high point in the stock market came on September 3, 1929, when the Dow reached 381.17—a 27.1 percent increase over 1928, and more than 300 percent higher than when the investing craze had begun in 1924. And here the market stalled, drifting slowly downward.

It was on Monday, October 21, that the number of shares traded increased dramatically, but at lower and lower prices; the stock ticker ran hours behind actual trades. On Thursday, October 24, forever after known as Black Thursday, nearly 13 million shares were traded as stocks declined by great leaps. The market did recover during the late afternoon, but no one really believed anything good was going to happen anytime soon.

The market did eventually, though temporarily, stop falling—but not for weeks. The low for the year was reached on November 13, when the

Dow closed at 198.69, nearly half what it had been just over two months before. Worse, during the drop, not only did investors see their investments shrink, but those who had borrowed to buy their stock saw their investments sold off to pay their broker debts or, just as bad, owed money for stock that was worth less and less.

What followed is now called the Great Depression, but the crash of the stock market did not cause the Depression, despite what President Hoover argued for some time afterward. The crash directly affected only the 1.5 million people who were "in the market," out of a total population of some 120 million. It was merely the psychological last straw on an increasingly weak camel.

The symbolic force of the stock market crash was intensified when the market just kept crashing. It would pause for a time, often for some months, rise tauntingly for a bit, and then would crash again. Seven times it did that before it finally hit bottom nearly three years later. From a high Dow Jones average of 381.17 in September 1929, the bottom was an appalling 41.22, a drop of nearly 90 percent.

In its shock, the nation was forced to see the now visible and public chasms in the rest of the economy. Within six months of Black Thursday, unemployment grew from 1.5 million to more than 3 million. President Hoover, who with the rest of his administration and the elite of the financial industry tried constantly to be reassuring, issued a statement that "all the evidence indicates that the worst effects of the crash upon unemployment will have passed during the next sixty days." [4]

On May 1, 1930, Hoover addressed the United States Chamber of Commerce in Washington. The *New York Times* front page headline read: WORST OF DEPRESSION OVER, SAYS HOOVER. And so he had said. In his opening, Hoover stated: "We have been passing through one of those great economic storms which periodically bring hardship and suffering upon our people. While the crash only took place six months ago, I am convinced we have now passed the worst and with continued unity of effort we shall rapidly recover." [5]

By this time, unemployment had passed 7.5 million. The phrase **"PROSPERITY IS JUST AROUND THE CORNER"** was increasingly attributed to the president, although he never said it then or afterward. What he had said implied it, though, and events increasingly proved him wrong.[6] By the end of 1932, unemployment would exceed 14 million, meaning that some 40 million people had no dependable family income.

No matter where one looked, things seemed worse. The banks started failing—256 of them in November 1930. In December, the United States

Bank, with deposits of more than $200 million, closed its doors, the largest bank failure in history. In 1932 nearly 1,500 banks failed; some 85,000 businesses had closed, 9 million savings accounts were gone, and $26 billion in wages had disappeared.[7]

There was no national means of helping the poor and the newly poor; there was not even the philosophy that the national government had any such responsibility. Cities and states tottered under the weight of the new demands. In New York City, for example, government spent $6 million for relief in 1930 and $25 million in 1931, and it faced an estimated $75 million to meet bare needs in 1932. Private charities, in which President Hoover placed his faith, soon found themselves similarly overwhelmed. For a brief time, men by the hundreds sold apples on city streets (though Hoover later claimed they had left their jobs for this more profitable occupation).

Fear replaced the relentless, blinding optimism of the past—fear of starving, fear of watching children die, fear of losing jobs that paid less and less every year, fear of losing homes and farms as mortgages were called in by banks and mortgage companies, fear of foreigners, fear of communism and fascism, and fear of the unknown that might yet happen. When thousands of veterans, calling themselves the Bonus Expeditionary Force, peacefully marched on Washington in mid-1932 in an effort to force Congress and the president to pay them their promised "bonus," not due until 1945, they were met first by a rebuff from the Senate and then by an armed force that a fearful government called out to disperse them. The nation saw newspaper photos of the U.S. Army fighting its own veterans.

Hoover's government tried to help, but his initiatives were always small, tardy, and ill-founded to boot. Indeed, in trying anything, Hoover was going against a deeply ingrained belief, widely held at the time, that government assistance of any kind would weaken the moral fiber of the individual and erode the very foundation of the nation. In 1932 Hoover decided that all attempts by his government were only making things worse as the budget deficit reached toward $1 billion. He decided instead that only balancing the budget could restore the nation to its old prosperity.

For many, hope lay in the presidential election of 1932. The Democrats nominated New York's governor, Franklin Delano Roosevelt. Roosevelt, an aristocrat from an old, wealthy Democratic family, was an activist governor, committed to using government to restore the nation and aid the poor. What he promised, above all, was federal government action.

The Republicans glumly renominated Hoover.

Roosevelt did not mistake the national mood. The election result was a landslide, as Roosevelt received 57.4 percent of the popular vote, more than 7 million more than Hoover, and won in the electoral college 472–59. From being in a minority, the Democrats controlled Congress: the Senate by 60–35 and the House by 310–117.

But there were months to go before Roosevelt was to be inaugurated, and the election did not change either the national mood or its economic slide. There were calls for strong, even dictatorial, leadership. Italy's dictator Benito Mussolini was held up as an example in places as different as the U.S. Chamber of Commerce and progressive magazines. The bank crisis, building for years, threatened to take down the entire financial system. In the first two months of 1933, another four thousand banks shut down, and state after state declared bank holidays, effectively closing all the banks within their borders. By inauguration day, more than half the states had closed their banks.

The inauguration of the new president on March 3, 1933, was held in a national atmosphere of near paralysis. Hoover's secretary of war had ordered a transfer of troops to Kentucky, presumably to protect Fort Knox and, in answer to a question in the Senate, had "referred to Reds and possible Communists that may be abroad in the land."[8]

With thousands watching in the cold and millions listening on the radio, Roosevelt was sworn in. Aware of the vital importance of the moment, Roosevelt began on a religious note, "This is a day of national consecration," then moved to differentiate himself sharply from the previous president and administration by promising frankness.

> I am certain that my fellow Americans expect that on my induction into the Presidency I will address them with a candor and a decision which the present situation of our Nation impels.

He moved quickly to reassurance:

> This great Nation will endure as it has endured, will revive and will prosper.

And then to the psychological core of his listeners:

> So, first of all, let me assert my firm belief that **THE ONLY THING WE HAVE TO FEAR IS FEAR ITSELF**—nameless, unreasoning, unjustified terror which paralyzes needed efforts to convert retreat into advance.

He would not ignore the obvious:

Values have shrunken to fantastic levels; taxes have risen; our ability to pay has fallen; government of all kinds is faced by serious curtailment of income; the means of exchange are frozen in the currents of trade; the withered leaves of industrial enterprise lie on every side; farmers find no markets for their produce; the savings of many years in thousands of families are gone. More important, a host of unemployed citizens face the grim problem of existence, and an equally great number toil with little return. Only a foolish optimist can deny the dark realities of the moment.[9]

But there was hope, he believed. It lay within and could be reached only with action: "This Nation asks for action, and action now." He promised to bring Congress back immediately into special session for action and pledged that if Congress failed to act he would ask for "broad Executive power to wage a war against the emergency, as great as the power that would be given to me if we were in fact invaded by a foreign foe."

Roosevelt closed by stressing the urgent and demanding need for the government to act.

We do not distrust the future of essential democracy. The people of the United States have not failed. In their need they have registered a mandate that they want direct, vigorous action. They have asked for discipline and direction under leadership. They have made me the present instrument of their wishes. In the spirit of the gift I take it.[10]

On March 5, the first business day after the inauguration, Roosevelt declared a national bank holiday. On March 9 Congress began meeting in special session and within hours approved an emergency banking act. The next day Roosevelt sent Congress a message on the economy, warning of imminent government bankruptcy and asking for wide power to cut government spending.

On March 12, nine days after becoming president, he broadcast the first of his "fireside chats" to the nation, in which he clearly explained the nature of the banking crisis and the steps to be taken over the next few days to reopen first the Federal Reserve banks and then those banks in some 250 cities that were found to be sound. As the days went on, more and more banks found to be solvent would be reopened until only those that needed financial reorganization were still closed. He ended the brief talk by telling his listeners what they could do.

There is an element in the readjustment of our financial system more important than currency, more important than gold, and that is the confidence of the people. Confidence and courage are the essentials of success in carrying out our plan. You people must have faith; you must not be stampeded by rumors or guesses. Let us unite in banishing fear. We have provided the machinery to restore our financial system; it is up to you to support and make it work.

It is your problem no less than it is mine. Together we cannot fail.[11]

In the next two and a half months, an unprecedented number of initiatives flowed from the White House to the Congress and back again. In what has since become known as "the first hundred days," Roosevelt proposed ten major initiatives. Each was passed by Congress, often within days, and all were passed by the end of May. Included in this unprecedented activity were the legalization of beer and wine sales (with substantial taxes on both), an agriculture bill to assist farmers, the creation of the Civilian Conservation Corps to put unemployed young men to work, federal relief grants to the states, reorganization of the banking and securities industries, the creation of the Tennessee Valley Authority to permit federal planning for natural resources, relief for hard-pressed homeowners, emergency railroad legislation, and a National Industrial Recovery Act to force industries to increase employment, mandate a shorter workweek with decent wages, and prevent unfair competition.

Although the Depression would last throughout the decade, the worst had indeed passed. Most important, people again believed that someone could do something, that someone would do something, and that things would get better. The fear had receded, though it was never forgotten by those who lived through those years.

WHO KNOWS WHAT EVIL LURKS
IN THE HEARTS OF MEN?

★ 1936 ★

By the end of World War I in November 1918, the United States was clearly a major world power. The great nations of Europe were devastated economically, politically, and militarily; much of a generation of their young men were dead or wounded. Only the United States survived with its factories intact, its population burgeoning, its finances strong, and its technological genius evident.

Yet for all its new international power, the United States remained in large measure what it had been: a collection of regions rather than a unified nation, focused internally and distrustful of international involvement. Regional cultures, regional politics, regional accents, and regional styles predominated.

True, the nation had experienced unifying—and divisive—political events: national elections. But the presidency, the one truly national office, was still largely captive to regional politics that resulted in decentralized policies both domestically and internationally.

True, too, the nation had experienced unifying—and divisive—military events, but except for the Civil War, the wars the nation engaged in were not dominant events that drew its people together as a nation, at least not for long.

Distance and tradition still left the United States a collection of disparate peoples. Technology, however, was slowly—and then quickly—shortening distance and eroding tradition. It was only a matter of time, and events were picking up speed.

By 1920 the network of railroads throughout the country was largely complete. Local railroads had been important for decades; the first transcontinental railroad had been completed in 1869, but now nearly everywhere was reachable from everywhere else. The trains carried almost twice as many passengers as they had at the turn of the century, and they carried them farther—passenger miles had tripled during the same period.

By 1920 there were more than 9 million cars on the roads, just twelve years after Henry Ford introduced the Model T. Although Ford's car had been inexpensive from the beginning—just $950—in 1924 a Ford without a self-starter cost just $290. As Ford's price fell, production and sales skyrocketed: from 18,000 cars in 1909-10 to 1,250,000 in 1920-21. For the first time families' choices for shopping or entertainment were not limited by the range of a horse.

Airplanes had made an appearance too, though not in as transforming a way as in later decades. Still, the Wright brothers had first flown at Kitty Hawk in 1903, and by World War I airplanes were seen over the battlefields of Europe.

The first technology that began to draw the country together culturally was moving pictures—the movies. In 1903 the first silent movie with a connected story, *The Great Train Robbery*, made its appearance. By the 1920s, there were movie houses in nearly every town in America.

The invention that was to bring the country together at the same time, and symbolically in the same place, began abroad. In 1895 Guglielmo Marconi created wireless telegraphy, which could transmit sounds without miles of wires strung on vulnerable poles. Through a series of inventions in England and the United States over the next twenty years, the ability to transmit and receive speech and music was gradually developed. For the first decades of the twentieth century, the radio was mostly an clumsy device built from kits or parts by young men and technically comfortable adults, who listened to see from how far away they could receive the broadcasts sent out by other equally amateurish but technically adventurous men, often transmitting from garages or rooftops.

Seeing the potential as few others did in 1916, David Sarnoff, then assistant chief engineer at the American Marconi Company (later RCA, with Sarnoff as its president), wrote a memo to his superiors: "I have in mind a plan of development which would make radio a 'household utility' in the same sense as the piano or phonograph. The idea is to bring music into the home by wireless."[1]

In 1922 Sarnoff introduced the Radiola, a radio console that required no assembly and no technical knowledge to operate. The set cost $75, not cheap for the time but within reach of the nation's large middle class. American Marconi sold $11 million worth of sets that year; three years later the total was $60 million.

What people listened to, though, were local broadcasts. There were more than 1,400 broadcasting stations in the country and more than 3 million sets to listen to them. What people heard was usually music, both recorded and live, sports, and news. The business potential was clear and not lost on major corporations.

In 1926 the first broadcasting network, NBC, was established. CBS was organized in 1927, and more networks came quickly.

The listeners were there; the advertisers were there; and the means to broadcast nationally was there. All that was needed was a program to attract the mass national audience.

That program came on August 19, 1929, aired on the NBC Blue Network. Created and acted by two white men, Freeman Gosden and Charles Correll, *Amos 'n' Andy* featured the comic adventures of two black men, their families, their friends, and their neighbors. It quickly grew to be the most popular program on the air, reaching an estimated 40 million listeners—one-third of the population. At first the show aired for fifteen minutes six days a week, and it was said that you could listen in by walking down any leafy street, hearing the voices of Amos and Andy coming from the living room in each house you passed.

The beginning, then, was a comedy linked to the old-time minstrel shows. But what started with comedy continued with dramas, now half an hour long as writers learned the hard way to condense literary staples like *David Copperfield* or "The Cask of Amontillado" to fit the time available. While radio drama suffered from time constraints, it enjoyed the freedom of being a medium of sound only. The visual component was supplied by the listeners whose imaginations were triggered by what they heard. Just a few sounds—a voice, a note of music, the slamming of a door—would do, and do better, than all the scenery on a stage or screen.

In the early 1930s the crime and mystery shows began, with *Eno Crime Club, Fu Manchu, Charlie Chan, Sherlock Holmes*—and *The Shadow*. First aired a year after *Amos 'n' Andy,* in August 1930, on CBS's *Detective Story, The Shadow*'s title character was at first merely the host and narrator, invisible and inaudible to the characters. The show's primary sponsor was the Blue Coal Company, but since there were few national brands, it had other sponsors in various regions of the country. In that form it lasted, moving from CBS to NBC and back again.

It was not until 1937 that *The Shadow* became a national phenomenon. Orson Welles was picked to be the Shadow, and Agnes Moorhead, later part of Welles's *Mercury Theatre,* joined him as his "friend and constant companion, the lovely Margo Lane."

In this rebirth, the Shadow was, in ordinary life, Lamont Cranston, a well-to-do man-about-town, student of the sciences, and master of a technique, learned in the Orient, for controlling people's minds. Cranston devotes his life to righting wrongs done to the powerless, bringing the guilty to justice, and solving crimes that have baffled the police. Because he can control minds, he can make himself invisible to those he stalks. As a crime fighter with an extraordinary power and a dual life, the Shadow prefigured Superman ("Up, up, and away"), Batman ("Holy moley, Batman"), and Captain Marvel ("Shazam").

The Shadow and Margo Lane were joined by the pompous and egotistical Commissioner Weston, who always took credit for the Shadow's triumphs. Lane developed an unfortunate tendency to be kidnapped or captured by the villain of each episode, complicating the Shadow's crime-solving task.

The show also developed its signature opening lines, "WHO KNOWS . . . WHAT EVIL . . . LURKS . . . IN THE HEARTS OF MEN? THE SHADOW KNOWS!" followed by an eerie, maniacal laugh. And it always ended with, "The weed of crime bears bitter fruit. Crime does not pay. The Shadow Knows." Strangely, Welles was unable to do the laugh maniacally enough, so the opening and closing lines were done with a recording of the original Shadow, Frank Readick.

Airing every Sunday, the show outlasted Welles, who left in the fall of 1938 when the *Mercury Theatre*'s "War of the Worlds" made him too famous for the part. The producers wanted an unknown and finally settled on Bill Johnstone. The show ran for nearly twenty years, with four other people playing the part, signing off finally on December 26, 1954.

Not surprisingly, attempts to use the character in movies—both in the 1940s and more recently—failed. Cranston's mind-altering technique was believable only on the radio, where the audience, not the visual special effects expert, would do the work of envisioning the story.

Over that same period of time, radio developed nearly every kind of show that now is seen on television, even some now thought to have been invented by the newer medium. Some direct transfers in the 1950s failed as soon as viewers could see what they had once imagined. Others continued and still continue, though with updating: the popular quiz show *The $64 Question* became *Who Wants to Be a Millionaire? Don McNeill's Breakfast Club* became *The Today Show, Ted Mack's Amateur Hour* became *American Idol,* and even the reality shows had an ancestor, *Queen for a Day.*

FRANKLY, MY DEAR, I DON'T GIVE A DAMN | TOMORROW IS ANOTHER DAY

★ 1939 ★

When Atlanta's Margaret Mitchell began writing her first and only novel in 1926, the landscape of American popular entertainment was in the midst of major changes. Movies were the rage all over the country.

The first flickering images had emerged from the workshop of Thomas Edison in the late 1880s; two decades later movies had become an increasingly important industry where technology both drove and was driven by popular demand. The first movie premier had been held in New York City just before the end of the nineteenth century. By the end of the first decade of the new century the nickelodeon amusement where people peered into a slot to watch films lasting a minute or so had given way to specially built theaters—eight to ten thousand of them—where people sat to watch movies that lasted sixty minutes or more. D. W. Griffith's three-hour-long Civil War epic *The Birth of a Nation* had opened in 1914—just as World War I was beginning in Europe. And before the end of the decade, a few movie stars signed million-dollar contracts.

Movies mortally wounded vaudeville; the addition of sound to the movie images in 1927 buried it. By the beginning of the Great Depression in 1929, there were tens of thousands of movie theaters, and tens of millions of Americans went to the movies every single week.

While all this was happening, Mitchell plugged along. She had lived all her life in Georgia, growing up on a heavy diet of Confederate history, largely absorbed through novels and the stories told to her by relatives and Civil War veterans. She had started her book with a clear vision of both the beginning and the end of her story, but she wrote in spurts, working on sections in somewhat random fashion, stuffing each finished chapter into a large manila envelope. By 1930 she was only two-thirds through and still had not settled on a title.

Five years later the book was still incomplete, though her friends knew about it and esteemed her storytelling. When Harold Latham, an editor at the Macmillan Company, visited Atlanta, a friend of Mitchell's told him about the novel and recommended it to him, though she herself had not seen it. When Latham met Mitchell and asked to see the book, she denied that it even existed. The next day, however, she appeared at Latham's hotel with a huge pile of envelopes—so big that he had to buy a suitcase to carry it back to New York City. Latham read the book on the train going home, ignoring Mitchell's telegram asking him to return the manuscript. When he arrived home, he finished reading and made her an offer for the book. Reluctantly Mitchell agreed, and the two of them worked for another six months to complete it.

Now more than a thousand pages long, the book, finally titled *Gone with the Wind*, was priced at a daringly expensive three dollars. Publication, originally scheduled for May, was delayed for a month to print another ten thousand copies. When the Book of the Month Club wanted it for its July selection, Macmillan printed yet another fifty thousand copies.

Gone with the Wind finally appeared at the end of June 1936 and was a runaway bestseller. The *New York Times* reviewed it twice, first on June 30 in its regular book column and again on the cover of the Sunday book review section. Ralph Thomson, the first reviewer, called the writing lively but never distinguished, "although now and then there flitters a dull rage at the upset that ended such a beautiful civilization and allowed Negroes for a time to 'live in leisure while their former masters struggled and starved.'"[1] However, J. Donald Adams, the Sunday reviewer, began his review, "This is beyond a doubt one of the most remarkable first novels produced by an American writer. It is also one of the best."[2]

What the reviewers said did not matter. As James A. Michener, then a junior editor at Macmillan and later a best-selling author, wrote, "It is difficult even now to comprehend what a staggering event *Gone With The Wind* was in that post-Depression year of 1936. . . . So great was the word of mouth publicity on *Gone With The Wind* that within twenty days of publication 176,000 copies had been sold. Over the summer months, when bookstores customarily fell into doldrums, sales rose to 700,000 copies, one New York store ordering 50,000 copies on one day. With a year of publication, 1,383,000 copies had been sold."[3]

Curiously, the reviewers stressed the quality of the history in the book, when in fact it is shot through with inaccuracies and misty legends of pre–Civil War southern living. Not the least of the myths, though perhaps comforting to the readers of the time, were that the slaves and their owners loved each other and that the tyrannical North had started the war. Mitchell later wrote that she had intended her book to be the South's answer to the lies of *Uncle Tom's Cabin*. "It makes me very happy to know that *Gone With The Wind* is helping refute the impression of the South which people abroad gained from *Uncle Tom's Cabin*."[4] In fact, the Civil War is never seen in the book except for its effects. The driving force is the romantic melodrama of the heroine, Scarlett O'Hara, a selfish, independent, determined beauty who is driven to survive and to save Tara, her family's plantation.

The romance was not lost on the booming movie business, and especially not on one of its most ambitious young producers, David O. Selznick. Early in 1936, before the book had even been published, Selznick had been sent a synopsis by his East Coast story editor. Although Selznick was taken with the story, he was leery of Civil War movies as box office flops; but after some weeks of thinking about it, he offered $50,000 for the movie rights, an enormous sum at a time when the nation's 30 million wage earners, according to the Social Security Board, averaged $890 a year.

As sales of the book boomed, news that there would be a movie similarly swept the nation. A storm of letters arrived on Selznick's desk, 90 percent of them demanding that Clark Gable play the key role of Rhett Butler. Gable did not want the part, but he needed the money. Selznick did not want Gable, if only because his contract was held by Selznick's father-in-law, who would demand a high price for his star. But Gable it had to be. He was not only the most popular male movie star, he had already demonstrated his ability to affect audiences in unexpected ways. In the 1934 film *It Happened One Night*, Gable undresses to his underwear, revealing that he is not wearing an undershirt. Within the year, undershirt sales plummeted, bankrupting that portion of the clothing industry.[5]

Making the movie would not be easy or pain-free. Indeed, the search for someone to play Scarlet O'Hara took years, in part because Selznick had to stall until his current film distribution deal ran out and in part because Selznick was notoriously hard to please. Indeed, just to get a final script, he ran through eight writers — and then rewrote everything himself.

Eventually Selznick had to start, and on December 10, 1938, still without a leading lady, he began shooting by assembling all the old sets on the lot and setting fire to them to represent the burning of Atlanta. Luckily, as the fire was being shot, Selznick's brother showed up to announce, "Here's your Scarlett O'Hara," introducing him to an English newcomer, Vivien Leigh.

The story of the filming became instant Hollywood legend. In addition to his eight writers, Selznick ran through three directors, two of them working simultaneously, though on different scenes. He shot the film in the still-new Technicolor, largely because one of his backers had invested in the process, and shot nearly half a million feet of film, of which only 160,000 feet was printed. He used 59 actors and 2,400 extras, 1,100 horses, 375 other animals, and 450 wagons and other vehicles, and he had 5,500 costumes made. The rough cut ran six hours. The total production cost was more than $4 million, a record for the time.

Extravagant as Selznick was, he knew what he wanted. Staying as close to the book as he could, he stayed closer to what he felt was critical— Scarlett: her struggle to survive and her attraction to and fear of Rhett Butler. Discarded from the book was any mention of the Ku Klux Klan and any of what he felt to be harmful stereotypes of African Americans.

The previews of the movie held in California at the end of September 1939 were wildly successful. That an audience would stay for a four-hour movie—even with an intermission—was unheard of at the time. A state holiday was declared in Georgia for the Atlanta premier on December 15, 1939.

What the ecstatic audience saw in *Gone with the Wind* was the love affair and a story of endurance. And the story resonated with a nation just beginning to emerge from the Depression, an act of national survival even for those who had kept their jobs.

In the movie, Scarlett lives through the privations of the war and then the privations of Reconstruction, always sacrificing both herself and others for survival. She is married twice, once for revenge and once for money, to men she does not love, all the while carrying on a love-hate relationship with the one person most like herself—Rhett. And Rhett, realistic and of uncertain morals though he is, stays loyal to her, always ready to help when he is most needed. When Scarlett finally marries him, Rhett cannot make her feel his love and absorbs rebuke and scorn until, when their daughter dies in a riding accident, he cannot take it anymore.

Characteristically, at the same time Scarlett realizes that she not only loves Rhett but must have him, and in the final moments of the movie she tells him so, just as he is about to leave her for good. As he turns to walk down the stairs and out of her life, she cries, "Rhett, if you go, where shall I go? What shall I do?"

He looks at her and says, **"FRANKLY, MY DEAR, I DON'T GIVE A DAMN."**

Scarlett collapses in despair, then remembers the one thing she does have to live for, the one thing she has always loved, has always fought for, and has always valued above all else–her family's plantation, Tara. "Tara! . . . Home. I'll go home, and I'll think of some way to get him back! After all, **TOMORROW IS ANOTHER DAY."**

And with that line the movie ends, pulling back to a silhouette of Scarlett against a red sunset with Tara in the distance. There was not a dry eye in the house.

Gone with the Wind was nominated for thirteen Academy Awards and won eight, including Best Picture, Best Actress for Vivien Leigh, and Best Supporting Actress for Hattie McDaniel (the first win for an African American). At least as important from Selznick's standpoint, the movie grossed more than $1.2 billion. It was banned in Europe by the Nazis, who clearly did not want a film showing the triumph of people under an occupation, but it ran for four years in England and was a major hit in Europe after the war was over. The film has since been released six times in the United

States. Theater receipts have now topped $2 billion domestically, leaving it still at the top of the all-time box office lists.

WAIT TILL NEXT YEAR

★ 1941 ★

The world knows New York loves a winner, but for more than half a century New York, or at least an important part of it, loved a loser. In fact the Brooklyn Dodgers were, and are, so loved in their home borough and city that many have never forgiven their owner for moving them three thousand miles away.

The Brooklyn professional baseball club entered the National League in 1890 while Brooklyn was still a separate city. The city had had a professional team since 1883, but it played in leagues like the Interstate League and the American Association. From the beginning the team was called the Dodgers, shortened from the Trolley Dodgers because of the rapidly increasing number of trolley cars that made getting to their ballpark a race between entertainment and injury. Dodgers may have been their first name, but it was hardly their only one as the team sought a permanent home and a clear identity.

Over the early years, the Dodgers were called the Bridegrooms (because six of the players on the 1889 team were newly married), the Superbas (because their manager had the same name as a popular vaudeville company called Hanlon's Superbas), the Robins (because their manager was Wilbert Robinson), and even the Infants. But they always returned to the Dodgers, a name that finally showed up on their uniforms in 1933.

No matter what the name, the Dodgers were generally mediocre. From 1903, when the two leagues settled into the form they would keep, until 1941, the Dodgers had a combined record of 2,696 wins and 3,048 losses, a winning percentage of 47 percent. During these thirty-eight years they finished in the first division (the top four teams in the eight-team league) only nine times.

They were, though, entertaining, loved, and very much a local team, for the players lived in Brooklyn, shopped in Brooklyn, and were greeted by name on the streets. Wilbert Robinson was known as "Uncle Robby" and his wife as "Ma." The seats were cheap enough that kids could, and did, collect bottles and return them to stores for enough so they could spend the afternoon watching the game at the bandbox of a stadium named Ebbets Field after Charles Ebbets, the club's president who built it.

Even when the team finished first in the National League in 1916 and 1920, both times under Uncle Robbie, they were snakebit. In 1916, coming into the World Series with a 94–60 record, the Dodgers faced a Boston Red Sox team featuring a starting pitching staff including Dutch Leonard, Carl Mays, and the rookie Babe Ruth. In fact, the highest ERA among the starting Boston pitchers was 3.06. The Dodgers lost four games to one, and in the following year plunged to seventh place.

Four years later the Dodgers were back, this time facing the Cleveland Indians in a best-of-nine series. The Indians were led by future Hall of Famer Tris Speaker, who hit .388 that year, and pitcher Jim Bagby, with a 31–12 won-loss record. This time the Dodgers lost in what would become a tradition of heartbreak mingled with slapstick. Off the field, the series saw Prohibition agents search the press box, which the Brooklyn team management had reportedly supplied with illegal liquor, and the arrest of Brooklyn's Rube Marquard for ticket scalping. On the field, the games featured the first-ever bases-loaded homer in a World Series, hit by Elmer Smith of Cleveland, and the first-ever unassisted triple play, by the wonderfully named Bill Wambsganss of Cleveland. The Dodgers went meekly, losing the series five games to two, and in the following year they plunged out of the first division. It would be twenty-one years before they saw first place and the World Series again.

During the years when the Yankees, Giants, and Philadelphia Athletics were fielding great teams and winning championships, the Dodgers muddled along, hitting their most beloved low during the late 1920s, when they became known as the Daffiness Boys. The Dodgers were not unusual for the time in being hard drinkers and curfew violators. Nor did they lack for some fine ballplayers; but under Uncle Robbie they never really gelled into a winning team, settling instead for bonehead plays and eccentric characters.

The Daffiness Boys were symbolized for all time by Babe Herman, who joined the club in 1926 as a great hitter, a terrible fielder, and a generally ill-starred player. One incident stood out even then and marked the Daffiness era. In Herman's rookie year, the Dodgers played an August double-header against the Boston Braves. Late in the game the Dodgers had the bases loaded with one man out when Herman hit cleanly to right field. The man on third scored, but the man on second held up, thinking that Herman's hit might be caught. When he saw the ball hit the ground, he ran for third and rounded the bag, but then he held up again and retreated to third. Meanwhile the man on first, believing Herman had hit at least a triple, rounded second and headed for third too. Herman, seeking to stretch a double into a triple and not watching what was happening around him, headed for third as well. In the blink of an eye, all three men piled up at third base.

Herman tried to get back to second as one of the others was tagged out, but with a quick throw from Boston's third baseman he too was tagged out. The *New York Times* reporter wrote, "Being tagged out was much too good for Herman."[1]

Things got so bad that when the New York Giants' manager, Bill Terry, was asked about the Dodgers' prospects in the upcoming 1934 season, he responded, "Brooklyn? Is Brooklyn still in the league?" The Dodgers got some measure of revenge for that comment when they beat the Giants in the last two games of the season so that the Cardinals could win the pennant. The Dodgers, though, finished solidly in the second division.

Things really did not begin to change until 1937, when Brooklyn hired Larry MacPhail as executive vice president with "full and complete authority over the operations of the club."[2] MacPhail had been a successful baseball executive with Columbus in the American Association and then with Cincinnati, where he had introduced night games into the National League and hired Red Barber to broadcast home games on radio. A George Steinbrenner long before George Steinbrenner was heard of, MacPhail had a fiery temper, was completely dedicated to winning, and was determined to spend whatever it took.

Within his first twelve months he acquired, borrowed, and spent the astronomical sum of $200,000 for improvements to Ebbets Field, professionalized the ushers and private police at the stadium, hired Babe Ruth as coach, discarded an agreement among the New York teams not to broadcast home games, and brought in Red Barber from Cincinnati to do it. And then, in a key move, MacPhail named his shortstop, Leo Durocher, as his new player-manager. That move would shortly bring baseball success and endless drama to the club as, over the years, MacPhail would fight with his manager publicly, endlessly fire and rehire him, and once more vow eternal loyalty.

In the next few years, as MacPhail brought in a succession of players, firing some quickly and keeping others, Durocher led the club to success. The Dodgers finished third in 1939, their first time in the first division in nine years. In 1940 they finished second, this time with a new shortstop,

Pee Wee Reese, who was so good that Durocher replaced himself with Reese at the position. And while MacPhail raged in his office, Durocher raged on the field, as he had always done as a player. But this time his conduct was so bad that he was fined and suspended by the president of the league for "prolonged argument and conduct on the field tending to incite riot."

Everyone sensed that 1941 was going to be the Dodgers' year. MacPhail brought in more key players. Red Barber's broadcasts of all the Dodgers' games had gained the team fans across the nation. In a furious pennant fight with the Cardinals, the Dodgers clinched the pennant on September 28. The team had drawn a club record of 1.2 million fans at home and another million on the road.

The Dodgers, though, had to face the New York Yankees in the first subway series, and no one had beaten the Yankees in a World Series since 1926. This was a Yankee club with Red Ruffing, Lefty Gomez, Bill Dickey, Joe Gordon, Jolting Joe DiMaggio, King Kong Keller, and the rookie Phil Rizzuto—five of them future Hall of Famers. But in 1941 only Di-Maggio and Rizzuto hit for more than .300. The Dodgers could counter with two twenty-two-game winners—Whit Wyatt and Kirby Higbe—and three .300 hitters, Joe Medwick, Dixie Walker, and Pete Reiser, at twenty-two the youngest player to win the National League batting championship.

The first two games were held at Yankee Stadium, though Dodger fans outnumbered Yankee fans in the park. The teams split the games, with the Yankees winning the opener 3-2 and the Dodgers winning the second with an identical score. The third game shifted to Ebbets Field, and the aging Dodger pitcher, Fat Freddie Fitzsimmons, was locked in a scoreless pitching duel until he was hit on the knee by a line drive and had to be helped off the field. The Yankees scored two runs in the eighth inning, and while the Dodgers countered once in their half of the inning, the Yankees held on to win 2-1 and lead the series two games to one.

In the fourth game, the Dodgers fell behind early but scored two in the fourth inning and two more in the fifth to go ahead four games to three. They looked to even up the series behind the solid relief pitching of Hugh Casey, especially when the first two Yankee batters in the ninth inning grounded out. The third batter, outfielder Tommy Henrich, battled Casey to a three and two count and then swung at a vicious low curve ball—and missed. That was the end of the game—except that Mickey Owen could not catch the ball. By the time he caught up to it, Henrich was safe on first. Years later in an interview, Pee Wee Reese intimated that the curve Casey had thrown and Owen could not catch was in fact a spitball. "It was a little wet slider, and the ball kind of broke real sharply to the right and kinda got by his glove."[3]

Whatever actually happened, Casey lost his composure. DiMaggio singled, Keller doubled, scoring both Henrich and DiMaggio, Bill Dickey walked, Gordon doubled, scoring two more, Rizzuto walked, and finally Murphy grounded out. The Yankees led 7–4, and the Dodgers went easily in the last of the ninth.

Their heart was gone. On the next day, Monday, October 6, the Yankees won the fifth game, and the series, 3–1. Curiously, and perhaps symbolically, the Yankees pitcher retired the Dodgers in the seventh inning on just three pitches. That night's final edition of the *Brooklyn Eagle* carried a banner headline, **"WAIT TILL NEXT YEAR!"**. But next year was World War II.

The Dodgers' next chance did not come until 1947. Branch Rickey had replaced MacPhail as general manager, had broken the color barrier by bringing in Jackie Robinson against the wishes of every other club owner, and had steadily improved the club during and after the war. Yet in this World Series and three that followed it—in 1949, 1952, and 1953—the Dodgers faced the much-hated Yankees with their tradition of World Series victories.

In the 1947 series, the Yankees won four games to three. Each game was close, and the sixth game featured Al Gionfriddo's historic running catch of Joe DiMaggio's near-certain home run that would have tied up the game. The fans had to wait until next year again.

In 1949 the Dodgers lost again, this time four games to one. The early games were close, the first three being decided by a single run. The later games were not. Once more, the fans had to wait until next year.

In 1952 they faced the Yankees again, no longer with DiMaggio but with Mickey Mantle. The series was even, three games to three, when, with the Yankees ahead 4–2, the Dodgers loaded the bases with two out. Jackie Robinson popped up in the infield, where no one seemed ready for it until second baseman Billy Martin raced across the infield to catch the ball on the run just as it was about to hit the ground. The Dodgers never threatened again and lost the series four games to three. And again the fans had to wait until next year.

The next year the two clubs faced each other again. The Dodgers fielded a club that featured what one writer has called an all-star at each position:[4] Roy Campanella as catcher, Gil Hodges at first, Junior Gilliam at second, Pee Wee Reese at shortstop, Billy Cox at third, and Jackie Robinson, Duke

Snider, and Carl Furillo in the outfield. But the Yankees were equally strong, with players like Billy Martin, Phil Rizzuto, Gil McDougald, Hank Bauer, Mickey Mantle, Gene Woodling, and Yogi Berra. The Yankee pitching staff was somewhat better.

And again the Dodgers lost, this time four games to two, despite Carl Erskine's striking out fourteen Yankees in the third game. Next year seemed a very long time coming.

In 1955 the Dodgers won the pennant again, and again they faced the Yankees, the sixth time in their eight times in the World Series. Again, on paper they had the better lineup, nearly the same as in 1953. The Yankee pitching staff looked better; their top four starters had ERAs below 3.15. The Dodgers had Don Newcombe, whose brilliant season included pitching for a 20-5 record and a .359 batting average with seven home runs. The Dodgers had clinched the National League pennant on September 9 and had finished first by thirteen and a half games over the Milwaukee Braves. Momentum seemed to be on their side, but they still had to face the Yankees.

And in the first two games history seemed to repeat itself. In the opener, the Yankees' Whitey Ford beat Newcombe 6-5. Newcombe developed a sore arm and never reappeared in the series. Tommy Byrne beat Billy Loes in the second game 4-2.

The series shifted to Ebbets Field, where in the third game Jackie Robinson took over. On third base as the Dodgers loaded the bases, Robinson bluffed stealing home so often that the Yankee pitcher Bob Turley walked in a run on four pitches. In the seventh inning, Robinson took third when outfielder Elson Howard threw behind him on a double. Johnny Podres held the Yankees to three runs as the Dodgers won 8-3.

The Dodgers won the next two games as well, but when the series shifted back to Yankee Stadium, the Yankees tied it up in the sixth game. Everything rested on the final game.

Facing Tommy Byrne again, the Dodgers jumped out in front, scoring one run in the fourth inning and another in the sixth. Holding a 2-0 lead, Dodger manager Walt Alston pinch hit for infielder Don Zimmer, moved Junior Gilliam from left field to second base, and put Sandy Amoros in left field. It was probably the most important managerial decision of his life.

Up to that point, Johnny Podres had held the Yankees scoreless. But in the Yankees' half of the sixth inning, the Yanks put two men on base with only one out. Podres was getting tired as he faced the next Yankee batter, Yogi Berra, with the tying runs on base. Anticipating that Berra would pull the ball, Alston moved his outfielders far to the right. On a Podres outside pitch, Berra for once swung late and lofted a ball high toward the left field line, where no one was remotely close enough to catch it.

Amoros, who had been positioned nearly in center field, took off in an obviously futile chase. He ran and ran and ran. Podres later said:

> The ball seemed to hang up in the air forever, and there was Amoros, still running. I wondered, "Is he going to get it?"
>
> As it turned out, he did, though just barely. I know Gilliam could not have made that catch, because he was a righty, and the only way Amoros got it was that he was left-handed, and didn't have to catch it backhanded. At the last moment, still going at top speed, Amoros reached out, and the ball dropped right into his glove. I let out a sigh. Like everyone else, I had been holding my breath.[5]

Then Amoros whirled and threw a perfect relay to Reese at shortstop, who in turn threw to first base for a double play.

The Yankees never threatened again. The Dodgers had won the World Series.

While the newspaper headlines screamed the expected in huge type (the *Daily News* front page blared "THIS IS NEXT YEAR"), it was Art Smith, a columnist for the *Daily News,* who said it best:

> Everything was crazy in Brooklyn last night. . . . Nobody went home to supper. Nobody talked any sense. . . . Everybody walked around with goofy expressions on their pans. . . . For the unbelievable, the incredible, the impossible had come about. . . . Them Dodgers had put them Yankees under the Stadium sod and now they was champions of the whole world.
>
> Saloonkeepers gave away booze to guys they never saw before. . . . Candy store owners played the big treat to neighborhood kids who'd been robbing 'em blind for years. . . . Women kissed neighbors they wouldn't be caught dead talking to. . . . Men hollered and slugged strangers on the back and guys who hadn't been known to lift a geezer in years rolled off the wagon and barked at the crescent moon.
>
> Never before had Brooklyn, that borough of perennial October gloom, gone so joyously screwy, so hysterically daffy, so ecstatically nuts. . . . Because this, at long last, was Next Year![6]

It was a joy that would have to last for eternity. The next year the Dodgers faced the Yankees again in the series and were beaten in seven games.

The year after that they slipped to third place amid the news that the owner was moving the club to Los Angeles. After the 1957 season, they were gone.

KILROY WAS HERE

★ 1942 ★

In the second half of the 1930s the guns sounded once again in Europe. The Great War, as it was called in England, had not been "a war to end all wars." In the United States the feeling was strong that the country would not again be drawn into a European conflict in which it had no stake or interest. Even with Italy actively at war in Africa and Germany announcing that it would no longer abide by the Versailles Treaty and would build an air force and a 550,000-man army, 50,000 World War I veterans marched on Washington in support of peace. A week later, 175,000 college students held a one-hour strike for peace. Congress passed the Neutrality Act of 1935 that embargoed all arms and munitions and forbade all loans to belligerents.

During the next five years, events in Europe slowly began to shift public opinion. As Germany, Italy, and then Russia seized more countries; as the Germans, repeating events of World War I, invaded Belgium and France; and as the bombing of London began, the United States had to do something, at least in its own defense. After all, the American army in 1939 ranked twentieth in the world and consisted of only 174,000 enlisted men operating with World War I equipment and augmented by 200,000 national guardsmen.

In response, and in the midst of a reelection campaign, Roosevelt called for the first peacetime draft in American history. The congressional debate on the resulting Burke-Wadsworth bill began in the Senate at the end of August 1940 and in the House of Representatives in early September. Although public opinion on the war was shifting rapidly, the debate in both houses was heated and framed by noisy demonstrations outside. Clearly, the growing catastrophe in Europe had not eclipsed the memories of 1917–19. The *New York Times* reported:

Just before the House adjourned at 10:45 the protracted sitting and conten-
tious debate frayed tempers to the breaking point. Representative Sweeney,
Democrat, of Ohio, speaking against the bill, accused President Wilson of
putting the United States in the World War and President Roosevelt of trying to involve the country in the present conflict.

He tried to sit down beside Representative Vincent, Democrat, of Kentucky, who, according to witnesses, told Mr. Sweeney that he was "a traitor"
and asked him to sit elsewhere.

After an exchange of roundhouse swings the contestants were separated.
Mr. Sweeney's face was slightly bruised.[1]

The bill was passed and signed by President Roosevelt on September
16 as the Selective Training and Service Act of 1940. The act limited the
number who could be drafted to 900,000; the men could be only ages
twenty-one to thirty-five, and their term of enlistment would be one year.
On October 16, some 17 million men would register for the draft. The first
draft call would come on November 7.

Despite concerns about registration, the men who would be liable for
the draft were largely in favor of it—or at least resigned to its necessity. In
October, *Reader's Digest* published George Gallup's summary of the results
of a Gallup poll that surveyed both the general population and the potential draft pool. The results, in light of later events, were heartening.

To the question, "Do you think every able-bodied young man 20 years
old should be made to serve in the Army, Navy or air force for a year,"
68 percent said yes. Gallup commented, "The majority explained they
favored preparedness for the defense of democracy; were for preserving
peace by impressing the world with our military strength; thought universal training prudent in view of our prospect of standing alone in a hostile
world."[2]

When only young men were asked, "Under selective conscription, will
you, personally, have any objection to spending a year in some branch of
the military service?" 76 percent said they would have no objection.[3]

And when asked, "What should the United States do if Hitler defeats
England and takes over the English navy—try to get along with Germany
or get ready to fight the Germans?" Gallup wrote, "Get ready to fight, declared 50 percent. Try to get along with Germany, said 29 percent. And the
remaining 21 percent said, 'do both!'" Continued Gallup, "Appeasement
seemed to be an extremely doubtful policy even to those who wanted to
'try to get along.'"[4]

The registration went smoothly, especially since the registration and the eventual draft lottery and selection were administered locally by 6,500 draft boards staffed by local people. The first calls were small, in part because Roosevelt was in the midst of a reelection campaign and in even greater part because the army was not ready for a flood of new enlistees. It took just over a year for the army to reach its legislated limit of 900,000. Before that point was reached, however, the one-year enlistment of the first draftees was due to expire. Army chief of staff George Marshall began lobbying Congress in the summer for a bill to extend the enlistment period and to remove the ban on using draftees overseas.

These steps were not easy, despite the worsening war in Europe and even the sinking of several United States ships by German submarines. Congress passed the bill that Marshall and Roosevelt wanted in August 1941—by a single vote.

Then in December came the Japanese attack on Pearl Harbor and Germany's declaration of war on the United States. Those already in the military, drafted or volunteer, had their terms of service extended "for the duration" plus six months. By 1945 the army had grown to 8,300,000 men and women, more than 7 million of whom had been drafted.

It was an unusual army. It was far better educated than the army in 1917; the soldiers came from the whole range of white American life; they were used to complaining when they were not happy; and they were not particularly subservient to their "superior" officers. It was not, however, representative of the whole country. Those of Japanese origin were not allowed to enlist, and blacks were drafted in far smaller numbers than their population would suggest and used only for manual labor. Later on, as personnel needs increased, both populations would see combat, and both would serve with distinction—except in the navy, which resisted any minorities as much as possible.

At heart, it was a civilian army.

General Marshall, perhaps alone among the senior officers in the service, recognized that his was both a military job and a political one. In his view the army had another task besides fighting, and that was to ensure the morale of its enlisted men by providing the food, shelter, and amenities they either were used to or wanted to be used to—at least when they were not in combat. To an extraordinary degree, and to the astonishment and envy of their allies, the American army succeeded.

The enlisted men also found ways to make their lives more bearable, often through a typical mocking American humor. As troops began moving overseas in 1942, they were greeted in unusual places by a sign that read

KILROY WAS HERE. At first the sign, scribbled in chalk or hastily painted, was just words. After a while in Britain, it began to include a face adopted from a British sign, its upper half peering over a wall, with fingers grasping the wall.

> Every GI must have carried a piece of chalk because the words "Kilroy Was Here" appeared on rocks, walls, tanks, and enemy helmets everywhere from Sicily to Okinawa. Generalmajor Franz Sensfuss of the 212th Volksgrenadier Division led his command into the Battle of the Bulge and told his men that if they captured a soldier named Kilroy, he wanted to interview the prisoner himself.[5]

After the war was over and the men began to return home, there was a spate of articles asking "Who's Kilroy?" So many people asked the question that on September 27, 1946, an officer in the army's adjutant general's office was reported to have "announced to the Associated Press that, though the Army had the complete low-down on 10,000,000 World War II G.I.'s, it knew absolutely nothing about Kilroy. 'As far as we are concerned,' the major concluded, 'this Kilroy simply doesn't exist.'"[6]

But the search went on, and there were many suggestions: a local steeplejack, a garage mechanic, or someone whom someone knew. The American Transit Association sponsored a radio contest asking for the answer. The winning entry came from James J. Kilroy of Halifax, Massachusetts.

> On December 5, 1941, I started to work for Bethlehem Steel Company, Fore River Ship Yard, Quincy Mass., as a rate-setter. . . . I started my new job with enthusiasm, carefully surveying every innerbottom and tank before issuing a contract. I was thoroughly upset to find that practically every test leader I met wanted me to go down and look over his job with him, and when I explained to him that I had seen the job and could not spare the time to crawl though one of these tanks again with him, he would accuse me of not having looked the job over.
>
> I was getting sick of being accused of not looking the jobs over and one day, as I came through the manhole of a tank I had just surveyed, I angrily marked with yellow crayon on the tank top, where the testers could see it, "KILROY WAS HERE." The following day a test gang leader approached me with a grin on his face and said, "I see you looked my job over."[7]

Was that really Kilroy? Possibly. Certainly the slogan spread and endured because it appealed to the GIs' sense of humor when humor was needed.

I SHALL RETURN

★ 1942 ★

There was never any question what Douglas MacArthur was going to be. Born in 1880, he grew up on a frontier army post at the end of the Indian wars. His father, Arthur MacArthur, was a Civil War hero — at age eighteen, the youngest major in the Union army and a winner of the Congressional Medal of Honor. As soon as Douglas was old enough, he attended West Texas Military Academy and then West Point, where he graduated first in his class and was first captain.

By the time the United States entered World War I, MacArthur was already a colonel and had seen duty in the Philippines, where his father was military governor, and in Vera Cruz, Mexico, where he was recommended for his own Congressional Medal of Honor. By the end of World War I he had won twelve medals, including two purple hearts, nine awards for heroism, and the Distinguished Service Medal, not counting the nineteen decorations he received from the other Allied nations. Promoted to major general, he was, at thirty-eight, the youngest general in all the Allied armies.

After the war, MacArthur's career did not languish like those of so many of his brother officers, who found themselves either out of the service or held in rank with little to do as the army shrank. MacArthur became superintendent of West Point for three years, was sent to the Philippines as military governor, and in 1930 went to Washington as army chief of staff. In each position he exhibited brilliance, energy, and an ability to get things done.

The American army, by this time, was the world's sixteenth largest, with only 132,000 men, antiquated equipment, and a small budget. Much of MacArthur's time was spent arguing in Congress and in public for a modern army, for the stockpiling of strategic materials, and for planning for industrial coordination and mobilization. In the face of the Depression and the great domestic needs of the time, his arguments were ignored, though at the end of his tour of duty he was awarded his second Distinguished Service Medal and was sent back to the Philippines as the military adviser to the new Commonwealth of the Philippines.

It was a welcome and fortunate return. It was welcome because MacArthur was popular among the Filipinos, many of whom had become close friends in his previous tour there. Indeed, his friend Manuel Quezon was about to become president of the new commonwealth, which had been promised eventual independence. It was fortunate because a few months before his arrival, Japan had begun its military expansion by successfully invading and occupying Manchuria and Jehol in the north of China.

MacArthur was so close to the new government that in 1936 he went on inactive army status to accept the title of field marshal of the Philippines, a position that brought with it the job of building a commonwealth army capable of defending the country. The need for such an army was much talked about in Washington but never acted on with equipment or money. Without much of either, MacArthur's efforts at defending a geographic area to which he alone was committed were doomed.

Japan's next step came soon. In 1937 the Japanese invaded China proper. Within two years, the quickly emerging nation had occupied all of eastern China, fighting against forces more interested in destroying each other than the invaders. After the fall of France, Japan moved to occupy the northern part of Vietnam and signed on with the German-Italian Axis. All the rest of East Asia, with its rich natural resources, was now threatened.

The Philippine government declared a state of emergency but failed to mobilize what defense forces it had or to provide the funds MacArthur needed. In Washington, the Philippines were considered expendable; Europe was the focus of attention, funds, and equipment. The one step that President Franklin D. Roosevelt did take was to order the merger of the American and Filipino troops on the islands and to reappoint MacArthur to the army, promote him to lieutenant general, and make him commander of all military forces there. The last part of the promotion was a title without much substance.

On December 7, 1941, Japan attacked Pearl Harbor, seeking to destroy any American threat in the Pacific. Only the two American aircraft carriers survived, because they had not been in port.

Sunday the seventh in Hawaii was Monday the eighth in the Philippines. At 3:40 a.m., MacArthur was informed of the attack by the chief of the army's War Plans Division in Washington. He was also warned that he should expect an attack "in the near future." But MacArthur did nothing—except make many of the same mistakes made at Pearl Harbor. The planes were lined up wing to wing on runways to prevent sabotage, and though the lone radar gave a warning of incoming planes, it was ignored. At noon on the eighth, Japanese planes struck all the United States' installations and destroyed all its aircraft. Two days later, another raid destroyed the United States naval base at Cavite and the only two battle-ships the Allies had west of Hawaii.

By this time MacArthur had begun to act. He had 16,000 American troops—though only two complete regiments—and the 12,000-strong combat-trained Philippine Scouts Division. Moreover, he believed he could successfully resist an invasion by Japanese troops. Yet when the Japanese did invade north of Manila on December 22, the largely untrained and hastily called up Filipino troops ran. Within hours the Japanese landed a second force southeast of Manila, putting the defenders in a trap and threatening the capital city.

Just in time, MacArthur's military genius emerged. He ordered a dou-ble retreat of 28,000 men who were 160 miles apart and had both evade the invading troops and avoid the bottlenecks created by refugees flooding out of Manila, all the while blowing up eighty-four bridges. The rallying point for the retreat was the twin garrisons of the Bataan peninsula and its offshore island of Corregidor. By the time the retreat was over and the last bridge was blown up, MacArthur had 80,000 soldiers safe, together with 26,000 refugees.

What MacArthur had failed to do, because he had been convinced that no invasion of the islands could succeed, was stockpile sufficient food. At once the defenders went on half-rations. He was temporarily in a strong military position, but he was alone. Elsewhere, the Japanese triumphed in quick order. The British fell in Hong Kong, in all of Malaya including Singapore, much of Burma, and Borneo; the French were forced to cede Indo-China; and the Dutch lost both their fleet and the Dutch East Indies. Australia was threatened. Only MacArthur's troops held out.

MacArthur spent the next months leading the resistance from the tun-nels of Corregidor, accompanied by his wife and young son. Imploring Washington for reinforcements and resupply, he was met with promises that could not be kept and were never meant as anything but a means to keep him fighting. Food dwindled and rations continued to be cut. The Japanese shelled continually, but to no avail. The United States chief of staff asked General Dwight D. Eisenhower, once MacArthur's second in command, what should be done. Eisenhower had two recommendations. First, the Philippines could not be saved, and Australia had to be the base for future United States operations. Second, MacArthur had to stay on Corregidor and go down with his men.

But MacArthur was already an international hero and a symbol of re-sistance. Moreover, the Australians, feeling the threat of the oncoming Japanese forces, demanded proof of the Allies' commitment to them or else they would withdraw their army from North Africa. The commitment they demanded was MacArthur.

In February 1942, Roosevelt agreed. When MacArthur was warned that he would be evacuated from Corregidor, his first impulse was to resign his commission so he could enlist as an ordinary soldier and fight on Bataan. The impulse gave way to the pressure from Roosevelt and MacArthur's own staff. He conceived of an evacuation by PT boat from the Philippines to the island of Mindanao to the south and from there by plane to Australia. That settled, he ordered food cut again, to one-third normal rations, planning to return with a counterattack within four months.

On the evening of March 11, MacArthur, with his wife, their son and his nanny, and a staff of sixteen men, boarded two PT boats and escaped. After a journey of 560 miles that took thirty-five hours, they arrived on Mindanao, and several days later three B-17 bombers took them all to Australia, some 1,500 miles away. When he arrived, MacArthur asked about the United States forces he believed were already in the country. There were none.

Newspapers throughout the United States trumpeted the news, carefully underlining that MacArthur had left the Philippines on the president's orders. Roosevelt, too, issued a statement emphasizing that fact.

> I know that every man and woman in the United States admires with me General MacArthur's determination to fight to the finish with his men in the Philippines. But I also know that every man and woman is in agreement that all important decisions must be made with a view toward the successful termination of the war. Knowing this, I am sure that every American, if faced individually with the question as to where General MacArthur could best serve his country, could come to only one answer."[1]

But it was MacArthur's statement made in Adelaide on his way by train to Melbourne that stayed in the public's mind.

> The President of the United States ordered me to break through the Japanese lines and proceed from Corregidor to Australia for the purpose, as I understand it, of organizing the American offensive against Japan. A primary purpose of this is relief of the Philippines. I came through and **I SHALL RETURN**.[2]

Though the War Information Office asked MacArthur to change his statement to "We shall return," he refused. The war was personal; it was his honor at stake. Moreover, the incentive for the statement came from Carlos Romulo, a future president of the nation, on Corregidor itself. "America has let us down and won't be trusted," he told a Filipino journalist. "But the people still have confidence in MacArthur. If *he* says *he* is coming back, he will be believed."[3] The slogan was used throughout the Philippines during the occupation, and in fact the only sustained guerrilla opposition to Japanese occupation in Asia was in the Philippines.

MacArthur's return, though, was a long time in coming. Bataan and Corregidor fell on May 6, 1942. It took two years for the U.S. Navy and MacArthur to fight their way back. MacArthur developed a new form of attack for this island war. He used planes to substitute for artillery and had elite landing troops follow massive invasion bombardments. Each island captured provided land for a new airfield that would enable the capture of the next island. He moved past well-defended islands to capture ones that were not as strongly held, forcing the Japanese to abandon those thus isolated. By August 1944, starting from nearly nothing two years earlier, MacArthur and his forces had moved nearly two thousand miles.

And finally, on October 20, 1944, two years and nine months after he had escaped, MacArthur invaded the Philippines. From the beach, he broadcast a short message to the people he loved.

> To the People of the Philippines:
> *I have returned.*
> By the grace of Almighty God, our forces stand again on Philippine soil—soil consecrated in the blood of our two peoples. We have come, dedicated and committed, to the task of destroying every vestige of enemy control over your daily lives, and of restoring, upon a foundation of indestructible strength, the liberties of your people. . . .
> Rally to me. Let the indomitable spirit of Bataan and Corregidor lead on. As the lines of battle roll forward to bring you within the zone of operations, rise and strike. Strike at every favorable opportunity. For your homes and hearths, strike! For future generations of your sons and daughters, strike! In the name of your sacred dead, strike! Let no heart be faint. Let every arm be steeled. The guidance of divine God points the way. Follow in His Name to the Holy Grail of righteous victory![4]

The war had become MacArthur's personal crusade; he had reached his Jerusalem.

NUTS!

★ 1944 ★

By mid-December 1944, the Allied forces in Western Europe had stalled in their effort to conquer Germany and bring an end to World War II. In the six months since the Normandy invasion, the combined British, Canadian, French, and American forces had achieved a great deal, slogging out difficult fighting in the hedgerows of Normandy, racing eastward across France and northward through Belgium and part of Holland. In September, though, the Allies had been forced to stop as their supply lines lengthened and as they fought a difficult and costly battle in Huertgen Forest.

Winter came on, and the weather turned extremely nasty–the coldest, some said, in memory. While the Germans were clearly on the defensive, the Allies had stalled out for a number of reasons, not the least being that they needed seven hundred tons of supplies each day while the Germans needed only two hundred tons.[1] The danger to the Allies was real, since the Germans were fast bringing on new weapons—ballistic missiles and jet aircraft—and had kept up their production of war materiel despite intense Allied bombing. As the weather turned bad, the Allies' ability to use aerial reconnaissance disappeared, and since they were sitting on the German border, civilian intelligence, so useful in France, largely dried up.

Well before the winter began, back in mid-September, Hitler had announced a new offensive that he believed would force the Allies back, perhaps off the Continent entirely, wreak havoc with the alliance, and retake the only real port that the enemy controlled—Antwerp. First code-named "Watch on the Rhine" and later "Autumn Mist," the plan as announced to his field commanders depended on surprise, speed, slow reaction by the enemy, bad weather, and the capture of enemy supplies, especially gasoline.

Despite the tactful opposition of several of his chief generals, Hitler's plan of launching his attack through the Forest of Ardennes actually had some chance of success. The front through which his tanks and infantry would attack was relatively lightly defended. To the north of the Ardennes Allied troops were spread out, one division for every 1.4 miles of front. To the south, in an area under the command of General Omar Bradley, there was one division for every nine miles of front. But in the line of the attack to come, the Americans had only one division for each twenty miles of front, and these troops were either battle-weary or almost completely new to the war.

By scraping up every nonessential soldier in Germany and enlisting boys as young as sixteen and men previously considered overage, the Germans amassed a huge army, outnumbering the Americans ten to one at the point of attack. They gathered 1,500 planes and got priority in shipments of new tanks. Hitler was taking a great gamble, endangering the German forces confronting the rapidly advancing Russian army to the east.

Beginning at 5:30 a.m. on December 16, well before dawn, the German attack began with a massive hour-long artillery barrage. Much of the Americans' communications and their defensive positions were destroyed. When the barrage ceased, troops and tanks, supported by aircraft flying below the clouds, smashed into the American lines. The spearhead of the attack was the First SS Panzer Division, whose first-day mission was to reach the Meuse River, fifty miles away.

At first the Germans had great success—moving quickly, creating panic, and profiting from the surprise Hitler had counted on. But almost from the first, and increasingly as time went on, isolated American units began to stiffen, holding up the advancing forces, destroying or moving much of the badly needed gasoline, blowing up bridges, and creating roadblocks that held up the pace of the German advance. Two regiments of American troops, though, ran out of ammunition and surrendered—the 7,500 prisoners were the biggest mass surrender of the war against Germany.

Hitler had also counted on a slow Allied reaction to the offensive. What he got was something else. Despite the lack of intelligence and a confusion in the front lines, by December 17 First Army Headquarters realized that something bigger than a diversion was going on. The commander of the First Army called his superior, General Bradley, reaching him in conference with commander in chief General Dwight D. Eisenhower at Eisenhower's headquarters. Bradley dismissed their alarm, but Eisenhower correctly saw the importance of events—even how the breakthrough might be turned against the attackers. The key, psychologically as much as militarily, was to hold on to the city of Bastogne, isolated in the center of the German breakthrough, the hub of a good road network westward that the Germans needed.

Eisenhower ordered that the 82nd and 101st Airborne Divisions be moved into the area, the 82nd to reinforce the northern side of the breakthrough and the 101st to move into Bastogne itself. The Germans' luck had begun to run out.

On the eighteenth there were breaks in the clouds. Allied planes not only got a sense of where and how strong the enemy was, they were able to attack for as long as the breaks held. On the nineteenth, at dawn, the 101st Division arrived in Bastogne, just ahead of the encircling German army.

Although surrounded and short of adequate clothing for the bitter winter weather, with no hot food and little shelter except foxholes, the Americans held out, though taking serious losses of men and equipment, especially tanks. But the Germans had fallen fatally behind schedule and were equally hampered by the weather—the rain, snow, and mud that limited tank mobility. The fate of Bastogne was becoming the stuff of headlines in American newspapers even as Eisenhower called a meeting of his senior officers to give orders to contain what was now called "the Bulge" and then to counterattack. In fact General George Patton, anticipating Eisenhower's plan and orders, left for the meeting only after ordering his staff to ready his troops for an attack northward against his side of the Bulge.

The weather grew even worse, with snow and with temperatures at night falling below zero degrees Fahrenheit. The Germans had captured much of the 101st's medical supplies and doctors, so that the wounded often went untreated. The ring around Bastogne grew tighter.

Then, on the morning of December 22, General Heinrich Freiherr von Lüttwitz, commander of the Forty-seventh Panzer Corps, wrote a letter to the commanding officer of the American troops inside Bastogne.

> The fortune of war is changing. This time the U.S.A. forces in and near Bastogne have been encircled by strong German armoured units. More German armoured units have crossed the River Our near Ortheuville, have taken Marche and reached St. Hubert by passing through Homores-Silbret-Tillet. Librimont is in German hands.
>
> There is only one possibility of saving the encircled U.S.A. troops from total annihilation: that is the honourable surrender of the encircled town. In order to think it over, a period of two hours will be granted, beginning with the presentation of this note.
>
> If this proposal should be rejected, one German artillery corps and six heavy anti-aircraft battalions are ready to annihilate the U.S.A. troops in and near Bastogne. The order for firing will be given immediately after this two-hour period.
>
> All the serious civilian losses caused by this artillery fire would not correspond with the well-known American humanity.[2]

The letter was given to Lieutenant Hellmuth Henke, who spoke English, to deliver to the senior officer inside Bastogne. The Germans ceased firing, as did the Americans. Waving white flags, Henke, another officer, and two enlisted men approached the American lines, where they were blindfolded and driven to General Anthony McAuliffe's headquarters.

Still blindfolded, Henke handed the letter to someone. While he stood, waiting for some sort of answer, Henke was asked questions to which he had no answer. Then a reply was put into his hand, and the group was driven back to the front. There the blindfolds were removed, and Henke read what McAuliffe had written — a terse, one-word response: **"NUTS!"**

> Henke turned to his escort, Col. Joseph Harper, and said, "Nuts?"
> "It means 'go to Hell,' said Harper. And that Henke understoood." [3]

McAuliffe's response became one of the most famous of the war, and certainly the most unpremeditated.

On the next day, December 23, the weather cleared. Allied warplanes filled the skies, dropping supplies into Bastogne, bombing German transport facilities, shooting up German vehicles and troops. On Christmas Day the Germans tried one last time to break into Bastogne, but it was too late. Taking heavy losses, they withdrew.

On December 26 the lead tanks of Patton's advance broke through the German lines around Bastogne, and the siege was over.

Halted everywhere, the German attempt at a breakthrough into France and to Antwerp had ended. Out of supplies, running out of tanks and soldiers, the Germans could only wait for the inevitable. And the inevitable began on January 3 in deep snow and bitter cold as the Allied counteroffensive began to push the Bulge back. Within two weeks, the Germans were back to their original lines.

The Battle of the Bulge, symbolized in the popular mind by the siege of Bastogne, was America's single largest battle of the war — and the most costly. The American forces suffered nearly 77,000 casualties, including more than 8,000 dead and more than 21,000 missing. The Americans also lost more than seven hundred tanks and tank destroyers. [4]

But grave as those losses were, the Americans could afford them. The Germans could not. The German troops suffered nearly 82,000 casualties, including more than 12,000 dead and more than 30,000 missing, and lost more than 350 tanks. [5] As General Friedrich Wilhelm von Mellenthin later wrote, "Our precious reserves had been expended, and nothing was available to ward off the impending catastrophe in the East." [6]

THE BUCK STOPS HERE

GIVE 'EM HELL, HARRY!

★ 1945 ★

★ 1948 ★

Harry S. Truman became president of the United States on April 12, 1945, a little less than two hours after the death of Franklin D. Roosevelt. Few outside Washington, DC, knew the new president; fewer inside Washington thought he was up to the job.

Indeed, Truman was unlike any president who had preceded him in the twentieth century. He was not from a prominent political family. He did not have a long, highly visible career in politics or government. He was not wealthy or successful in private life. He was not college educated. Harry Truman was a calculated political accident.

Born in 1884 into a struggling family in rural Missouri, Truman left business college after a year when he was needed to work on the family farm, doing the hard labor of farm work for ten years. In 1916 he joined the army as part of the 129th Field Artillery. When the United States entered the war, Truman's regiment was sent to France, where he was promoted to captain and commanded an artillery battery in combat.

After the war Truman, with a war buddy, opened a men's store that was briefly successful until the recession in 1922, when the partners had to file for bankruptcy. Out of a job, Truman turned to Democratic political boss T. J. Pendergast and was elected to his first political office, a judicial administrative job that gave him the title of judge. Although he was defeated for reelection, he was elected again in 1926, and his eight-year tenure was noted for his efficiency and honesty in office.

In 1934 Truman, again with the support of the Pendergast machine, defeated the Republican incumbent for United States senator. Although he was initially known as the senator from Pendergast, he earned a reputation for hard work, accuracy, honesty, and gregariousness, the last a prized quality in the Senate. When he won reelection in 1940, without any support from President Franklin D. Roosevelt or from the party and without any real financial backing from anyone but his friends, he was enthusiastically welcomed back to the Senate.

It was in his second term in the Senate that Truman's national stature began to grow. He was given the chairmanship of the Senate Special Committee to Investigate the National Defense Program by Roosevelt, who thought he would be an ally and make few waves. Truman, though, wangled enough money to staff the commission with investigators and began holding hearings into a wide range of areas, from the performance of military aircraft suppliers to the production of farm machinery. So great was his effect on the way business and government acted that *Time* put his picture on the cover in early 1943 and wrote, "For a Congressional committee to be considered the first line of defense—especially in a nation which does not tend to admire its representatives in Congress assembled—is encouraging to believers in democracy. So is the sudden emergence of Harry Truman, whose presence in the Senate is a queer accident of democracy."[1]

As the Democrats were getting ready for the 1944 presidential election, there was no doubt that Roosevelt would again be the nominee. However, a number of senior members of the party, aware that Roosevelt's health was deteriorating, united against the renomination of Henry Wallace as vice president. It was likely that Roosevelt would not live out this next term in office, and Wallace was not someone they wanted as the next president. Truman was among those being considered, but when Roosevelt eventually agreed to his selection, it was more because of what Truman was not. He was not from a big city or the East, he was not a noted liberal—he was not, in short, someone who might overshadow the president. Only the liberals were opposed, but they would not fight Roosevelt.

Truman it was. He was nominated and elected. Yet as vice president he was kept completely in the dark. Roosevelt ran things as he always had, by himself. And when Roosevelt died and Truman was sworn in, he was as unprepared for the presidency as he could possibly have been. He did not know that he would soon have to make crucial decisions about things he knew nothing about—the use of the atomic bomb, the ongoing negotiations with Winston Churchill and Joseph Stalin about the conduct of the war, and the future organization of the postwar world.

Though Truman asked for the nation's prayers and professed to be thunderstruck by his sudden elevation, he was not, in fact, unready. A month into the job of president, Truman met with the British foreign minister, Anthony Eden, to prepare for the upcoming meeting with Churchill and Stalin at Potsdam. "I am here to make decisions," Truman told him, "and whether they prove right or wrong, I am going to make them."[2]

And make decisions he did. For the next two years, faced with the end of the war in Europe and then in the Pacific, faced with the need to reintegrate large numbers of soldiers back into the life of the nation, faced with labor unrest and strikes, faced with rising inflation, faced with a newly resurgent Republican Party that seized control of both houses of Congress in the 1946 elections, Truman acted. He left Roosevelt's cabinet largely intact, though as secretary of state he selected General George Marshall, who was universally loved and respected. His administration created the Central Intelligence Agency, recommended Alaska and Hawaii for statehood, secured the passage of the Employment Act that got the government into the business of fostering employment, set up the President's Economic Council, and brought Herbert Hoover back to do a report on the world food shortage. Truman also was the first president to address the NAACP, calling for comprehensive civil rights for all Americans.

He also made mistakes. He waited too long to act when his friends got him into trouble. He allowed members of his cabinet to undercut him. He acted rashly when he thought the nation was in danger, as when national strikes threatened the economy.

But no one was in doubt that he acted, and no one was in doubt as to where he stood.

Making decisions and taking responsibility were, as Truman saw it, the essence of the presidency. It was to some degree part of his personality and to some degree a result of his military service, where he acted, even against directions, when he thought it imperative for the good of his men and the outcome of a battle. In the fall of 1945, one of his closest friends on his staff gave him a copy of a sign he had seen on the desk in the head office of a federal reformatory in Oklahoma. The sign read, **THE BUCK STOPS HERE**. Although the sign remained on Truman's desk only a short time, it was a motto he never forgot. Nor did the press.[3]

He paid a real price for his outspokenness and his decisiveness. By April 1948, with the next presidential election looming, Truman's approval rating was down to 36 percent, and more than half of those surveyed said they actively disapproved of him. The Gallup polls in March revealed that at that time Truman would lose to almost any Republican candidate. The newspaper and magazine political columnists almost as a body were writing him off, and there was a move by many in his own party to replace him as the Democratic candidate.

Truman, though, did not care. He had already decided to seek the nomination for president and to run, probably against Governor Thomas E. Dewey of New York. He was determined to do what he felt was right, no matter what the consequences. His State of the Union address in January called for a national health insurance program, a massive housing program, increased support for education and for farmers, greater protection of natural resources, and a raise in the minimum wage from forty cents an hour to seventy-five cents.

In February Truman, as he had promised, sent a civil rights message to Congress calling for a federal antilynching law, federal protection for the right to vote, anti-poll-tax legislation, a Fair Employment Practices Commission with the power to stop discrimination by employers and unions, and action by Congress on claims by Japanese Americans for their mistreatment during the war.

These initiatives enraged the Republicans as well as members of his own party, chiefly in the South.

By accident, though, one of Truman's major weaknesses found a cure. Truman was a poor speaker in front of large audiences—wooden in his delivery and in his body movements. In April it dawned on his staff that when Truman spoke to small groups without a full speech script, he was comfortable and effective. Truman agreed to try a new approach, and after delivering a prepared speech at a convention of newspaper editors, he spoke off the cuff and was a great success. Each time he tried it afterward he improved. He was now ready to take this new self on the road.

Early in June Truman embarked on a "nonpolitical" train tour of eighteen western states. It was a rehearsal for the campaign to come. And it was on this trip that Harry Truman found his style, his audience, and his campaign themes. His style was combative, slashing, no-holds-barred; others may have conceded the election before he had even been nominated, but not Truman.

His audience was anyone who would come out to see him, and even this early, before the campaign had begun, people turned out. The press, then and later, dismissed the crowds as just curious to see the president. What the press did not understand until after the election was over was that the crowds listened to what Truman had to say and increasingly responded, breaking into his talk with comments and even yells like "Pour it on, Harry."

In just over fifteen days, Truman had traveled to eighteen states, covering more than nine thousand miles, and delivered seventy-three speeches. His performance should have alarmed his opponents.

Six days after Truman's return to Washington, Dewey was nominated by the Republican Party. On that same day, June 24, 1948, the Russians blockaded Berlin in a move to force the Americans, British, and French out of the city. Truman immediately announced that the Allies would remain, and four days later the Americans began what became known as the Berlin Airlift to provide food, fuel, and medical supplies for the entire Allied-governed population. The next world war threatened just as the American political scene was turning hot.

In the middle of July the Democrats met in Philadelphia, sure of their coming defeat. There was a desperate attempt to enlist General Dwight D. Eisenhower as the nominee, though no one knew if he even was a Democrat. Eisenhower refused several times before they gave up. No other viable alternative to Truman could be found, so Truman was nominated, with his prospects even gloomier than before the convention began. He would face not only Dewey with his united Republican Party, but also a Progressive Party headed by former vice president Henry Wallace, the darling of the liberals, and a States' Rights Party headed by South Carolina governor Strom Thurmond, the staunch defender of segregation.

Only Truman really believed. He not only believed, he was willing to do anything to succeed. And he began his fight right in the middle of his speech accepting the nomination, when he called Congress back to Washington for a special session to deal with the problems facing the country. "Now, my friends, if there is any reality behind the Republican platform, we ought to get some action from a short session of the 80th Congress. They can do this job in 15 days, if they want to do it. They will still have time to go out and run for office." [4]

The trap was set. The Republican-controlled Congress met, and despite pleas from Dewey, their own nominee, refused to give the president any action. Harry Truman's point was made, and he never let the voters forget it. In a press conference shortly after the end of the special session, Truman agreed with a reporter that it had been a "do-nothing" session and a "do-nothing" Congress. In every speech thereafter, a high point would be Truman's denunciation of the "do-nothing Eightieth Congress."

It did not seem to matter, though. The campaign began with the polls showing that Dewey held an overwhelming lead. George Gallup's poll reported that Dewey had 48 percent of the voting public; Truman had 37 percent, Wallace had 5 percent, and 10 percent were undecided. Elmo Roper's poll gave Dewey 46.3 percent, Truman 31.5 percent, and Wallace 3 percent; 19.2 percent were undecided.

So strong was Dewey's lead that two key decisions were made. First, Dewey and his advisers strengthened their commitment to a campaign that made no mistakes and lost no votes. His theme would be national unity. Second, Roper announced that the race was already decided and that he would make no more polling results public; they would reveal no differences and would not be newsworthy.

And still Truman continued to believe. On September 17, 1948, he, his family, his aides and campaign staff, and the press boarded the presidential train to begin a "whistle-stop" campaign. He planned to travel nearly 22,000 miles in three phases: first across the country to California for fifteen days, then through the Midwest for six days, and finally to the big cities in the Northeast, ending back in Missouri for ten days — a total of nearly thirty-three days of nonstop traveling, speaking, and campaigning.

As Truman was preparing to board for the train's departure from Washington, the vice presidential nominee, Senator Alben Barkley of Kentucky, posed with him for photographers and told him, "Mow 'em down, Harry." Truman flashed his wide grin and replied, "I'm going to fight hard. I'm going to give 'em hell."

Truman's words made the newspaper accounts, in one form or another, around the nation.

As he crossed the nation to California, making scheduled and unscheduled stops along the way, Truman drew crowds far beyond what anyone anticipated. At each place where he had no formal speech prepared, but where people had assembled at the railroad station, Truman's train would stop, and he would come out and speak. Working from carefully prepared notes about local candidates and local issues, Truman was combative and involved the audience. Often he would tell the crowd that they were to blame for the nation's problems because they had stayed home during the last election. He would storm about the "do-nothing Eightieth Congress," and, often someone in the crowd would yell, "GIVE 'EM HELL, HARRY!" Energized anew, he would excoriate the special interests that dominated the Republican Party.

On and on he rolled, while Dewey kept up his nonconfrontational speeches, demonstrating his fitness for high national office and his desire to avoid offending anyone. Dewey was even pictured with his wife in a national magazine with a caption, "The future President and his first lady."

Yet Truman was having an effect. He had given some 275 speeches and reached millions of voters. Indeed, with two weeks to go before election day, a new Gallup poll showed Dewey's lead down to six points. Surely, the Republicans thought, it was just too late for Truman. Dewey even suggested through the media that some mechanism should be created for new Republican administration to have a strong say in national policy after the election but before Dewey was sworn in. It was just too dangerous to leave Truman in charge even for a few months.

On November 2, 1948, Harry Truman voted, as did millions of other American voters. Near midnight, the noted radio announcer H. V. Kaltenborn told listeners that though Truman was ahead by 1,200,000 votes, he was clearly the loser. Four hours later Kaltenborn announced that Truman was ahead by 2 million votes, but that Dewey was the likely winner, since key GOP states like Illinois and Ohio had yet to be counted.

By 9:30 the next morning, Truman had been declared the winner in Illinois, Ohio, and California—and thus had won the election, while the Democrats had won control of both houses. Shortly after 11:00, Dewey conceded. The unthinkable Republican nightmare had become reality, and Dewey was dubbed "the man who snatched defeat from the jaws of victory."

The victory was Truman's. His confidence never faltered. His energy never flagged. He had given them hell in spades, though as he said later, "I never gave anybody hell. I just told the truth and they thought it was hell."[5]

NICE GUYS FINISH LAST

★ 1947 ★

It was more a statement of personality than philosophy, but it was seized on as an American reality, or at least as a statement of American belief. And the person who first made it, Leo Durocher, spent his whole life embodying those four words.

From a poor family on the wrong side of the tracks in Springfield, Massachusetts, Durocher joined the Yankees in 1928 for spring training, already the fully formed personality that would become famous. With his well-tailored clothes, his aggressive style of play, and his constant mouthing off to teammates and opponents, the rookie was instantly disliked by all the Yankees except the one who counted most—manager Miller Huggins. In his first regular season game, he tried to pick a fight with the most pugnacious player of the time, Ty Cobb, but was saved by the intervention of Babe Ruth. Despite hitting well, he continued to be an outcast. During the off-season, there were persistent rumors that Leo had stolen Babe Ruth's watch and Lou Gehrig's World Series ring. Indeed, rumors that Durocher stole from teammates persisted for decades, but they were likely just an indication of how much he was disliked.

Leo's position as Yankee scapegoat was not improved in 1929 when he beat out the popular Mark Koenig for shortstop and Koenig was moved to third base. Some of his teammates told reporters that he was dishonest and hung around with gamblers. Others threw him curve balls in the infield to force him into making errors. Worse, Huggins, Leo's only supporter on the team, died at the end of the season. Four months later Durocher was gone, put on waivers. American League teams, familiar with his personality, did not respond, and he was eventually traded to the Cincinnati Reds.

Durocher's three seasons with the Reds were marked by a steadily declining batting average, superb fielding, arguments on and off the field, and frequent visits to the fleshpots and gambling joints across the river from staid Cincinnati. He did, though, get married—but the marriage, the resulting child, and a subsequent divorce disappeared from his later autobiography.

Traded again, to St. Louis early in the 1933 season, Durocher found himself with a winning club and one that, for once, suited his prickly personality. He feuded constantly with player-manager Frankie Frisch and continued taunting opponents and fighting with teammates. The Cardinals, though, were a good home for him, filled with aggressive, eccentric characters and with a new general manager, Branch Rickey, who played the role of Leo's father, filling his contracts with incentive clauses for good behavior, bill paying, and child support. His hitting improved, though it was never great. His best year was 1936, when he hit .286 and was named the starting shortstop for the All-Star Game.

Leo had become a favorite of the press, a source of stories and stand-out quotations. He was credited with coming up with the club's nickname, the Gas House Gang. Though the term had been used by sportswriters previously, it was his use of the phrase, quoted during the 1935 spring training, that stuck.

Traded to the Brooklyn Dodgers just after the 1937 season, Durocher found the place suited him even better than St. Louis. Brooklyn loved his attitude, his readiness to scrap with opponents and umpires, and his willingness to do anything to win. The Dodgers, though, were also perennial losers, consistently finishing deep in the second division. That was about to change.

At the beginning of 1938, Larry MacPhail was named general manager of the Dodgers. He began to buy the best players he could find, and at the end of another losing season he fired the manager and named Durocher player-manager. It was the beginning of a tumultuous but fabulously successful relationship.

Before the season even began, MacPhail fired Leo for gambling during spring training (it turned out to be bingo) and for fighting (a scrap with his caddy during an off-day round of golf), but the firing was forgotten by the next day. It was the just the first of many times MacPhail would fire Durocher during their years together.

The 1939 season was also the first time Durocher was fined by the National League president, Ford Frick, a fine that was incurred by a fight Leo had during a game against the Giants at the Polo Grounds. Like his firings by MacPhail, this was just the beginning of Leo's league fines and, eventually, suspensions.

Yet for all his fisticuffs and verbal abuse of opponents and umpires, Durocher was a great success as a manager. MacPhail got him the players, and Durocher led the Dodgers to their first winning season in seven years, finishing third in the league. The next year the team finished second, though Leo was fined and suspended by the league "for prolonged argument and conduct on the field tending to incite riot." In 1941 the Dodgers finished first. MacPhail fired Durocher for failing to stop the team train on the way into New York so that he could board it and share in the adulation of the crowds waiting to meet the team. The firing, as usual, was rescinded, but the Dodgers lost a heartbreaker of a series to the hated Yankees.

Leo's troubles began in earnest. During the war years, he raged on and off the field. He was briefly suspended by the league and constantly thrown out of games. On his orders, the Dodger pitchers were throwing beanballs to intimidate opposing batters, and President Frick responded by announcing an automatic fine for Durocher each time it happened. The Dodger clubhouse had by now become notorious for gambling and cardplaying and as a hangout for Durocher's friends, notably the gambler Memphis Engleberg and the actor George Raft, who openly associated with mob figures.

MacPhail was fired at the end of the 1942 season, and Branch Rickey succeeded him in his role as both general manager and steward of Durocher's behavior. Durocher's fighting and antagonism got so bad that in 1943 he faced a revolt and barely avoided having to forfeit a game for lack of players. It was at this time that Durocher got his second divorce.

In 1944 the Dodgers had their first and only losing season under Durocher, followed by a formal investigation of a crooked dice game that George Raft hosted in Leo's New York City apartment. Though Leo was not implicated, his name's being involved did not help him with Rickey. In 1945 Durocher and a friend beat up a newly returned veteran, breaking his jaw. Only the efforts of actor Danny Kaye, another friend of Leo's, kept the case out of court.

With the players coming home from the war, the Dodgers looked to return to their winning ways. They had the hitting and the pitching, and just as important, they shared Leo's on-field attitudes. On July 5, 1946, the Dodgers were at the Polo Grounds for two games. Durocher was in the dugout with a group of people watching batting practice. Frank Graham, a columnist for the *New York Journal American* and the only reporter that Durocher ever respected, wrote about it the next day in a story headlined "Leo Doesn't Like Nice Guys." The subhead read, "Isn't One Himself He Loudly Admits; Says They Wind up in Seventh Place":

> It was twilight at the Polo Ground and, in the Dodgers' dugout, Red Barber was needling Leo Durocher about the home runs the Giants had hit the day before.
>
> "Home runs! Leo said. "Some home runs! Line drives and pop flies that would have been caught on a bigger field! That's what they were!"
>
> "Why don't you admit they were real home runs?" Red asked, sticking the needle in a little deeper. "Why don't you be a nice guy for a change?"
>
> Leo had been reclining on the bench, watching the Dodgers at batting practice. Now he leaped to his feet.
>
> "A nice guy!" he yelled. "A nice guy! I've been around in baseball for a long time and I've known a lot of nice guys. But I never saw a nice guy who was any good when you needed him. . . ."
>
> "Nice guys!" he said. "Look over there. Do you know a nicer guy than Mel Ott? Or any of the other Giants? Why, they're the nicest guys in the world! And where are they? In seventh place!"
>
> He walked up and down again, beating himself on the chest.
>
> "Nice guys! I'm not a nice guy—and I'm in first place. Nobody helped me get there, either, except the guys on this ball club and they ain't nice guys. . . ."
>
> "The nice guys are all over there," he said. "In seventh place."[1]

As far as anyone knows, that is the closest Durocher ever came to making the statement attributed to him. One biographer stated that the back-page headlines the next day screamed, **"NICE GUYS FINISH LAST—LEO**," though a careful review of the papers has not turned up any of those headlines. The only other publication the statement did appear in was the weekly *Sporting News,* which reprinted Graham's column with a new headline, "'Nice Guys' Wind Up in Last Place, Scoffs Lippy."[2]

In fact the Dodgers lost that series to the Giants two games to one, but they finished the season tied with the Cardinals for first place, losing the pennant in the playoff.

And in 1947 Durocher was suspended for the whole season, but not for fighting, not for gambling, and not for flouting a court order not to marry actress Larraine Day until her California divorce became final in 1948. He was suspended for telling an unwelcome truth.

Before the 1947 season began, Commissioner A. B. "Happy" Chandler met with Durocher to get him to clean up his act. The constant rumors of Durocher's unsavory associates, his well-publicized romance with the still-married Day, and the threats by right-wing newspaper columnist Westbrook Pegler to expose Durocher's moral and ethical shortcomings had put Chandler, urged on by Branch Rickey, in a position where he had to do something. Armed with the results of a private investigation, Chandler confronted Durocher with a list of people, including mobsters Bugsy Siegel and Joe Adonis, whom Durocher immediately had to stop seeing. He also insisted that Leo had to stop staying in George Raft's house when in Los Angeles. Leo, feeling the heat, agreed.

But he did not agree to stay out of the news. First, he and Day violated a court order and went to Mexico for her divorce and their marriage. Then, before a March exhibition game against the Yankees in Havana, Leo spotted two of the people he had been forbidden to associate with—gamblers Memphis Engleberg and Connie Immerman—sharing the Yankees' box with Yankees general manager Larry MacPhail. His next day's ghostwritten column "Durocher Says" in the *Brooklyn Eagle* claimed, "MacPhail was flaunting his company with known gamblers right in the players' faces. If I even said 'Hello' to one of those guys, I'd be called before Commissioner Chandler and probably barred."[3]

MacPhail filed a complaint with Chandler against Durocher for actions "detrimental to baseball," and the Brooklyn Catholic Youth Organization announced that it would withdraw its affiliation with the Dodgers' Knothole Club on the grounds that "the present manager of the Brooklyn Baseball Team is not the kind of leader we want for your youth to idealize and imitate." On April 9, 1947, to the distress of Dodgers fans, Chandler suspended Durocher for the entire 1947 season. The reason given was "an accumulation of unpleasant incidents detrimental to baseball."[4]

Although he returned as manager for the 1948 season, Durocher's days were numbered. Club president Walter O'Malley wanted him out, and Branch Rickey suggested that he leave. Durocher did but was immediately hired by the hated New York Giants. Here too his fire and baseball acumen pushed a Giants team that had a winning percentage of only .415 to play .573 ball for the rest of the year.

Durocher's career with the Giants was marked, as always, by winning teams and trouble with the authorities. In seven full seasons under Durocher, the Giants won two pennants and one World Series. But burned out and lured by the possibilities of being a television star, Leo quit after the 1955 season, spending the next ten years in a variety of television roles and hanging out with Frank Sinatra's "Rat Pack." And he got divorced from Larraine Day, his third divorce.

He may have been gone from baseball, but he was not forgotten. Hired in 1966 to manage the Chicago Cubs, for the third time Durocher turned a perennial losing team into a winner. He also got married again.

Six years later, the Cubs fired Durocher for failing to win a pennant, though he had finished second three times and had never finished out of the first division. He was hired in midseason to manage the Houston Astros, but he had had enough and lasted only until the end of the 1973 season. He was divorced for a fourth and last time in 1981.

His heart's desire, to be elected to the Hall of Fame during his lifetime, went unfulfilled. Despite his record as a manager, with a winning percentage of .540 (better than half the managers in the Hall of Fame at his death), he had just made too many enemies along the way. One of those who consistently voted against his admission was Cardinal Hall of Famer Stan Musial, who had, it was said, never forgiven Durocher for ordering his pitchers to throw at his head. Typically, Durocher told the friend who was to be his executor that if he was elected posthumously he should refuse the election. Here too he failed. Leo Durocher was elected to the Hall of Fame in 1994 — three years after his death — and his election was accepted.

SPAHN, SAIN, AND PRAY FOR RAIN

★ 1948 ★

The Boston Braves, the National League team in Boston, may not have been the worst baseball team of the twentieth century, but they were certainly in the running. So bad were they that in 1936 the club president changed the name to the Boston Bees. The change did not help, and the name was changed back in 1941.

The Braves had not always lost. In fact, from their inception in 1876 through the turn of the century, they finished first eight times and second four times. The new century, though, was a bad one. Until after World War II, the Braves finished eighth—last—in the league nine times and next-to-last thirteen times. There was one bright spot in 1914, however, when they went from a fifth-place finish the year before to win the pennant and face the Philadelphia Athletics in the World Series. Though not given a chance against owner-manager Connie Mack's powerhouse, the Braves swept the A's, and, some say in revenge, Mack traded all his good players over the winter to start again.

Thereafter the Braves wallowed in mediocrity. As one Boston sportswriter, Al Hirshberg, wrote, "If ball players of the 'twenties were given the choice of going to the minor leagues or going to the Boston Braves, they would have chosen the minor leagues. From the sticks, at least, they had a chance to come back again."[1]

Constantly short of money to the point of near bankruptcy, the Braves developed the habit of trading for players who were well past their prime. In 1935 the club hired Babe Ruth both as a player and as the club's "second vice president" and "assistant manager." Ruth hit his last few home runs with the Braves but never had a chance to become their manager.

But Ruth was not the only over-the-hill player to join the Braves. Future Hall of Famers Paul Waner, Ernie Lombardi, Billy Herman, and Rabbit Maranville all ended their careers at Braves Field, known to sportswriters and fans as the Wigwam. The Braves did hire one of the DiMaggio brothers, but Vince DiMaggio was the brother who could not hit, specializing instead in strikeouts. When they traded for St. Louis Cardinal pitching ace Mort Cooper, Cooper won his first six games, then injured his arm and was never effective again. They hired Casey Stengel as manager, but Stengel had not yet become a genius and never led the club higher than fifth in the league.

The Braves' fortunes turned in 1944 when three Boston contractors led by Lou Perini bought out the other shareholders and assumed control of the team. For the first time, the Braves were solvent and had owners who were determined to spend money on the aging ballpark and on players. It took time for their efforts to show, since many of the players were off in the armed forces, but Perini started by hiring the best manager in baseball, Billy Southworth, and giving him full control of the team.

With the end of the war, Braves fans began to see new and better players on the field. In 1946, under Southworth for the first time, the Braves finished with their first winning record in eight years. And 1947 was even better, as the team compiled an 86–68 record and finished third. By the time the 1948 season opened, the Braves line-up was strong in the field, at the plate, and on the mound.

The first six weeks of the season, though, belied this improvement. The Braves struggled, barely gaining a break-even record. Then, beginning on June 6, the Braves began a six-game winning streak that moved them from fourth place to first. While they moved very briefly into second place immediately thereafter, the club regained first place and stayed there for the rest of the season, with only an occasional lapse.

In their June winning streak, their two pitching stars, Warren Spahn and Johnny Sain, won three of the six games, but it was not just pitching that kept them in first place. The team was hitting, and by the end of the season had a team batting average of .275, the best in the National League. The combination was working, and throughout the year the Braves did what good teams always do—win the close games and win in the late innings, several times with two out in the ninth.

Yet it was pitching that caught the fans' attention. When the Braves went on another winning streak in early September, Spahn and Sain were able to win four of those six games because rain-canceled games allowed them to share pitching duties in consecutive double-headers.

It was at this point in the season, with the Braves still fighting to stay on top, that manager Billy Southworth told Boston sportswriters his pitching plans for the remainder of the season. "A favoring schedule will enable the Tribe's field boss," wrote Howell Stevens, "to use both of his ace flingers, Johnny Sain and Warren Spahn, six more times in case the pennant race is not mathematically decided before the first week in October." [2]

That same day, The *Boston Post* carried a column by sports columnist Gerry Hern, headlined "BRAVES BOAST TWO-MAN STAFF" with the subhead

PITCH SPAHN AND SAIN, THEN PRAY

FOR RAIN — But every Day is a
Dark Day for Tribe

Hern's column began with a short poem, attributed to the nonexistent "collected writings of W. Southworth, 1948."

First we'll use Spahn, then we'll use Sain,
Then an off day, followed by rain.

Back will come Spahn, followed by Sain
And followed, we hope, by two days of rain.[3]

The column spent three paragraphs on the Braves' pitching staff and the rest on the wonders of rookie shortstop Alvin Dark, who hit .322 for the year and became the National League's Rookie of the Year. Dark's name provided the pun at the end of the subhead.

Strangely enough, through the end of the month, what was a piece of doggerel became a prophecy passing into baseball legend. It did rain when needed, and Spahn and Sain won three games each and soon won the pennant, finishing in first place by six and a half games.

Yet it was the Braves' fate always to share the city's excitement, since the Red Sox were locked in a three-way race for first place in what was then still called "the junior league." Even on the day the Braves clinched the National League title, the front-page banner headline read: "Braves Clinch Pennant, Sox in Second Place."

The Braves might have faced the Boston Red Sox in the World Series, but the Red Sox finished the season tied with the Cleveland Indians and lost a one-game playoff.

As in 1914, the Braves were given little chance to win the series. The Indians had five future Hall of Famers in the lineup, including the American League's 1948 Most Valuable Player, Lou Boudreau, and two pitching greats, Bob Feller and Bob Lemon. The Indians also fielded the first two black players to play in a World Series, outfielder Larry Doby and relief pitcher Satchel Paige.

The first game brought hope to Boston, as the Braves, behind the pitching of Johnny Sain and a disputed pickoff play at second base, won 1-0. But the Indians took the next three games, lost one, and finished the Braves off in Boston. It was a closely fought series; four of the six games were decided by two runs or fewer, but it was the end of the line for the Braves. They never again finished higher than fourth place.

Not only did the Braves never recover from the loss, neither did the fans. As it became clear that the Braves were not going to contend again, attendance at the ballpark slumped. In 1948 the Braves drew nearly 1.5 million fans to their games. Two years later, attendance had dropped below a million. When the club sold the rights to show their games on the newly popular television in 1951, attendance plummeted to 487,000, and to 281,000 in 1952.

In March 1953, with the behind-the-scenes encouragement of the Dodgers' Walter O'Malley and the New York Giants' Horace Stoneham, Lou

Perini moved the club to Milwaukee. They lasted in Milwaukee until 1964, when the club again moved to Atlanta to become the Atlanta Braves. The only thing that remains of the old Boston Braves is their uniform, which, with the city name changed and the Indian chief's head removed from the arm, remains the same.

DUCK AND COVER

★ 1951 ★

At the end of each war the United States had fought, the nation drastically reduced its army and turned all its energies toward individual and national development. The nation had defeated its adversaries — or in the War of 1812, achieved a stalemate — and secured its borders; there was nothing more to fear or to be gained by looking outward.

The end of World War II in 1945 was different.

Europe lay in ruins: cities destroyed, factories in shambles, economies at subsistence level, and populations near starvation. It took the next three years and a massive aid program to rescue Western Europe and restore its economic vitality while at the same time enabling Greece and Turkey to stave off civil wars that threatened to bring in Communist governments. Soviet-occupied Eastern Europe had refused any participation in American aid. Czechoslovakia fell to a Communist coup just as the aid program was beginning.

As that aid program, called the Marshall Plan after George C. Marshall, President Harry S. Truman's secretary of state, was getting under way, the Russian occupation force in its sector of Berlin blockaded the city, denying food and fuel to the residents in the Allied sectors. Again the American government stepped in, launching a massive airlift that supplied the city for nearly a year until the Russians ended the embargo.

There was still no security, though. On September 21, 1949, Mao Tse-tung formally announced that his Red Army had taken control of China and proclaimed the sovereignty of the People's Republic of China. At this unexpected development, cries went up in Congress: Who Lost China?

But all these events were occurring somewhere else. And though vaguely troubled, Americans were busy at home, rebuilding lives interrupted by the war, converting their economy to a peacetime one capable of meeting massive, pent-up consumer demand, and above all creating families and having children, lots of children. The military planners, the diplomats, and the politicians might be greatly concerned with the emergence of a new global threat, but after all, there were still the oceans and thousands of miles between these events and the United States.

And besides, America had a weapon no one else did: the atomic bomb.

Then, on September 23, 1949, President Truman issued a press statement.

> I believe the American people to the fullest extent consistent with the national security are entitled to be informed of all developments in the field of atomic energy. That is my reason for making public the following information.
>
> We have evidence that within recent weeks at atomic explosion occurred in the U.S.S.R.[1]

The *New York Times* article stressed the importance of Truman's announcement, saying that it "ranks only next to his original announcement of the explosion of the first atomic bomb over Hiroshima on Aug. 6, 1945. It marks the end of the first period of the atomic age and the beginning of the second."[2]

If one wanted a date when American international insecurity began, September 23, 1949, would be as good a date as any.

Much of the public was well aware of the atomic bomb and what it could do. John Hersey's *Hiroshima* had been printed in its entirety in an issue of the *New Yorker* magazine two years earlier, read in full over ABC radio, published as a best-selling book, and sent free to the subscribers of the enormously popular Book of the Month Club. Hersey's vivid description of the devastation visited on the Japanese city was graphic and, now, terrifying.

As a response to this Russian development, Truman took two significant steps. First, he ordered the development of the next generation of nuclear weapons, the fusion, or hydrogen, "H-bomb," stepping up what came to be called the arms race. The United States would rely on a massive nuclear weapons stockpile coupled with a strong air force to deliver those weapons and deter Soviet aggression.

Second, to protect the public in case deterrence would not work, he proposed creating the Federal Civil Defense Administration (FCDA) and signed the resulting Federal Civil Defense Act in early 1951. Though the Democrats controlled both houses of Congress, the trend in politics was conservative and opposed to large-scale government programs. Funding for the FCDA was small, forcing it to concentrate on small-scale, privately funded efforts at the family level. For its first years, from 1951 to 1953, Truman requested $1.5 billion; he got $153 million. The same philosophy continued under Dwight D. Eisenhower, who was elected president in 1951. States and cities were left to fund whatever programs they needed.

What the FCDA could do was teach Americans how to create their own civil defense and assure them that surviving a nuclear attack was not only possible but easy. The key was to convince people that nuclear weapons were not qualitatively different from conventional weapons–just bigger.

In March 1951 the FCDA enlisted the help of the Advertising Council, an organization of advertising agencies and major corporate advertisers, to institute a massive public education campaign. Booklets were distributed, a twelve-part series on civilian defense ran in 2,168 newspapers,[3] television networks ran specials scripted by the FCDA, and opinion leaders from scientists to entertainers were enlisted in the effort.

To educate the nation's children, the FCDA hired Archer Productions to produce a film to be shown in schools. The film featured a cartoon character, Bert the Turtle, and a song:

> There was a turtle by the name of Bert
> And Bert the turtle was very alert;
> When danger threatened him he never got hurt
> He knew just what to do.
> He ducked!
> And covered!
> Ducked!
> And covered!

The refrain was repeated throughout the movie as children and adults, seeing a bright flash of light, demonstrated how easy it was to "DUCK AND COVER." A hallway at school would do; under a desk was fine; even a roadside curb would work in a pinch. The nine-minute movie was followed by class lessons on civil defense and later by surprise drills. It is significant, however, that the film largely shows suburban and rural scenes and almost entirely white adults and children.

When President Eisenhower took office, he appointed Val Peterson, former governor of Nebraska, as the head of the FCDA. Peterson continued the relationship with the Advertising Council and eventually wove in a series of federally sponsored annual civil defense rehearsals for an attack.

Called Operation Alert, these events began in 1954 and included simulated nuclear attacks on the nation's cities and practice of disaster plans.

Events, though, were putting real stress on civil defense plans. The American effort to develop an H-bomb had paid off, demonstrated by the test of the first one on November 1, 1952. That explosion on the Pacific island of Elugelab in the Marshall Islands was an enormous success. The ball of fire created rose five miles into the sky; Elugelab burned, broke in two, and sank. A mile-long, 175-foot-deep crater had been gouged in the ocean floor.

The report on the test leaked out the following year. One of the results reported was that the H-bomb's "four-mile wide fireball would have vaporized all of downtown Spokane or San Francisco, most of St. Louis or Pittsburgh, or everything in Manhattan from Central Park to Washington Square."[4] Once again the United States had unquestionable nuclear deterrence.

Not for long. Nine months later, on August 9, 1953, a banner headline in the *New York Times* declared:

MALENKOV CLAIMS THE HYDROGEN BOMB;

DECLARES MONOPOLY OF U.S. IS BROKEN;

LEADERS IN WASHINGTON ARE SKEPTICAL

But it was true, and the development exposed the inherent contradictions in America's civil defense policies.

First, offensive technology was greatly outpacing any developments in civil defense. In 1952 the FCDA had estimated that only 4 million people would die from a nuclear attack. Nearly double that number would be injured, but those could easily be cared for by local and state volunteers. Recovery from any attack would take just two weeks. Now, one year later, the FCDA listed forty-two cities as "critical target areas," and the only real defense, as Val Peterson testified in Congress and repeated in speeches across the nation, was for people "not to be there."[5]

Second, evacuation of the nation's forty-two target cities would mean getting 62 million people out before an attack. Though Peterson told a civil defense conference that evacuation was easy—after all, "New Yorkers and Chicagoans were already seasoned evacuees by virtue of their daily retreat from city to suburb"—such a movement of people took time that missiles and jet bombers did not allow and condemned city dwellers to death.[6]

Third, the home bomb shelters that had been built were shelters against a bomb's blast, not against nuclear fallout. Only in 1956 did the FCDA provide bomb shelter plans that included radiation defenses.

Fourth, no one was listening anyway. Since 1951 the Survey Research Center at the Institute for Social Research had conducted an annual survey of public attitudes on civil defense. Its fourth such survey, published in 1954, reported some surprising data. To the question, "How likely do you think it is that we're in for another world war?" respondents who thought World War III was either certain or probable were 47 percent of those polled, down 6 percent from 1952's survey. Another 9 percent in both years thought World War III was a fifty-fifty proposition. Yet 24 percent of those polled were apathetic toward civil defense, and another 34 percent did not know anything about it.[7]

When the survey asked, "Is there anything in particular you have already done for your own (or your family's) safety in case of an atom bomb attack?" 71 percent said they had done nothing, and another 22 percent said that they had gotten no information on the subject. Only 1 percent had fixed some kind of a shelter area.[8]

Even before the survey was published, government officials were worried. Val Peterson proposed that the FCDA needed to "scare the American people out of their indifference" and make them take civil defense seriously. Robert Cutler, Eisenhower's special assistant for national security affairs, argued that Peterson was right. Eisenhower got angry and categorically rejected scare tactics as a marketing technique.[9]

Gradually the civil defense effort dwindled into lip service. In September 1954 the FCDA was transferred from Washington, DC, to Battle Creek, Michigan, and many of its seasoned employees refused to move. Civil defense was not only out of mind, it was now out of sight.

OLD SOLDIERS NEVER DIE; THEY JUST FADE AWAY

★ 1951 ★

Five years after the end of World War II, General Douglas MacArthur had every right to feel superior, even omnipotent. He had amassed an unparalleled series of military victories, fighting in two world wars and on three continents. His military success, though, was now nearly equaled by his achievements as de facto ruler of Japan. The Japanese people revered him, and he had won that reverence by leading a complete transformation of Japanese society. He had written their constitution, introduced democracy and women's rights, forced the economy into a reasonable semblance of competitive capitalism, and led the occupation with a very light hand. Having lived in the Philippines and having fought the Japanese, MacArthur believed that he alone understood the Asian mind.

The Asian-Pacific world in 1950 was not a quiet place, but trouble did not come in the obvious spots. It came in Korea, between two governments that were almost a historical accident. Korea had been annexed by Japan in 1910 and invaded in the last days of World War II by the Russians, who had managed to occupy Seoul. When American troops arrived after the Japanese surrender, the Russians moved their forces back across the thirty-eighth parallel. A division had to be made between the two armies, thus setting up two separate governments, and the thirty-eighth parallel became the border between North Korea and South Korea. The Russians established the Democratic People's Republic of Korea, led by its newly installed premier Kim Il Sung, a major in the Red Army. The Americans established the Republic of Korea with its capital in Seoul, led by its newly elected president, Syngman Rhee. Neither the Russians nor the Americans recognized the others' client government.

And all was quiet, or what passed for quiet in those tumultuous days. The United Nations was charged with monitoring the uneasy situation, which to all expectations would last indefinitely.

On June 24, 1950, the North Korean army attacked in force across the thirty-eighth parallel. President Harry S. Truman had just arrived in Independence, Missouri, for a weekend with his family. MacArthur was with his family in Tokyo. When Truman was notified of the invasion, his first thought was that this could well be the outbreak of World War III. By the time Truman flew back to Washington the next day, Seoul was about to fall and the South Korean army was retreating on all fronts.

At a meeting of his senior advisers and cabinet members, Truman ordered several immediate steps, among them that MacArthur send ammunition and supplies to the South Korean army; that American civilians be evacuated under the cover of United States planes from Japan; and that the Seventh Fleet sail from the Philippines to the Formosa Strait to prevent any Chinese attack.

That same day the United Nations, at the urging of the United States, called an emergency session of the Security Council and voted 9–0 to condemn the aggression. A second resolution, drafted by the United States, called on all United Nations members to give assistance, including military assistance, to the Republic of Korea. That resolution was passed 7–1. Ironically, the Russians who could have vetoed both resolutions were absent, boycotting the Security Council over its refusal to seat Communist China as a permanent member.

MacArthur, who had initially downplayed the significance of the North Korean attack, believed that the South Koreans would hold and that only a few small ships were needed to evacuate Americans who wanted to leave. However, as soon as he was named commander in chief, Far East, and told to provide support to the defenders, MacArthur became pessimistic, predicting a collapse at any moment.

There was reason for this assessment. The North Koreans surged forward against the outgunned and outnumbered South Koreans and Americans fighting in tropical heat and intense rain. Casualties ran upward of 30 percent. It was not until the first week of August that the defenders, with support from rapidly arriving British, French, Turkish, Dutch, and Filipino troops, as well as tanks, supplies, and ammunition, established and held a perimeter. The line, a 145-mile arc around the port of Pusan, was the scene of fierce fighting throughout August and September, and it looked as if an evacuation was only a matter of time.

MacArthur constantly threatened to use Chinese troops from Formosa either to assist in Korea or to open a second front against the Chinese Communists. In mid-August Truman sent Averell Harriman, his national security adviser, to Tokyo to make it clear that there was to be no widening of the war. Harriman reported back that MacArthur understood and accepted the limit. Still, a few days later MacArthur sent a speech to be read at the Veterans of Foreign Wars convention in which he promoted the use of Formosa as a base of operations not only in Korea but in the rest of Asia. Though MacArthur was forced to withdraw the speech, it was too late; the full text was printed in at least two national magazines.

Now, for the first time, Truman considered removing MacArthur from command. The man seemed either unwilling to accept the president's limits or incapable of doing so.

However, MacArthur had a plan—a risky and daring plan that made the Joint Chiefs of Staff extremely nervous. He wanted to take troops from the Pusan perimeter and use them to make an amphibious landing behind enemy lines at Inchon. The plan was daring because it split MacArthur's forces, always a dangerous maneuver. It was risky because Inchon, with its strong currents and extremely high tides, had no beaches and could be easily defended from both the land and the sea.

MacArthur, in a hurried meeting with two members of the Joint Chiefs in Tokyo, got his way, in part because he persuaded them in a compelling thirty-minute presentation and in part because Truman himself, when he had been briefed on the plan, thought it was brilliant.

And so on September 15, 1950, with MacArthur on the command ship, 262 ships and 70,000 men invaded Inchon. The results were all that MacArthur had promised. Inchon fell in less than two full days, defeating more than 30,000 defenders at a cost of 536 dead, 2,550 wounded, and 65 missing. Within eleven days Seoul was retaken, and General Walton Walker's Eighth Army had broken out of the Pusan perimeter and moved rapidly northward. By late September, more than half the North Korean army was caught between the two forces. Those who did not surrender fled north without their weapons. By October 1 the United Nations forces were at the thirty-eighth parallel, where it had all begun.

But there were ominous signs amid the triumph. Preparations for modern jet aircraft—which the North Koreans did not have—were discovered outside Inchon, suggesting that the Chinese might be preparing to intervene. MacArthur's head of intelligence dismissed the idea. Chou En-lai, Communist China's foreign minister, using diplomatic channels, warned that China would come in to assist its ally if the United Nations troops crossed the thirty-eighth parallel. This warning too was dismissed as a bluff both in Tokyo and in Washington. When the United Nations voted to pursue the unification of Korea, Chou specifically broadcast that China's security was being threatened.

MacArthur asked for orders allowing him to move into North Korea. Both the United Nations and Washington agreed to let him, in effect, unify Korea, but with two conditions: he could not send planes into Chinese or Russian airspace, and only South Korean troops could be used near the Yalu River, the border between China and Korea.

South Korean troops moved across the thirty-eighth parallel on October 1, and the American Eighth Army followed on October 9. What they did not know was that Chinese troops were already moving across the Korean border. Indeed, MacArthur told Truman there was nothing to fear from the Chinese.

Had they intervened in the first or second months, it would have been decisive. We are no longer fearful of their intervention. . . . The Chinese have only 50,000 or 60,000 troops across the Yalu River. They have no air force. Now that we have bases for our Air Force in Korea, if the Chinese tried to get down to Pyongyang there would be the greatest slaughter.[1]

And for a while it seemed that MacArthur, as usual, was right. After capturing Pyonyang, MacArthur said publicly that the war was nearly over, and against explicit instructions, he sent United States troops in a split movement north into areas bordering both China and Russia. The Joint Chiefs of Staff asked for an explanation, but he brushed them off.

On November 28 the Chinese attacked with a force of 260,000, and the United Nations forces were suddenly in desperate straits. MacArthur's mood changed drastically. He called for heavy reinforcements, including forces from Formosa, a naval blockade of China, and permission to bomb the Chinese mainland. "The command . . . is now faced with conditions beyond its control and its strength."[2]

Truman refused all his demands. The retreats of both the United States Tenth Corps and the Eighth Army were heroic and successful despite sub-zero weather and extremely hard fighting, with the Chinese attacking in what were called "human waves." In Washington, Truman's civilian and military advisers both worried openly about MacArthur's deteriorating morale and his questionable strategy. Truman again considered relieving his commander but decided against it, for it would seem that he had turned against MacArthur for a single mistake.

For his part, MacArthur began to speak of his movement north toward the Chinese and Russian borders as a reconnaissance in force that had, in fact, disrupted the Chinese plans for a spring invasion. He attacked the press for aiding and abetting unpatriotic elements at home and enemies abroad. He published letters in United States newspapers and magazines, never admitting error and always finding blame elsewhere. Truman was furious. "Every second lieutenant knows best what his platoon ought to do. He thinks the higher-ups are just blind when they don't see things his way. But General MacArthur—and rightly too—would have court-martialed any second lieutenant who gave press interviews to express his disagreement."[3]

Then MacArthur's commander of the Eighth Army was killed in a highway accident. He was succeeded by General Matthew Ridgeway, at MacArthur's request and with Truman's enthusiastic endorsement. With the United Nations forces now below the thirty-eighth parallel once again, Ridgeway at first had to continue the retreat. MacArthur kept reporting that the situation continued to worsen, that the troops' morale continued to erode, and that the limitations placed on him jeopardized lives. Ridgeway, however, rejected MacArthur's assertion that four new United States divisions were needed to stem the tide. Truman held fast against MacArthur's attempts to widen the war to the whole of the Asian continent.

The Chinese, though, had exhausted their effort. After Chinese troops seized Seoul on January 4, 1951, Ridgeway's troops finally found a place to hold, and they did. Indeed, by the end of the month the Americans counterattacked and drove the Chinese back across the thirty-eighth parallel, once more recapturing Seoul.

The new victories only gave MacArthur new grounds for pressing on. He sent a new plan to Washington, recommending massive air attacks across the top of North Korea, laying a field of radioactive waste across the enemy's supply lines, and landing troops at the upper end of both coasts of North Korea. In Washington, however, the time had come to seek a cease-fire.

In early March Truman instructed both the State Department and the Pentagon to draft a cease-fire proposal that was sent for review to all the seventeen other nations in the United Nations coalition. A copy of the most important parts was sent to MacArthur as well. MacArthur's next move was to openly issue his own proclamation, an ultimatum that the Chinese should either settle the dispute in meetings with him or face certain defeat. His statement issued from Tokyo on March 24, 1951, read in part:

> The enemy, therefore, must by now be painfully aware that a decision of the United Nations to depart from its tolerant effort to contain the war to the areas of Korea, through an expansion of our military operations to his coastal areas and interior bases, would doom Red China to the risk of imminent military collapse.

He ended:

> I stand ready at any time to confer in the field with the commander in chief of the enemy forces in an earnest effort to find any military means whereby the realization of the political objectives of the United Nations in Korea, to which no nation may justly take exceptions, might be accomplished without further bloodshed.[4]

MacArthur's action was unilateral, inexplicable, unexpected, and openly insulting, and it undercut any cease-fire attempt. It was also contrary to his direct instructions, contrary to the facts in the field, and insubordinate. It could not be ignored.

While Truman, his cabinet, and the Joint Chiefs tried to decide not what to do, but how and when to do it, MacArthur continued his unilateral effort. A conservative magazine quoted him as saying that political decisions had led to a failure to recruit more South Koreans into their army, when in fact he himself had made that decision. A London newspaper quoted MacArthur as saying that the politicians were preventing him from winning the war. And a leading Republican congressman stood up in the House to read a letter from MacArthur saying that the Chinese Nationalists should be allowed to attack mainland China.

On April 6, 1951, Truman instructed the Joint Chiefs to come to a decision on MacArthur; the next day they unanimously agreed that he had to be dismissed because "the military must be controlled by civilian authority in this country."[5] That same day, Truman told his cabinet that he had come to the same decision a few days earlier.

Orders were cut relieving MacArthur of all his commands. Though Truman had wanted to spare MacArthur any public embarrassment and to inform him privately through emissaries, a series of communications failures and leaks meant that the general learned of his firing only when he was given a Signal Corps envelope containing a radio news report. In Washington, Truman issued a statement announcing his decision that began:

> With deep regret I have concluded that General of the Army Douglas MacArthur is unable to give his wholehearted support to the policies of the United States Government and of the United Nations in matters pertaining to his official duties.
>
> In view of the specific responsibilities imposed upon me by the Constitution of the United States and the added responsibility which has been entrusted to me by the United Nations, I have decided that I must make a change of command in the Far East.[6]

It was not an easy move politically on Truman's part. His own approval rating in the Gallup poll was reaching its all-time low of 26 percent. National elections were looming in November, and the Republicans seemed likely to regain control of Congress for the first time in twenty years. Although a consummate politician, Truman felt strongly that, in challenging him, MacArthur was challenging the constitution itself.

Immediately the Republicans, with Democratic consent, invited MacArthur to address a joint session of Congress. They also announced that there would be a congressional investigation of the conduct of the war and that they were considering impeachment hearings on a number of administration officials, including the president.

For once, though, MacArthur was silent. He left Tokyo on Monday, April 16. The Japanese were crushed to lose a man they revered; the Europeans were ecstatic to lose the man they feared would start the next world war. The American public was split in its response, but General Dwight D. Eisenhower, now president of Columbia University, defended the president's action. Most newspapers, even some of the more conservative, endorsed the action as well. Significantly, a Gallup poll found that, though 69 percent of those polled supported MacArthur, only 30 percent were ready to fight in China.[7]

Arriving first in Hawaii, then in California, and last in Washington, MacArthur was everywhere greeted by huge crowds. He arrived at the House of Representatives to speak on April 19 and entered to a standing ovation. Conspicuously absent were the president, his cabinet, and the Supreme Court justices. Conspicuously present were 30 million television viewers and millions more radio listeners. The moment was electrifying, and rhetorically the speech was riveting. MacArthur was interrupted by applause and cheers thirty times in his thirty-four-minute speech. But the speech was characteristically self-justifying, admitting no errors, conceding no ground, embracing the Joint Chiefs, who he said fully supported him, and blaming only the blind politicians who thought they were in charge.

And finally winding up, MacArthur brought tears to the eyes of many:

> I am closing my 52 years of military service. When I joined the Army, even before the turn of the century, it was the fulfillment of all of my boyish hopes and dreams. The world has turned over many times since I took the oath on the plain at West Point, and the hopes and dreams have long since vanished, but I still remember the refrain of one of the most popular barrack ballads of that day which proclaimed most proudly that **"OLD SOLDIERS NEVER DIE; THEY JUST FADE AWAY."**
>
> And like the old soldier of that ballad, I now close my military career and just fade away, an old soldier who tried to do his duty as God gave him the light to see that duty.
>
> Good Bye.[8]

So great was the emotion in the room at the close that Republican congressman Dewey Short of Missouri, a former minister, exclaimed, "We heard God speak here today. God in the flesh, the voice of God!"[9]

Truman was not impressed. After reading the speech later that day, he said he thought it "a bunch of bullshit." [10]

There were more huge parades in Washington and in New York City, but this moment in Congress was MacArthur's public high point and, indeed, the beginning of his long fade. The congressional hearing petered out once he displayed his lack of concern with any larger significance of his war plans and once the members of the Joint Chiefs testified that they did not approve of his plans, his public statements, or his challenge to presidential authority. MacArthur's popularity began dropping, the crowds got smaller, and his brief presidential aspirations came to naught.

He lived on in New York City, patiently listened to and then ignored by Presidents Eisenhower and Kennedy. He died on April 5, 1964.

THREE YARDS AND
A CLOUD OF DUST

★ 1957 ★

In the last decades of the nineteenth century, the growth of the cities and of business engendered a rising worry in the middle and upper classes about the loss of "the manly virtues." City life and business life were, it was believed, eroding the very qualities that had enabled the nation to be formed and mature against all odds.

In 1886 Theodore Roosevelt, having recently returned from his cattle ranching in North Dakota and having just lost a bid to become mayor of New York City, wrote that there was, in the land, a "general tendency among people of culture and education . . . to neglect and even look down upon the rougher and manlier virtues, so that an advanced state of intellectual development is too often associated with a certain effeminacy of character." [1] His concerns were echoed by historians, civic leaders, academics, and clerics.

One result of this concern for the nation's manliness was the development of football, a game consciously used to toughen the future leaders of the nation, to build manly character, and to transform the image and reality of America's secular colleges. Baseball was already fabulously popular, but from the beginning it was largely a working-class sport, played by artisans and clerks, and had a raffish image. Football was quickly to become *the* college sport.

Though football in a primitive form had been present at some colleges as a freshman hazing rite, and though the first intercollegiate game was played between Princeton and Rutgers in 1869, the game took on its importance to colleges and the nation only with the stress laid on it by Yale and by its true founder, Walter Camp.

Camp was an undergraduate at Yale from 1876 to 1882 and a fervent member of the Yale football team. After graduating, he stayed at Yale to study medicine and continued to play on the Yale team. No rule forbade graduate students or even faculty members from playing. He stayed on as an informal coach and athletic director even after he joined the New Haven Clock Company and rose to become the company's president and chairman of the board.

All during this time, Camp was laying down the rules of play: limiting the number of players on the field and establishing how the game would be played and scored. He continued to revise his rules until he died in 1928; not only were they accepted by all colleges, but Camp himself acted as adviser to many colleges besides his alma mater. Yale, though, was the powerhouse: from 1883 to 1898 the team had nine undefeated seasons, and in the three seasons from 1891 through 1893 the team scored at will while shutting out its opponents completely.[2]

It was Camp's system of team organization—of coaching coordinated team play, designing plays that were called at the line of scrimmage, and insisting on the subordination of the individual to the team—that became the envy and model of everyone else. Camp was also quick to see the relation of the lessons learned on the gridiron to those needed in later life.

> Finding a weak spot through which a play can be made, feeling out the line with experimental attempts, concealing the real strength till everything is ripe for the big push, then letting drive where least expected, what is this—an outline of football or business tactics? Both, of course.[3]

Others saw different lessons, no less important, in football's social mission—lessons that tied football to warfare:

> And they are but shining examples
> Of the lads we all love and admire,
> Ready with muscles of iron

For the scrimmage of blood and fire;
Ready to tackle the foeman
Alike upon land and on sea,
Columbia, these are thy jewels,
Thy heroes of battles to be![4]

By the 1890s football had become the rage on campus and in college life. The annual Big Game was created. There was the original Big Game between Yale and Harvard, but now Stanford and the University of California played for the "Axe," the Universities of Minnesota and Michigan vied for the "Little Brown Jug," and Purdue met Indiana in the contest for the "Old Oaken Bucket." These and other Big Games determined each team's success or failure for the whole season, regardless of their won-loss record.

As the popularity of college football soared, the football team became crucial as a moneymaker for the colleges and for fund-raising among alumni. By 1900 Yale's annual revenue from football reached $100,000, one-eighth of the school's total income. The alumni, being called on for donations, began demanding a successful team, one they could support and take pride in. Faculties and college presidents began to worry about the increasing importance of the sport.

The stress on producing a winning team inevitably meant hiring full-time professional coaches. Harvard, tired of being trounced by Yale every year, finally did so in 1905. Others followed until every college in the country had one and paid him well—as long as his team won. A study by the Carnegie Commission in 1929 revealed that the average full professor earned $5,000; the average head football coach made 20 percent more. On the other hand, college professors tended to stay in their jobs; head football coaches had a median tenure of three years.[5]

It was during these formative years of the game that Wayne Woodrow Hayes was born in a little town in Ohio. Known then and later as Woody, he was an enthusiastic athlete, an avid student of military history, and a firm believer in the character-building strict discipline of football. From his beginnings as a high school football coach, Hayes used his fiery temper and people's fear of it to build winning teams, though he also used his love of his players and his insistence on their well-being—as long as they conformed to his ideas—to form strong bonds with those who fit in. And when that happened, his teams won.

Returning from World War II, Hayes took the job of head coach at his alma mater, Denison College, where he began the patterns that would characterize his career. Denison had stopped its football program during the war, and Hayes had to begin anew with a mixture of true freshmen and returning veterans. He decided to use the newfangled T formation instead of the single-wing that was both common and familiar to his players. He also stressed hard, long practices, but his players' mistakes and their slowness in learning the new formation kept him in a near-constant state of rage. The returning veterans on the squad rebelled; one threatened to fight him, the others sullenly ignored him. The season was a failure.

For the 1947 season Woody backed off a bit, and the players grew more comfortable both with their coach and with his system. As he had done successfully at New Philadelphia High School before the war, Hayes used an offense that stressed a straight-ahead running attack, physical dominance of the other team, and as little passing as possible. It worked. Denison went undefeated. They were undefeated again in 1948, and Hayes's reputation as a coach began to grow in football-mad Ohio.

Offered a chance to be head coach at Miami University of Ohio, a school five times the size of Denison and far more committed to football, Hayes left Denison without notice to succeed a popular coach who ran a wide-open offense stressing speed, open-field running, and passing.

Within the first week of football practice, Hayes had alienated his team. The practices not only were long and hard, they were always in full pads with full-speed contact, and no breaks or water were allowed. Rather than forgetting their previous coach as Woody had expected, the team longed for him. Once again Hayes's first season was a failure, though Miami did win more games than it lost—barely.

Again Woody had to relent—a bit. For the 1950 season he began to use passes a little more, though still at only half the rate of his predecessor. Once again the players who survived and returned learned to adapt to his ways. This year the team lost only one game and went to the deliciously named Salad Bowl in Phoenix, where Miami beat Arizona State handily. Once again Hayes's reputation grew in Ohio and even nationally.

And once again Woody took a new job, leaving Miami for the most prestigious and most pressured job in Ohio, head coach at Ohio State University.

That football was wildly popular at OSU, no one doubted. More fans had come to see the annual Big Game—OSU versus Michigan—in a blinding blizzard than had attended the professional Cleveland Browns team playing in the conference championship game and in the league championship game—combined. That OSU was a hothouse that demanded winning against Michigan was also doubted by no one. The fans had driven out the previous coach for his "mediocre" four-year record of 21–13–2; Hayes would be the school's fifth coach in a decade.

Woody faced an irate and skeptical city and a team that included Vic Janowicz, the previous year's Heisman trophy winner, around whom the offense had been built. The first year was, as always, a torment for the team and for their coach. As he had at his last two jobs, Hayes disappeared from his family for six or seven months to work sixteen hours a day. Practices were run with Woody's usual rages and demands for full pads and full contact in Ohio's summer heat. Morale crashed; Janowicz's place in the offense was drastically reduced, and the players rebelled, even locking Hayes out of the locker room before one of the games. The season ended with OSU's record at 4–3–2, including a shut-out loss to Michigan.

Things improved a bit in the 1952 and 1953 seasons, but just a bit, as the Buckeyes went 6–3 in both years. They did, however, beat Michigan once in that period.

During this period, as Hayes wrote in 1957, his philosophy of football strategy was put in place for good.

> A well-coached and well-manned running attack is the most consistent fact in football. We use the word "consistency" to denote the success of a play, for a "consistent" play is one which has gained at least three yards. If each play gains three yards, it is almost a mathematical certainty that at least one of the three plays will gain considerably more than three yards so that possession of the ball is the net result.
>
> It is a fallacy to believe that we can "three-yard" a good team the length of the field and score consistently, for some misfortune usually will befall us before we cross the goal line. However, it is an even greater fallacy to assume that the above described offense is simply a dull, "three-yard" offense, for this is definitely not true. This style of attack puts such great pressure on the defense that eventually the defense over-commits itself up front and a long run or a well-placed pass results in a score.[6]

With the recruitment of players who could and would deal with Hayes's anger and his stringent demands—most notably at this point the superb running back Howard "Hopalong" Cassady—OSU began to roll. The 1954 team not only saved Hayes's job, it silenced his critics and his home telephone. The team went undefeated, beat Michigan, went to the Rose Bowl, where it beat USC, and was named national champion by the Associated Press.

From then on Ohio State and Woody Hayes were major forces in the world of football. His "theory of consistency" became known in the press as **"THREE YARDS AND A CLOUD OF DUST"** and was either derided as boring or lauded as triumphant, but it was always there, to be as feared by opponents as Woody often was feared by his players.

Within a year of the appearance of his book on his football theories, reporters were asking him about his "three yards and a cloud of dust" offense, and one noted that Murray Warmath, coach of the University of Minnesota football team, had called it Hayes's "three yards through concrete offense."[7]

Yet what this "theory of consistency" actually signified and what Hayes achieved so well was what football coaches—hired, paid, and retained for winning—had striven for since the days of Walter Camp: control. Players came and went, and the coaches had to remain generals, controlling the players and the flow of the game in ways that baseball managers could not and cannot do. Baseball is a sport of individuals who play on a team; the action is always and essentially one-on-one. There is little a manager can do to control the flight of the pitch or the swing of the bat.

Football is a sport of teams that individuals play on. It is a sport of mass formations, and the action is essentially a group action in which individuals can momentarily stand out. Here the coach can act as the controller, demand perfection of execution, call the plays, and achieve what has come to be called his "system." Hayes did not invent this style of coaching, but he did become its embodiment at a time when football's popularity began to surpass that of the American "national game."

ICH BIN EIN BERLINER

★ 1963 ★

The end of World War II did not bring a peace treaty with Germany. It brought an armistice; the peace treaty would come later. Germany was divided into four zones, each governed by one of the occupying powers: the United States, Great Britain, France, and the USSR. Berlin, the capital of the defeated nation, though deep in the Russian zone, was itself split into four similar zones with guaranteed land, canal, and air routes to each of the Western zones.

As a short-term measure, it was the best the Western powers could get, given that the Russians had conquered the city and the surrounding territory. As a longer-term measure, it was nothing but trouble.

The first major sign of that trouble came in 1948 when the Russians stopped all road access to Berlin, blockading the city and preventing both food and fuel from getting to the population. Only a constant airlift of supplies for more than a year, an airlift ordered by President Harry S. Truman even though it risked another global war, preserved both the citizens and the rights of the Western powers.

For the next decade Berlin was a site of constant Russian attempts to erode the freedoms of the West Berliners and the rights of their nominal occupiers. It was also the place where millions of East Germans, now with their own Soviet-bloc German Democratic Republic, could and did flee from their increasingly oppressive government. A massive East German workers' revolt in 1953, the first in a Soviet-bloc country, was violently put down by GDR and Russian troops.

The situation in Berlin remained both fragile and unchanged until the Russian premier Nikita Khrushchev announced on November 10, 1958, that it was long past time for a peace treaty to be signed. That treaty would recognize the division between East and West Germany as permanent and require the Western powers to leave Berlin immediately. He gave the West six months to accept the offer, after which Russia would alone sign a treaty and the East German government would become sovereign over all its territory. The access routes to Berlin would, sooner or later, be closed.

The West held firm, Khrushchev backed down, and the number of people fleeing the German Democratic Republic increased.

Soon after his inauguration in January 1961, President John F. Kennedy sent former secretary of state Dean Acheson to Europe to prepare a report on Berlin. In April Acheson reported back, saying that a crisis was imminent—

> that the allies were divided, the neutrals unhelpful, that the West was unprepared to counter effectively any Soviet interruption of access, and that West Berlin's importance might require us to use all-out force to maintain three basic American objectives: (1) the freedom of the people of West Berlin to choose their own system; (2) the presence of Western troops as long as the people required and desired them; and (3) uninterrupted access from the West across the East German Autobahn, air lanes, and canals.[1]

A summit meeting between Kennedy and Khrushchev was set to take place in Vienna in June. Kennedy was not in a strong position, for he was new to the job, inexperienced in foreign affairs, and fresh from the disaster of the Bay of Pigs invasion of Cuba. Khrushchev had his own problems, particularly with the increasingly independent Chinese, who were demanding a more aggressive approach in spreading communism around the world.

Still, the two needed to meet, Kennedy felt, so that they could personally work on a number of critical issues: the status of Laos in Southeast Asia, disarmament, the Russian desire to replace the secretary general of the United Nations, the German peace treaty, and Berlin. The night before the summit was to begin, June 3, 1961, Khrushchev told Kennedy that Berlin was high on his agenda. "The main problem is a peace treaty. If the United States refuses to sign it, the Soviet Union will do so and nothing would stop it." [2]

The next day, Khrushchev and Kennedy spent time by themselves. The Russian leader was bellicose, openly angry and threatening. He repeated his demand for a treaty and for East German sovereignty over all access routes to Berlin. If the United States wanted a war, he said, Russia would oblige.

Though no decisions on any of the issues were made, and though the talks were characterized publicly as "frank and courteous," Kennedy was shaken.

Back in Washington, his unease did not abate. A review of the diplomatic situation yielded no new options for him to propose. Worse, a review of the military contingency plans and state of readiness revealed that the United States had no real ability to counter combined GDR-USSR aggression except by starting a nuclear war. He told an aide, "We go immediately from a rather small military action to one where nuclear weapons are exchanged, which of course means . . . we are also destroying this country." [3]

A number of immediate actions were taken. The draft calls were greatly increased, Congress authorized mobilizing up to 250,000 men from the Reserves and National Guard; new air units were sent overseas; and a supplemental defense budget was approved. The United States was alone, however. The French were opposed to any negotiations; the British would not risk war without them, and the West Germans were opposed to both options.

On July 25, 1961, Kennedy addressed the nation on television, outlining the situation, stressing the United States' willingness to talk about the problems, but restating the position that the freedom of Berlin was "not negotiable."

> We cannot and will not permit the Communists to drive us out of Berlin, either gradually or by force. For the fulfillment of our pledge to that city is essential to the morale and security of Western Germany, to the unity of Western Europe, and to the faith of the entire free world.[4]

He also offered to put the status of Berlin to a vote of the city's citizens.

The fact was that a vote had been taking place for years, and the Russians were well aware of it. In the ten years from the end of the Berlin Blockade to 1958, more than 3 million East Germans and East Berliners had moved west, badly damaging the East German economy. Getting to the West was relatively easy. Most just traveled to Berlin and took a subway or train a few stops.

As people sensed that a crisis was coming, the East Germans' movement west increased. In February 1961 more than 13,000 had left, a 38 percent increase from the same month in 1960. In March more than 16,000 fled; in April, nearly 20,000. By July the number had increased to more than 30,000; in the first week in August, it was some 12,000.

The GDR government was both furious and terrified. Its leader, Walter Ulbricht, flew to Moscow in early August with a plan to stop the outflow. After some worried discussion and a quick trip home to check the readiness of his troops and the availability of supplies, he got permission. He would move at midnight, the night of Saturday, August 12.

Everyone knew of Ulbricht's absence, and rumors flew about what he would do. The flight from the East intensified, flooding the refugee center in West Berlin.

Ulbricht's plan, though, was a complete surprise, astonishing in a city filled with spies. At midnight the usually regular trains became erratic and then stopped. The subways too. At 2:00 a.m. Sunday, soldiers and policemen were seen rushing to install fence posts and barbed wire across the Brandenberg Gate. A new decree announced that the GDR was now assuming the border controls throughout the country and the "borders of the western sectors of Greater Berlin." The decree, though, carefully avoided any interference with the rights and powers of the western powers.[5]

By midday Sunday the closure was complete, and there was little anyone could do about it short of risking outright war. Soviet troops and tanks, known to be in the city, were carefully kept out of sight. Crowds from both sides came to see what had happened, to try last-minute escapes, to wave at friends and families, and to throw stones. They were dispersed by police in the West and by soldiers in the East. The Western powers were slow to react, their leaders on summer vacations. And when they did react, they sent protest notes that barely covered up their relief that the crisis had come and was not as threatening—to them—as it might have been.

In Berlin, however, the feeling of betrayal and abandonment grew hourly. The mayor of West Berlin, Willy Brandt, called a mass meeting of his citizens for Wednesday, August 16. A quarter of a million people came to stand in the rain, carrying signs like Betrayed by the West and The West Is Doing a Second Munich.[6] The *New York Times* reported that a group of students had sent Kennedy a note and a black umbrella. The note read: "We are sorry to say, Mr. President, that because of your reserved reaction to the happenings in Berlin you have at the moment become the most worthy possessor of this symbol of a fatal policy."[7] And in case the *Times* readers did not catch the reference, the article concluded, "The umbrella carried by the British Prime Minister, Neville Chamberlain, became known as a symbol of appeasement after his 1938 meeting in Munich with Hitler."

As he announced at the mass meeting, Brandt had sent a letter directly to Kennedy. The letter, and the confirmation of its contents by Edward R. Murrow, then head of the U.S. Information Agency, convinced Kennedy that some action had to be taken to reassure the Berliners. He ordered a convoy of 1,500 troops sent to the city immediately and sent both Vice President Lyndon B. Johnson and General Lucius Clay as his personal emissaries.

Johnson and Clay arrived on August 19, 1961. For the Germans, Clay was the most impressive sign of United States resolve, since he had commanded the city during the Berlin Blockade. The troop convoy arrived the following day in 350 vehicles and was met by a crowd of one million cheering Berliners.

Tensions abated somewhat, though the barbed wire was quickly replaced by concrete blocks and by lines of fortifications two and three deep, complete with antitank defenses. Escapes continued and would, in fact, never be entirely halted, but they became more and more dangerous and fewer.

Over the next twelve months, morale in the city improved. The wall eventually extended twenty-nine miles, rising nine to twelve feet high. Western resolve continued to be tested in mostly minor ways, but the East Germans became more irritating than threatening.

Meanwhile Kennedy waited for the "real" Soviet-induced crisis in Berlin. It came, though not in Berlin but in Cuba, with a crisis over Russian missiles during two weeks of October 1962. This time Kennedy, smarter about international affairs and more experienced in dealing with them, acted swiftly and successfully.

In the spring of 1963 Berliners were tiring of the siege and anxious about Western commitment, since attention had gone elsewhere—to the Caribbean and to Southeast Asia. This time President Kennedy, warned that Berlin was in danger of losing all confidence in America and its commitment to the city, came to the city himself.

He landed in Berlin on June 15, 1963, and was met by three-quarters of the population, who lined the streets.[8] He went first to the Berlin Wall, where a small crowd of East Berliners waved to him from the other side, then walked through crowds at the Brandenburg Gate, where the East Germans had hung massive red curtains to prevent him from seeing their part of the city.

Then Kennedy mounted the platform set up in the Rudoph Wilde Platz to speak to the crowd, estimated to be more than one million Berliners. As *Times* reporter Tom Wicker reported, "There seemed no doubt that Mr. Kennedy was moved by the greeting of the West Berliners. In the Rudolph Wilde Plaza he spoke with a passion he has seldom displayed."[9]

It was a short speech, but one of Kennedy's best.

There are many people in the world who really don't understand, or say they don't, what is the great issue between the free world and the Communist world. Let them come to Berlin.

There are some who say that communism is the wave of the future. Let them come to Berlin.

And there are some who say in Europe and elsewhere we can work with the Communists. Let them come to Berlin.

And there are even a few who say that it is true that communism is an evil system, but it permits us to make economic progress. Lass' sie nach Berlin kommen. Let them come to Berlin.

And he ended,

All free men, wherever they may live, are citizens of Berlin, and, therefore, as a free man, I take pride in the words **"ICH BIN EIN BERLINER."**[10]

The applause and the cheers lasted twenty minutes—twice as long as the speech itself.

I HAVE A DREAM

★ 1963 ★

The 1963 March on Washington began when police used dogs and high-powered fire hoses on children in Birmingham. The march began with Rosa Parks's refusal to sit in the back of the bus in Montgomery. It began with the Supreme Court decision outlawing school segregation. It began with decades of lynching, decades of separate water fountains, decades of shootings, bombings, and Ku Klux Klan terrorism. It began with decades of poor schools, poor jobs, poor housing, and daily humiliations throughout the nation. It began when Abraham Lincoln's Emancipation Proclamation became effective on January 1, 1863, but never really did.

The 1955 Supreme Court decision outlawing school segregation was first enforced only with the assistance of federal troops in 1957 at Central High School in Little Rock, Arkansas. Four months later a fourteen-year-old from Chicago, Emmett Till, was lynched in Mississippi. Three months after that, Rosa Parks refused to move, and the Reverend Martin Luther King Jr. led a bus boycott in Montgomery. The pace of what came to be called the civil rights movement picked up slowly—and then rapidly.

Each attempt to register voters, to integrate schools and public facilities, to get a meal at a lunch counter, or to sit where one pleased on a bus, in a terminal, in a theater was met with arrests, jail, prison complete with torture, injuries, home burnings, church bombings, and death. And the violence increased at a steady pace.

A. Philip Randolph, a longtime pioneer in the civil rights struggle, the founder and president of the Brotherhood of Sleeping Car Porters and of the Negro American Labor Council, addressed the council at its 1961 annual meeting. His remarks centered on "the slow progress, even the loss of ground, in black achievement since the beginning of the 'revolution.'" More blacks attended segregated schools in 1961 than in 1952; more were unemployed than in 1954, and median black income had dropped from 57 percent of white income to 54 percent.[1] Something had to be done.

Randolph met with Bayard Rustin, the most prominent and experienced political strategist and tactician in the civil rights movement. He asked him to devise a plan for a massive march on Washington to honor the centenary of the Emancipation Proclamation and to demonstrate dramatically the nation's failure to live up to its social and economic promises.

In January 1963 Rustin gave him a plan, and Randolph, clearing it with his Labor Council, sought the support of the other civil rights leaders.

The more activist Congress of Racial Equality led by James Farmer and the Student Nonviolent Coordinating Committee led by John Lewis were quick to join. King, now head of the Southern Christian Leadership Conference, was dubious about joint action and was then heavily involved in demonstrations in Birmingham, Alabama.

In fact, King's work in Birmingham was showing signs of petering out. It was getting harder and harder to recruit adults willing to march and go to jail. The breakthrough came from an unexpected source. James Bevel, who had been brought to the city to lead daily youth meetings for King, proposed using the teenagers who were crowding his meetings. On May 2, 1963, Bevel marched fifty youths two abreast into the police ranks and the waiting police vans. More followed quickly that day until nearly a thousand, some as young as six years old, had been sent to jail.

The next day another thousand young people emerged to march, but this time the Birmingham police, led by Chief Bull Connor, cracked. Police dogs attacked children; fire hoses knocked them off their feet. Not only had a moral victory been won as the photos and television pictures horrified the world, but the civil rights movement captured the news for weeks to come.

King himself now proposed joining Randolph's march, and Randolph renamed his proposed event the "March on Washington for Jobs and Freedom." The National Association for the Advancement of Colored People and the National Urban League quickly joined.

In Washington, President John F. Kennedy too had been shocked by the photos from Birmingham and was pushed to take a stand, one as politically dangerous as it was morally right. On the evening of June 11, 1963, Kennedy went on television to announce that he would present a major civil rights bill to Congress.

> We face a moral crisis as a country and as a people. It cannot be met by repressive police action. It cannot be left to increased demonstrations in the streets. It cannot be quieted by token moves or talk. It is time to act. . . . Those who do nothing are inviting shame as well as violence. Those who act boldly are recognizing right as well as reality.[2]

Kennedy sent his bill to Congress the following week and, at the same time, privately opposed the March on Washington for fear that it would either incite counterproductive violence in the streets or provoke obstinacy in Congress. He met privately with the leaders of the march to persuade them to stop. They told him that they understood his political problems but had their own problems too. The separatist Nation of Islam was pulling them in one direction while those already in the streets—the younger, more militant civil rights organizations—were becoming more and more impatient. The young, now leading the younger, were forcing the adults to catch up. The march had to go on; the date was now firmly set for August 28, 1963, in time, perhaps, to force the pace of congressional action on Kennedy's bill.

With time running short, Rustin and his staff in Harlem, some paid, most volunteer, had a crushing amount of work and endless details to accomplish to accommodate the 100,000 people he hoped to get to Washington. He arranged for 2,000 policemen to be deployed in the city, but he also enlisted a black police sergeant from New York City to train a large number of volunteer parade marshals. He told demonstrators to bring box lunches, but he also arranged to make and sell 80,000 ham-and-cheese sandwiches. Water had to be easily available, as did portable toilets, clinics, ambulances, and first-aid stations. Buses had to have staggered arrival times to reduce the chance of gridlock. The cost of the march quickly outstripped the budget, but the Taconic Foundation came through with enough funds to make up the difference.

By August 24 Rustin's transportation director knew of more than 1,500 arriving buses, twenty-one special trains, and three chartered passenger planes. She told Rustin that the planned-for 100,000 would be at least double that number. Though elated, he told her to keep the information to herself lest expectations get out of hand.

On the outside, though, the mood was not elation but fear. National guardsmen were mobilized to assist the police; 4,000 army troops were moved to stations just outside the city. Newspapers ran scare editorials warning of violence. The bars and liquor stores were ordered closed for the day. People, whether scared of the "invasion" or of the traffic jams, planned to stay home.

Some 1,700 newsmen were sent to cover the march, not counting the normal Washington bureaus. Reporters from around the world had come to see and hear. The television networks planned to broadcast the event live. Kennedy watched too, shuttling between a television set and an urgent top-level meeting on the political situation in South Vietnam, where there were some American troops but little American attention.

At first light on August 28, Rustin went to the Washington Monument, the starting place for the parade to the Lincoln Memorial, where the rally would take place. He expected to see crowds already assembling. To his shock, hardly anyone was there, but Rustin told newsmen that everything was "exactly according to plan."[3]

The police knew he was right. They could see large numbers of cars and buses just outside the city. By 9:30 a.m., some 40,000 people had arrived. By 10:30 their numbers had doubled, and more were coming. A lot more. By the beginning of the march, more than 250,000 people were there.

It took nearly two hours for everyone to march to the Lincoln Memorial. After the singing and the benedictions, Randolph spoke first:

> We are the advance guard of a massive moral revolution for jobs and freedom. . . . Those who deplore our militancy, who exhort patience in the name of a false peace, are in fact supporting segregation and exploitation. They would have social peace at the expense of social and racial justice.[4]

Following Randolph were seven-minute speeches from all the other leaders of the march. Dr. King came last, because Randolph knew his speech would be the most anticipated by the crowd and also because none of the other speakers wanted to go after him.

At last Dr. King took the podium:

> Five score years ago, a great American, in whose symbolic shadow we stand today, signed the Emancipation Proclamation. This momentous decree came as a great beacon light of hope to millions of Negro slaves who had been seared in the flames of withering injustice. It came as a joyous daybreak to end the long night of their captivity.
>
> But one hundred years later, the Negro still is not free. One hundred years later, the life of the Negro is still sadly crippled by the manacles of segregation and the chains of discrimination. One hundred years later, the Negro lives on a lonely island of poverty in the midst of a vast ocean of material prosperity. One hundred years later, the Negro is still languishing in the corners of American society and finds himself an exile in his own land.

He spoke not for his allotted seven minutes, but for nineteen, and the audience before him and at home stayed riveted. He spoke of the nation's default "on this promissory note" on Lincoln's Proclamation and of the need to continue the struggle "on the high plane of dignity and discipline." He spoke of the need for those who heard him to go back to the struggle in the North as well as the South, and above all he spoke of the need for belief "that somehow this situation can and will be changed."

And then he moved into his famous peroration.

> I say to you today, my friends, that in spite of the difficulties and frustrations of the moment, I still have a dream. It is a dream deeply rooted in the American dream.
>
> **I HAVE A DREAM** that one day this nation will rise up and live out the true meaning of its creed: "We hold these truths to be self-evident: that all men are created equal."
>
> I have a dream that one day on the red hills of Georgia the sons of former slaves and the sons of former slave owners will be able to sit down together at the table of brotherhood.

He echoed and reechoed that phrase, moving to the repeated phrase of "Let freedom ring," and finishing his speech with,

> When we allow freedom to ring, when we let it ring from every village and every hamlet, from every state and every city, we will be able to speed up that day when all of God's children, black men and white men, Jews and Gentiles, Protestants and Catholics, will be able to join hands and sing in the words of the old Negro spiritual, "Free at last! Free at last! Thank God almighty, we are free at last!"[5]

For the whites who listened across the nation, it was probably the first time they had ever heard a sermon from a black minister or had learned of the urgency and the glory of the goal.

At 4:30 p.m. the marchers left, singing the anthem of the civil rights movement, "We Shall Overcome." By nightfall they had left the city.

There is an enduring argument over whether the march was effective in any practical way. Kennedy's civil rights bill stayed bottled up in Congress. Passing it took the president's assassination and pressure from the next president, Lyndon Johnson from Texas, a former Confederate state, who successfully took up the torch.

There were decades of struggle to come, decades of legislation, years of unrest, killings, and violence, before the dream could be glimpsed as a real future.

Yet King knew the real meaning of the march and its practical effect before it ever took place. James Farmer later recounted a conversation between King and an angry, and jealous, Roy Wilkins, head of the NAACP:

> Wilkins leaned across the table and said to King, "One of these days, Martin, some bright reporter is going to take a good look at Montgomery and

discover that despite all the hoopla, your boycott didn't desegregate a single city bus. It was the quiet NAACP-type legal action that did it."

"We're fully aware of that, Roy," Martin replied with simple poise. . . .

Roy appeared to ignore the reply and pressed the point. "In fact, Martin, if you have desegregated anything by your efforts kindly enlighten me."

"Well," said Martin, "I guess about the only thing I've desegregated is a few human hearts."[6]

And he had and he did.

FLOAT LIKE A BUTTERFLY, STING LIKE A BEE

★ 1964 ★

Of all the professional sports in the United States, boxing has the oldest pedigree, going back to the ancient Greeks, and probably further. What we think of as boxing, however, began in 1867 with the publication in England of the Marquis of Queensberry rules. These rules eliminated the older forms of boxing, which had no rules, no time limits, no gloves, and no ring except that created by the spectators. Fights ended only when one man could no longer get up. Such barely controlled two-man riots differed little from street fighting and attracted, in the words of one newspaper, a crowd characterized by "rowdyism, villainy and scoundrelism, and boiled-down viciousness, concentrated upon so small a space."[1]

The new rules, mandating the size of the ring, the kinds of gloves to be used, and three-minute rounds with one minute in between, and banning from the ring anyone except the fighters themselves, were gradually adopted in the United States in the 1880s and were first used in a heavyweight championship fight in 1892. This new form of boxing not only cemented the reputation of the most idolized champion of the century, John L. Sullivan, but also became fashionable and respectable both as a spectator sport and among amateur athletics for the nation's elite.

Yet in securing a place for prizefighting among the nation's popular entertainments, Sullivan also ensured that it would be a segregated sport: "I will not fight a Negro," he declared, and his successors agreed.[2]

It was Jack Johnson who brought an end to the racial ban, though a temporary one, and he did it by pursuing Tommy Burns, the reigning champion in 1908, around the world, publicly challenging him—daring him—to fight. Burns gave in when an Australian guaranteed him $30,000 for the fight. So it was in Sydney, Australia, on December 26, 1908, that Johnson knocked out Burns and began his own reign as champion.

One "great white hope" after another tried to wrest the championship from Johnson. Even a former champion, Jim Jeffries, was induced to come out of retirement, but he too was beaten as Johnson toyed with him for fifteen rounds. The victory set off wild celebrations in the black community and retaliatory race riots in six states and Washington, DC.

Though a black man as heavyweight champion was source enough for white rage, it was Johnson himself who made the rage unbearable. He was a proud and highly visible champion, a lover of fast living, fast cars, and fast women—fast white women. He was cultured, literate, and loud. He insisted on being heard and being seen. Retribution of some sort was inevitable. In 1912 the government tried to convict him for violating the Mann Act (transporting women across state lines for immoral purposes). The first attempt failed; the second did not, as Johnson was convicted by an all-white jury. While his case was on appeal, Johnson jumped bail and left the country.

Finally, in 1915 at age thirty-seven and running out of money, Johnson fought another great white hope, Jess Willard, in Havana, Cuba, and was knocked out in the twenty-sixth round. When he returned to the United States, Johnson was sent to jail to serve his sentence of a year and a day, then spent the rest of his life scrambling for money in vaudeville shows, lecture halls, and sparring rings.

Boxing, at least at the recognized championship level, returned to being an all-white affair. And so it remained for twenty-two years.

Appropriately enough, money again broke the color barrier. After Gene Tunney retired as heavyweight champion in 1928, there were five different—and indifferent—champions, all white. Interest in the division and the money that fights brought in declined; the only solution was to allow the dominant black boxer, Joe Louis, to meet James Braddock for the championship. Louis, who was unbeaten in fights against both black and white fighters, easily captured the championship.

Outside the ring, Louis was no Jack Johnson, and that was no accident. He had been careful to follow a code of conduct drawn up by his manager that included such rules as:

- He was never to have his picture taken alongside a white woman
- He was never to go to a nightclub alone
- He was never to gloat over a fallen opponent
- He was to keep a deadpan in front of the cameras[3]

Louis kept the championship for twelve years, and those black fighters who followed him as champion—Ezzard Charles, Jersey Joe Walcott, Floyd Patterson, and Sonny Liston—stayed in his mold.

Then came Cassius Marcellus Clay. In 1960 Clay won a gold medal at the Olympics in the heavyweight division, and he turned professional a few months later. From his earliest years it was clear that he was not in the Louis pattern. After his first amateur fight, he stormed around the ring boasting that he would be "the greatest of all time." He was twelve. At the same age, he also began forecasting his fights in poetry.

This guy must be done
I'll stop him in one.[4]

In the two years after turning pro, Clay won consistently, if not always handily, and became a top contender in the division. His speed and his relatively small size for a heavyweight, coupled with his flamboyant manner, his constant trumpeting of his prowess, and the bumptious doggerel he used to predict the outcome of his fights, all deceived the sportswriters and fans. The older writers resented his manner, and the fans thought he was no real challenge for the reigning champion, Sonny Liston, whose size and power had demolished all comers.

No one, fan or writer or boxing official, particularly wanted a title fight for Clay, at least not anytime soon. So, like Johnson before him, Clay had to taunt the champion into a fight. He began his campaign in the relative privacy of a Las Vegas casino where Liston was training and put it into high gear after the champion's easily successful rematch with former champion Floyd Patterson. Patterson and Liston were still in their corners when Clay jumped into the ring to attract the cameras and microphones and began shouting, "The fight was a disgrace! . . . Liston is a tramp! I'm the champ. I want that big ugly bear!" He lunged at Liston, but three policemen held him back. "I'll whup him in eight!" he cried, holding up eight fingers. "Don't make me wait! I'll whup him in eight."[5] It worked. Liston said to his trainer, "Can you believe this guy? He's next."[6]

The fight was scheduled for February 25, 1964. No one gave Clay a chance except Clay himself, because he had a strategy for winning before he ever got into the ring.

> "Everyone predicted that Sonny Liston would destroy me. And he was scary. But it's lack of faith that makes people afraid of meeting challenges, and I believed in my self. I was confident I could whup him. So what I did was, I studied his style, I trained hard, and I watched Liston outside the ring. I went to his training camp and tried to understand what went on inside his head so later on I could mess with his mind. And all the time, I was talking, talking. That way, I figured Liston would get so mad that, when the fight came, he'd try to kill me and forget everything he knew about boxing.[7]

Nearly a year earlier, Clay had met his secret weapon, a man named Bundini Brown who was a navy veteran and a member of boxing entourages. He quickly became the only man who worked for Clay who could tell him what to do and make him do it. He relaxed Clay and energized him at the same time. He would say that the fighter and the entourage were like a cake, made with flour, eggs, and sugar, and that Bundini was the nutmeg that gave it that little extra taste.[8] If anyone was meant to join Clay in his campaign to unhinge Liston, it was Bundini Brown.

Clay's strategy of working on Liston's mind culminated on the morning of the Miami fight. He and his group arrived at the weigh-in ceremony and immediately created chaos. In the midst of it, Clay and Bundini were shouting Bundini's latest advice over and over: **"FLOAT LIKE A BUTTERFLY! STING LIKE A BEE!"**

And more: "I'm the champ! I'm ready to rumble! Tell Sonny I'm here! He ain't no champ! Round eight to prove I'm great! Bring that big ugly bear on!"[9]

By the time the ceremony was over, everyone including Liston was convinced that Clay was either crazy, terrified, or both. Only Mort Sharnik of *Sports Illustrated* suspected otherwise, because he had seen something no one else had.

> I was there, and it looked to me like Cassius was having a seizure, all gathered up in his own hysteria, going on and on, totally out of control. . . . Then, right in the middle of everything—and I don't know how many people saw this—he winked at Robinson. People were screaming and shoving and

jockeying for better camera angles, and Cassius was probably having a ball."[10]

That night the fighters entered the ring with the betting odds seven to one in Liston's favor. In fact, there was far more betting on which round Liston would win in than on who would emerge victorious. The last thing Clay said to the champion before the start of the fight was, "I've got you now, sucker!"[11]

So he did. The first round was Clay's. He hit Liston eight times in a row as the round drew to a close, and the two continued fighting after the bell. The second round was a draw; the third went to Clay as he bloodied the champion and hit him hard. In the fourth round, Clay took it easy, trying to tire his older opponent. Near the end of the round, though, something got in his eyes and, nearly blinded, he panicked. Only fast doctoring got him up for the next round, and he struggled to see just enough to stay out of danger.

By the end of round five Clay's eyes had cleared; his speed and reflexes had kept him out of trouble. In round six a revived and furious Clay attacked Liston relentlessly. Liston had no energy or punch left to answer.

As the bell rang for the beginning of round seven, Liston refused to come out, to the amazement of his trainer and disbelief of the crowd. Clay came out, though, shouting at the top of his lungs to the fans and writers in the front rows, "I am the King! I am the King! King of the World! Eat Your Words! Eat! Eat your words!"[12]

But the fight was not the end of Clay's ability to shock and enrage. The day after the fight, February 26, 1964, Clay announced that he believed "in Allah and in peace." The next day, reporters found him having breakfast with Malcolm X, the best-known member of the Nation of Islam — the Black Muslims, as the white world called them. A few days later the leader of the Nation of Islam, Elijah Muhammad, gave Clay a new name, a non-slave name, Muhammad Ali, and welcomed him into the Nation.

The public and the sportswriters had a new reason to dislike the champion. He had always rejected the way they had expected him to behave — as a fighter and as a black man. Now he had accepted a creed they feared.

In the ring, though, Ali was invincible. He beat Liston in a rematch that did not get beyond the first round. He demolished, even punished, the former champion Patterson, who had sworn to return the title to "an American." He beat everyone, and he became for many in the black community a sports hero and a cultural symbol.

It would never become easy, though it would always seem so from the outside. Ali was reclassified to be eligible for the draft and Vietnam. He refused, telling a reporter, "I ain't got no quarrel with them Vietcong," and became a hero to the growing number of those opposed to the war. He was tried and convicted for draft evasion, then stripped of his title. Eventually his conviction was unanimously overturned by the Supreme Court, but by that time he had not fought for more than three years.

Ali won back his title in 1974, retired in 1978, and returned a few months later to win it again. By that time and ever since, Ali had gained the admiration of most, if not all, of those who had reviled him over the years. In part, he became widely admired and loved not because of his fighting prowess (though that did not hurt) but because he had remained insistently true to his own vision of himself, true to his pride in his craft and his race. He insisted on the visibility that Jack Johnson had flaunted half a century before, to his eventual downfall. Ali had resurrected the past to create and demand a cultural future.

BURN, BABY, BURN

★ 1965 ★

In 1962 Magnificent Montague arrived in New York City to play the kind of music his young black audience wanted to hear. An increasingly popular black disc jockey, Montague had enthusiasm and energy to match the music.

Somewhere during my tenure in New York, I started to shout it when I got moved: "Burn, baby! Burn!" Nothing calculated, just another collision between emotion and alliteration. Don't remember how or when it came to me, just that the good ideas seemed to stick.[1]

[It's] just a way of signifying that rare, glorious, sanctified moment in which a record or anything else had taken its art to a new level. Out on the playground a young man might make a twisting hang-in-the-air shot, and you'd hear it from the brothers on the sidelines: "Burn, baby!"[2]

Montague moved to a Chicago station in 1964 and then to KGPJ in Los Angeles in February, where his popularity continued to soar. He encouraged his listeners to call in, give their names and schools, and say his phrase, "Burn, baby!"

Los Angeles was a deceptive place. Though California had been a Union state during the Civil War, Los Angeles had been a center of Confederate sympathizers, and later the county was a center of Ku Klux Klan activity. Black immigrants during World War II, arriving for work in the defense industry, had settled in three nominally integrated but actually segregated neighborhoods, and the city's black population exploded from 63,000 in 1940 to 171,000 in 1950 and 335,000 in 1960. The housing was generally poor, the schools were poor, and employment was poor. Los Angeles built five low-income housing projects after the war, all of them in the increasingly all-black areas. As was true throughout American cities, the income gap between blacks and whites was increasing, and the black unemployment rate in the ghettos of Los Angeles had grown too, from 12.6 percent in 1960 to nearly 20 percent in 1964. Jobs were not only hard to come by but nearly impossible to get in union-dominated trades and in some civil service occupations, especially the police and fire departments.

Report after report warned of the situation in black ghettos, which by 1965 had grown together into a massive segregated, impoverished area at the center of Los Angeles County. Not only was it huge, to the white majority it was both invisible and terrifying.

In 1962 and again in 1964, there had been violent confrontations between the police and ghetto residents. Regardless, the police chief, William H. Parker, told the California Advisory Committee to the U.S. Commission on Civil Rights, "I do not believe that there is any difficult problem existing in the relationship between the Los Angeles Police Department and the Negro community."[3] When three black city councilmen warned that the situation in their districts was becoming dangerous, they were berated by the CBS radio station on the grounds that they were "encouraging violence in the Negro community."[4]

A Louis Harris poll in 1964 revealed that 60 percent of the white population of Los Angeles thought that Negroes smelled different, and more than half did not want blacks living next door. Not too surprisingly, the voters passed a ballot proposition that year effectively repealing a new law prohibiting discrimination in the sale or rental of housing. At the same time, a survey of the black neighborhoods found that not one Negro felt any equality with whites, two-thirds thought they were not treated well, and one-third thought they were treated very badly. Nearly three-quarters of those interviewed said that Negro leaders were ineffective, and nearly two-thirds said "there were times when they really hated white people."[5]

The tinder was dry; only the spark was needed.

An assistant attorney general sent a memo to the state attorney general warning that something bad could happen, and that if it did the results could be calamitous. The memo was ignored, and when asked about it, the governor said it did not exist. But nothing happened in 1964–nothing out of the ordinary.

The spark was struck a year later. In the late afternoon of Wednesday, August 11, 1965, during a brutal heat wave, a motorcycle policeman in the Watts section of the black ghetto pulled over a young black man on suspicion of drunken driving. A second policeman arrived, along with a curious crowd that assembled to watch. At first the confrontation was calm. The young man's mother arrived to make sure that the car, which belonged to her, was not impounded and to advise her son to go along with the police in a patrol car. Suddenly realizing that he was going to be taken away, the young man resisted. His brother tried to intervene. The police now faced two men, one daring them to shoot him, and a constantly growing crowd. They called for assistance. As reinforcements arrived with weapons drawn, the crowd grew and the officers now on the scene began to force the driver, his brother, and their mother into patrol cars.

The police drove off with their prisoners, but rumors flew about real and imagined police brutality. The crowd threw rocks and bottles first at the departing police, then at any cars on the street. By 7:45 p.m. a riot had begun.

As the night wore on they stoned anything that moved, often injuring drivers. News crews and reporters were attacked. Looting had begun. The police reaction was often uncoordinated, ineffective, and undirected.

By early Thursday morning, however, the riot had subsided, and the police declared the disturbance over. There had been some twenty-five serious injuries among civilians in addition to the seventeen among the police. The Los Angeles deputy chief of police, Roger Murdock, told reporters, "It was just a night to throw rocks at policemen."[6]

The Los Angeles Times was not so sure. In its early editions, the event got coverage inside the paper. In later editions the story moved to page three; the final edition carried a banner headline on page one: "1,000 RIOT IN L.A.; POLICE AND MOTORISTS ATTACKED." The story dominated the page with text and pictures. It made good reading; its tone was reassuring. On the other hand, the newspaper could rely only on official sources; it had never hired a black reporter.

The police believed they had everything under control. They were wrong. For the next three nights the crowds were ever larger, the violence ever more destructive, and the inability of the authorities to deal with the rioting became ever more apparent.

At dawn on the second day, eighteen cars and seventy-six buildings had been looted or burned down; seventy-four injuries had been reported, including gunshot wounds. The governor of California was on vacation in Greece; the lieutenant governor, having been assured that the riot was contained, left town for a meeting in Berkeley. All editions of the *Times* carried the story on page one under a banner headline: "7,000 IN NEW RIOTING; TROOPS ALERTED."

Magnificent Montague went to sleep early that night, since he had to get up early to do his radio show.

> I'm falling asleep in my home in Brentwood, fifteen miles and a universe away from the madness, when all of a sudden I hear that chant on the TV news.
>
> *Burn, baby!* BURN!
>
> Wait a minute. That's mine! The rioters are screaming it! They can't do that! They can't steal what I invented. They can't turn it around, make it sound like what it's not. . . . These rioters, they've got it all wrong, and I can feel something terrible in my bones: everybody else is gonna get it all wrong too.[7]

The National Guard was alerted, but its help was not formally requested. The lieutenant governor was reluctant to act, and the governor had to be found in Greece to make that decision. He did make it, but it would take time for the Guard to be assembled, transported, and put into action.

While the government was struggling to respond, bad got worse.

Crowds no longer waited until evening. They began assembling in the morning; rioting began in the early afternoon. The riot had moved far beyond its original area and seemed to be spreading quickly. Despite increased numbers of police, the situation was out of control from the start. Fire alarms overwhelmed the system, and the Fire Department was relying on pictures from a television station's helicopter. The police radio could barely keep up with the calls.

> The police radio crackled constantly with emergency calls: "Manchester and Broadway, a mob of 1,000 . . . 51st and Avalon, a mob of 1,000 . . . Vernon and Central, looting . . . 88th and Broadway, gun battle . . . 84th and

Vermont, juvenile dispensing guns . . . 48th and Avalon, . . . And on into the night.[8]

The police could not estimate the number of rioters, except to say that it "far surpassed the previous night when the estimate was 7,000."[9] About 10:00 that night, the police calculated that before dawn the riot would reach the center of Los Angeles.

Just before 11:00 p.m., the National Guard arrived. The first units began patrolling in Watts. Their appearance in combat uniforms and with rifles at port arms began to stay the violence.

By this time the *Times* had found a black reporter—a trainee in the paper's advertising department—who was sent in on Friday night and promptly phoned in his story. His page one article ran on Sunday, headlined: "PASSWORD GAINS SAFE PASSAGE: 'BURN, BABY, BURN' SLOGAN USED AS FIREBUGS PUT AREA TO TORCH."

> Negro arsonists raced autos through otherwise deserted Los Angeles streets flinging Molotov cocktails into store after store and shouting a hep slogan borrowed from a radio disc jockey:
> "Burn, baby, burn!"[10]

The riot was ended in Los Angeles, or nearly so, with the full deployment of the National Guard. On Sunday it shifted to Long Beach, where it lasted another day. Riots, though, had broken out in Chicago and in Springfield, Massachusetts, rendering the situation more than just a West Coast aberration. What was left in the black ghetto in Los Angeles were smoking ruins, thirty-two dead, 1,100 wounded, 4,000 arrested, more than seven hundred buildings damaged or destroyed by fire, and lots of bitterness and blame.

Everyone agreed that what had happened was terrible. But why had it happened? The police captain who commanded the division in Watts knew—it was modern moral laxness:

> A lack of moral character has become evident throughout the United States. Bookstores are full of pornography that is stomach turning. Movies try to outdo each other in sexual suggestiveness. There is a lack of respect for living by the rules. Crime in Watts is simply an aggravated manifestation of what is happening elsewhere.[11]

Police Chief Parker knew—it was the civil rights movement:

Terrible conflicts are building up within these people. You can't keep telling them that the Liberty Bell isn't ringing for them and not expect them to believe it. You cannot tell people to disobey the law and not expect them to have a disrespect for the law. You cannot keep telling them that they are being abused and mistreated without expecting them to react.[12]

A rioter knew, pointing to the burning buildings:

"That's the hate that hate produced, white man," the Negro owner of a service station declared.

"This ain't hurting us none. We have nothing to lose. Negroes don't own the buildings. You never did a decent thing in your life for us, white man."[13]

The next day the *Times* ran a page one boxed editorial titled "A Time for Prayer," pleading for reflection on how to ensure that the rioting would never recur. On its editorial page, however, it ran a racist cartoon showing a group of civil rights leaders carrying a "We shall Overcome" sign as they watch a rampaging mass of black, thick-lipped apemen carrying bottles and clubs. The caption read, "We Shall Overwhelm." The bigotry of the North was becoming visible; so too was the rage of the ignored, the invisible in the North's inner cities. Many more riots would break out in many more cities in the ensuing years.

Montague stopped using his trademark phrase. It survived as a slogan with a different, ominous meaning.

HELL NO, | **AMERICA:**
WE WON'T GO | **LOVE IT**
 | **OR LEAVE IT**

★ 1966 ★

By the time of the presidential election of 1960, there were fewer than a thousand United States troops in Vietnam. As part of the strategy of containing communism around the world, both President Harry S. Truman and President Dwight D. Eisenhower had sent money and noncombat troops to the noncommunist South Vietnam. Few noticed or cared about this minor effort in a minor area far, far away.

In May 1961 the newly elected president John F. Kennedy sent Vice President Lyndon B. Johnson to Southeast Asia to report on the situation there. Johnson reported that things looked bad, that the Vietcong insurgents were slowly winning. There was hope, but to reverse the situation would take more money and more American troops. Two more missions reached the same conclusion, and Kennedy reluctantly authorized both money and men, though he limited the combat role of United States troops to a defensive one.

The increased support was temporarily successful. The South Vietnamese leadership, however, had proved dictatorial, increasingly unpopular, and corrupt. By the time Kennedy was assassinated in November 1963, the number of United States troops involved had been increased to more than 16,000, and casualties had begun to mount: 16 killed in 1961, 53 in 1962, and 123 in 1963.[1]

Still, few noticed at home, and still fewer cared. The civil rights movement in the South attracted the national attention; so did the crises over missile bases in Cuba and the Berlin Wall. The arrival of the Beatles in New York and their appearance on national television early in 1964 attracted even more notice.

Lyndon B. Johnson was now president. Although advised by a White House task force to increase United States military involvement in Vietnam or risk a takeover of the country, Johnson resisted the pressure, though he did increase financial aid to the country, authorize clandestine operations against North Vietnam, and begin limited bombing of the enemy's supply lines in Laos. By the end of the year, just over two hundred Americans had been killed.

In the presidential election of 1964, Johnson faced the Republican senator Barry Goldwater. Goldwater insisted that the war in Vietnam was like any other war and must be fought by attacking the source—North Vietnam. Johnson opposed widening the war and increasing American involvement in the struggle: "We are not about to send American boys nine or ten thousand miles away from home to do what Asian boys ought to be doing."[2] Not to look weak, however, months before the election he did increase the number of American troops there by 5,000.

Johnson won the election with the greatest percentage margin in United States history and the largest plurality of votes—16.9 million. The election was in large part a referendum on the war.

Exactly what the referendum concerned or what the vote meant, however, was far from clear. A month before the polling places opened, the navy reported that two of its destroyers operating in international waters off the coast of North Vietnam had been attacked by enemy torpedo boats. The attacks had not in fact ever taken place and the reports were the result of combatant confusion, but that information did not surface for years afterward.

Congress acted immediately, though. On August 7, 1964, it approved what was popularly called the Gulf of Tonkin Resolution giving Johnson the power to order military operations in the area without declaring war. Johnson's popularity surged to an approval rating of 72 percent, and support for his military policies in Vietnam was even higher—85 percent.

By this time there had been a scattering of small antiwar protests from old-line pacifist groups. The seeds for more were planted in December 1964 when the large campus-based Students for a Democratic Society announced it would sponsor a major Vietnam protest march in Washington, DC, in April 1965.

In November 1964 and January 1965, the Vietcong, supported by troops from the north, attacked two United States airbases, inflicting serious casualties on the defenders. The United States response was one that had been debated for several years. It began a bombing campaign designed to mount steadily and move northward if the aggression continued: Operation Rolling Thunder. Polls taken at the time showed overwhelming public support.

Protests followed immediately, though the groups generally were in the hundreds. Picketing and marches took place in some ten cities; so did arrests. Ads were placed in newspapers. But the real spark of growth in this antiwar movement did not come in the streets; it came on the campuses.

A group of concerned faculty at the University of Michigan conducted what they called a teach-in, a clear reference to the sit-in tactics important to the civil rights movement. It took place on March 24, 1965, from 8:00 p.m. until 8:00 a.m. More than three thousand attended the opening session; more than six hundred were still there at its close. Within weeks, teach-ins were held at colleges and universities around the country; the largest was held in Washington, DC, with 122 schools connected to it by telephone lines. The events heightened awareness of the war among a crucial audience, people who were ready to take action, to emulate their peers in the civil rights struggle—people who were of an age to be drafted.

For the rest of the year, everything escalated.

President Johnson quietly announced that troops would be increased by 50,000 and, a month later, that American soldiers would take on an active combat role. In fact, by the end of the year Johnson had approved increasing the troops by 100,000—to more than 184,000. Bombing sorties rose to 117,000 during the same time, 18,000 over North Vietnam. By year's end a quarter of a million bombs had been dropped, destroying bridges and cutting supply roads. With an increase in troops, there was a nearly tenfold increase in United States casualties, from just over two hundred to just under two thousand.[3]

Casualties among the Vietcong and the North Vietnamese soared. The north, though, countered by increasing its infiltration into the south—from 800 men a month during the summer of 1965 to 1,500 a month by late fall. By early 1966 the number was up to 4,500 a month.[4]

The pace of the antiwar activity in the United States picked up as well. There were more protest marches and more people marching. A march in Washington, DC, in April attracted some 20,000; the International Days of Protest in October brought a reported 100,000 into the streets of some ninety cities.

Public support for Johnson's Vietnam actions remained strong. The protests had no effect on public policy, and the protesters' mood was one of frustration. Some despaired. Others decided that more than a show of concern was needed to get the public's attention. In November, in two separate incidents, two pacifists poured gasoline on themselves and committed suicide by setting themselves on fire. It was dramatic and shocking; it echoed what a few Buddhist monks had done in Saigon; it made headlines, but it was not an answer.

The first shift in tactics came in the South, significantly from the civil rights workers. In January 1966 a civil rights worker was murdered in Tuskegee. Three days later John Lewis, the head of the Student Non-violent Coordinating Committee announced, "The murder of Samuel Younge in Tuskegee, Alabama, is no different than the murder of people in Vietnam, for both Younge and the Vietnamese sought, and are seeking, to secure the rights guaranteed them by law."[5] Shortly afterward, SNCC announced its opposition to the draft to provide troops for Vietnam.

Then, on August 17, 1966, SNCC sponsored a demonstration at an army induction center in Atlanta. As the *New York Times* reported in a small buried story, "About 20 Negroes shouting anti-Vietnam war slogans barged into an Army induction center today with a group of recruits but were quickly shoved outside by soldiers."[6] Prominent among the slogans was HELL NO,

WE WON'T GO. Their leaflets stated, "We are tired of the spilling of black men's blood in white men's wars."[7] The slogan spread quickly around the nation, as did the picketing and sit-ins at recruitment and induction centers.

Still the war went on and on. By the end of 1966, American forces numbered 385,000, double the previous year's. Still the fighting continued and the number of American soldiers killed tripled to more than 6,000. Still a majority of the public supported the war.

In Washington, however, more senators had begun to ask questions. The administration lost an important ally when the Senate Foreign Relations Committee chairman, William Fulbright, turned against the war and began to hold hearings on its conduct. In February 1966 General Maxwell Taylor testified that the war was being won and that the enemy's losses would place them in difficulty by the next year. Fulbright countered by noting that the numbers of Vietcong, according to United States intelligence, kept rising, doubling to 243,000 despite the loss of 44,000 killed or captured.[8]

From a high point in 1965, President Johnson's approval ratings in 1966 began a steady decline, and dissatisfaction with the war showed a steady increase. In the midterm elections the Democrats lost forty-seven House seats, three Senate seats, and eight governorships. The nightly scenes of the war on television news programs and the mounting casualties were, in fact, having more of an effect than the antiwar protests—turning opinion not necessarily against the fact of the war itself but against the way it was going. The new Congress easily passed a $12.2 billion supplemental appropriations bill for the war in March 1967.

A major new protest effort was planned for April 15, 1967. At the site of the primary march, New York City, a huge crowd began assembling before dawn. In one corner of Central Park, more than 175 draft cards were burned. The overt act of defiance had begun on a small scale in mid-1965 and had immediately been made a federal offense by an act of Congress, incurring five years in prison and a $10,000 fine. Hundreds more cards would be burned in the future.

The police estimated that 125,000 people marched to the United Nations; organizers estimated 300,000 to 400,000. The march, though, attracted significant, sometimes threatening, opposition as the war was beginning to split the country. At one point construction workers threw steel reinforcing rods and cups filled with sand at the marchers; eggs rained down from some apartment buildings. People threw red paint; clusters of onlookers shouted epithets. The story made the front page of the *New York*

Times, which noted that younger demonstrators used the slogans Hell No, We Won't Go and Hey, Hey, LBJ, How Many Kids Did You Kill Today?[9] In San Francisco, the other major march site, some 65,000 people filled a stadium in Golden Gate Park.[10]

Two weeks later, in response to the antiwar march, the Veterans of Foreign Wars held Loyalty Day parades in Manhattan and Brooklyn. Though the VFW had predicted a turnout of 150,000, the *Times* reporters counted just over 7,000. Along the line of march, one viewer held up a sign reading: "One country, one flag. Love it or leave it."[11] That slogan, too, spread rapidly, though usually in the form **AMERICA: LOVE IT OR LEAVE IT.**

The social fabric, it seemed, was breaking down. The division over the war mirrored societal divisions on a host of issues.

In July 1967 major riots broke out in Newark, New Jersey, and in Detroit that dwarfed the 1965 Watts riot in Los Angeles. These were followed by riots in other cities that exploded with inner city blacks' frustration over social and economic problems intractable to the kinds of nonviolent tactics used in the South.

Whites involved in the civil rights movement were effectively ordered out of activist organizations as the black power movement grew, grew militant, and often became violent. Rock-and-roll record albums were burned by ministers and town officials outraged at the growing popularity of "degenerate" Negro music and dance. Boys wearing "hippie" clothes and sporting long hair were the object of catcalls and physical attacks merely for their appearance. College students were urged to "tune in, turn on, and turn off" as drug use became more prevalent.

Nothing was working as expected. The draft calls increased, the troops sent to Vietnam increased, and the dead returning in body bags increased too. By the end of 1967 more than 485,000 troops were in Vietnam; more than 11,000 had been killed. As the end of the year approached, the peace marches grew smaller. A major march in October attracted only 50,000 to 75,000, but though numbers were smaller, there was violence from demonstrators and police, keeping everyone on edge.

For some the only way to turn these energies to productive uses was the upcoming presidential election in November 1968. President Johnson clearly had the power to take the Democratic nomination; but the election was going to center on the war and its destruction at home and abroad, and a candidate who opposed the war and Johnson's administration of it had some slim chance of influencing the outcome of the election or the war. Yet only Senator Eugene J. McCarthy of Minnesota would, reluctantly, agree to oppose Johnson for the nomination and would, equally reluctantly, campaign.

Then on January 30, 1968, the Vietcong and North Vietnamese forces launched a major offensive at the end of Tet, the Vietnamese New Year celebration. Attacking government facilities and military bases throughout the south, the fighting lasted nearly three weeks. For the attackers, the offensive was a military disaster. They were repulsed, with 40,000 killed. For the defenders, it was the very definition of a Pyrrhic victory: the United States lost 1,100 killed, the South Vietnamese army, 2,300. In the whole of South Vietnam, 14,000 civilians were killed, 224,000 were wounded, and 600,000 were made homeless.

The senior network evening news anchorman, CBS's Walter Cronkite, went to Vietnam and returned to tell his audience: "To say that we are closer to victory today is to believe, in the face of the evidence, the optimists who have been wrong in the past." A story in the *New York Times* in March revealed a Pentagon plan to send more than 200,000 additional soldiers.

Public opinion, which just a month before had supported the war 60 percent to 24 percent, plummeted. Now those opposed to the war led 42 percent to 41 percent. And in the New Hampshire Democratic primary Senator McCarthy, led by a legion of college student volunteers, got 42 percent of the vote against a sitting president of his own party.

The end for Johnson was written on the wind. A review of the Vietnam situation conducted by a group of former government officials and senior military officers at the behest of the secretary of defense concluded that no new troops should be dispatched and that the president should seek a negotiated settlement.

On Sunday night, March 31, 1968, President Johnson spoke to the public on national television. He announced that the United States would immediately reduce its war efforts unilaterally and asked for meetings with the enemy to seek peace. In his conclusion, he made a statement whose content had been known to a very few of his closest aides.

> I have concluded that I should not permit the Presidency to become involved in the partisan divisions that are developing in this political year. . . . I do not believe that I should devote an hour or a day of my time to any personal partisan causes or to any duties other than the awesome duties of this office—the Presidency of your country.
>
> Accordingly, I shall not seek, and I will not accept, the nomination of my party for another term as your President.[12]

The divisions within the country were too great to be healed even by this personal sacrifice. Political activity was dwarfed by the assassination of Reverend Martin Luther King Jr. on April 4, the subsequent riots in more than a hundred cities across the nation, a student and community uprising against Columbia University that was put down only after a week, with violent police action, and Senator Robert F. Kennedy's assassination on June 8.

The American involvement in the war and the negotiations would continue for another six years under another president, a Republican. Another 37,000 American soldiers would die. And the divisions in the country have not fully healed to this day.

YOU'VE COME A LONG WAY, BABY

★ 1972 ★

By the beginning of Dwight D. Eisenhower's first term as president in 1953, the nation's societal arrangements of ethnicity, race, class, religion, and gender had changed little since the end of the Civil War. True, the number of people had grown, as had the places from which they or their ancestors had come; the religions they avowed had multiplied; their racial backgrounds had diversified; the various classes had waxed and waned with the economy. But the basic assumptions on which the nation managed its public and private affairs had not changed. America was still, at the heart of all it did and believed, an Anglo-Saxon, white, Christian, male society. It would not be so much longer.

The civil rights movement was the first tremor of the coming earthquake, signaled by the Montgomery, Alabama, bus boycott in 1955. The rest of the decade saw ever-increasing protests, demonstrations, violence, and national attention.

There was more to come, on a subject far from men's minds.

Once the right of women to vote had been secured by the ratification in 1920 of the Nineteenth Amendment to the Constitution, nothing much happened. Women, it turned out, did not vote in great numbers, and when they did, they did not vote in a bloc. In fact the position of women in society worsened in the four decades after they achieved the vote. The percentage of women in colleges relative to men had dropped, as had the percentage who held bachelor's degrees and doctorates.[1] By 1960 the number of married women in the workforce had jumped, a third of them with children still at home, but their earnings and career prospects were severely limited. They were, people assumed, largely married, mothers of families, and content.

Then came the publication in 1963 of *The Feminine Mystique* by Betty Friedan. Friedan had begun with a study of her graduating class of 1942 at Smith College that revealed a massive, silent discontent. Further examination of the content of women's magazines and her own social and psychological insights produced a surprise publishing phenomenon. Within a year the book sold more than a million copies.

The reaction from most readers was, first, relief that they were not alone, that others felt as they did, and then anger at what the author and they saw as the limits on their lives and energies. Not everyone loved the book. As Friedan said, "I was cursed, pitied, told to get psychiatric help, to go jump in the lake and accused of being 'more of a threat to the United States than the Russians.'"[2]

As the ferment bubbled, Congress took up what would become the Civil Rights Act of 1964, a response both to President John F. Kennedy's assassination and to the civil rights movement roiling both the South and then the North. Virginia's Democratic congressman Howard W. Smith, the chairman of the powerful House Rules Committee, was an ardent defender of segregation but, far less known, an equally ardent proponent of women's rights. Smith moved an amendment to Title VII, the section of the bill that sought to prohibit discrimination in employment. To the list of the categories protected—race, color, religion, and national origin—Smith added sex.

The reaction by many of "Judge" Smith's colleagues was to make his addition a joke. But Smith was serious, supported by both President Lyndon B. Johnson and his wife, Lady Bird, and he was powerful. The amendment and the bill passed, creating the Equal Employment Opportunity Commission to enforce Title VII.

Hardly anybody outside the swiftly coalescing women's rights movement even noticed. The act, after all, was primarily meant to correct abuses for black men and women. The EEOC's new director belittled any use of Title VII on behalf of women. It was, after all, a joke that got made into law, and that was not something new in Congress. "There are people on this commission who think that no man should be required to have a male secretary and I am one of them."[3] No one was surprised, then, in August 1965 when the EEOC, in response to complaints from women's groups, ruled that sex-segregated want ads in the newspapers were legal.

The following year a number of attendees at the Third Annual Conference on the Status of Women in Washington, DC, Betty Friedan among them, decided that the EEOC had to be confronted over its refusal to enforce Title VII. When their resolution was not even allowed to come to a vote, the group caucused informally at lunch and decided to form a new pressure group. Friedan wrote on her paper napkin, "the National Organization for Women." As she later explained, the new organization was "to take action to bring women into full participation in the mainstream of American society *now*."[4]

NOW promptly took on the unsuspecting EEOC. It held a national day of picketing the EEOC's offices, dumped piles of newspaper want ads on the doorsteps, picketed the *New York Times* for its want ads, and, finally sued both the *Times* and the EEOC. The newspaper and, in 1968, the EEOC gave in, not only in this specific case but, soon, in others without prompting. NOW's victory established it as powerful in the eyes of the government and the media. With its new reputation, it attracted ever more members and ever more hostility.

For the next several year NOW moved quickly, and change came in its wake with surprising speed—at restaurants and bars that had banned women, at airlines that had made stewardesses resign when they married or reached age thirty-two, and at large corporations that had denied women specific jobs. To gain national recognition for the women's rights movement, NOW announced a Women's Strike for Equality on August 26, 1970, the fiftieth anniversary of the ratification of the Nineteenth Amendment. Politicians rushed to endorse the event. President Richard M. Nixon issued a supporting presidential proclamation.

On that day thousands of women from all walks of life marched in cities across the nation. Teach-ins and picketing were held in support of a range of women's issues. In New York City, a huge crowd (the police said 10,000, organizers said 50,000) jammed the streets.

Some of the media and those they interviewed sneered:

At ABC, Howard K. Smith began his report . . . with this snide introduction: "Three things have been difficult to tame. The ocean, fools, and women. We may soon be able to tame the ocean, but fools and women will take a little longer." Smith gave the last word to West Virginia's senator Jennings Randolph, who described the women's movement as "a small band of bra-less bubble heads." [5]

The *New York Times,* though, had learned its lesson. Its editorial supported the march, the marchers, and their demands.

While the women's movement was growing and becoming more and more visible, it was not only the politicians and the media who noticed. There was another group always willing to exploit social trends in its own interests—marketers and advertising agencies.

In 1968 some unknown marketer persuaded the giant Philip Morris company to introduce a new cigarette meant for the modern woman. Named Virginia Slims, connoting both the cigarette's shape and the kind of modern women it was meant for, the product first used the slogan You've Come a Long Way. After taking a poll to see if adding one more word would offend their market, the Leo Burnett ad agency produced a series of ads contrasting the plight of old-timey women with a beautiful, stylish, rakish woman of the present. In each ad was the new slogan, **YOU'VE COME A LONG WAY, BABY.**

The addition of the last word brought protests from some feminists. In a defense betraying either naïveté or cynicism, but in either case denying any commercial motive, the advertising account executive in charge of the account told the *Chicago Tribune:* "I've always had a feeling—and it may be just my own opinion—that Virginia Slims may have helped the women's movement. We've put a lot of dollars behind this one theme. It promotes awareness of women in particular. It is a woman's product. And the ads did portray the suffragette movement." [6]

With, or perhaps despite, this sign of cultural acceptance, the women's movement seemed to be going endlessly from victory to victory. More legislation on women's issues passed Congress in 1972 than had been passed in the previous two decades. The newspapers were filled with articles on women who had just broken new professional or job barriers. Not the least of these victories, at least as far as the movement was concerned, was the passage in Congress of a new constitutional amendment that stated, "Equality of rights under the law shall not be denied or abridged by the United States or by any State on account of sex."

This, the Equal Rights Amendment, or ERA to which it was quickly shortened, had a long history; it was first introduced to Congress in 1923 and had been occasionally considered and rejected, but more usually ignored, in the intervening years. This time, though, it sailed through Congress with few dissenting votes and on March 22, 1972, was sent to the states for ratification. Hawaii, the first state to act, ratified the ERA within minutes of learning of its passage.

By the following April, thirty states had ratified the ERA. It looked like a sure winner.

When Congress passed the ERA in 1972, Phyllis Schlafly took notice. Part of the conservative wing of the Republican Party, Schlafly had made her reputation and gained her following with her book supporting Senator Barry Goldwater for the GOP presidential nomination against New York's governor Nelson Rockefeller. For Schlafly, the ERA was nothing less than a liberal attack on what have since become known as traditional family values; the women's movement was nothing less than a revolution meant to destroy womanhood itself. She started an organization named StopERA and went to work.

Schlafly had picked her timing and issues shrewdly. To amend the Constitution requires the approval of three-quarters of the states; ERA's supporters needed thirty-eight states to approve the ERA. Schlafly and StopERA needed only twelve to reject it, a far easier task for a state-based organization than for the nationally driven NOW. Moreover, NOW, whatever its beginnings, had become something of an elitist group. NOW's own representative survey of its members in 1974 found that only 17 percent called themselves "homemakers" as opposed to 52 percent of all adult women in the country.[7] NOW's issues had the most appeal for women who not only entered the workforce but had the education and the desire to make work into a career.

Feminist literature saw housework as something anyone could do, even men. The homes in the suburbs were, in Friedan's own words, nothing more than "comfortable concentration camps."[8] Unwittingly, NOW and the other feminist organizations from centrist to radical had turned what had been a societally honored role into a plight.

> Women's libbers are trying to make wives and mothers unhappy with their career, make them feel that they are "second-class citizens" and "abject slaves." Women's libbers are promoting free sex instead of the "slavery" of marriage. They are promoting Federal "day-care centers" for babies instead of homes. They are promoting abortions instead of families.[9]

With ideology now squared off against ideology, the campaigns for and against the ERA got both ugly and silly, focused on peripheral though emotive issues: Could women be drafted and forced into deadly combat? Would men be free to divorce women and leave them defenseless and unsupported to raise their children alone? Would women have their Social Security payments reduced to the level of men's? Would men and women have to share cells in prison? Would separate public restrooms be made illegal?

By the end of 1977—one year before the deadline for ratification—thirty-five states had ratified the ERA. In desperation, supporters of the ERA got Congress to extend the deadline to 1982. It did not make any difference. The amendment died in 1982.

Feminism, though, did not die; progress toward equality in law, in the workplace, and in society continued and continues. In many ways, one of the arguments of state legislatures that an equal rights amendment to the Constitution was unnecessary turned out to be right. The laws of the nation and the results of numerous lawsuits were already sufficient to gain women the kinds of equality that the government could, on its own, enforce. Social change and time would have to do the rest.

In fact, by 1975 the ERA had ceased to be a political issue over which reasonable people could reasonably disagree. It had, for both sides, become a symbol. For one it was a symbol of national recognition of a long disregarded history of slights, oppression, derision, and suppression. For the other it was a symbol of unwanted, dangerous, threatening sexual, social, and political change that was happening faster than anyone could control or many could assimilate.

ERA was, in fact, the opening battle of the culture wars.

MR. GORBACHEV, TEAR DOWN
THIS WALL!

★ 1987 ★

At the end of World War II, the world powers had been reduced to two: the United States and the Soviet Union. The United States wanted to shrink its military, reduce its spending, and go home. But the Soviet Union, a difficult ally during the war, was now being more than difficult. It was threatening.

In Europe, the Soviets had taken over all the countries they had overrun in chasing the Germans back to Berlin, except for Czechoslovakia (soon to be swallowed up) and the jointly occupied Austria and Germany. Russian troops lingered in Iran and refused to give up a base in Finland. Communists directed from Moscow were an increasingly powerful political force in Italy and France and were involved in attempts to overthrow the governments of Greece and Turkey.

In Asia the Chinese Communists were moving swiftly to destroy Chiang Kai-shek's government; there was constant friction between northern and southern Korea, and the Vietnamese nationalists under Ho Chi Minh's leadership were resisting the return of the French colonialists.

Everywhere Russian leaders were making increasingly derogatory remarks about the West in private and increasingly hostile speeches in public.

Having tried to treat the Soviets and its leader, Joseph Stalin, as ordinary politicians and diplomats, having tried to build trust, and having tried to use political pressure, the American leaders, particularly the State Department, were at a loss.

In response to a request from Washington, George Kennan, the deputy chief of the United States mission in Moscow, provided his analysis of the situation and the beginnings of a strategy for how to manage United States–Soviet relations. The document Kennan sent to Washington on February 22, 1946, immediately dubbed "the long telegram," argued that everything the United States had done with the Russians during and after the war was completely wrong because we did not understand who they were or what they wanted.

The contents of Kennan's telegram circulated around Washington with furious speed; within weeks, one man had changed the course of American foreign policy and the course of history. When he expanded his thoughts under the name "X," in an article in *Foreign Affairs* titled "The Sources of Soviet Conduct," no one doubted who X was.

Kennan argued, both from his reading and from his eight years' experience in Russia, that the Russian leaders needed enemies in order to continue their rule. Having done away with their internal enemies and having defeated the Germans at a terrible cost in lives and sacrifice, Stalin had now turned to the West to supply the needed enemy. More, to increase the only kind of allies who could be trusted—Communists who looked only to Moscow for leadership—meant to push outward from the center. The Communist ideology was the means to this end, not an end in itself. The end they sought was the continuation of their totalitarian state that would perpetuate and justify their rule. War against the West was not necessary; other means were available, and they knew history was on their side.

Kennan provided more than an explanation of Soviet behavior; he provided an answer to this new and hostile force: "In these circumstances it is clear that the main element of any United States policy toward the Soviet Union must be that of a long-term, patient but firm and vigilant containment of Russian expansive tendencies."[1]

The key word here was containment, and containment became the dominant United States foreign policy for the next three decades, though how it was implemented and what was emphasized changed as internal political winds shifted, administrations changed, and external challenges altered. The adoption of the containment strategy was, if not the beginning of the cold war, then certainly the United States' official recognition that the cold war already existed.

The new policy succeeded at first, stabilizing affairs in Iran, Turkey, Greece, western Europe, and Japan. On March 12, 1947, Harry S. Truman announced the public expression of containment—the Truman Doctrine: "It must be the policy of the United States to support free peoples who are resisting attempted subjugation by armed minorities or outside pressures." Significantly, there was no suggestion of going to the rescue of countries like Poland or eastern Germany that were already within the Soviet orbit.

Within two years, though, events made changes to the containment policy internationally necessary and domestically vital. The western European nations were feeling increasingly insecure, with thirty Soviet army divisions across their borders faced by fewer than ten American, British, and French divisions. At the end of August 1949 the Soviets tested their first atomic bomb, stripping the United States of its nuclear monopoly. On October 1, 1949, the Chinese Communists formally established the People's Republic of China, swelling the landmass and the population under Communist control and enraging Republicans in Congress. President Truman ordered a review of American foreign policy and military strategy, a review that would take into account the new threats as well as the limited national resources available to counter them.

The completed National Security Council review, contained in a document called NSC-68 and submitted to Truman at the end of January 1950, first reviewed the new international environment in bleak terms and summarized:

> For a free society there is never total victory, since freedom and democracy are never wholly attained, are always in the process of being attained. But defeat at the hands of the totalitarian is total defeat. These risks crowd in

on us, in a shrinking world of polarized power, so as to give us no choice, ultimately, between meeting them effectively or being overcome by them.[2]

To prevent such a future and to "win the peace," NSC-68 altered Kennan's containment policy in significant ways. No longer could the nation defend only selected strongpoints; it had to defend against any Soviet incursion anywhere. All losses were vital losses, not necessarily strategically but certainly for their effect on the morale of our allies and their determination to stand with us. The original object of Kennan's policy—effecting a change in Soviet behavior—was quietly abandoned. Containment itself became the goal.

To accomplish this task, to contain the Soviet Union everywhere, meant that our military forces had to be greatly expanded, not allowed to diminish, relative to those of our adversary. For a nation only half a decade removed from world war, such a turnabout would be hard; for a cost-conscious Republican Congress and an equally cost-conscious president, funding that military expansion might well prove even harder.

Then, on June 24, 1950, the North Korean army attacked South Korea and quickly drove the defenders back. Within weeks Truman, who had originally asked Congress for a defense budget of $13.5 billion, now went back for more, and he went back again and again as the Korean War expanded and as the recommendations of NSC-68 began to be implemented. By the end of the fiscal year, Congress had authorized $48.2 billion.[3] Truman also approved the development of the hydrogen bomb. The arms race within the cold war had begun.

Each administration that followed over the ensuing three decades made its own reexamination of military and defense policy. Each administration changed Kennan's original policies to a greater or lesser degree, but always in the means used, never in the result sought—the containment of Soviet power. Wars, large and small, were fought in places Americans had never heard of before; governments were overturned, repressive governments were supported, and occasionally the use of nuclear weapons was threatened. From the perspective of the present we can see that mistakes were made, some disastrous. Developments that were of little importance were seen as critical, and political fear of underreacting—the fear of howls of "who lost . . ." often determined action. However, the ultimately consistent direction of Republican and Democratic administrations alike was, in fact, reasonable and understandable in the face of the clear near-term totalitarian threat.

In 1980 Ronald Reagan was elected president. He found America's military depleted in strength and arguably less potent than the Soviets'. Much like George Kennan, Reagan believed that the Soviets would respond only to power and could never be trusted in their agreements. As a consequence, a military buildup across the services was started, at a projected cost of $1.5 trillion. And Reagan's hostility to what he termed the "evil empire" kept pace. "The West won't contain communism. It will transcend communism. It will dismiss it as some bizarre chapter in human history whose last pages are even now being written."[4] Reagan was not content merely to strengthen the United States in order to keep the status quo of containment. First he would match threat with threat. When the Soviets placed operational intermediate-range missiles in eastern Europe, he ordered the deployment of United States intermediate-range ballistic and cruise missiles, an order that caused considerable unrest among NATO nations.

Second, Reagan would force changes in Soviet behavior—in effect returning to the original aim of Kennan's ideas. Such behavioral changes were critical, since Reagan believed that containment was inherently unstable. Moreover, he was personally horrified by nuclear weapons and the thought of nuclear warfare. The decades-old pattern had to be broken.

The first real sign that something different was going to happen came in 1983 when Reagan announced that the United States would begin a Strategic Defense Initiative, a program to develop an antimissile shield for the nation that would make nuclear weapons irrelevant. He was even willing to give the completed defensive system to any nation.[5] The president's program was widely derided, nicknamed "Star Wars," and called "a projection of fantasy into policy."[6] The Soviets, though, took it seriously indeed, since they too had been doing antimissile research and were worried that they could not match the United States technologically or even afford to try.

After his reelection in 1984, Reagan also announced that he was not interested in arms limitations and that the United States would no longer abide by an arms limitation treaty, SALT-II, that had never been ratified. What he was interested in, he said, was arms reduction, even arms elimination.

But the president was not the only source of intense pressure on the Soviets. They were trapped in a quagmire in Afghanistan, which, like the United States in Vietnam, they could not leave and they could not win. Their finances were being drained by the cost of supporting their increasingly unreliable and uncontrollable dependent states—Cuba, Angola, and the Warsaw Pact nations. Their industrial and transportation infrastructure was deteriorating from lack of maintenance; the explosion of a nuclear power reactor at Chernobyl exposed the dire weaknesses of their technology.

In October 1986 Reagan and the Russian leader Mikhail Gorbachev met in Iceland at the Russian's request to seek ways of reducing tensions. Gorbachev suggested that each side could reduce its strategic missiles by half within five years. In addition, both sides could remove all intermediate-range missiles from Europe and agree to eliminate all ballistic missiles within ten years. Reagan was indeed interested, but he discovered that in exchange Gorbachev wanted an end to the Star Wars program. Furious, Reagan ended the talks. The possibility of a successful United States missile shield was his guarantee of any agreement with Gorbachev, no matter how much they personally liked each other. Gorbachev was astonished, and perhaps disheartened.

In early June 1987 President Reagan was going to be in Europe for a series of meetings. The West German government asked him to visit Berlin, if only for a few hours, since the city was celebrating its 750th anniversary. He agreed.

Berlin in 1987 was a different place strategically than it was in 1948, 1953, and 1961. Past crises had left it divided but settled, a place that no longer threatened to lead to immediate United States–Soviet warfare, even nuclear annihilation. Still, Berlin had remained a potent symbol for both sides in the cold war, a divided city that represented the nature of the endless confrontation and its human cost.

One of the president's speechwriters, Peter Robinson, went to Berlin to gather material. As part of his visit he arranged to have dinner with a group of Berliners; after the initial small talk, Robinson asked if it was true, as he had heard, that the Berliners had gotten used to the wall.

Our hostess broke in. A gracious women, she had grown angry, Her face was red. She made a fist with one hand, then pounded it into the palm of the other. "If this man Gorbachev is serious with his talk of glasnost and perestroika," she said, "he can prove it. He can get rid of this wall."[7]

And that idea was the key to the speech that Robinson wrote and then defended against seemingly endless attempts to soften it. On June 12, 1987, the president mounted the podium overlooking the Berlin Wall and the Brandenburg Gate. He spoke to an audience that the police estimated at 20,000. Several minutes into his remarks, Reagan came to the subject of the Wall.

We welcome change and openness; for we believe that freedom and security go together, that the advance of human liberty can only strengthen the cause of world peace. There is one sign the Soviets can make that would be unmistakable, that would advance dramatically the cause of freedom and peace.

General Secretary Gorbachev, if you seek peace, if you seek prosperity for the Soviet Union and Eastern Europe, if you seek liberalization; Come here to this gate! Mr. Gorbachev, open this gate! **MR. GORBACHEV, TEAR DOWN THIS WALL!**[8]

The statement was buried in the middle of the speech, but Reagan knew how to punch up a line, and his words made the headlines.

Over the next two years, the Soviets shed—and were deserted by—their empire. On December 31, 1991, the Union of Soviet Socialist Republics dissolved itself. In its place was the Commonwealth of Independent States, a loosely organized, much diminished successor. The cold war and the arms race were officially over.

NOTES

INTRODUCTION

1 Noah Webster, *An American Selection of Lessons in Reading and Speaking, Calculated to Improve the Minds and Refine the Taste of Youth: And Also, to Instruct Them in the Geography, History, and Politics of the United States, to Which Is Prefixed Rule of Elocution* (Philadelphia: Young and M'Culloch, 1787), 5.

2 David Ramsay, *History of the United States from Their First Settlement as English Colonies in 1607, to the Year 1808*, 2nd ed. (Philadelphia: M. Carey, 1818), 1:iv.

3 Benson J. Lossing, *The National History of the United States: From the Period of the Union of the Colonies against the French, to the Inauguration of Washington* (New York: E. Walker, 1855), 22.

4 Charles A. Goodrich, *A History of the United States of America on a Plan Adapted to the Capacity of Youth and Designed to Aid the Memory by Systematick Arrangement and Interested Associations* (New York: Collins, 1823), 76.

5 Charles Altschul, *The American Revolution in Our School Textbooks* (New York: George H. Doran, 1917), 22–25.

6 William Harlan Hale, *Horace Greeley: Voice of the People* (New York: Harper, 1950), 144, 174.

7 Albert J. Beveridge, *The Life of John Marshall* (Boston: Houghton Mifflin, 1916), 2:349.

8 For an interesting discussion of the crucial value of a culture's historical memory see William H. McNeill, "Mythistory, or Truth, Myth, History, and Historians," *American Historical Review* 91, no. 1 (February 1986): 6.

WE SHALL BE AS A CITY UPON A HILL

1 Edmund S. Morgan, *The Puritan Dilemma: The Story of John Winthrop* (Boston: Little, Brown, 1958), 41; spelling modernized.

2 John Winthrop, "A Modell of Christian Charity," quoted in Robert C. Winthrop, *Life and Letters of John Winthrop* (New York: Da Capo Press, 1971), 2:18.

3 Winthrop's allusion is to Matthew 5:14: "You are the light of the world. A city set on a hill cannot be hid."

4 Winthrop, *Life and Letters*, 19.

5 Although even as important a late nineteenth-century American historian as George Bancroft, who discusses Winthrop in his *History of the United States of America* and quotes from this sermon, stops his quotation just before "the city upon a hill" sentence, concentrating instead on "the Lord make it like that of New England." George Bancroft, *History of the United States*, author's last revision (New York: D. Appleton, 1885), 1:236.

6 John F. Kennedy, "Address of President-Elect John F. Kennedy Delivered to a Joint Convention of the General Court of the Commonwealth of Massachusetts," January 9, 1961, http://www.jfklibrary.org/Historical+Resources/Archives/Reference+Desk/Speeches/JFK/003POFOGeneralCourt01091961.htm, 1–2.

7 Ronald Reagan, "Farewell Address to the Nation," January 11, 1989, http://www.reaganfoundation.org/reagan/speeches/farewell.asp, 5.

NO TAXATION WITHOUT REPRESENTATION

1 Samuel Eliot Morison, Henry Steele Commager, and William E. Leuchtenberg, *The Growth of the American Republic*, 6th ed. (New York: Oxford University Press, 1969), 1:143.

2 Quoted in A. J. Langguth, *Patriots: The Men Who Started the American Revolution* (New York: Simon and Schuster, 1988), 25.

3 Morison, Commager, and Leuchtenberg, *Growth of the American Republic*, 144.

4 James Otis, "The Rights of the British Colonies Asserted and Proved," in *Pamphlets of the American Revolution*, vol. 1, *1750–1776*, ed. Bernard Bailyn (Cambridge, MA: Harvard University Press, 1965), 446, 447.

5 *The Works of John Adams*, ed. Charles C. Little and James Brown (Boston, 1850), 10:319. It is also worth noting that Adams wrote elsewhere that his minutes or notes of the Otis arguments at the trial were done "in a very careless manner . . . , and that "I was much more attentive to the information and the eloquence of the speaker than to my minutes" (*Works*, 7:124). The famous slogan does not, in fact, begin to appear in school history textbooks until very late in the nineteenth century.

DON'T FIRE UNTIL YOU SEE THE WHITES OF THEIR EYES

1 Quoted in Samuel B. Griffith II, *In Defense of the Public Liberty* (New York: Doubleday, 1976), 138.

2 Quoted in Page Smith, *A New Age Now Begins* (New York: McGraw-Hill, 1976), 1:524–25.

3 Quoted in ibid., 1:533.

GIVE ME LIBERTY OR GIVE ME DEATH

1 Quoted in Richard R. Beeman, *Patrick Henry: A Biography* (New York: McGraw-Hill, 1974), 49.

2 Quoted in ibid., 60.

3 Patrick Henry, "Patrick Henry Ignites the American Revolution," in *Lend Me Your Ears: Great Speeches in History*, selected and introduced by William Safire (New York: W. W. Norton, 1992), 87.

4 Ibid., 88–89.

WE MUST ALL HANG TOGETHER, OR MOST ASSUREDLY
WE SHALL ALL HANG SEPARATELY

1 Thomas Paine, *Common Sense*, in *Thomas Paine: Collected Writings* (New York: Literary Classics of the United States, 1995), 36.

2 *Letters of Delegates to Congress, 1774–1789*, ed. Paul H. Smith (Washington, DC: Library of Congress, 1976), 3:523.

3 David G. McCullough, *John Adams* (New York: Simon and Schuster, 2001), 107–8, 138. McCullough also tells the story of John Hancock's saying that he wrote his

name large so that the king wouldn't need his spectacles to read it, and he cites Rhode Island's Stephen Hopkins's remark on signing as well. Hopkins, who suffered from palsy, is supposed to have said after signing, "My hand trembles, but my heart does not."

4 Quoted in Page Smith, *A New Age Now Begins*, (New York: McGraw-Hill, 1976), 1:686–87.

5 Quoted in McCullough, *John Adams*, 118.

6 Quoted in Samuel B. Griffith II, *In Defense of the Public Liberty* (New York: Doubleday, 1976), 291.

7 Quoted in Smith, *New Age*, 1:700.

8 Both Jefferson and Adams would go to their graves insisting that the Declaration had been signed on July 4. And, as every trivia buff knows, Adams and Jefferson both died on that same day, July 4, in 1826.

9 Jared Sparks, *The Works of Benjamin Franklin*, rev. ed. (Philadelphia: Childs and Peterson, 1840), 1:810.

10 Carl Van Doren, *Benjamin Franklin* (New York: Viking, 1938), 551.

I ONLY REGRET THAT I HAVE BUT ONE LIFE TO LOSE FOR MY COUNTRY

1 Morton Pennypacker, *The Two Spies: Nathan Hale and Robert Townsend* (New York: Houghton Mifflin, 1930), 2.

2 Henry Phelps Johnston, *Nathan Hale 1776: Biography and Memorials* (New Haven, CT: Yale University Press, 1914), 136 n. 1.

3 Alexander Rose, *Washington's Spies: The Story of America's First Spy Ring* (New York: Bantam Dell, 2006), 31–32.

4 Quoted in Johnston, *Nathan Hale*, 137.

5 Quoted in Pennypacker, *Two Spies*, 5. In later versions of her book, Adams left out the final two sentences of the quotation, substituting the following: "Neither the expectation of promotion, nor of pecuniary reward, induced him to the attempt. A sense of duty, a hope that, in this way he might be useful to his country, and an opinion which he had adopted, that every kind of service necessary to the public good became honourable by being necessary, were the great motives which induced him to engage in an enterprise by which his connexions lost a most amiable friend, and his country one of its most promising supporters." See Hannah Adams, *An Abridgement of the History of New England for the Use of Young Persons* (Boston, 1805, 1807; London, 1806). In all editions, Adams credits "general Hull, of Newton, for this interesting account of captain Hale." It is significant that the version Hull told her is not the version credited to Hale.

6 More recently, F. K. Donnelly suggested another possible source for Hale's words in the words of Englishman John Lilburne, a leader of the Levellers, who said in court, "I am sorry I have but one life to lose, in maintaining the truth, justice, and righteousness, of so gallant a piece." According to Donnelly, Lilburne's words were known in American political literature of the eighteenth century. "A Possible Source for Nathan Hale's Dying Words," *William and Mary Quarterly*, 3rd ser., 42, no. 3 (July 1985): 394–96.

7 The best discussion of Hale's capture and execution in the light of recent evidence is contained in Rose's *Washington's Spies*. As Rose points out, Hale's fame grew slowly—always linked with some version of the slogan–beginning with Hannah Adams's book and culminating with a major biography by I. W. Stuart in 1856.

THESE ARE THE TIMES THAT TRY MEN'S SOULS

1 Quoted in Samuel B. Griffith II, *In Defense of the Public Liberty* (New York: Doubleday, 1976), 314.
2 Thomas Paine, "The American Crisis, Number 1, December 19, 1776," in *Thomas Paine: Collected Writings* (New York: Literary Classics of the United States, 1995), 91.
3 Ibid., 98–99.

MILLIONS FOR DEFENSE, BUT NOT A CENT FOR TRIBUTE

1 Jean Edward Smith, *John Marshall: Definer of a Nation* (New York: Henry Holt, 1996), 210.
2 Ibid., 236–37.

FIRST IN WAR, FIRST IN PEACE, AND FIRST IN THE HEARTS
OF HIS COUNTRYMEN

1 Quoted in Willard Sterne Randall, *George Washington: A Life* (New York: Henry Holt, 1997), 284.
2 Ibid., 425.
3 Ibid., 463.
4 Ibid., 462.
5 Ibid., 482.
6 John Alexander Carroll and Mary Wells Ashworth, *George Washington*, vol. 7, *First in Peace* (completing the biography by Douglas Southall Freeman) (New York: Charles Scribner's Sons, 1977), 651.
7 Charles A. Goodrich, *A History of the United States of America on a Plan Adapted to the Capacity of Youth and Designed to Aid the Memory* (New York: Collins, 1826), 219. So well known did these words become and so lasting was their effect that more than a century later they could be used—and be recognized—about the chronically hapless Washington Senators: "First in war, first in peace, and last in the American League."

REMEMBER THE ALAMO

1 Quoted in Randolph B. Campbell, *Gone to Texas: A History of the Lone Star State* (New York: Oxford University Press, 2003), 117.
2 Quoted in ibid., 144; emphasis in the original.
3 Quoted in Alfred M. Williams, *Sam Houston and the War of Independence in Texas* (Boston: Houghton Mifflin, 1893), 193.
4 Quoted in M. K. Wisehart, *Sam Houston: American Giant* (Washington, DC: Robert B. Luce, 1962), 224.
5 Quoted in Campbell, *Gone to Texas,* 157–58.

I'D RATHER BE RIGHT THAN BE PRESIDENT

1 Quoted in Robert V. Remini, *Henry Clay: Statesman for the Union* (New York: W. W. Norton, 1991), 178.
2 Quoted in Samuel Eliot Morison, Henry Steele Commager, and William E. Leuchtenberg, *The Growth of the American Republic,* 6th ed. (New York: Oxford University Press, 1969), 1:398–99.
3 Remini, *Henry Clay,* 272.
4 *Niles National Register,* March 23, 1839, 55. At least one historian has called Clay's statement the most egregious example of political sour grapes in American history.

The point in Clay's career when he made the statement makes it clearly not sour grapes. After all, he ran for president once more and tried for the nomination one other time. Although difficult for a modern sensibility to understand, Clay's statement was meant seriously.

5 Quoted in Remini, *Henry Clay*, 659.

6 Quoted in Morison, Commager, and Leuchtenberg, *Growth of the American Republic*, 563.

TIPPECANOE AND TYLER TOO

1 William Nisbet Chambers, "Election of 1840," in *History of American Presidential Elections, 1789–2001*, vol. 2, *1828–1844*, ed. Arthur M. Schlesinger Jr. (Philadelphia: Chelsea House, 2002), 651.

2 Not only does the slogan have poetic qualities of a sort, it is far superior to those of the campaign that have disappeared from memory, like "Harrison, two dollars a day, and roast beef." Quoted in William Harlan Hale, *Horace Greeley, Voice of the People* (New York: Harper, 1950), 56.

3 Letter from Nicholas Biddle to a Harrison adviser, quoted in Paul F. Boller Jr., *Presidential Campaigns* (New York: Oxford University Press, 1985), 70.

4 Chambers, "Election of 1840," 675.

5 Ibid., 677.

FIFTY-FOUR FORTY OR FIGHT!

1 Quoted in Charles Sellers, "Election of 1844," in *History of American Presidential Elections, 1789–2001*, vol. 2, *1828–1844*, ed. Arthur M. Schlesinger Jr. (Philadelphia: Chelsea House, 2002), 149.

2 Quoted in Thomas M. Leonard, *James K. Polk: A Clear and Unquestionable Destiny* (Wilmington, DE: Scholarly Resources, 2001), 38.

3 Sam W. Haynes, *James K. Polk and the Expansionist Impulse* (New York: Addison-Wesley, 1997), 67.

GO WEST, YOUNG MAN

1 Ray Allen Billington, *Westward Expansion: A History of the American Frontier* (New York: Macmillan, 1974), 240.

2 Quoted in William Harlan Hale, *Horace Greeley: Voice of the People* (New York: Harper, 1950), 41.

3 Quoted in ibid., 195.

4 In fact, Greeley was not the first to use the expression, though it became his forever. The editor of the *Terre Haute Express*, John Babson Lane Soule, first used it in his newspaper in 1851. See Glyndon G. Van Deusen, *Horace Greeley: Nineteenth-Century Crusader* (Philadelphia: University of Pennsylvania Press, 1953), 176 n. 44.

5 Quoted in Samuel Eliot Morison and Henry Steele Commager, *The Growth of the American Republic*, 4th ed. (New York: Oxford University Press, 1950), 2:82.

6 Quoted in Frederick Jackson Turner, "The Significance of the Frontier in American History," in his *The Frontier in American History* (Tucson: University of Arizona Press, 1986), 1.

7 Wyoming, with 60,000 people, was admitted into the Union in 1890, but Utah, with a population of 211,000, was not and would not be until 1896, when the state relinquished polygamy.

8 Billington, *Westward Expansion*, 657.

A HOUSE DIVIDED AGAINST ITSELF CANNOT STAND

1 Quoted in Samuel Eliot Morison, Henry Steele Commager, and William E. Leuchtenberg, *The Growth of the American Republic*, 6th ed. (New York: Oxford University Press, 1969), 586–87.

2 Quoted in David Herbert Donald, *Lincoln* (New York: Simon and Schuster, 1995), 187–88.

3 Abraham Lincoln, "House Divided Speech," Springfield, Illinois, June 16, 1858, in *American Speeches: Political Oratory from the Revolution to the Civil War* (New York: Literary Classics of the United States, 2006), 634.

DAMN THE TORPEDOES, FULL SPEED AHEAD

1 Quoted in A. T. Mahan, *Admiral Farragut* (New York: D. Appleton, 1892; St. Clair Shores, MI, 1970), 272.

2 Quoted in James P. Duffy, *Lincoln's Admiral: The Civil War Campaigns of David Farragut* (New York: John Wiley, 1997), 245.

3 Mahan, *Admiral Farragut*, 277.

4 Foxhall A. Parker, *The Battle of Mobile Bay* (Boston: A. Williams, 1878). In an appendix to the short book, Parker, who was a commodore in the Union navy, provides a list, by ship, of all the officers of all the Union ships that passed the forts. His own name is not among them.

5 John Coddington Kinney, *Battles and Leaders of the Civil War, Being for the Most Part Contributions by Union and Confederate Officers* (New York: Century, 1884, 1888), 4:390–91. Kinney was a first lieutenant in the Thirteenth Connecticut Infantry and acting signal officer, USA. The article is "based upon the officer's paper in 'The Century' for May, 1881, entitled, 'An August Morning with Farragut,' revised and extended for the present work."

6 Loyall Farragut, *The Life of David Glasgow Farragut, First Admiral of the United States Navy, Embodying His Journal and Letters* (New York: D. Appleton, 1879), 416–17.

WITH MALICE TOWARD NONE, WITH CHARITY FOR ALL

1 Quoted in T. Harry Williams, *The Life History of the United States*, vol. 5, *1849–1865: The Union Sundered* (New York: Time-Life Books, 1963), 36.

2 Samuel Eliot Morison, Henry Steele Commager, and William E. Leuchtenberg, *The Growth of the American Republic*, 6th ed. (New York: Oxford University Press, 1969), 1:653 n. 1.

3 Quoted in Russell F. Weigely, *A Great Civil War: A Military and Political History, 1861–1865* (Bloomington: Indiana University Press, 2000), 111.

4 Quoted in Morison, Commager, and Leuchtenberg, *Growth of the American Republic*, 704.

5 Abraham Lincoln, "Second Inaugural Address," Washington, DC, March 4, 1865, in *American Speeches: Political Oratory from the Revolution to the Civil War* (New York: Literary Classics of the United States, 2006), 734.

6 Ibid.

7 David Herbert Donald, *Lincoln* (New York: Simon and Schuster, 1995), 574.

8 Jean Edward Smith, *Grant* (New York: Simon and Schuster, 2001), 406.

9 Joshua Lawrence Chamberlain, *The Passing of the Armies* (New York: Bantam Books, 1993), 200.

WAR IS HELL

1 Abner R. Small, *The Road to Richmond*, ed. Harold Adams Small (Berkeley: University of California Press, 1939). Quoted in Eric T. Dean Jr., "'Dangled over Hell': The Trauma of the Civil War," in *The Civil War Soldier: A Historical Reader*, ed. Michael Barton and Larry M. Logue (New York: New York University Press, 2002), 409.

2 Robert S. Robertson, *Diary of the War*, ed. Charles N. Walker and Rosemary Walker (Fort Wayne, IN: Allen County-Fort Wayne Historical Society, 1965). Quoted in Dean, "'Dangled over Hell,'" 406.

3 U. S. Grant, *Personal Memoirs of U. S. Grant and Selected Letters, 1839–1865* (New York: Library of America, 1990), 479.

4 William T. Sherman, "Address by William Tecumseh Sherman (1820–1891), Presented in Salem, Illinois, on July 4, 1866," researched by James R. Heintze, American University, Washington, DC, at www.american.edu/heintze/Sherman.htm.

5 Theodore F. Upson, *With Sherman to the Sea: The Civil War Letters Diaries and Reminiscences of Theodore F. Upson*, ed. Oscar Osburn Winther (Baton Rouge: Louisiana University Press, 1943), entry dated October 4, 1864; spelling as in original.

6 *Ohio State Journal*, August 12, 1880, photostat in Lloyd Lewis, *Sherman: Fighting Prophet* (New York: Harcourt, Brace, 1932), opposite 635. Sherman, as Lee Kennett points out, also celebrated the army and its wartime glories. In a speech to the Knights of Saint Patrick, an undated newspaper clipping records him as saying, "Many of us . . . well remember when we had real armies, with their hundreds of thousands of men in serried ranks in all the majesty of glorious war, with a holy cause and a foe worthy of our steel." Cited in Lee B. Kennett, *Sherman: A Soldier's Life* (New York: HarperCollins, 2001), 328.

7 Upson, *With Sherman to the Sea*, 181.

GIVE ME YOUR TIRED, YOUR POOR

1 Quoted in Mary J. Shapiro, *Gateway to Liberty: The Story of the Statue of Liberty and Ellis Island* (New York: Vintage Books, 1986), 11.

2 Quoted in ibid., 14.

3 "Admiring Objects of Art," *New York Times*, December 4, 1883, 2.

4 It is widely believed that the contents of the portfolio were auctioned off, not raffled, as the *New York Times* reported. But had there been an auction among the luminaries present at the show's opening, the *Times* would surely have reported that, not to mention telling who had bid on and won many of the items in the portfolio. The word "raffle" meant then what it means today.

5 *New York Times*, December 4, 1883, 2.

6 Quoted in Shapiro, *Gateway to Liberty*, 49–50.

7 "In Memory of Emma Lazarus," *New York Times*, May 6, 1903, 9.

IF NOMINATED I WILL NOT RUN; IF ELECTED I WILL NOT SERVE

1 Lee B. Kennett, *Sherman: A Soldier's Life* (New York: HarperCollins, 2001), 310.

2 Lloyd Lewis, *Sherman: Fighting Prophet* (New York: Harcourt, Brace, 1932), 615.

3 Ibid., 629–30.

4 Ibid., 630.

5 William Tecumseh Sherman, *Memoirs of General William T. Sherman*, 2nd ed. (New York: D. Appleton, 1904), 2:466.

6 "Gen. Sherman Will Not," *New York Times,* June 5, 1884, 1.

7 Lewis, *Sherman,* 631.

8 Quoted in Samuel Eliot Morison, Henry Steele Commager, and William E. Leuchtenberg, *The Growth of the American Republic,* 6th ed. (New York: Oxford University Press, 1969), 1:160–61.

9 Quoted in Mark D. Hirsch, "The Election of 1884," in *History of American Presidential Elections,* ed. Arthur M. Schlesinger Jr. (Philadelphia: Chelsea House, 2002), 4:1575.

YOU SHALL NOT CRUCIFY MANKIND UPON A CROSS OF GOLD

1 Quoted in Michael Kazin, *A Godly Hero: The Life of William Jennings Bryan* (New York: Alfred A. Knopf, 2006), 47.

2 William Jennings Bryan, "Democratic Candidate William Jennings Bryan Delivers His 'Cross of Gold' Speech," in *Lend Me Your Ears: Great Speeches in History,* selected and introduced by William Safire (New York: W. W. Norton, 1992), 771, 772.

3 Quoted in Kazin, *A Godly Hero,* 61.

4 "Bryan's Bid for First Place," *New York Times,* July 10, 1896, 3.

YES, VIRGINIA, THERE IS A SANTA CLAUS

1 Quoted in Penne L. Restad, *Christmas in America: A History* (New York: Oxford University Press, 1996), 45.

2 Quoted in ibid., 128.

3 "The Seamy Side of Christmas," *New York Tribune,* December 23, 1894, 6. Quoted in Restad, *Christmas in America,* 131.

4 "Yes Virginia, There Is a Santa Claus," *New York Sun,* September 21, 1897, 6.

REMEMBER THE *MAINE!*

1 Quoted in Ivan Musicant, *Empire by Default: The Spanish-American War and the Dawn of the American Century* (New York: Henry Holt, 1998), 9.

2 Quoted in ibid., 34.

3 W. A. Swanberg, *Citizen Hearst* (New York: Charles Scribner's Sons, 1961), 107–8.

4 Irving Werstein, *Turning Point for America: The Story of the Spanish-American War* (New York: Julian Messner, 1964), 65.

FIRE WHEN READY, GRIDLEY

1 Quoted in Ivan Musicant, *Empire by Default: The Spanish-American War and the Dawn of the American Century* (New York: Henry Holt, 1998), 153.

2 Quoted in ibid., 193.

3 Quoted in ibid., 202.

4 George Dewey, *Autobiography of George Dewey, Admiral of the Navy* (New York: Charles Scribner's Sons, 1913), 214.

5 John Barrett, *Admiral George Dewey: A Sketch of the Man* (New York: Harper, 1899), 66.

SPEAK SOFTLY AND CARRY A BIG STICK

1 Edmund Morris, *The Rise of Theodore Roosevelt* (New York: Coward, McCann and Geoghegan, 1979), 527.

2 Kathleen Dalton, *Theodore Roosevelt: A Strenuous Life* (New York: Alfred A. Knopf, 2002), 165.

3 Elting E. Morrison and John Blum, eds., *The Letters of Theodore Roosevelt* (Cambridge, MA: Harvard University Press, 1951–54), 2:1474 (letter dated 3/19/1913).

4 American Treasures of the Library of Congress, www.190c.gov/exhibits/treasures/trm139.html.

5 Morris, *Rise of Theodore Roosevelt*, 724.

6 "Col. Roosevelt Talks to the Minnesotans," *New York Times*, September 3, 1901, 10.

7 After his exploits in the Spanish-American War, Roosevelt preferred this title to all others.

8 Theodore Roosevelt, *Theodore Roosevelt: Letters and Speeches*, ed. Louis Auchincloss (New York: Literary Classics of the United States, 2004), 772.

9 H. H. Kohlsaat, *From McKinley to Harding* (New York: Charles Scribner's Sons, 1923), 100–101.

10 "Speak Softly; Carry Big Stick; Says Roosevelt," *Chicago Tribune*, April 3, 1903, 1.

11 "Speak Softly, Carry a Big Stick, and Wear a Fierce Mustache; Is the Advice of Inspector Shea to the West Side Policemen," *Chicago Tribune*, April 13, 1903, 3.

12 *Chicago Tribune*, April 21, 1903.

13 *New York Times*, July 9, 1904, 3.

HIT 'EM WHERE THEY AIN'T

1 Quoted in Burt Solomon, *Where They Ain't* (New York: Free Press, 1999), 95.

2 The Beaneaters became the Boston Doves, the Boston Bees, and finally the Boston Braves before they were moved to Milwaukee and eventually to Atlanta.

3 "Games Yesterday," *Brooklyn Eagle*, August 7, 1901, 11. That this is the long-sought first appearance of Keeler's axiom in print is reinforced by a letter printed in the *Brooklyn Eagle* on August 27. The letter is from Henry Chadwick, long-time baseball writer and historian, the only baseball writer elected to the Hall of Fame itself. The letter begins, "The *Eagle* recently had an interesting story in its base ball columns describing an interview its reporter had with that champion of scientific batsmen, Willie Keeler, for the champion Brooklyn team, in which William told of a letter he had received." The rest of the letter is Chadwick's elaboration on Keeler's "Treatise on Batting" and makes it clear that Chadwick had first learned of Keeler's words in the *Eagle* article.

THERE'S HONEST GRAFT AND THERE'S DISHONEST GRAFT

1 Lincoln Steffens, *The Autobiography of Lincoln Steffens* (New York: Harcourt, Brace, 1931), 618.

2 Barber Connable and Edward Silberfarb, *Tigers of Tammany: Nine Men Who Ran New York* (New York: Holt, Rinehart and Winston, 1967), 155. In the 1868 election, which featured both presidential and New York State gubernatorial races, the fraudulent votes probably carried the state for the Democratic presidential candidate and elected the Democratic candidate for governor.

3 Samuel P. Orth, *The Boss and the Machine* (New Haven, CT: Yale University Press, 1920), 71.

4 Connable and Silberfarb, *Tigers of Tammany*, 207.

5 William L. Riordon, *Plunkitt of Tammany Hall*, introduction by Arthur Mann (New York: E. P. Dutton, 1963), 49.

6 Ibid., 3.

7 Ibid., 6.

8 "G. W. Plunkitt Ill, Famous Politician," *New York Times*, November 8, 1924, 15.

9 "Politicians at Bier of Geo. W. Plunkitt," *New York Times*, November 23, 1924, E7.

WE STAND AT ARMAGEDDON, AND WE BATTLE FOR THE LORD

1 Nathan Miller, *Theodore Roosevelt: A Life* (New York: William Morrow, 1992), 441.

2 Ibid., 487.

3 James Chace, *1912: Wilson, Roosevelt, Taft and Debs — the Election That Changed the Country* (New York: Simon and Schuster, 2004), 34.

4 Theodore Roosevelt, speech in Osawatomie, Kansas, August 31, 1910, in *The Penguin Book of Twentieth-Century Speeches*, ed. Brian MacArthur (New York: Viking, 1992), 21.

5 H. W. Brands, *T.R.: The Last Romantic* (New York: Basic Books, 1997), 699.

6 Ibid., 700.

7 Ibid., 702.

8 Chace, *1912*, 117.

9 "Colonel Here to Stop 'Theft' of Presidency," *Chicago Daily Tribune*, Sunday, June 16, 1912, 1.

10 Miller, *Theodore Roosevelt*, 524.

11 "Roosevelt Warns of Peril to Nation; Throng Acclaims His Fight for Right," *Chicago Daily Tribune*, June 18, 1912, 1. A banner headline across the entire front page read, "The Eighth Commandment: 'Thou Shalt Not Steal.'"

12 *Chicago Daily Tribune*, June 18, 1912, 1.

13 *Chicago Daily Tribune*, June 18, 1912, 2.

14 *New York Times*, June 23, 1912, quoted in Chace, *1912*, 121.

15 "Chicago and Baltimore with the Political Scene Shifters," *American Magazine*, September 1912, 526. (There is no byline, but the article is said to have been written by Finley Peter Dunne.)

HE KEPT US OUT OF WAR *AND* MAKE THE WORLD SAFE FOR DEMOCRACY

1 August Heckscher, *Woodrow Wilson* (New York: Charles Scribner's Sons, 1991), 450.

2 Ibid., 339.

3 Arthur S. Link, ed., *The Papers of Woodrow Wilson*, vol. 33 (Princeton, NJ: Princeton University Press, 1980), 154. Wilson attempted in a press conference the following day to take back that next-to-last sentence, but the words had been spoken and notice taken. Besides, the last sentence essentially says the same thing.

4 Arthur S. Link, ed., *The Papers of Woodrow Wilson*, vol. 36 (Princeton, NJ: Princeton University Press, 1984), 47.

5 "Glynn Eulogizes Wilson as Patriot," *New York Times*, June 15, 1916, 2.

6 Arthur S. Link and William M. Leary Jr., "The Election of 1916," in *History of American Presidential Elections, 1789-2001*, ed. Arthur M. Schlesinger Jr. (Philadelphia: Chelsea House, 2002), 6:2280.

7 Heckscher, *Woodrow Wilson*, 424-25.

8 Woodrow Wilson, "President Woodrow Wilson Presents an Ideal to the War Congress," in *Lend Me Your Ears: Great Speeches in History*, selected and introduced by William Safire (New York: W. W. Norton, 1992), 115.

LAFAYETTE, WE ARE HERE

1 John Keegan, *The First World War* (New York: Alfred A. Knopf, 1999), 372.
2 "Independence Day Celebrated in Both London and Paris," *New York Tribune,* July 6, 1917, 2.
3 John J. Pershing, *My Experiences in the World War* (New York: Frederick A. Stokes, 1931), 1:92.
4 Charles E. Stanton, original handwritten speech, Hoover Institution Archives, Stanford University, Palo Alto, CA. Both the original version and the scribbled shorter version are there.
5 Lawrence Stallings, *The Doughboys: The Story of the AEF, 1917–1918* (New York: Harper and Row, 1963), 203.
6 Ibid., 15–16.

SAY IT AIN'T SO, JOE

1 Eliot Asinof, *Eight Men Out* (New York: Henry Holt, 1963), 46.
2 *Chicago Herald and Examiner,* September 30, 1920, quoted in ibid., 121. William A. Cook, an avid Cincinnati fan, has argued that "there is no record of any newsboy confronting Joe Jackson with [these] legendary words." Cook, *The 1919 World Series: What Really Happened* (Jefferson, NC: McFarland, 2001), 118. The newspaper story is a record, but a questionable one.
3 So strong was the feeling of betrayal that within months of the players' confessions the group was popularly and journalistically known as the "Black Sox."
4 Asinof, *Eight Men Out,* 270.

THE BUSINESS OF AMERICA IS BUSINESS

1 Quoted in T. H. Watkins, *The Great Depression: America in the 1930s* (New York: Little, Brown, 1993), 26.
2 Jules Abels, *In the Time of Silent Cal: A Retrospective History of the 1920s* (New York: G. P. Putnam's Sons, 1969), 19.
3 Expressed in 1929 dollars; *U.S. Gross National Product in 1929 Prices,* series 08166 (Ann Arbor, MI: National Bureau of Economic Research, 1980).
4 Abels, *In the Time of Silent Cal,* 43.
5 Quoted in Donald R. McCoy, *Calvin Coolidge: The Quiet President* (New York: Macmillan, 1967), 202.
6 "Coolidge Declares Press Must Foster America's Idealism," *New York Times,* January 18, 1925, 19.
7 A decade later, William Allen White wrote in his biography of Coolidge: "Dr. Claude M. Fuess, official biographer of Calvin Coolidge, writes that 'one day President and Mrs. Coolidge were having guests, one of whom was endeavoring to pry out of the President what he meant when he said "I do not choose to run in 1928." Cal's answer was the same one that he used on many occasions — Silence. But Mrs. Coolidge supplied the answer with: "Poppa says there's a depression coming."'" William Allen White, *A Puritan in Babylon: The Story of Calvin Coolidge* (New York: Macmillan, 1938), 362 n. 15. It is unclear at just what date this event took place. Mrs. Coolidge's statement has an apocryphal air, especially when the date of her supposed comment is unknown. More significantly, Fuess's biography of Coolidge was published a year after White's and makes no mention of any such

event or comment from Mrs. Coolidge. Claude M. Fuess, *Calvin Coolidge: The Man from Vermont* (New York: Little, Brown, 1939). As Robert Sobel, another Coolidge biographer, observes, "There is scant evidence for this. [Coolidge's] public statements of this time were invariably optimistic. As for private statements, these were always aired years after the fact, and of doubtful provenance." Robert Sobel, *Coolidge: An American Enigma* (Washington, DC: Regenery, 1998), 373.

PROSPERITY IS JUST AROUND THE CORNER *AND* THE
ONLY THING WE HAVE TO FEAR IS FEAR ITSELF

1 Dixon Wecter, *A History of American Life*, vol. 13, *The Age of the Great Depression: 1929–1941* (New York: Macmillan, 1948), 1.
2 Ibid., 7.
3 Frederick Lewis Allen, *The Big Change: America Transforms Itself, 1900–1950* (New York: Harper, 1952), 144; italics in original.
4 John Kenneth Galbraith, *The Great Crash, 1929* (New York: Houghton Mifflin, 1961), 51.
5 "Text of the President's Speech," *New York Times*, May 2, 1930, 1.
6 President Hoover denied in his memoirs that he had used the phrase: "This bit of optimism was later distorted by our opponents to make me say, 'Prosperity is just around the corner,' which I never did say. It was no doubt a political mistake on my part to open the way for such an attack if things went wrong—which they did." Herbert C. Hoover, *The Memoirs of Herbert Hoover*, vol. 3, *The Great Depression, 1929–1941* (New York: Macmillan, 1952), 58. Indeed, the sentiment, whether whistling past the graveyard or sincerely felt, was in the air of the time. On April 24, 1930, a week before Hoover made his Chamber of Commerce speech, the president of the Silk Association of America addressed the American Raw and Thrown Silk Association and ended his speech with the statement, "It, therefore, is timely for the silk industry to put its house in order promptly so that we may enjoy the benefits of prosperity that is just around the corner." *New York Times*, April 25, 1930, 47.
7 Wecter, *History of American Life*, 17.
8 Arthur M. Schlesinger Jr., *The Age of Roosevelt: The Crisis of the Old Order: 1919–1933* (Boston: Houghton Mifflin, 1957), 4.
9 Franklin Delano Roosevelt, "President Franklin D. Roosevelt's First Inaugural Instills Confidence in a Depression-Racked Nation," in *Lend Me Your Ears: Great Speeches in History*, selected and introduced by William Safire (New York: W. W. Norton, 1992), 779.
10 Roosevelt, Inaugural Address, 782–83.
11 *FDR's Fireside Chats*, ed. Russell D. Buhite and David W. Levy (Norman: University of Oklahoma Press, 1992), 16–17.

WHO KNOWS WHAT EVIL LURKS IN THE HEARTS OF MEN?

1 Quoted in Leonard Maltin, *The Great American Broadcast* (New York: Penguin Putnam, 1997), 2.

FRANKLY, MY DEAR, I DON'T GIVE A DAMN *AND* TOMORROW
IS ANOTHER DAY

1 Ralph Thompson, Books of the Times, *New York Times*, June 30, 1936, 17.

2 J. Donald Adams, "A Fine Novel of the Civil War," *New York Times Book Review*, July 5, 1936, 1.

3 James A. Michener, introduction to the anniversary edition of *Gone with the Wind* (New York: Macmillan, 1975), vii.

4 Quoted in Bruce Chadwick, *The Reel Civil War* (New York: Alfred A. Knopf, 2001), 211.

5 Lyn Tornabene, *Long Live the King: A Biography of Clark Gable* (New York: G. P. Putnam's Sons, 1976), 174–75.

WAIT TILL NEXT YEAR

1 Frank Graham, *The Brooklyn Dodgers: An Informal History* (New York: G. P. Putnam's Sons, 1947), 106.

2 Ibid., 156.

3 Peter Golenbock, *Bums: An Oral History of the Brooklyn Dodgers* (New York: G. P. Putnam's Sons, 1984), 74.

4 Ibid., 342.

5 Ibid., 403–4.

6 Art Smith, "Brooklyn Pinches Itself, Goes Crazy," *Daily News*, October 5, 1955, 3, 6.

KILROY WAS HERE

1 Harold B. Hinton, "Draft Call Nov. 7, Wadsworth Says," *New York Times*, September 5, 1940, 14.

2 George Gallup, "American Youth Speaks Up," *Reader's Digest*, October 1940, 52.

3 Ibid., 51–52.

4 Ibid., 53.

5 Chester G. Hearn, *The American Soldier in World War Two* (London: Salamander Books, 2000), 29–30.

6 Bill Davidson, "Who's Kilroy," *Collier's*, December 28, 1946, 20.

7 James J. Kilroy, letter, *New York Times Magazine*, January 12, 1947, 30.

I SHALL RETURN

1 Charles Hurd, "General Flies Out," *New York Times*, March 18, 1942, 1.

2 Byron Darnton, "General Tells Aim," *New York Times*, March 21, 1942, 1.

3 William Manchester, *American Caesar: Douglas MacArthur, 1880–1964* (Boston: Little, Brown, 1978), 271.

4 Quoted in Courtney Whitney, *MacArthur: His Rendezvous with History* (New York: Alfred A. Knopf, 1956), 158.

NUTS!

1 John Keegan, *The Second World War* (New York: Penguin Books, 1989), 439.

2 Kenneth S. Davis, *Experience of War: The United States in World War II* (Garden City, NY: Doubleday, 1965), 964–65.

3 Stephen E. Ambrose, *Citizen Soldiers* (New York: Simon and Schuster, 1997), 224–25.

4 Davis, *Experience of War*, 578.

5 Ibid., 578.

6 Ibid., 968.

THE BUCK STOPS HERE *AND* GIVE 'EM HELL, HARRY!

1 David McCullough, *Truman* (New York: Simon and Schuster, 1992), 285.

2 Ibid., 384.

3 The motto plays on the popular expression "Passing the Buck," said to derive from Truman's favorite game, poker; it widely meant, and means, avoiding responsibility.

4 McCullough, *Truman*, 643.

5 Ibid., 663–64.

NICE GUYS FINISH LAST

1 Frank Graham, "Graham's Corner," *New York Journal American*, Saturday, July 6, 1946, second page of sports section.

2 Frank Graham, *Sporting News*, July 17, 1946, 9.

3 Gerald Eskenazi, *The Lip: A Biography of Leo Durocher* (New York: William Morrow, 1993), 206–7.

4 Ibid., 208.

SPAHN, SAIN, AND PRAY FOR RAIN

1 Al Hirshberg, *The Braves: The Pick and the Shovel* (Boston: Waverly House, 1948), 25.

2 Howell Stevens, "Sain and Spahn Hope of Braves," *Boston Post*, September 14, 1948, 18.

3 Gerry Hern, "Pitch Spahn and Sain, Then Pray for Rain—But Every Day Is a Dark Day for Tribe," *Boston Post*, September 14, 1948, 18.

DUCK AND COVER

1 United Press, "Truman Statement on Atom," *New York Times*, September 24, 1949, 1.

2 William L. Laurence, "Soviet Achievement Ahead of Predictions by Three Years," *New York Times*, September 24, 1949, 1.

3 Laura McEnaney, *Civil Defense Begins at Home* (Princeton, NJ: Princeton University Press, 2000), 35.

4 William Manchester, *The Glory and the Dream: A Narrative History of America, 1932–1972* (Boston: Little, Brown, 1973–74), 1:703.

5 McEnaney, *Civil Defense*, 48.

6 Ibid., 51.

7 Stephen B. Withey, *Fourth Survey of Public Knowledge and Attitudes concerning Civil Defense: A Report of a National Study in March 1954* (Ann Arbor: Survey Research Center, Institute for Social Research, University of Michigan, 1954), 54, 81.

8 Ibid., 78.

9 Guy Oakes, *The Imaginary War: Civil Defense and American Cold War Culture* (New York: Oxford University Press, 1994), 149.

OLD SOLDIERS NEVER DIE; THEY JUST FADE AWAY

1 William Manchester, *American Caesar: Douglas MacArthur, 1880–1964* (Boston: Little, Brown, 1978), 592.

2 Quoted in McCullough, *Truman* (New York: Simon and Schuster, 1992), 816.

3 Manchester, *American Caesar*, 615.

4 "Text of MacArthur's Korea Statement," *New York Times*, March 24, 1951, 2.

5 Manchester, *American Caesar*, 641.

6 "Truman's Statement of Regret in Announcing the Relieving of MacArthur," *New York Times*, April 11, 1951, 8.

7 Manchester, *American Caesar*, 651.

8 Douglas MacArthur, "General Douglas MacArthur Moves Congress with "Old Soldiers Never Die," in *Lend Me Your Ears: Great Speeches in History*, selected and introduced by William Safire (New York: W. W. Norton, 1992), 379.

9 McCullough, *Truman*, 852.

10 Ibid., 852.

THREE YARDS AND A CLOUD OF DUST

1 Theodore Roosevelt, "Machine Politics and New York City," *Century Magazine* 23 (November 1886): 76; quoted in Clifford Putney, *Muscular Christianity: Manhood and Sports in Protestant America, 1880–1920* (Cambridge, MA: Harvard University Press, 2001), 26.

2 Benjamin G. Rader, *American Sports from the Age of Folk Games to the Age of Televised Sports*, 2nd ed. (Englewood Cliffs, NJ: Prentice Hall, 1990), 101.

3 Quoted in Elliott J. Gorn and Warren Goldstein, *A Brief History of American Sports* (New York: Hill and Wang, 1993), 158.

4 John Paul Bocock, "The Foot-Ball Heroes," *Leslie's Weekly* 88 (January 5, 1899): 7; quoted in Putney, *Muscular Christianity*, 47.

5 Rader, *American Sports*, 184–85.

6 Woody Hayes, *Football at Ohio State* (1957); quoted in Bill Levy, *Three Yards and a Cloud of Dust*, 2nd ed. (Columbus, OH: Nicholas Ward, 2004), 329.

7 Kaye Kessler, "Woody Didn't Put Neck in a Noose," *Columbus Citizen*, September 14, 1958, 3C.

ICH BIN EIN BERLINER

1 Theodore C. Sorensen, *Kennedy* (New York: Harper and Row, 1965), 583–84.

2 Ibid., 584.

3 Ibid., 588.

4 Ibid., 592.

5 Ann Tusa, *The Last Division: A History of Berlin, 1945–1989* (Reading, MA: Addison-Wesley, 1997), 272.

6 Alexandra Richie, *Faust's Metropolis: A History of Berlin* (New York: Carroll and Graf, 1998), 724.

7 "German Students Send an Umbrella to Kennedy," *New York Times*, August 17, 1961, 10.

8 Richie, *Faust's Metropolis*, 771.

9 Tom Wicker, "Berliners' Welcome Filled with Emotion," *New York Times*, June 16, 1963, 1, 12.

10 John F. Kennedy, "President John F. Kennedy Assures West Germany of America's Steadfastness," in *Lend Me Your Ears: Great Speeches in History*, selected and introduced by William Safire (New York: W. W. Norton, 1992), 494–95. A myth has grown up, repeated in popular and scholarly media alike, that Kennedy, not knowing German, made the mistake of referring to himself as a "jelly doughnut," whereupon the crowd laughed. The facts are that no Berliner used that word to refer to his favorite pastry, that the crowd laughed at a different point in his speech, and that Kennedy's use of the article *ein* does not change the meaning of the word *Berliner* any more than saying "I am an American" is any different from saying "I am American." Most important, no Berliner in that huge crowd at that tense time would have mistaken Kennedy's meaning or found it amusing.

I HAVE A DREAM

1 Paula F. Pfeffer, *A. Philip Randolph: Pioneer of the Civil Rights Movement* (Baton Rouge: Louisiana State University Press, 1990), 240.

2 Jervis Anderson, *Bayard Rustin: Troubles I've Seen; a Biography* (New York: Harper-Collins, 1997), 244.

3 Ibid., 255.

4 Ibid., 257.

5 Reverend Martin Luther King Jr., "Reverend Martin Luther King Jr. Ennobles the Civil Rights Movement at the Lincoln Memorial," in *Lend Me Your Ears: Great Speeches in History,* selected and introduced by William Safire (New York: W. W. Norton, 1992), 498–99, 500.

6 Anderson, *Bayard Rustin,* 246.

FLOAT LIKE A BUTTERFLY, STING LIKE A BEE

1 Elliott J. Gorn and Warren Goldstein, *A Brief History of American Sports* (New York: Hill and Wang, 1993), 73.

2 David Remnick, *King of the World* (New York: Random House, 1998), 222.

3 Ibid., 225–26.

4 Ibid., 96.

5 Ibid., 77.

6 Ibid.

7 Thomas Hauser, *Muhammad Ali: His Life and Times* (New York: Simon and Schuster, 1991), 60.

8 Ibid., 136.

9 Remnick, *King of the World,* 178.

10 Hauser, *Muhammad Ali,* 70.

11 Remnick, *King of the World,* 190.

12 Ibid., 200.

BURN, BABY, BURN

1 Magnificent Montague and Bob Baker, *Burn, Baby! Burn! The Autobiography of Magnificent Montague* (Urbana: University of Illinois Press, 2003), 92.

2 Ibid., 4.

3 Robert Conot, *Rivers of Blood, Years of Darkness* (New York: Bantam Books, 1967), 96.

4 Ibid., 97.

5 Ibid., 100.

6 Jack McCurdy and Art Berman, "1,000 Riot in L.A.; Police and Motorists Attacked," *Los Angeles Times,* August 12, 1965, 1.

7 Montague and Baker, *Burn, Baby! Burn!* 1–2.

8 Art Berman, "Scenes of Fire Rage Unchecked; Damage Exceeds $10 Million," *Los Angeles Times,* August 14, 1965, 12.

9 Ibid., 12.

10 Robert Richardson, "Password Gains Safe Passage: 'Burn, Baby, Burn' Slogan Used as Firebugs Put Area to Torch," *Los Angeles Times,* August 15, 1965, 1. Richardson's article contained a boxed identification: "Robert Richardson, 24, a Negro, is an advertising salesman for The Times."

11 Conot, *Rivers of Blood,* 224.

12 "Races," *Time,* August 20, 1965, 19.

13 Richardson, "Password Gains Safe Passage," 2.

HELL NO, WE WON'T GO *AND* AMERICA: LOVE IT OR LEAVE IT

1 Vietnam War Casualties by Month, Prepared by Washington Headquarters Services, Directorate for Information Operations and Reports, www.vietnam.ttu.edu/virtualarchive/statistics/VietnamWarDeathsbyMonthYearand Branch.pdf.

2 Thomas Powers, *The War at Home: Vietnam and the American People, 1964–1968* (New York: Grossman, 1973), 16.

3 Ibid., 95.

4 Ibid.

5 Ibid., 148.

6 "Atlanta Negroes Protest," *New York Times,* August 18, 1966, 22.

7 "Negroes and Police Scuffle in Atlanta," *New York Times,* August 19, 1966, 22.

8 Powers, *War at Home,* 112-13.

9 Douglas Robinson, "100,000 Rally at U.N. Against Vietnam War," *New York Times,* April 16, 1967, 1.

10 Powers, *War at Home,* 183.

11 Murray Schumach, "2 Veterans' Parades Here Hail American Soldiers Fighting in Vietnam," *New York Times,* April 30, 1967, 1.

12 Quoted in Powers, *War at Home,* 314. President Johnson kept this last announcement so much to himself and a very few that in his rehearsal videotape for the broadcast he says only something to the effect that at this point he will insert a response to a letter he received.

YOU'VE COME A LONG WAY, BABY

1 Ruth Rosen, *The World Split Open: How the Modern Women's Movement Changed America* (New York: Viking Penguin, 2000), 41-42.

2 Ibid., 6.

3 Ibid., 72.

4 Ethel Klein, *Gender Politics: From Consciousness to Mass Politics* (Cambridge, MA: Harvard University Press, 1984), 14.

5 Rosen, *World Split Open,* 296.

6 Robert Cross, "Scanning the Ads with Karen Boehning," *Chicago Tribune,* March 11, 1973, 23.

7 Jane J. Mansbridge, *Why We Lost the ERA* (Chicago: University of Chicago Press, 1986), 109.

8 Quoted in Rachael Donadio, "Betty Friedan's Enduring 'Mystique,'" *New York Times Book Review,* February 26, 2006, 23.

9 Phyllis Schlafly, "What's Wrong with 'Equal Rights' for Women," quoted in Mansbridge, *Why We Lost the ERA,* 104.

MR. GORBACHEV, TEAR DOWN THIS WALL!

1 "X," "The Sources of Soviet Conduct," *Foreign Affairs* 25, no. 4 (July 1947): 575.

2 "NSC-68: United States Objectives and Programs for National Security: A Report to the President Pursuant to the President's Directive of January 31, 1950," found at www.mtholyoke.edu/acad/intrel/nsc68-2.htm.

3 John Lewis Gaddis, *Strategies of Containment* (New York: Oxford University Press, 1982), 113.
4 Dinesh D'Souza, "How the East Was Won," *American History*, October 2003, 39.
5 Peggy Noonan, *When Character Was King: A Story of Ronald Reagan* (New York: Viking, 2001), 284.
6 D'Souza, "How the East Was Won," 40.
7 Peter Robinson, *How Ronald Reagan Changed My Life* (New York: HarperCollins, 2003), 98.
8 Ronald Reagan, Speech at the Brandenburg Gate, Berlin, June 12, 1987, in *American Speeches: Political Oratory from Abraham Lincoln to Bill Clinton* (New York: Literary Classics of America, 2006), 759.

RECOMMENDED READING

Unless noted, all the recommended readings are in print, though a few have been reprinted by other publishers. Those few not in print may be available in larger libraries or, often, in the used book market.

WE SHALL BE AS A CITY UPON A HILL

A recent and detailed biography of John Winthrop is Francis J. Bremer's *John Winthrop: America's Forgotten Founding Father* (New York: Oxford University Press, 2003). It places Winthrop in the context of his Puritan roots in England as well as the Puritan mission in the new world. Bremer's *The Puritan Experiment: New England Society from Bradford to Edwards* (Hanover, NH: University Press of New England, 1995) puts Winthrop in a longer historical context. Not to be forgotten—and still in print—is Edmund S. Morgan's *The Puritan Dilemma: The Story of John Winthrop* (Boston: Little, Brown, 1958). Morgan's book may be older, but it is still as valuable and insightful as it is readable.

NO TAXATION WITHOUT REPRESENTATION *THROUGH* FIRST IN WAR, FIRST IN PEACE, AND FIRST IN THE HEARTS OF HIS COUNTRYMEN

In the past decades there has been an explosion of writing about the American Revolutionary period, to the point where the literature threatens to rival that on the Civil War. A good place to start is in the broad histories of the period that include both the political and the military struggles: John Ferling, *A Leap in the Dark: The Struggle to Create the American Republic* (New York: Oxford University Press, 2003); David Hackett Fischer, *Washington's Crossing* (New York: Oxford University Press, 2004); and Robert Middlekauff, *The Glorious Cause: The American Revolution, 1763–1789* (New York: Oxford University Press, 2005).

Also valuable are books that concentrate on group biography as a way of seeing events, specifically Joseph J. Ellis's *Founding Brothers: The*

Revolutionary Generation (New York: Alfred A. Knopf, 2000) and Gordon S. Wood's *Revolutionary Characters: What Made the Founders Different* (New York: Penguin Press, 2006).

David McCullough's *1776* (New York: Simon and Schuster, 2005) concentrates on the single, arguably most crucial, year and does it with his usual flair.

There are two key books for those interested in deeper reading about the momentous Declaration of Independence. The long-time classic in the field first published in 1922, and still in print, is Carl L. Becker's *The Declaration of Independence: A Study in the History of Political Ideas* (New York: Alfred A. Knopf, 1958). Becker stresses the origins of the Declaration in English late-seventeenth-century philosophy, particularly John Locke. A more recent and valuable book is Garry Wills's *Inventing America: Jefferson's Declaration of Independence* (New York: Doubleday, 1978). Wills concentrates on Jefferson's original draft and locates the intellectual origins in the Scottish Enlightenment of the eighteenth century. Recent and valuable is Pauline Maier, *American Scripture: Making the Declaration of Independence* (New York: Alfred A. Knopf, 1997).

Some of the best, most recent work has been in individual biographies of key actors in the revolutionary drama. Perhaps the most popular of these is David McCullough's *John Adams* (New York: Simon and Schuster, 2001), but valuable too are Walter Isaacson's *Benjamin Franklin: An American Life* (New York: Simon and Schuster, 2003) and Joseph J. Ellis's *American Sphinx: The Character of Thomas Jefferson* (New York: Alfred A. Knopf, 1998). James MacGregor Burns and Susan Dunn's short *George Washington* (New York: Henry Holt and Company, 2004), is particularly good on Washington's contribution to the concept of the office of the president. While older, and a condensation of his long-standard four-volume Washington biography, James Thomas Flexner's *Washington: The Indispensable Man* (Boston: Little, Brown, 1974; reprint, Newtown, CT: American Political Biography, 2003) is still valuable.

Those interested in the postrevolutionary years would do well to turn to Stanley M. Elkins and Eric L. McKitrick's *The Age of Federalism: The Early American Republic, 1788–1800* (New York: Oxford University Press, 1993). The waning and waxing role of the navy during these years—and through the War of 1812—is best found in Nathan Miller's *Broadsides: The Age of Fighting Sail, 1775–1815* (New York: John Wiley, 2000). William M. Fowler Jr.'s *Jack Tars and Commodores: The American Navy, 1783–1815* (New York: Houghton Mifflin, 1984) is, unfortunately, out of print.

The Constitutional Convention in 1787 that sought to cure the potentially fatal flaws in the first constitution has been widely examined. David O. Stewart's *The Summer of 1787: The Men Who Invented the Constitution* (New York: Simon and Schuster, 2007) concentrates on the politics of those months and does it well, and Carol Berkin's *A Brilliant Solution: Inventing the American Constitution* (New York: Harcourt, 2002) conveys both the importance of the issues and the atmosphere in which the convention took place. Catherine Drinker Bowen's *Miracle at Philadelphia: The Story of the Constitutional Convention, May to September 1787* (Boston: Little, Brown, 1966) remains in print and still makes for wonderful, evocative reading.

REMEMBER THE ALAMO *THROUGH* GO WEST, YOUNG MAN

There are two key books covering the whole of 1836–51—and beyond. For the political developments, Sean Wilentz's *The Rise of American Democracy: Jefferson to Lincoln* (New York: W. W. Norton, 2005) is invaluable. For the inexorable movement of America westward from the outset until the beginning of the twentieth century, *the* definitive book is Ray Allen Billington's *Westward Expansion: A History of the American Frontier* (New York: Macmillan, 1974). Only an abridged version is still in print, but the full book is usually available in larger libraries.

Two books on Texas, and its epochal moment in San Antonio, are particularly good. The first, Randolph B. Campbell's *Gone To Texas: A History of the Lone Star State* (New York: Oxford University Press, 2003) is detailed and strong. The second, by the great Texas historian Joe B. Frantz, *Texas: A History* (New York: W. W. Norton, 1984), conveys both information and a flavor of the state in wonderful style. It is not in print.

In the national politics during the years when disunion constantly threatened, The Great Triumvirate of Senators Henry Clay, Daniel Webster, and John Calhoun dominated Washington and national policy to a greater extent than the presidents in the White House. These three have been the subject of superb biographies: Robert V. Remini's *Henry Clay: Statesman for the Union* (New York: W. W. Norton, 1991) and *Daniel Webster: The Man and His Time* (New York: W. W. Norton, 1997), and John Niven's *John C. Calhoun and the Price of Union: A Biography* (Baton Rouge: Louisiana State University Press, 1988). Merrill D. Peterson treats all three and their complex interaction in his *The Great Triumvirate: Webster, Clay, Calhoun* (New York: Oxford University Press, 1987).

The election of 1840, which is notable more for its campaign than for its result, is best covered by William Nisbet Chambers's essay "Election of 1840," in *History of American Presidential Elections, 1789–2001*, vol. 2, *1828–1844*, ed. Arthur M. Schlesinger Jr. (Philadelphia: Chelsea House, 2002). The drawback is that these books are found only in libraries. However, Paul F. Boller Jr.'s *Presidential Campaigns* (New York: Oxford University Press, 1985) is excellent, if not as detailed, and Robert Gray Gunderson's *The Log Cabin Campaign* (Lexington: University of Kentucky Press, 1957), once out of print, is now available in reprint form (Ann Arbor, MI: Books on Demand, n.d.).

For a good background on the political and societal trends underlying the push westward, see Tomas R. Hietala's *Manifest Design: Anxious Aggrandizement in Late Jacksonian America*, rev. ed. (Ithaca, NY: Cornell University Press, 2003). Horace Greeley, who was known eventually as "Go West Greeley," is also important in his role as newspaper editor and political dabbler. He is the subject of a new biography by Robert Chadwell Williams, *Horace Greeley: Champion of American Freedom* (New York: New York University Press, 2006).

A HOUSE DIVIDED AGAINST ITSELF CANNOT STAND *THROUGH* WAR IS HELL

The Civil War is a subject that has dominated—some would say obsessed—the nation since its conclusion. The literature, both scholarly and popular, is voluminous and difficult to pick from. A very good place to start are two books by James M. McPherson: *Battle Cry of Freedom: The Civil War Era* (New York: Oxford University Press, 1988), a single-volume history that is both solid and well written, and his earlier *Ordeal by Fire: The Civil War and Reconstruction*, which has been revised and reprinted (New York: McGraw-Hill Higher Education, 2000). Even more recent, and very rewarding, is Russell Weigley's *A Great Civil War: A Military and Political History, 1861–1865* (Bloomington: Indiana University Press, 2000). Though Weigley's book does not specifically treat the subject of slavery, Peter Kolchin's *American Slavery: 1619–1877*, rev. ed. (New York: Farrar, Straus and Giroux, 2003) is the book with which to begin reading on this subject.

As a famously brutal war, the Civil War is not often viewed through the eyes of the rank and file. A wonderful place to get that perspective is Michael Barton and Larry M. Logue, eds., *The Civil War Soldier: A Historical Reader* (New York: New York University Press, 2002).

The figure of Lincoln towers over events in this era and in historical memory. David Herbert Donald's *Lincoln* (New York: Simon and Schuster,

1995) is a superb biography. Doris Kearns Goodwin's *Team of Rivals: The Political Genius of Abraham Lincoln* (New York: Simon and Schuster, 2005) concentrates on an aspect of Lincoln that is often overlooked: his masterful political skills.

General Sherman has received less attention than Grant or Lee or a host of other military figures and is more remembered by readers of *Gone with the Wind.* Lee Kennett's biography, *Sherman: A Soldier's Life* (New York: HarperCollins, 2001) is a very well done book by a military historian. John F. Marszalek's *Sherman: A Soldier's Passion for Order* (New York: Free Press, 1993) is the general's most comprehensive biography but is out of print.

The navy's role, more important than is often recognized—then or now—can be first and best approached in James P. Duffy's *Lincoln's Admiral: The Civil War Campaigns of David Farragut* (New York: John Wiley, 1997).

GIVE ME YOUR TIRED, YOUR POOR

Several books were published for the centennial of the Statue of Liberty; the best of these is Mary J. Shapiro's *Gateway to Liberty: The Story of the Statue of Liberty and Ellis Island* (New York: Vintage Books, 1986). Emma Lazarus, whose only lasting fame derives from the poem, part of which is inscribed on the statue, has received little attention then or now. Esther H. Schor's biography, *Emma Lazarus* (New York: Schocken Books, 2006), is a welcome updating of Heinrich Eduard Jacob's *The World of Emma Lazarus* (New York: Schocken Books, 1949).

For the larger story, that of the waves of immigration in the nineteenth and early twentieth centuries, see the section "The Century of Immigration—1820-1924" in Roger Daniels's *Coming to America: A History of Immigration and Ethnicity in American Life* (New York: HarperCollins, 1990). John Higham's *Strangers in a Strange Land: Patterns of American Nativism, 1860-1925* (New Brunswick, NJ: Rutgers University Press, 2002) was first published in 1955. It was a landmark study then and is still a valuable place to go for an understanding of the social, political, and legal resistance to large-scale immigration.

IF NOMINATED I WILL NOT RUN; IF ELECTED I WILL NOT SERVE

An excellent overview on the politics and society in what is known as the Gilded Age can be found in Vincent F. DeSantis's *The Shaping of Modern America, 1877-1920* (Wheeling, IL: Harlan Davidson, 2000), an expansion of his earlier book, *The Gilded Age: 1877–1896*. The two biographies noted in the "War Is Hell" section are good on this period of Sherman's life as well.

YOU SHALL NOT CRUCIFY MANKIND UPON A CROSS OF GOLD

If not for the 1955 play and 1960 movie *Inherit the Wind*, Bryan would have vanished from all but scholarly memory. He survived, though, in a theatrical and distorted caricature. Robert W. Cherny's *A Righteous Cause: The Life of William Jennings Bryan* (Boston: Little, Brown, 1985) emphasizes Bryan's influence on American public policy in ways that help pave the way for the Progressive movement in the early twentieth century. The more recent Bryan biography by Michael Kazan, *A Godly Hero: The Life of William Jennings Bryan* (New York: Alfred A. Knopf, 2006), convincingly refutes the lingering aspects of the Bryan stick figure, arguing that he was neither an agrarian reactionary, an anti-intellectual, nor a sad buffoon.

The Populist movement, which is so crucial both politically and socially during this time, is well covered in Lawrence Goodwyn's *The Populist Revolt: A Short History of the Agrarian Revolt in America* (New York: Oxford University Press, 1978). For the best book-length study of the election of 1896, turn to Stanley Jones's *The Presidential Election of 1896* (Madison: University of Wisconsin Press, 1964; reprint, Ann Arbor, MI, Books on Demand, n.d.). Gilbert C. Fite's "Election of 1896," in *History of American Presidential Elections, 1789–2001*, ed. Arthur M. Schlesinger Jr., 5:1787–1871 (Philadelphia: Chelsea House, 2002), and Paul F. Boller Jr.'s *Presidential Campaigns* (New York: Oxford University Press, 1985) are good substitutes; the former is available only in libraries and the latter is in print, though it is not as detailed.

YES, VIRGINIA, THERE IS A SANTA CLAUS

There are two very good recent books on the development of Christmas in America first, reluctantly, as a religious celebration and later as the full-blown folk holiday and commercial event it has become. Penne L. Restad's *Christmas in America: A History* (New York: Oxford University Press, 1996) is a slim volume, but it is particularly good on the historical development of Christmas and is organized chronologically. Karal Ann Marling's *Merry Christmas: Celebrating America's Greatest Holiday* (Cambridge, MA: Harvard University Press, 2000) is organized thematically and provides an overview of all aspects of Christmas from its origins to giftwrap, from sentiment to commercialism.

The Spanish-American War is usually seen as a major expression of America's belief in its "Manifest Destiny" first to settle in its full continental ocean-to-ocean boundaries and then to control the Western Hemisphere. This view is taken by Anders Stephanson in *Manifest Destiny: American Expansionism and the Empire of Right* (New York: Hill and Wang, 1995). Robert Kagan's *Dangerous Nation* (New York: Alfred A. Knopf, 2006) takes the case even further, arguing that from its inception the country was expansionist, considered dangerous by other nations, and often ruthless.

On the other hand, Ivan Musicant's *Empire by Default: The Spanish-American War and the Dawn of the American Century* (New York: Henry Holt, 1998) argues that the "empire" that resulted was not planned but an accident of events. Musicant is a naval historian and is particularly good on this central aspect of the war. A more scholarly, though older, military history is David F. Trask's *The War with Spain in 1898* (New York: Macmillan, 1981).

HIT 'EM WHERE THEY AIN'T

The origins of what was once called "the national pastime" have long been disputed. The only thing certain is that Abner Doubleday did not invent it. Benjamin G. Rader's *Baseball: A History of America's Game* (Urbana: University of Illinois Press, 1992) covers the whole history of the sport from its earliest counterparts on the greens of colonial towns to the modern unionized, televised, professionalized sport.

Burt Solomon's *Where They Ain't* (New York: Free Press, 1999) concentrates on the history of the first team called Baltimore Orioles and gives the best biographical treatment of Willie Keeler, whose first name seems permanently to be Wee.

THERE'S HONEST GRAFT AND THERE'S DISHONEST GRAFT

Political groups called machines by their enemies and tightly run organizations by their friends were long a feature of America's political scene—and not just in the cities of the Northeast. A good overview is provided by John M. Allswang in his *Bosses, Machines, and Urban Voters: An American Symbiosis* (Baltimore: Johns Hopkins University Press, 1986). Alfred Connable and Edward Silberfarb's *Tigers of Tammany: Nine Men Who Ran New York* (New York: Holt, Rinehart and Winston, 1967) is an excellent history of the most famous of political machines from its birth to its demise. Unfortunately the book is no longer in print, but it can be found in larger libraries. The classic treatment of the philosophy and operations of Tammany is preserved in William L. Riordon's collection and printing of *Plunkitt of Tammany Hall,* with its introduction by Arthur Mann (New York: E. P. Dutton, 1963), which is still in print and still in use in political science classes.

WE STAND AT ARMAGEDDON, AND WE BATTLE FOR THE LORD

There are a number of excellent biographies of Theodore Roosevelt: John Morton Blum's *The Republican Roosevelt,* 2nd ed. (Cambridge, MA: Harvard University Press, 1977); Nathan Miller's *Theodore Roosevelt: A Life* (New York: William Morrow, 1992); and Edmund Morris's *The Rise of Theodore Roosevelt* (New York: Coward, McCann and Geoghegan, 1979) and his *Theodore Rex* (New York: Random House, 2001). All provide a good background for even further reading.

James Chace's *1912: Wilson, Roosevelt, Taft and Debs—the Election That Changed the Country* (New York: Simon and Schuster, 2004) is a lively telling of that campaign, which saw four credible political parties vying for the stage. Chase provides good profiles of all the protagonists.

HE KEPT US OUT OF WAR *AND* MAKE THE WORLD SAFE FOR DEMOCRACY

One authoritative, eminently readable biography of President Wilson is August Heckscher's *Woodrow Wilson* (New York: Charles Scribner's Sons, 1991; reprint, Newtown, CT, American Political Biography, 2000). The prominent Wilson scholar Arthur S. Link published an earlier book, *Woodrow Wilson: Revolution, War, and Peace* (Arlington Heights, IL: Harlan Davison, 1979), that concentrates on Wilson's changing attitudes toward war with Germany and the subsequent peace.

An excellent study of Wilson's presidency, especially on his political reform initiatives, is Kendrick A. Clements's *The Presidency of Woodrow Wilson* (Lawrence: University Press of Kansas, 1992).

LAFAYETTE, WE ARE HERE

An exceptional overview of the war is provided by John Keegan, one of the finest military historians. His *The First World War* (New York: Alfred A. Knopf, 1999) treats both the strategy and the tactics of the war with his usual clarity and ends by seeing the seeds of the next world war in the treaty ending that one.

For a good introduction to the American role in the war see David F. Trask's *The AEF and Coalition Warmaking, 1917–1918* (Lawrence: University Press of Kansas, 1993). Trask seeks to correct the traditional view that the United States' entry into the war was the single decisive factor in the victory of the Allies.

SAY IT AIN'T SO, JOE

Besides Benjamin Rader's *Baseball*, recommended above under "Hit 'Em Where They Ain't," Steven A. Riess's *City Games: The Evolution of American Urban Society and the Rise of Sports* (Urbana: University of Illinois Press, 1989) covers both the development of baseball and that of other sports, but it also discusses the role of business, government, and unsavory elements from the beginnings of professional sports. The standard and definitive history of the 1919 Black Sox scandal is Eliot Asinof's *Eight Men Out* (New York: Henry Holt, 1963).

THE BUSINESS OF AMERICA IS BUSINESS

An excellent background on the interwar period is presented by William E. Leuchtenberg in *The Perils of Prosperity, 1914–1932* (Chicago: University of Chicago Press, 1993). Worthwhile too is Ellis W. Hawley's *The Great War and the Search for a Modern Order: A History of the American People and Their Institutions, 1917–1933* (New York: St. Martin's Press, 1992).

Presidents Harding and Coolidge have been belittled, even scorned, since their years in office. Robert K. Murray's *The Politics of Normalcy: Governmental Theory and Practice in the Harding-Coolidge Era* (New York: Norton, 1973) takes a more favorable view of their administrations. William Allen White's *A Puritan in Babylon: The Story of Calvin Coolidge* (New York: Macmillan, 1938; reprint, Phoenix, AZ, Simon, 2001) is stimulating, informative, and biased against the man that the author, an influential newspaper editor of the time, saw as overmatched and ill-suited for the job.

PROSPERITY IS JUST AROUND THE CORNER

For understanding the stock market crash there is no better place to start than John Kenneth Galbraith's *The Great Crash, 1929* (New York: Houghton Mifflin, 1961). It is often very funny and always clear and formidable in its analysis of what happened and why. Charles P. Kindleberger's *The World in Depression, 1929–1939* (Berkeley: University of California Press, 1973) places the events in the United States in a world context as the economic disaster spread globally.

President Herbert Hoover's reputation has recovered somewhat in the decades since the crash and the Great Depression. Martin L. Fausold's *The Presidency of Herbert C. Hoover* (Lawrence: University Press of Kansas, 1985) is a balanced assessment of the man who was elected as "the great humanitarian" for his work in post–World War I Europe. Still, Fausold sees Hoover's failure in the economic crisis as a failure of leadership.

Arthur M. Schlesinger Jr.'s *The Age of Roosevelt: The Crisis of the Old Order, 1919–1933* (Boston: Houghton Mifflin, 1957) is a bit dated but still provides an excellent overview of events leading up to and during the early years of the Great Depression.

THE ONLY THING WE HAVE TO FEAR IS FEAR ITSELF

The literature on Franklin Delano Roosevelt is enormous. A good place to start is Frank Burt Freidel's one-volume scholarly biography, *Franklin D. Roosevelt: A Rendezvous with Destiny* (Boston: Little, Brown, 1990). Not to be overlooked is the (out of print) classic work on FDR by James Mac-Gregor Burns, *Roosevelt: the Lion and the Fox* (New York: Harcourt Brace, 1956), a vivid picture of the man and his presidency. Valuable too is the second volume of Arthur M. Schlesinger Jr.'s *The Age of Roosevelt*. This volume, *The Coming of the New Deal* (Boston: Houghton Mifflin, 1959), covers the first two years of FDR's first term with Schlesinger's customary style.

WHO KNOWS WHAT EVIL LURKS IN THE HEARTS OF MEN?

Susan Smulyan's *Selling Radio: The Commercialization of American Broadcasting, 1920–1934* (Washington, DC: Smithsonian Institution Press, 1994) traces the development of radio during its key years, focusing on the interaction between the technology and society and the influence of advertising on the new medium. Erik Barnouw's *A History of Broadcasting in the United States*, especially volume 1, *A Tower in Babel* (New York: Oxford University Press, 1966), is also excellent on these formative years. John Dunning's *Tune in Yesterday* (Englewood Cliffs, NJ: Prentice-Hall, 1976) is particularly worthwhile for many of the specific programs, including *The Shadow*.

The noted film critic and historian Richard Schickel's *Movies: The History of an Art and an Institution* (New York: Basic Books, 1964) remains the single best introduction to film and the film industry. It is out of print, however, though generally available in libraries. A later book, David Nasaw's *Going Out: The Rise and Fall of Public Amusements* (New York: Basic Books, 1993), is broader in scope and more analytical but necessarily more limited in depth. Nasaw skimps on sports but is worthwhile for his treatment of vaudeville, early theater, and movies.

Gavin Lambert's *GWTW: The Making of "Gone with the Wind"* (Boston: Little, Brown, 1973) is superb in its concentration on a single film and rich in its treatments of the personalities involved. Surprisingly for someone who wrote only a single book, albeit a blockbuster best-seller, Margaret Mitchell has been the subject of three biographies in the past fifty years. The out-of-print *Road to Tara: The Life of Margaret Mitchell* (New Haven, CT: Ticknor and Fields, 1983) by Anne Edwards is the best of them, though journalistic in style and content. A more scholarly biography is Darden Asbury Pyron's *Southern Daughter: The Life of Margaret Mitchell and the Making of "Gone with the Wind"* (New York: Oxford University Press, 1991; reprint, Athens, GA, Hill Street Press, 2006).

WAIT TILL NEXT YEAR

Beyond the baseball background books recommended earlier, there are two particular books on the Brooklyn Dodgers. The earlier one is by a prominent sportswriter of the time: Frank Graham's *The Brooklyn Dodgers: An Informal History* (New York: G. P. Putnam's Sons, 1947; reprint, Carbondale: Southern Illinois University Press, 2002). The later book, occasioned by nostalgia for Brooklyn's lost team, is all reminiscence, though wonderfully so: Peter Golenbock's *Bums: An Oral History of the Brooklyn Dodgers* (New York: G. P. Putnam's Sons, 1984).

KILROY WAS HERE

The literature on World War II, both scholarly and popular, is voluminous. A very good one-volume overview of the war from its causes to its conclusion is John Keegan's *The Second World War* (New York: Penguin Books, 1989). Keegan's book begins long before the United States entered the war and is able to keep clear for readers what was going on and why on many fronts with many armies and many strong personalities.

An excellent and broader overview of the effect of the war in the United States is William L. O'Neill's *A Democracy at War: America's Fight at Home and Abroad in World War II* (Cambridge, MA: Harvard University Press, 1998). Besides his attention to the battlefield, O'Neill's discussion includes racial minorities and women and addresses the changes mass mobilization wrought on the home front.

The story of Kilroy is really the story of the enlisted man in World War II combat, at least the enlisted man in the American army who had been, only a short time before, just another civilian. Lee Kennett's *GI: The American Soldier in World War II* (Norman: University of Oklahoma Press, 1987) describes the process of creating an army from a horde of civilians in compelling as well as scholarly fashion. Stephen E. Ambrose's *Citizen Soldiers* (New York: Simon and Schuster, 1997) provides a close look at the enlisted men's combat experience based on a large number of interviews. Another valuable perspective is provided by David Reynolds, *Rich Relations: The American Occupation of Britain, 1942–1945* (New York: Random House, 1995).

I SHALL RETURN

Douglas MacArthur was once the most celebrated of American generals; he was also, less obviously then and more obviously since, one of the most controversial, attracting ardent defenders and fervent detractors—both of whom are right. An evenhanded treatment of MacArthur in World War II is Ronald H. Spector's *Eagle Against the Sun: The American War with Japan* (New York: Free Press, 1985). This single-volume history of the Pacific Theater is especially good in dispassionately weighing the rival strategies of MacArthur and Admiral Ernest King and then describing how the strategies were worked together.

The best of MacArthur's defenders is William Manchester's *American Caesar: Douglas MacArthur, 1880–1964* (Boston: Little, Brown, 1978). While Manchester does not ignore his subject's many flaws, he does stress his virtues—an interesting approach since Manchester was a marine who fought under the general. Indeed, his *Goodbye, Darkness: A Memoir of the Pacific War* (Boston: Little, Brown, 1980) is a riveting personal account of the experience of island fighting from the perspective of an enlisted man. For the opposing view, Michael Schaller's *Douglas MacArthur: The Far Eastern General* (New York: Oxford University Press, 1989; reprint,

Bridgewater, NJ, Replica Books, 2000) stresses the general's weaknesses and mistakes but tends to ignore why he was successful and intensely popular with the public and his troops.

NUTS!

Danny S. Parker's *The Battle of the Bulge: Hitler's Ardennes Offensive, 1944–1945* (Philadelphia: Combined Books, 1991) is one of the best concentrated studies of this key battle. Somewhat more scholarly is Trevor Nevitt Dupuy's *Hitler's Last Gamble: The Battle of the Bulge, December 1944–January 1945* (New York: HarperCollins, 1994). Dupuy traces the battle through each individual unit engaged, with close attention to both the commanders and the embattled troops.

THE BUCK STOPS HERE *AND* GIVE 'EM HELL, HARRY!

David McCullough's biography *Truman* (New York: Simon and Schuster, 1992) is a warm and admiring view of the man no one expected to follow FDR. For a politician's appreciation of him by a prominent Labour and Social Democratic politician who, like many in Europe, came to admire Truman, see Roy Jenkins's now out of print *Truman* (New York: Harper-Collins, 1986). Robert H. Ferrell's *Harry S. Truman and the Modern American Presidency* (Boston: Little, Brown, 1983) is admiring but critical about the administration's application of the new containment policy.

The best account of the 1948 presidential election is out of print but worth finding: Irwin Ross's *The Loneliest Campaign: The Truman Victory of 1948* (New York: New American Library, 1968). Ross conveys the clear sense of Truman against all odds, virtually alone and relentlessly confident in the face of received Washington opinion.

NICE GUYS FINISH LAST

Beyond Benjamin Rader's *Baseball*, recommended for any of the baseball slogans, there are two key books dealing with Leo Durocher. The first published was an "as told to" autobiography, *Nice Guys Finish Last*, written with Ed Linn (New York: Simon and Schuster, 1975), which provides a sense of what Durocher was actually like while skipping over details that he neither remembered nor wanted remembered. A recent fine treatment of the man, Gerald Eskenazi's *The Lip: A Biography of Leo Durocher* (New York: William Morrow, 1993), manages to keep the flavor while retrieving the facts, misdeeds, and successes. Unaccountably, it is no longer in print.

Beyond brief mentions in baseball histories (best in Benjamin Rader's *Baseball*), almost nothing has been written about the Boston Braves. Al Hirshberg, a Boston sportswriter who covered the team in the forties, wrote the only book of note, *The Braves: The Pick and the Shovel* (Boston: Waverly House, 1948), just after the best season the team ever had in the twentieth century. The book is a good read, in part because of the style of sportswriting of the day, which has long disappeared. It is out of print, though, and hard to find. Two books are in print: Richard A. Johnson's *Boston Braves* (Mount Pleasant, SC: Arcadia, 2001) and Harold Kaese's *The Boston Braves, 1871–1953* (Boston: Northeastern University Press, 2004). Kaese's book contains contributions from Johnson and from Warren Spahn.

DUCK AND COVER

The 1950s are largely ignored by social historians as a breathing period between World War II and the turbulence of the sixties. William O'Neill's *American High: The Years of Confidence, 1945–1960* (New York: Free Press, 1986), though a popular history, gives a good sense of the period and the insecurities that lay beneath the caricatured blandness. It is out of print, though. David Halberstam's assessment of the period makes superb reading: *The Fifties* (New York: Random House, 1993).

Vivid descriptions and analyses of the civil defense policies and activities during this protonuclear age are provided in Guy Oakes's *The Imaginary War: Civil Defense and American Cold War Culture* (New York: Oxford University Press, 1994) and in Laura McEnaney's *Civil Defense Begins at Home* (Princeton, NJ: Princeton University Press, 2000). Oakes's book is particularly interesting in its focus on the essential contradiction between convincing the public that civil defense was needed because of the risk of nuclear warfare and assuring them that our military defenses were superb. McEnaney explores the social effects of civil defense mobilization, which were not always what policy planners expected.

OLD SOLDIERS NEVER DIE; THEY JUST FADE AWAY

In addition to the dueling biographies of MacArthur cited in "I Shall Return" above, C. A. MacDonald's history of the Korean War, *Korea: The War Before Vietnam* (New York: Free Press, 1987), provides a much-needed overview of the war and the actions of the British and Canadian troops as well as the Americans. MacDonald, whose analysis of both the tactics and the strategies employed by the United Nations forces, stresses the difficulties of fighting a limited war. Rosemary Foot's out-of-print book *The Wrong War: American Policy and the Dimensions of the Korean Conflict, 1950–1953* (Ithaca, NY: Cornell University Press, 1985) is particularly strong on the effect the war had on America's international relations, especially with China. It is the conflict with China that figures so largely in the conflict between Truman and MacArthur.

THREE YARDS AND A CLOUD OF DUST

A good broad overview of the history of American sports can be found in Elliott J. Gorn and Warren Goldstein's *A Brief History of American Sports* (New York: Hill and Wang, 1993). Gorn and Goldstein begin in the colonial era and examine both college and professional sports from boxing to football. Two books take a narrower and more scholarly approach: First, Ronald A. Smith's *Sports and Freedom: The Rise of Big-Time College Athletics* (New York: Oxford University Press, 1988) concentrates on the development of intercollegiate athletics in the late nineteenth and early twentieth centuries. Smith describes the shift from student-dominated sports, particularly football, to alumni and professional coaches, a shift that set the stage for the major "programs" of today. Second, Clifford Putney traces the beginning of intercollegiate sports in the importation of the British theology of muscular Christianity. Putney's *Muscular Christianity: Manhood and Sports in Protestant America, 1880–1920* (Cambridge, MA: Harvard University Press, 2001) convincingly presents the rise of sports in collegiate life as a means of combating what many saw as the growing effeminacy of college graduates.

Bill Levy's popular history of Ohio State football, *Three Yards and a Cloud of Dust*, 2nd ed. (Columbus, OH: Nicholas Ward, 2004), culminates with the tenure of Woody Hayes and is predictably adulatory, though detailed and informative. It is a fan's history.

ICH BIN EIN BERLINER

John Lewis Gaddis's *The Cold War: A New History* (New York: Penguin Books, 2005) is a superb overview of postwar foreign policy. His earlier *Strategies of Containment* (New York: Oxford University Press, 1982) is more detailed and somewhat more scholarly but still eminently readable.

Either one provides the background for a full understanding of the early trials of President Kennedy—and those presidents who followed. For a specific perspective from Berlin, Ann Tusa's *The Last Division: A History of Berlin, 1945–1989* (Reading, MA: Addison-Wesley, 1997) is detailed and evocative. The Berlin crisis that Kennedy faced is superbly analyzed by Michael R. Beschloss in *The Crisis Years: Kennedy and Khrushchev, 1960–1963* (New York: Burlingame, 1991). This last book is out of print but can be found in libraries.

I HAVE A DREAM

Robert Weisbrot's *Freedom Bound: A History of America's Civil Rights Movement* (New York: Norton, 1990) is a sweeping overview from the early sit-in movement through the 1980s. It is, unfortunately, out of print but is available in libraries. Weisbrot provides a clear sense of all the factions involved and increasingly in conflict within the movement. Dauntingly massive, but superb, is Taylor Branch's trilogy *America in the King Years*. For this slogan, Branch's second volume, *Pillar of Fire* (New York: Simon and Schuster, 1998), is central, and Branch is particularly good at evoking the swirl of events around his central focus.

The Reverend Martin Luther King Jr. is central here, and David J. Garrow's *Bearing the Cross: Martin Luther King, Jr., and the Southern Christian Leadership Conference* (New York: William Morrow, 1986) is a detailed picture of this iconic figure. Garrow presents a balanced understanding of King in and beyond the civil rights movement. Two figures who were essential to the success of the March on Washington tend to be overlooked but should not be: A. Philip Randolph and Bayard Rustin. Fortunately there are good recent biographies of both: Paula F. Pfeffer's *A. Philip Randolph: Pioneer of the Civil Rights Movement* (Baton Rouge: Louisiana State University Press, 1990) and John D'Emilio's *Lost Prophet* (Chicago: University of Chicago Press, 2004).

FLOAT LIKE A BUTTERFLY, STING LIKE A BEE

Gorn and Goldstein, *A Brief History of American Sports*, recommended above under "Three Yards and a Cloud of Dust," is good for a brief background on the history of this sport, including ancient history. Thomas Hauser's biography *Muhammad Ali: His Life and Times* (New York: Simon and Schuster, 1991) is told almost entirely through interviews with those who knew or know him. It is colorful but offers little analysis or independent insight. David Remnick's later book, *King of the World* (New York: Random House, 1998), relies to some extent on Hauser's. It is done with Remnick's usual style, intellect, and verve, though, and with real insight into the man.

BURN, BABY, BURN

Taylor Branch's third volume of *America in the King Years*, *At Canaan's Edge* (New York: Simon and Schuster, 2006), provides superb insight into the civil rights movement in the midst of which the Watts riot erupted. Though journalistic in style, Robert Conot's *Rivers of Blood, Years of Darkness* (New York: Bantam Books, 1967) stands up as the best detailed treatment of the racial strife that made banner headlines and magazine covers, forcing the country to confront the problems that the North shared with the South. Conot's book is out of print, though available in libraries.

To put the events of Watts into a larger historical context, Paul A. Gilje's *Rioting in America* (Bloomington: Indiana University Press, 1999) surveys urban riots from colonial times to modern, from ethnic strife to labor warfare.

HELL NO, WE WON'T GO *AND* AMERICA: LOVE IT OR LEAVE IT

George C. Herring's *America's Longest War: The United States and Vietnam, 1950–1976* (New York: McGraw-Hill, 1996) is an excellent study of the war that focuses on its context within American foreign policy under a series of presidents. For a more popular history as an introduction to this internally divisive conflict, Stanley Karnow's *Vietnam, a History* (New York: Penguin Books, 1997) is excellent and evenhanded, and it begins further back, in its French colonial history.

Tom Wells's *The War Within: America's Battle over Vietnam* (Berkeley: University of California Press, 1994) is a voluminous study, rich in detail, that includes both the politics and the street battles of the time. A fine book, though now out of print, is Thomas Powers's *The War at Home: Vietnam and the American People, 1964–1968* (New York: Grossman, 1973). While journalistic in style, the book is a clear, well-written, detailed examination of the growing and changing domestic reaction to the war, done early enough to catch the conflicts over tactics and strategies within the peace movement.

The book that coalesced the women's liberation movement, Betty Friedan's *The Feminine Mystique* (New York: Norton, 1963), is still in print and worth reading for an understanding of why this movement caught fire so quickly. Cynthia Harrison's *On Account of Sex: The Politics of Women's Issues, 1945–1968* (Berkeley: University of California Press, 1989) begins slightly further back to see the women's movement as a backlash against the social and economic effects of the end of World War II and the return home of millions of men. Susan Browmiller's *In Our Time: Memoir of a Revolution* (New York: Dial, 1999) is an excellent view from the inside.

For the effects wrought in American society, Ruth Rosen's *The World Split Open: How the Modern Women's Movement Changed America* (New York: Viking Penguin, 2000) is excellent. Jane J. Mansbridge's examination of the struggle over the Equal Rights Amendment in *Why We Lost the ERA* (Chicago: University of Chicago Press, 1986) is thoughtful and politically astute.

MR. GORBACHEV, TEAR DOWN THIS WALL!

Ronald Reagan as president is in the midst of a more dispassionate assessment—or reassessment—since nearly a generation has passed. Though recent, Peggy Noonan's *When Character Was King: A Story of Ronald Reagan* (New York: Viking, 2001) is by a former member of Reagan's White House and a passionate loyalist. Indeed, her book is valuable for just that view. More scholarly, balanced, and often sympathetic is Michael Schaller's *Reckoning with Reagan: America and Its President in the 1980s* (New York: Oxford University Press, 1992). Schaller is critical of many of Reagan's policies but recognizes his achievement of restoring American self-confidence. Lou Cannon's *President Reagan: The Role of a Lifetime* (New York: Public-Affairs, 2000) is based on the author's years covering the White House.

For a close examination of Reagan's relations with Gorbachev and the events that led to the dissolution of the Soviet Union, see the scholarly and readable Warren I. Cohen, *The Cambridge History of America's Foreign Relations,* vol. 4, *America in the Age of Soviet Power* (New York: Cambridge University Press, 1993).

INDEX

Body of Liberties, The, 14
Bonus Expeditionary Force, 185
Book-of-the-Month Club, 233
Borneo, 210
Boston, 14, 20, 27, 30, 50
Boston Beaneaters, 145
Boston Bees, 229
Boston Braves, 198, 228–32
Boston Massacre, 27
Boston Post, 230
Boston Red Sox, 176, 198, 231
Boston Tea Party, 27
Boudreau, Lou, 231
Bowie, Jim, 59, 60
Braddock, James, 261
Bradley, Omar, 213, 214
Brandeis, Louis D., 159
Brandt, Willy, 253
Brandywine Creek, 50
Braxton, Carter, 32, 36
Breed's Hill, 22–24
Brodie, Walter, 144
Brooklyn Atlantics, 143
Brooklyn Bridegrooms, 197
Brooklyn Dodgers, 197–204, 224–27
Brooklyn Eagle, 146, 201, 227
Brooklyn Infants, 197
Brooklyn Robins, 197
Brooklyn Superbas, 145, 197
Brooklyn Trolley Dodgers, 197
Brooks, Rep. Preston, 90
Brooks, Rev. Phillips, 125
Brotherhood of Sleeping Car Porters, 255
Brouthers, Dan, 144
Brown, Drew "Bundini," 263
Bryan, William Jennings, 118–23, 129, 152
Buchanan, James, 90
Bulge, Battle of the, 213–16
Bull Moose Party, 159
Bunker Hill, battle of, 22–25, 116
Burma, 210
Burns, Tommy, 261
Butler, Gen. Benjamin Franklin, 100
Butler, Rhett, 195, 196
Butler, Sen. Andrew Pickens, 90
Byrne, Tommy, 202

Calhoun, Sen. John C., 4, 70, 78
Camp, Walter, 245, 249

Campanella, Roy, 201
Captain Marvel, 191
Carnegie Commission, 246
Casey, Hugh, 200–1
Cassady, Howard "Hopalong," 248
Central Intelligence Agency, 219
de Céspedes, Carlos Manuel, 128
Chamberlain, Gen. Joshua, 103
Chamberlain, Neville, 253
De Chambrun, Col. Jacques Adelbert, 167
Charlie Chan, 191
Chandler, A. B. "Happy," 227
Charles, Ezzard, 262
Chase, Hal, 177
Chicago Cubs, 228
Chicago Daily Tribune, 156
Chicago Herald and Examiner, 173, 176
Chicago Tribune, 280
Chicago White Sox, 172–77
China, People's Republic of (Communist),
    232, 238, 239–40, 284
Chinese Exclusion Act of 1882, 113
Chou En-lai, 239
Church, Francis P., 126
Churchill, Winston, 218
Christmas, 123–27
    cards, 125
    carols, 125
    legal holiday, 125
    trees, 125
Cicotte, Eddie, 172, 173, 174, 175, 176
Cincinnati Reds, 172–75
Cincinnati Red Stockings, 143
Civil Rights Act of 1964, 278
    Title VII, 278
Clay, Cassius Marcellus, 262–64. *See also*
    Ali, Muhammad
Clay, Gen. Lucius, 253
Clay, Henry, 4, 5, 63–70, 72–73, 78, 79, 88
Cleveland, Grover, 114, 117–18, 120, 121,
    129, 130
Cleveland Indians, 198, 231
Cobb, Rep. Thomas W., 64
Cobb, Ty, 172, 223
Coercive Acts, 27, 28
Collins, Eddie, 172
Columbia Broadcasting Company (CBS),
    190
Columbia University, 243

Littleton, Martin, 143
Livingston, Robert, 34
Lodge, Sen. Henry Cabot, 128, 138, 142
Lomasney, Martin, 148
Lombardi, Ernie, 229
London Remembrancer, 40
Long, John D., 132, 133–34, 135
Longfellow, Henry Wadsworth, 125
Louis XVI, 55
Louisiana Territory, 84
Loes, Billy, 202
Los Angeles Times, 267, 268, 269, 270
Lusitania, 160

MacArthur, Gen. Arthur, 208
MacArthur, Gen. Douglas, 208–11, 236–44
Maceo, Antonio, 129
Mack, Connie, 229
MacKensie, Capt. Frederick, 39
MacMillan Company, 193
MacPhail, Larry, 199–200, 201, 224–25
Mahan, Capt. Alfred Thayer, 127, 138
Maine, USS, 129, 130–32, 133, 137
Malaya, 210
Malcolm X, 264
Manila Bay, battle of, 135–37, 139
Mantle, Mickey, 201, 202
Mao Tse Tung, 232
Maranville, Rabbit, 229
March on Washington for Jobs and Freedom, 256–59
Marconi, Guglielmo, 190
Marquand, Rube, 198
Marshall, Gen. George C., 206, 232
Marshall, John, 45, 46, 47, 48
Marshall Plan, 232
Marti, José, 128–29
Martin, Billy, 201
Massachusetts Bay Colony, 12, 13, 18
Mays, Carl, 198
McAuliffe, Gen. Anthony, 216
McCarthy, Sen. Eugene J., 275, 276
McCullough, David, 33
McDaniel, Hattie, 196
McDougald, Gil, 202
McGraw, John, 144, 145, 147
McKean, Thomas, 36
McKinley, William, 122–23, 129, 130, 138, 139, 140, 142, 152

McMullin, Fred, 172, 174
Meade, Gen. George, 100
Medwick, Joe, 200
Mercury Theatre, 191, 192
Mexico, 57–59, 159, 163, 164, 178, 208
Miami University of Ohio, 247
Michener, James A., 194
Milwaukee Braves, 202
Missouri Compromise, 64–66, 70, 89–90, 91
Mitchell, Margaret, 192–94
Mobile Bay, battle of, 92–98
Monroe, James, 25, 166
Monroe Doctrine, 141
Montague, Magnificent, 265–66, 268, 270
Montojo, Adm. Patricio, 135
Montressor, Capt. John, 39
Moore, Clement Clarke, 124
Moore's Creek Bridge, 32
Moorhead, Agnes, 191
Morris, Robert, 35
Murdock, Roger, 267
Murphy, William, 150, 151
Murrow, Edward R., 253
Musial, Stan, 228
Mussolini, Benito, 186

Nast, Thomas, 124, 149
National Association for the Advancement of Colored People (NAACP), 219, 256, 259
National Broadcasting Company (NBC), 190
National Organization for Women, 279
National Republican Party, 147
National Union Party, 101
National Urban League, 256
Nation of Islam, 257, 264
Naturalization Act of 1795, 112
Negro American Labor Council, 255
"New Colossus, The," 111, 112, 113
Newcombe, Don, 202
New Philadelphia High School, 247
New York City, 37–39, 171
New York Daily News, 203
New York Evening World, 176
New York Giants, 144, 177, 198, 199
New York Highlanders, 146
New-York Historical Society, 124

New York *Journal*, 131
New York *Journal American*, 226
New York *Sun*, 126–27
New York *Times*, 110, 111, 194, 233, 235, 253, 273, 274, 276, 279, 280
New York *Tribune*, 6
New York *World*, 112, 130, 160
New York Yankees, 147, 176, 198, 200–3, 223
Nicaragua, 159
Nixon, Richard M., 118, 279
Norfolk, 32
NSC-68, 284–85

O'Hanlon, Virginia, 126
O'Hara, Scarlett, 194, 195, 196
Ohio State University, 247–49
Olive Branch Petition, 29, 31
O'Malley, Walter, 227, 231
Operation Alert, 235
Oregon Territory, 76–78, 79–81
Otis, James, 17–20
Otis, Joseph, 23
Owen, Mickey, 200–1

Paige, Satchel, 231
Paine, Tom, 31–32, 42–43
Panic of 1837, 72, 85
Parker, Alton B.143
Parker, William H., 266, 269–70
Parks, Rosa, 255
Patterson, Floyd, 262, 264
Patton, Gen. George, 215, 216
Payn, Louis, 140
Pearce, Dicky, 143
Pedestal Fund Art Loan Exhibition, 110–11
Pegler, Westbrook, 227
Pendergast, Thomas J., 217
Perini, Lou, 229, 231
Pershing, Gen. John J., 167, 168, 169–70
Peterson, Val, 234, 235, 236
Philadelphia Athletics, 198, 229
Philadelphia Centennial Exhibition, 109
Philip Morris Corporation, 280
Philippines, the, 134–36, 208, 209–12
Pickering, Timothy, 47, 48
Pinckney, Charles, 45, 46, 47, 48

Pintard, John, 124
Plainfield Crescents, 144
Platt, Thomas, 138, 139–41
Plunkitt, George Washington, 150–51
Podres, Johnny, 202, 203
Poland, 284
Polk, James K., 69, 70, 79–80
Populist Party, 199, 122
Porter, Adm. David, 102
Portsmouth, 29
Prang, Louis, 125
presidential elections
    1824, 4–5, 66–67
    1828, 6
    1832, 68
    1836, 72
    1840, 68, 72–75, 118
    1844, 69, 78–80
    1848, 69
    1864, 101
    1884, 114–18
    1896, 118–23, 129
    1900, 141
    1904, 143, 152
    1912, 153–57, 159
    1916, 162–64
    1920, 179
    1924, 179
    1928, 182
    1932, 185–86
    1944, 218
    1948, 219–23
    1952, 118
    1960, 270–71
    1964, 271
    1968, 275–76
Prescott, Col. William, 22
Preston, Sen. William C., 68
Princeton University, 42, 50, 245
Proctor, Sen. Redfield, 133
Progressive Party, 159, 162
Pronunciamento de Yara, 128
Providence, 42
Puerto Rico, 129
Pulitzer, Joseph, 122, 130
Pullman Rail Strike, 120
Purdue University, 249
Puritans, 11–12
Putnam, Israel, 22, 23, 39